A Concise Companion to Modernism

Blackwell Concise Companions to Literature and Culture

General Editor: David Bradshaw, University of Oxford

The aim of this series is to provide accessible, innovative approaches to major areas of literary study. Ranging from between ten and twelve newly commissioned chapters, the volumes provide an indispensable companion for anyone wishing to gain an authoritative understanding of a given period or movement's intellectual character and contexts.

Modernism	Edited by *David Bradshaw*
Romanticism	Edited by *Jon Klancher*
Restoration and 18th Century	Edited by *Cynthia Wall*
Feminist Theory	Edited by *Mary Eagleton*
The Victorian Novel	Edited by *Francis O'Gorman*

A Concise Companion to Modernism

Edited by David Bradshaw

Blackwell
Publishing

© 2003 by Blackwell Publishing Ltd

BLACKWELL PUBLISHING
350 Main Street, Malden, MA 02148-5020, USA
9600 Garsington Road, Oxford OX4 2DQ, UK
550 Swanston Street, Carlton, Victoria 3053, Australia

First published 2003 by Blackwell Publishing Ltd

2   2005

Library of Congress Cataloging-in-Publication Data

A concise companion to modernism / edited by David Bradshaw.
    p. cm. — (Blackwell concise companions to literature and culture)
    Includes bibliographical references and index.
    ISBN 0-631-22054-2 (alk. paper) — ISBN 0-631-22055-0 (pbk. : alk. paper)
    1. English literature—20th century—History and criticism—Handbooks, manuals, etc.
2. Modernism Literature)—Great Britain—Handbooks, manuals, etc. I. Bradshaw, David.
II. Series.

PR478 .M6 C66 2003
820.9'112—dc21

                                                                2002066419

ISBN-13: 978-0-631-22054-1 (alk. paper) — ISBN-13: 978-0-631-22055-8 (pbk. : alk. paper)

A catalogue record for this title is available from the British Library.

Set in 10 on 12.5 pt Meridien
by Ace Filmsetting Ltd, Frome, Somerset

The publisher's policy is to use permanent paper from mills that operate a sustainable forestry policy, and which has been manufactured from pulp processed using acid-free and elementary chlorine-free practices. Furthermore, the publisher ensures that the text paper and cover board used have met acceptable environmental accreditation standards.

For further information on
Blackwell Publishing, visit our website:
www.blackwellpublishing.com

Contents

Contents

Acknowledgments

The publishers gratefully acknowledge the following for permission to reproduce copyright material.

Cambridge University Press and the London School of Economics for permission to reproduce extracts from N. Mackenzie, ed., *The Letters of Beatrice and Sidney Webb. Volumes I—III*, Cambridge University Press, 1978. © London School of Economics.

Carcanet Publishers for permission to reproduce "The Eugenist" by Robert Graves. From: Beryl Graves and Dunstan Ward, eds., Robert Graves, *Complete Poems* Vol ii, Manchester: Carcanet, 1997, p. 156.

The National Library of Scotland for permission to quote from the letters of Elizabeth Frances McFall (Sarah Grand)

University College London for permission to quote from the Galton archive.

Notes on Contributors

Tim Armstrong is a Reader in Modern English and American Literature at Royal Holloway, University of London. His publications include *Modernism, Technology and the Body: A Cultural Study* (1998) and *Haunted Hardy: Poetry, Memory, History* (2000), as well as the edited volumes *American Bodies* (1996) and (co-edited) *Beyond the Pleasure Dome: Writing and Addiction from the Romantics* (1993), and a selection of Hardy's poetry for Longman Annotated Texts.

Todd Avery is Assistant Professor of English at the University of Massachusetts, Lowell, where he teaches late-Victorian and twentieth-century British literature and culture. He has published essays on Virginia Woolf, the Bloomsbury Group, and Victorian ethics, and a monograph, *Close and Affectionate Friends: Desmond and Molly MacCarthy and the Bloomsbury Group* (1999). His current research projects include books on Bloomsbury's ethics and British modernists' involvement with the BBC.

Michael Bell is Professor of English and Comparative Literary Studies at the University of Warwick. He has taught in France, Germany, Canada and the USA and writes mainly on modernism, European fiction since Cervantes, and philosophical themes such a primitivism, myth, and the history of sentiment. His books include *D. H. Lawrence: Language and Being* (1992), *Modernism and Myth* (1997), and *Sentimentalism, Ethics and the Culture of Feeling* (2000). He is currently working on a study of the theme of *Bildung* in Rousseau, Goethe, and Nietzsche.

Patrick Brantlinger is Rudy Professor of English at Indiana University. He served as Editor of *Victorian Studies* from 1980 to 1990 and his most recent books are *The Reading Lesson* (1998) and *Who Killed Shakespeare? What's Happened to English since the Radical Sixties* (2001).

David Bradshaw is Hawthornden Fellow and Tutor in English Literature at Worcester College, Oxford, a Fellow of the English Association and an Editor of the *Review of English Studies*. He has edited *The Hidden Huxley* and *Brave New World* (both 1994); Oxford World Classics editions of *The White Peacock* (1997), *Women in Love* (1998), *Mrs. Dalloway* (2000) and Virginia Woolf's *The Mark on the Wall and Other Short Fiction* (2001); the Penguin Classics editions of *Decline and Fall* (2001) and *The Good Soldier* (2002), and has published widely on modernist literature and thought.

Stephen Frosh is Professor of Psychology and Director of the Centre for Psychosocial Studies in the School of Psychology at Birkbeck College, University of London. His numerous academic publications include *For and Against Psychoanalysis* (1997), *Sexual Difference* (1994), *Identity Crisis* (1991), and *The Politics of Psychoanalysis* (2nd edn 1999). His most recent books are *Young Masculinities* (with Ann Phoenix and Rob Pattman, 2002) and *After Words* (2002).

Mary Ann Gillies is an Associate Professor of English at Simon Fraser University, Vancouver, Canada. Her main areas of interest are Anglo-American modernism and cultural studies. She is the author of *Henri Bergson and British Modernism* (1996), has recently completed a book on the literary agent in Britain, 1880—1920, and is currently at work on a project that investigates the ways in which literary reputations were constructed (and destroyed) in the first half of the twentieth century.

Peter D. McDonald is a Fellow of St Hugh's College and a Lecturer in English at the University of Oxford. He is the author of *British Literary Culture and Publishing Practice* (1997) and the co-editor of *Making Meaning: "Printers of the Mind" and Other Essays by D. F. McKenzie* (2002).

Jeremy MacClancy is a Professor of Social Anthropology at Oxford Brookes University. He has carried out fieldwork in the Southwest Pacific, Basque Spain, Nigeria, and the London auction rooms. His most recent books are *The Decline of Carlism* (2000) and *Exotic No More: Anthropology Today* (2002). Besides teaching the anthropologies of art, food, and Europe, he has a particular interest in the history of British social anthropology and its interfaces with writers and the public.

April McMahon is Professor of English Language and Linguistics at the University of Sheffield. Her main research interests involve language classification; the contribution phonological theories can make to explaining sound change; and the history of English, especially Scots. She is the author of *Understanding Language Change* (1994), *Lexical Phonology and the History of English* (2000), *Change, Chance, and Optimality* (2000), and *An Introduction to English Phonology* (2001).

Angelique Richardson is a Lecturer in Victorian Literature and Culture at the University of Exeter. She is the author of *Love and Eugenics in the Late Nineteenth Century: Science, Fiction, and Rational Reproduction* (2003), editor of *Women Who Did: Stories by Men and Women 1890–1914* (2002), and co-editor of *The New Woman in Fiction and in Fact: Fin-de-Siècle Feminisms* (2001). She is a contributing editor of *Critical Quarterly*.

Michael H. Whitworth is a Lecturer in English Literature at the University of Wales, Bangor, and is the author of *Einstein's Wake: Relativity, Metaphor, and Modernist Literature* (2001). He is currently writing a book on Virginia Woolf and her socio-political contexts, and is editing an anthology on modernism.

Sarah Wilkinson completed her D.Phil. thesis, "Perceptions of Public Opinion in British Foreign Policy-Making about Nazi Germany, 1933—1938," in 2000. She has taught British and international history at Oxford and Reading universities but is currently training to become a barrister. She is a Fellow of All Souls College, Oxford.

Chronology

Death of Flaubert. Death of George Eliot. Birth of Lytton Strachey. Birth of Apollinaire. Gladstone becomes Prime Minister for the second time (–1885). First Anglo-Boer War (–1881).	**1880**	Gilbert and Sullivan, *The Pirates of Penzance*. Meredith, *The Tragic Comedians*. Gissing, *Workers in the Dawn*. Hardy, *The Trumpet-Major*. Dostoevsky, *The Brothers Karamazov*.
Death of Disraeli. Death of Carlyle. Death of Dostoevsky. Birth of Picasso. Birth of Bartók.	**1881**	Gilbert and Sullivan, *Patience*. James, *The Portrait of a Lady; Washington Square*. Christina Rossetti, *A Pageant and other Poems*. D. G. Rossetti, *Ballads and Sonnets*. Shaw, *Love Among the Artists*. E. B. Tylor, *Anthropology*. Wilde, *Poems*. Ibsen, *Ghosts*.
Death of Darwin. Death of Emerson. Death of D. G.	**1882**	Froude, *History of the First Forty Years of Carlyle's Life*.

Rossetti. Death of Trollope.
Death of James Thomson.
Birth of Virginia Woolf.
Birth of James Joyce. Birth
of Stravinsky. Society for
Psychical Research founded.
Second Married Women's
Property Act.

Gilbert and Sullivan,
    Iolanthe.
Jefferies, *Bevis.*
Shaw, *Cashel Byron's
    Profession.*
Stevenson, *Treasure Island.*
Wagner, *Parsifal.*

Death of Wagner. Death of   **1883**
    Marx. Birth of W. C.
    Williams. Birth of Mussolini.

Carpenter, *Towards
    Democracy.*
Shaw, *An Unsocial Socialist.*
Schreiner, *The Story of an
    African Farm.*

Birth of Sean O'Casey. *Oxford*   **1884**
English Dictionary begins to appear
(–1928)

*The Century Guild Hobby
    Horse* (1884–92).
Gilbert and Sullivan,
    Princess Ida.
Gissing, *The Unclassed.*
Twain, *Huckleberry Finn.*
Ruskin, *The Storm-Cloud of the
    Nineteenth Century.*
Huysmans, *A Rebours.*

Death of Hugo. Birth of Pound.   **1885**
    Birth of D. H. Lawrence.
    Radio waves discovered.
    Internal combustion
    engine invented.

Jefferies, *After London.*
Gilbert and Sullivan, *The
    Mikado.*
Meredith, *Diana of the
    Crossways.*
Pater, *Marius the Epicurean.*
Ruskin, *Praeterita* (1885–9).
Zola, *Germinal.*

Defeat of Gladstone's first   **1886**
    Irish Home Rule Bill.

Gissing, *Demos.*
Rider Haggard, *King
    Solomon's Mines.*
James, *The Bostonians, The
    Princess Casamassima.*

		Stevenson, *Dr. Jekyll and Mr Hyde, Kidnapped.*
		Hardy, *The Mayor of Casterbridge.*
Queen Victoria's Golden Jubilee.	**1887**	Conan Doyle, *A Study in Scarlet.*
		Frazer, *Totemism.*
		Gilbert and Sullivan, *Ruddigore.*
		Rider Haggard, *Allan Quartermain, She.*
		Hardy, *The Woodlanders.*
		Pater, *Imaginary Portraits.*
		"Mark Rutherford," *The Revolution in Tanner's Lane.*
		Stevenson, *Underwoods.*
		Verdi, *Otello.*
Death of Matthew Arnold. Birth of T. S. Eliot.	**1888**	Arnold, *Essays in Criticism* (Second Series).
		Kipling, *Plain Tales from the Hills.*
		Gilbert and Sullivan, *The Yeomen of the Guard.*
		Moore, *Confessions of a Young Man.*
		Morris, *Signs of Change, A Dream of John Ball.*
		Mrs. Humphry Ward, *Robert Elsmere.*
Death of Robert Browning. Death of Wilkie Collins. Death of Gerard Manley Hopkins. Birth of Hitler.	**1889**	Booth, *Life and Labour of the People in London* (17 vols., –1903).
		Gilbert and Sullivan, *The Gondoliers.*
		Gissing, *The Nether World.*
		Pater, *Appreciations.*

		"Mark Rutherford," *Catherine Furze*.
		Stevenson, *The Master of Ballantrae*.
		Yeats, *The Wanderings of Oisin and Other Poems*.
Death of Newman.	**1890**	Frazer, *The Golden Bough* (12 vols., 1890–1915).
Death of van Gogh.		Morris, *News from Nowhere*.
Fall of Parnell.		Booth, *In Darkest England*.
		Ibsen, *Hedda Gabler*.
Death of Rimbaud.	**1891**	Gissing, *New Grub Street*.
Death of Melville.		Hardy, *Tess of the D'Urbervilles*.
Birth of Prokofiev.		Wilde, *The Picture of Dorian Gray*.
Death of Tennyson.	**1892**	First English translation of Ibsen, *Peer Gynt*.
Birth of Ivy Compton-Burnett.		First English translation of Zola's works.
Birth of Vita Sackville-West.		Gissing, *Born in Exile*.
		Kipling, *Barrack-Room Ballads*.
		Yeats, *The Countess Cathleen*.
Death of Maupassant.	**1893**	Pinero, *The Second Mrs. Tanqueray*.
Second Irish Home Rule Bill rejected.		Shaw, *Mrs. Warren's Profession*.
Formation of the Independent Labour Party (ILP).		
Death of Stevenson.	**1894**	The *Yellow Book* (–1897).
Death of Pater.		Moore, *Esther Waters*.
Death of Christina Rossetti.		Shaw, *Arms and the Man*.
Birth of Aldous Huxley.		Debussy, *L'après-midi d'un faune*.
Trial and conviction of Dreyfus.		

Death of T. H. Huxley.	**1895**	Wilde, *The Importance of*
Trials and conviction of Oscar		*Being Earnest.*
Wilde.		Wells, *The Time Machine.*
Röntgen's discovery of X-rays.		Hardy, *Jude the Obscure.*
Marconi invents wireless		Chekhov, *The Seagull.*
telegraphy.		Conrad, *Almayer's Folly.*
Invention of the		
cinematograph.		
Death of William Morris.	**1896**	Housman, *A Shropshire*
Death of Verlaine.		*Lad.*
Birth of F. Scott Fitzgerald.		*Daily Mail* founded.
		Puccini, *La Bohème.*
		Wells, *The Island of Dr.*
		Moreau.
Queen Victoria's Diamond	**1897**	Conrad, *Tales of Unrest.*
Jubilee.		Stoker, *Dracula.*
		James, *What Maisie Knew.*
		Shaw, *Plays Pleasant and*
		Unpleasant.
		Wells, *The Invisible Man.*
Death of Mallarmé.	**1898**	Hardy, *Wessex Poems.*
Death of Gladstone.		Wells, *The War of the Worlds.*
Death of "Lewis Carroll".		Wilde, *The Ballad of Reading*
Birth of Hemingway.		*Gaol.*
The Curies discover radium		
and plutonium.		
Birth of Nabokov.	**1899**	Yeats, *The Wind among the*
Second Anglo-Boer War		*Reeds.*
(–1902).		Tolstoy, *Resurrection.*
Death of Nietzsche.	**1900**	*Daily Express* founded.
Death of Wilde.		Conrad, *Lord Jim.*
Death of Ruskin.		Freud, *The Interpretation of*
Boxer Rebellion (–1901).		*Dreams.*
Relief of Mafeking.		

Death of Queen Victoria; accession of Edward VII.	**1901**	Mann, *Buddenbrooks.* Strindberg, *Dance of Death.* Kipling, *Kim.*
Death of Zola.	**1902**	Bennett, *Anna of the Five Towns.* Gide, *The Immoralist.* Conrad, *Heart of Darkness.* Hobson, *Imperialism.* James, *The Wings of the Dove.* William James, *Varieties of Religious Experience.* *Times Literary Supplement* (*TLS*) founded.
Death of Whistler. Death of Gauguin. Death of Gissing. Death of Herbert Spencer. Birth of "George Orwell". Birth of Waugh. First aeroplane flight. Women's Social and Political Union (WSPU) founded by Emmeline Pankhurst.	**1903**	Butler, *The Way of All Flesh.* Childers, *The Riddle of the Sands.* James, *The Ambassadors.* Shaw, *Man and Superman.* Moore, *Principia Ethica.* *Daily Mirror* founded.
Death of Chekhov. Death of Leslie Stephen. Franco-British Entente. Russo-Japanese War (–1905).	**1904**	Synge, *Riders to the Sea.* Chekhov, *The Cherry Orchard.* James, *The Golden Bowl.* Conrad, *Nostromo.* Hardy, *The Dynasts* (–1908). Puccini, *Madame Butterfly.*
Birth of Sartre. Special Theory of Relativity. Sinn Fein founded in Dublin.	**1905**	Richard Strauss, *Salomé.* Wilde, *De Profundis.* Wharton, *The House of Mirth.* Forster, *Where Angels Fear to Tread.*
Death of Ibsen.	**1906**	Galsworthy, *The Man of*

Death of Cézanne.		*Property.*
Birth of Beckett.		Kipling, *Puck of Pook's Hill.*
Liberal Government elected.		Sinclair, *The Jungle.*
		"Everyman's Library" begun.
Death of Huysmans.	**1907**	Picasso, *Les Demoiselles*
Birth of Auden.		*d'Avignon.*
Cubist exhibition, Paris.		Conrad, *The Secret Agent.*
		Synge, *The Playboy of the*
		Western World.
		Forster, *The Longest Journey.*
		Bergson, *L'Evolution créatrice.*
Old Age Pensions Act.	**1908**	Stein, *Three Lives.*
		Bennett, *The Old Wives' Tale.*
		Forster, *A Room with a View.*
		Pound, *A Lume Spento.*
		Sorel, *Reflections on Violence.*
		Elgar, *First Symphony.*
		Bartók, *First String Quartet.*
Death of Meredith.	**1909**	Marinetti, *Futurist Manifesto.*
Death of Swinburne.		Mahler, *Ninth Symphony.*
Blériot flies across English		Matisse, *The Dance.*
Channel.		Frank Lloyd Wright, *Robie*
Freud lectures on		*House.*
psychoanalysis in the USA.		Pound, *Personae.*
		Schoenberg, *Five Orchestral*
		Pieces.
		Wells, *Tono-Bungay.*
Death of Edward VII; accession	**1910**	Stravinsky, *The Firebird.*
of George V.		Forster, *Howards End.*
Death of Twain.		Wells, *The History of Mr. Polly.*
Death of Tolstoy.		Russell and Whitehead,
Death of Florence Nightingale.		*Principia Mathematica*
First Post-Impressionist		(–1913).
Exhibition, London.		

Death of Galton. Death of Gilbert. Death of Mahler. National Insurance Act. Suffragette agitation.	**1911**	Beerbohm, *Zuleika Dobson*. Bennett, *Hilda Lessways*. Conrad, *Under Western Eyes*. Douglas, *Siren Land*. Lawrence, *The White Peacock*. "Mansfield", *In a German Pension*. Pound, *Canzoni*. Wells, *The New Machiavelli*. Wharton, *Ethan Frome*.
Death of Scott of the Antarctic. Birth of Pollock. Second Post-Impressionist Exhibition, London. National Dock Strike. Sinking of the *Titanic*.	**1912**	Pound, *Ripostes*. *Daily Herald* founded. Mann, *Death in Venice*. Marcel Duchamp, *Nude Descending a Staircase*. Shaw, *Pygmalion*. Schoenberg, *Pierrot Lunaire*.
Second Rejection of Irish Home Rule Bill by Lords. Suffragette demonstrations, London.	**1913**	*New Statesman* founded. Cather, *O Pioneers!* Lawrence, *Sons and Lovers*. Frost, *A Boy's Will*. Proust, *A la recherche du temps perdu* (–1927). Stravinsky, *Le Sacre du printemps*. Husserl, *Phenomenology*.
Birth of Dylan Thomas. Irish Home Rule Bill passed by Parliament. Outbreak of World War I.	**1914**	Joyce, *Dubliners*. Conrad, *Chance*. Bell, *Art*. Frost, *North of Boston*. Founding of *BLAST*.
Sinking of *SS Lusitania*. General Theory of Relativity. Air attacks on London.	**1915**	Woolf, *The Voyage Out*. Lawrence, *The Rainbow*. Maugham, *Of Human Bondage*. Pound, *Cathay*. Ford, *The Good Soldier*.

Richardson, *Pointed Roofs.*
D. W. Griffith, *Birth of a Nation.*

Death of Henry James.	**1916**	Joyce, *A Portrait of the Artist as a Young Man.*
First Battle of the Somme (July–November).		Pound, *Lustra.*
Easter Rising in Dublin.		
Gallipoli.		
Lloyd George Prime Minister.		
Dada.		

Passchendaele (July–November).	**1917**	Eliot, *Prufrock and Other Observations.*
USA enters War.		Valéry, *La Jeune parque.*
Balfour Declaration.		Lowell, *Tendencies in Modern American Poetry.*
Russian Revolution.		Jung, *The Unconscious.*
		Yeats, *The Wild Swans at Coole.*

Death of Owen.	**1918**	Joyce, *Exiles.*
Armistice (11 Nov.).		Lewis, *Tarr.*
Influenza pandemic (–1919).		Strachey, *Eminent Victorians.*
Votes for women aged thirty and over in Britain.		West, *The Return of the Soldier.*
		Hopkins, *Poems.*
		Paul Klee, *Gartenplan.*

Bauhaus founded at Weimar by Walter Gropius.	**1919**	Picasso, *Pierrot and Harlequin.*
Treaty of Versailles.		Hardy, *Collected Poems.*
Atlantic flown by Alcock and Brown.		Sinclair, *Mary Olivier.*
Relativity scientifically proved.		Anderson, *Winesburg, Ohio.*
First woman MP elected (Nancy Astor).		Keynes, *The Economic. Consequences of the Peace.*
		Mencken, *The American Language.*
		Woolf, *Night and Day.*

League of Nations established.	**1920**	Lawrence, *Women in Love.*

American women achieve the vote.

Eliot, *The Sacred Wood.*
Shaw, *Heartbreak House.*
Wharton, *The Age of Innocence.*
Pound, *Hugh Selwyn Mauberley.*
"Mansfield", *Bliss and Other Stories.*
Lewis, *Main Street.*
O'Neill, *The Emperor Jones.*
Fry, *Vision and Design.*
Matisse, *L'Odalisque.*

Irish Free State established.

1921

Pirandello, *Six Characters in Search of an Author.*
Dos Passos, *Three Soldiers.*
Huxley, *Crome Yellow.*
Picasso, *Three Musicians.*
Munch, *The Kiss.*

Death of Proust.
Birth of Larkin.
Fascists in power in Italy.
Founding of the British Broadcasting Company (BBC).

1922

Eliot, *The Waste Land.*
Joyce, *Ulysses.*
Woolf, *Jacob's Room.*
Lewis, *Babbit.*
Wittgenstein, *Tractatus Logico-Philosophicus.*
Fritz Lang, *Dr. Mabuse.*
Friedrich Murnau, *Nosferatu.*
Criterion founded.

Death of "Mansfield".
BBC radio begins transmission.
President Coolidge elected.

1923

Huxley, *Antic Hay.*
Lawrence, *Kangaroo.*
Macaulay, *Told by an Idiot.*
Stevens, *Harmonium.*

Death of Lenin.
Death of Kafka.
Death of Conrad.
First Labour Government.
Surrealist Manifesto.

1924

Forster, *A Passage to India.*
Mann, *The Magic Mountain.*
O'Casey, *Juno and the Paycock.*
Ford, *Some Do Not.*
Cecil B. de Mille, *The Ten Commandments.*

1925 Woolf, *Mrs. Dalloway.*
Stein, *The Making of Americans.*
Huxley, *Those Barren Leaves.*
Ford, *No More Parades.*
Fitzgerald, *The Great Gatsby.*
Dreiser, *An American Tragedy.*
Hemingway, *In Our Time.*
Kafka, *The Trial.*
Eisenstein, *Battleship Potemkin.*
Chaplin, *The Gold Rush.*
Picasso, *Three Dancers.*
Whitehead, *Science and the Modern World.*
Hitler, *Mein Kampf* (–1926).

Death of Rilke.
General Strike (Britain, May 3–12).

1926 Hemingway, *The Sun Also Rises* (*Fiesta* in England, 1927).
T. E. Lawrence, *The Seven Pillars of Wisdom.*
D. H. Lawrence, *The Plumed Serpent.*
Ford, *A Man Could Stand Up.*
Faulkner, *Soldier's Pay.*
Tawney, *Religion and the Rise of Capitalism.*
Fritz Lang, *Metropolis.*
Jean Renoir, *Nana.*
Moore, *Draped Reclining Figure.*

Lindbergh flies Atlantic solo.
First "talkies".

1927 Woolf, *To the Lighthouse.*
Hemingway, *Men without Women.*
Epstein, *Madonna and Child.*
Heidegger, *Being and Time.*
Wilder, *The Bridge at San Luis Rey.*

Death of Hardy.

1928 Yeats, *The Tower.*

Women's suffrage extended to women over 21 in Britain.		Bell, *Civilization*. Lawrence, *Lady Chatterley's Lover*. Huxley, *Point Counter Point*. Waugh, *Decline and Fall*. Woolf, *Orlando*. Hall, *The Well of Loneliness*. Eisenstein, *October*.
Second Surrealist Manifesto. Opening of the Museum of Modern Art, New York. Wall Street Crash.	**1929**	Aldington, *Death of a Hero*. Bridges, *The Testament of Beauty*. Faulkner, *The Sound and the Fury*. Graves, *Goodbye to All That*. Hitchcock, *Blackmail*. Woolf, *A Room of One's Own*.
Death of Lawrence. Death of Conan Doyle. Global Depression. Television begins in USA. Photo flashbulb invented.	**1930**	Auden, *Poems*. Eliot, *Ash Wednesday*. Crane, *The Bridge*. Faulkner, *As I Lay Dying*. Lewis, *Apes of God*. Waugh, *Vile Bodies*. Leavis, *Mass Civilisation and Minority Culture*. Freud, *Civilisation and its Discontents*.
National Government formed (UK). Abandonment of Gold Standard (UK).	**1931**	O'Neill, *Mourning Becomes Electra*. Matisse, *The Dance*. Fritz Lang, *M*. Charlie Chaplin, *City Lights*. Woolf, *The Waves*.
President Roosevelt elected.	**1932**	*Scrutiny* started. Brecht, *The Mother*. Céline, *Voyage au bout de la nuit*.

Auden, *The Orators.*
Huxley, *Brave New World.*

Hitler becomes Chancellor of Germany.	**1933**	Stein, *The Autobiography of Alice B. Toklas.* Malraux, *La Condition humaine.* Eliot, *The Use of Poetry and the Use of Criticism.* Orwell, *Down and Out in Paris and London.* Wells, *The Shape of Things to Come.* Yeats, *Collected Poems.*
Radioactivity discovered.	**1934**	Beckett, *More Pricks Than Kicks.* Eliot, *The Rock, After Strange Gods.* Fitzgerald, *Tender is the Night.* Pound, *ABC of Reading.* Waugh, *A Handful of Dust.* Miller, *Tropic of Cancer.*
Italian Invasion of Abyssinia (Nov).	**1935**	Eliot, *Murder in the Cathedral.* Auden and Isherwood, *The Dog Beneath the Skin.* Isherwood, *Mr. Norris Changes Trains.* Gershwin, *Porgy and Bess.* Dali, *Giraffe on Fire.* Shostakovich, *First Symphony.* Odets, *Waiting for Lefty.*
Death of George V; accession of Edward VIII; abdication crisis; accession of George VI. Death of Chesterton. Death of Housman.	**1936**	Auden, *Look, Stranger!* Faulkner, *Absalom, Absalom!* Thomas, *Twenty-five Poems.* Smith, *Novel on Yellow Paper.* Mondrian, *Composition in Red and Blue.*

Death of Kipling.
Spanish Civil War (–1939).
Moscow Show Trials.
BBC Television begins
 (Nov).

Huxley, *Eyeless in Gaza*.
Orwell, *Keep the Aspidistra Flying*.
Chaplin, *Modern Times*.
Ayer, *Language, Truth and Logic*.
Keynes, *General Theory of Employment, Interest and Money*.

Death of Barrie.
Death of Wharton.
Chamberlain Prime Minister.
Destruction of Guernica,
 Spain.

1937

Jones, *In Parenthesis*.
Orwell, *The Road to Wigan Pier*.
Woolf, *The Years*.
Tolkien, *The Hobbit*.
Picasso, *Guernica*.
Steinbeck, *Of Mice and Men*.

Munich agreement
 (Sept 30).
First jet engine.

1938

Beckett, *Murphy*.
Bowen, *The Death of the Heart*.
Green, *Brighton Rock*.
Mumford, *The Culture of Cities*.
Orwell, *Homage to Catalonia*.
Dos Passos, *U.S.A.*
Picasso, *Woman in Easy Chair*.
Bartók, *Violin Concerto*.
Yeats, *New Poems*.
Picture Post begins.

Death of Freud.
Death of Yeats.
Death of Ford.
Russo-German Pact.
Beginning of World War II
 (Sept 3).

1939

Joyce, *Finnegans Wake*.
MacNeice, *Autumn Journal*.
Orwell, *Coming Up for Air*.
Steinbeck, *The Grapes of Wrath*.
Eliot, *The Family Reunion*.
Isherwood, *Goodbye to Berlin*.
Picasso, *Night Fishing at Antibes*.
Jean Renoir, *The Rules of the Game*.
Yeats, *Last Poems and Two Plays*.

Introduction

David Bradshaw

This innovative collection of specially commissioned essays is essential reading for anyone wishing to come to terms with the intellectual matrix of Anglo-American literary modernism. In making available to non-specialist readers twelve expert overviews of some of the most significant fields and phenomena – such as physics, anthropology, psychoanalysis, and Nietzscheanism – which impacted on the "revolution of the word" between (roughly) 1880 and 1939, the companion provides both a range of contexts for modernist literature and a series of essays which are accessible and authoritative in their own right. Together they comprise the story of an age.

For the first time, material condensed from a formidable array of technical books and learned articles has been brought together in a single volume, and while the companion's main target reader is the literary student, it is anticipated that its scope and reach will also appeal to specialists in a number of other disciplines and, indeed, to any general reader with an interest in discovering more about the remarkable intellectual milieu of an extraordinary cultural epoch.

An enhanced awareness of the efflorescence of ideas which occurred in twelve major fields in the late nineteenth and early twentieth centuries can only intensify the reader's appreciation of the radical and iconoclastic environment in which literary modernism emerged and flourished. Most of the essays foreground individual modernist writers who registered the contiguous upheavals in science, philosophy, and language with particular vividness and relish, and in all the chapters the stress falls on the effects which specific breakthroughs, concepts, and paradigm shifts had on the wider intellectual community rather than on a more narrow and insular account of the specialist topic in question.

If contextual knowledge can release textual meanings, none of the authors of this compilation would wish to claim that the relationship between imaginative writing and the ideas it embodies, shadows, or kicks against is anything but complex, multiplex, and sensitive. However, there are so many instances of modernist writers appropriating aspects of and even whole areas of specialist knowledge which in turn transformed the shape and tenor of their work – Yeats and eugenics, H. D. and psychoanalysis, Graves and myth, are obvious examples – that this collection needs no more justification, perhaps, than that it will undoubtedly further an understanding of such modernist bending, borrowing, and bricolage. Among other things, these essays will reinvigorate the reader's thinking about such core issues as the Nietzschean inflection of modernism, the advent and appeal of Bergsonism, the modernist state, publishing and the modernist reader, the interface between technology and modernism, eugenics and the life sciences, the institutions and market conditions of modernism, and that more precise revolution of the word instigated by Saussure, Bloomfield, and their fellow-linguists.

It is now universally accepted that the Anglo-American modernist movement comprised much more than a largely white, male avant-garde conscientiously detached from and contemptuous of both the literary mainstream and modernity at large. We also know that human character did not change in 1910 (despite Virginia Woolf's claim that it did), just as a decade earlier (despite the death of Nietzsche) the new century had dawned without incident, culturally speaking, apart from the appearance (in German) of Freud's *Interpretation of Dreams*. Indeed, critical speculation about when, precisely, modernism burst forth and when it petered out looks more and more futile as time goes on: no period of cultural activity is airtight and all watersheds form part of more extensive upland systems that are fed by rain carried from far away. This volume's attempt to isolate and elucidate the major intellectual developments which assumed importance for modernist writers has been made with an acute awareness that the temper of a historical period is always and inevitably continuous with the past as well as being fissiparous, contradictory, manifold, and fugitive. Preoccupations which appear to have colonized the mind of one writer show no sign of having had any influence at all on the vast majority of his or her contemporaries, making any attempt to capture an era's "turn of mind" or "climate of opinion" all the more fraught with conceptual, procedural, and terminological difficulty. Like Patricia Waugh, the authors of these essays would forcefully reject "the notion of *Zeitgeist* as a seamless and overarching historical unity binding literature to philosophy and scientific discovery in a straightforward reflectionist chain" (Waugh 1997: 6). But, to a greater or lesser extent, they all share a conviction that it can only benefit students of the period in general, and students of its literature in particular, to become more familiar with specialist fields of knowledge which are patently in play, one way or another, in the diverse writings of the modernist age, a remarkably distinct, though far from stand-alone cultural era.

If each of these essays is concerned to facilitate the reading of modernist texts by bringing on the reader's receptivity to what they may enclose, an even greater aspiration of the volume is to be dependable without being reductive. Background or contextual knowledge may amplify our understanding of a text by indicating new possibilities of interpretation, but contexts must never be configured as cordons beyond which contextually "unauthorized" readings are barred from progressing. This companion is conceived as a guidebook, not a code book, and its chief aim is to provide a free-standing, probing, and reliable supplement to modernism which avoids the pitfalls of superficiality, over-prescriptiveness, and oversimplification.

Neither the editor nor any of the contributors would wish to argue that the twelve topics covered by the essays are the *only* modernist preoccupations which the reader should consider. Another, longer book might have contained additional essays on, among other things, the occult, social credit, aviation, race, historiography, skyscrapers, dance, censorship, Russia, America, rejuvenation, cinematography, telephony, music hall, and ecology, yet even so it would have been hardly less selective for all its extra bulk. Taken together, these twelve new essays explore what are probably the most significant of the ideas which were "in the air" (to borrow a phrase of Grant Allen's quoted in Angelique Richardson's chapter) during the modernist epoch. However, the mentality of modernism was so thick with novelty and discovery that it would be unwise to be too categorical about this. Moreover, there have already been numerous studies of the great structural issues which spanned the period, such as feminism, imperialism, and war, and this is the only reason why chapters have not been dedicated to those key concerns in this volume.

One of the most interesting aspects of the book, perhaps, is the way it will help promote an understanding of the cross-fertilization of ideas in the period. The eugenist R. A. Fisher, for example, "one of the most important and productive thinkers in statistics of [the twentieth] century"

3

(Mazumdar 1991: 96), was also deeply read in Nietzsche. "An interest in Nietzsche," indeed:

> was not uncommon among the eugenists. Maximilian Mügge . . . who occasionally lectured for the Eugenics Education Society, wrote in 1909 in the first volume of the *Eugenics Review* that Galton had founded a racial religion: the ideal of the super-man would supply the religious feeling of responsibility which would give the science its popular support. Havelock Ellis, another founding member of the [Eugenics Education] Society, was also one of Nietzsche's most prolific exponents in English . . . . The commentators at this time generally saw Nietzsche as the philosopher of Darwinism and evolution whose *Übermensch* was the forerunner of a new human race, a master race. (Mazumdar 1991: 104)

Similarly, Oscar Levy, the man responsible for the first complete and authorized translation of the works of Nietzsche into English, was also a degenerationist and dedicated eugenist, as was his fellow Nietzschean, the anti-democrat and misogynist Anthony Ludovici (for more on both of them see Michael Bell's chapter on Nietzscheanism). The reader of the first three chapters of this collection, therefore, will have been introduced to the mindset of a common intellectual type in the modernist period, the post-Darwinian, Nietzschean, eugenist and elitist, and it is hoped that other chapter clusters will offer similar insights. Equally valuable is the way in which the essays will encourage the reader to look at the same text from a number of perspectives: for example, *The Waste Land* as seen through the eyes of Jeremy MacClancy, Mary Ann Gillies, Stephen Frosh, and myself.

"Literature undeniably reflects in some sense the life and thought of its time," Michael Bell began his Introduction to the *1900–1930* volume of "The Context of English Literature" series in 1980, "but to determine how it does so is the delicate and continuing function of criticism." He continued:

> It may address itself to "life" in a greater or lesser degree but its value as literature is not in any simple sense contingent on such a criterion. The vitality or meaningfulness of literature hinges on its internal intensity rather than the quantity of historical information in a factual sense that it may include. It is a delicate matter, therefore, to mediate pertinently between literary experience and its putative contexts; to discuss "influences" and preoccupations without collapsing the tension of this vital heterogeneity. (1980: 1)

These cautionary words are as relevant today as they were when Michael

Bell first wrote them, and they are especially germane to a period in which the autonomy of the writer was established as a "vital" aesthetic principle. Even though the once-dominant concept of the modernist text as inviolably formalist is no longer tenable, it remains true that any approach to the "putative contexts" of a modernist text should be made tentatively and "delicate[ly]," and in full recognition of the limitations of such an enterprise as well as its value. Michael Bell' s essay for this present volume is not the only one which seeks to bring into play all the tact and circumspection required of the specialist contributor attempting to negotiate between the "vital heterogeneity" of literature and its specific historical contexts.

References and Further Reading

Bell, Michael, ed. 1980. *The Context of English Literature 1900–1930*. London: Methuen.
Mazumdar, Pauline M. H. 1991. *Eugenics, Human Genetics and Human Failings: The Eugenics Society, its Sources and its Critics in Britain*. London: Routledge.
Waugh, Patricia, ed. 1997. *Revolutions of the Word: Intellectual Contexts for the Study of Modern Literature*. London and New York: Arnold.

1

The Life Sciences: "Everybody nowadays talks about evolution"

Angelique Richardson

In the first year of the third millennium, Charles Darwin replaced Charles Dickens on the British ten-pound note. He is celebrated again by the state, just as, over a century earlier, though his ideas had shocked and dismayed his contemporaries, no less than they had fascinated them, he was buried with Christian ceremony in Westminster Abbey. In 1889 the biologist and popular, prolific writer Grant Allen remarked: "everybody nowadays talks about evolution. Like electricity, the cholera germ, woman's rights, the great mining boom, and the Eastern Question, it is 'in the air'" (1889: 31). Stringing together apparently unrelated concerns of the late nineteenth century, Allen could not have chosen a more consanguineous group. Social and scientific progress, and questions of race, race failure, gender, and disease were converging under the umbrella of "evolution" (see also Chapter 2).

The politics of evolution had shifted radically over the course of the nineteenth century. In the early decades, on the edge of the hungry forties, atheistic revolutionaries were evangelizing bottom-up evolution, and the ideas of the French zoologist Jean-Baptiste de Lamarck (1744–1829) were appearing in the pauper press; the idea that an animal could transform itself into a higher being and pass on all its gains (without godly intervention) appealed to militant members of the working class. Lamarck put forward the idea of the "inheritance of acquired characteristics" or "use-inheritance" in his evolutionary treatise, *Philosophie zoologique* (1809).

This theory attempted to account for the transmutation of species, and posited that in responding to environmental changes, organisms were constantly susceptible to structural and functional changes. Each generation, in learning to cope with its environment, would transmit its learning, as acquired characteristics, to successive generations. It drew upon the materialist belief in spontaneous generation, the ascent of a scale of organization – a biological reworking of the great chain of being – and the idea of environmental influence, primarily *education*, which a number of Enlightenment thinkers had accepted in different forms. Darwin would harness the radical potential of evolution for bourgeois ends, redefining humans as material beings, and nature as a competitive free-for-all (Desmond and Moore 1992: 44). Looking back half a century in 1907, Edmund Gosse remarked in *Father and Son: A Study of Two Temperaments*:

> This was the great moment in the history of thought when the theory of the mutability of species was preparing to throw a flood of light upon all departments of human speculation and action. It was becoming necessary to stand emphatically in one army or the other . . . . The reactionaries, although never dreaming of the fate which hung over them, had not been idle. In 1857 the astounding question had for the first time been propounded with contumely, "What then, did we come from an orang-outang?" (1907: 102–3)

Robert Owen, President-elect of the British Association for the Advancement of Science, put humanity in a special sub-class, distinct from all (other) animals (1858); "I wonder what a chimpanzee would say to this?" responded Darwin (*Correspondence* 6: 419; Desmond and Moore 1992: 453). In the wake of the withdrawal of God, a new space opened for causal explanations of history, and the search for new social, political, and, now, scientific authorities, for determining forces, intensified. By the second half of the nineteenth century, the dramatic achievements of the experimental and theoretical sciences had brought a new prestige to science. Science had become a major source of military, industrial, and economic strength, and this lent it a new political status, increasing its potential as a form of social control.

Thomas Huxley concluded his review of *The Origin of Species* (1859): "we do not believe that . . . any work has appeared calculated to exert so large an influence . . . in extending the dominion of Science over regions of thought into which she has, as yet, hardly penetrated" (1864: 336). Darwin had left his readers with a cliffhanger: "In the distant future I see open fields for far more important researches. Psychology will be based on a new foundation, that of the necessary acquirement of each mental power and capacity by gradation. Light will be thrown on the origin of man and his history" (Ch. 14). Direct light would be thrown on human origin in Darwin's *The Descent of Man, and Selection in Relation to Sex* (1871).

Biology and Sociology

There were several camps in the evolutionary debates, but the precise makeup and goals of these camps shifted during the course of the nineteenth century, as various biological and social agendas modified, concurred, and diverged. Biology is uniquely positioned among the sciences. As Heschel noted in *Who is Man?*: "A theory about the stars never becomes a part of the being of the stars . . . we become what we think of ourselves" (1965: 7). Biology is not overtly concerned with social transformation but, perhaps because it shares with other sciences a claim to enjoy a value-free objectivity, its potential to change how we perceive ourselves is even greater. Social thought before Darwin had stressed the inevitability of society and nature taking the forms they did: for example, William Paley's *Natural Theology* (1802) and the *Bridgewater Treatises* (1835) were attempts to reconcile the observations of science with what Wordsworth had termed "Nature's holy plan." By 1891, Hardy could say in *Tess of the D'Urbervilles*: "some people would like to know whence the poet whose philosophy is in these days deemed as profound and trustworthy as his song is breezy and pure, gets his authority for speaking of 'Nature's holy plan'" (Wordsworth, "Lines Written in Early Spring," 1, 22; Hardy 1891: 62).

Early in the nineteenth century Enlightenment systems of classification were called into question; the image of the tree was usurping the great chain of being. In 1836, Darwin returned from his five-year trip around the world in *HMS Beagle*, laden with material refutation of static, linear systems of classification. Natural sciences, as Foucault observes in *The Order of Things*, were replaced by social sciences as static analytical taxonomies were replaced with functional organic systems. Darwin's branching evolution undid fixity for good; with *The Origin of Species*, hierarchies became blurred and essentially problematic.

In the middle years of the nineteenth century, as the Creation Story was called into question, concern and excitement focused on alternative possibilities for the origin of humanity. "Hurrah, the Monkey Book has come," rejoiced Darwin in a letter to Huxley (Thomas Huxley Papers 5: 173) as Huxley's forthright *Evidence as to Man's Place in Nature* (1863) appeared.

But, in the decades that followed, biology became increasingly preoccupied with where humankind was *going*. This was partly because Darwin's theory of evolution was anti-teleological; it destroyed the idea of determinism. Here, barnacles played a key role; their life story refuted the idea of evolution as progress, recapitulating by a move from free-swimming larvae to sessile animals the possibility that evolution could move backwards as indifferently as forwards: life was in flux. As Huxley pointed out in 1894,

> the word "evolution", now generally applied to the cosmic process, has had a singular history, and is used in various senses. Taken in its popular signification it means progressive development, that is, gradual change from a condition of relative uniformity to one of relative complexity; but its connotation has been widened to include the phenomena of retrogressive metamorphosis, that is, of progress from a condition of relative complexity to one of relative uniformity. (6)

Like Darwin, Karl Marx explained human existence in terms of causal historical processes. At Marx's graveside in Highgate cemetery in London in 1883, Friedrich Engels said: "just as Darwin discovered the law of development of organic nature, so Marx discovered the law of development of human history" (Marx and Engels 1968: 429–30). Drawing on the Malthusian idea that population growth will inevitably outstrip food and space, Darwin defined life as struggle without a goal. Marx and Engels saw *The Origin of Species* as a "bitter satire" on man and nature; Marx remarked that "Darwin recognizes among beasts and plants his English society" (Desmond and Moore 1992: 485).

Natural selection worked toward adaptation, not progress; it was opportunistic, and ungoverned. Various thinkers grappled with the implications of the undirected nature of biological development. Wilde in *De Profundis* celebrated uncertainty – a version of Keats's "negative capability," but he could do so with a new language and backing. He embraced "the dynamic forces of life"; and "those in whom such forces become incarnate": "people whose desire is solely for self-realization never know where they are going. They can't know" (180). In 1911, in *Creative Evolution*, the French moral philosopher Henri Bergson posited a constant state of tension between the original creative life-force, the *élan vital*, and the resistance of the inert matter from which that force must construct living bodies (see Bowler 1983: 241; see also Chapter 5 in this volume); the irregular pattern of biological development, progress, even derives from this tension. Inherent in every particle of life was this rebel force.

With the new focus on what the future might hold, biology gave birth to sociology. Scratch the surfaces of sociology and biology and it soon becomes clear that both disciplines have had, from their inception, as much to do with prescription as with description. In 1853 Auguste Comte, who coined the term "sociology," wrote "the subordination of social science to biology is so evident that nobody denies it in statement, however it may be neglected in practice" (1853: II, 112). Comte held that the biological sciences were the immediate historical precursors of sociology and the logical base upon which the theories of the social sciences could be built. The organic metaphor of a functional society was a powerful catalyst for advancing the division between the sociologically normal and the pathological, a division which first appeared in the work of Comte. Comte was drawing on Claude Henri de Saint-Simon's idea that society, like the human body, had its own physiology. European sociology is grounded in analogical organicist reasoning (see D. Porter 1997: 8; T. M. Porter 1990). Herbert Spencer, sociologist and intellectual ally of George Eliot, did more than anyone to popularize the term "evolution." Integrating popular biology with social argument through analogy, he condensed laws of society and laws of physiology, and argued that life (including the life of society) was moving inevitably toward higher forms. Spencer opposed any state intervention, aggressively promoting, instead, *laissez-faire* capitalism as the social form most likely to allow each individual to exercise their powers fully in the service of the community. The pressures of competition would, he believed, ensure optimum adaptation and hence progress. For example, in "The Social Organism," he argued that "the changes going on" and "social organization in its leading peculiarities . . . are consequent on general natural causes." Responsible for the glib tautology "the survival of the fittest" (1864: ss. 164; 165), Spencer's ideas lent themselves to a biologization of racial and social hierarchies which would underpin late nineteenth-century "social Darwinism" – the selective application of Darwinian ideas to society. The spaces between Darwinism and Social Darwinism would prove fertile ground for the emergence of contradictory theories and agendas. Political groups of all persuasions had a field day, finding in Darwin's ideas justification for competition as well as cooperation. By 1904, speaking before the Sociological Society with Charles Booth, the businessman, shipowner, social investigator, and author of *Life and Labour of the People in London* (17 vols. 1889–1903), in the chair, the evolutionary biologist and sociologist Patrick Geddes would stress the importance of tapping contemporary enthusiasm for eugenics, the self-conscious control of human evolution through selective breeding (see Chapter 2 in this volume):

Since Comte's demonstration of the necessity of the preliminary sciences to social studies, and Spencer's development of this, still more since the evolution theory has become generally recognised, no one disputes the applicability of biology to sociology. Many are, indeed, vigorously applying the conceptions of life in evolution, in geographical distribution and environment, in health and disease, to the interpretations of the problems of the times; while with the contemporary rise of eugenics to the first plane of interest, both social and scientific, these lines of thought, bio-social and bio-geographic, must needs be increasingly utilised and developed. (Meller 1979: 122)

Chance

In the *Origin of Species* Darwin had introduced a radically new emphasis, grounding evolution in organic variation, placing chance at the center of the universe. Variation was central to his thesis on the origin of and preservation of species:

> owing to [the] struggle for life, any variation, however slight and from whatever cause proceeding, if it be in any degree profitable to an individual of any species, in its infinitely complex relations to other organic beings and to external nature, will tend to the preservation of that individual, and will generally be inherited by its offspring. (1859: 115)

In fact, Darwin defined natural selection as the preservation of these slight variations (1859: 115). He wrote conclusively in *Variation of Plants and Animals under Domestication:*

> no shadow of reason can be assigned for the belief that variations, alike in nature and the result of the same general laws, which have been the groundwork through natural selection of the formation of the most perfectly adapted animals in the world, man included, were intentionally and specially guided. However much we may wish it, we can hardly follow Professor Asa Gray in his belief that "variation has been led along certain beneficial lines", like a stream "along definite and useful lines of irrigation." (1868, II: 428)

The incessant construction of variety for survival is deterministic, but determined, itself, by chance.

It was the essential chanciness of nature, the randomness of life that biology revealed, that most exercised the nation, quickening the search for new sources of authority. The new disciplines of sociology and biology

11

were filling up the spaces opened up by Darwin's dangerous ideas. Chance is difficult to handle. Hardy's post-Darwinian poems form a sustained lament for the loss of divine agency:

> Has some Vast Imbecility, Mighty to build and blend,
> But impotent to tend,
> Framed us in jest, and left us now to hazardry?
> Or come we of an Automaton
> Unconscious of our pains?
> ("Nature's Questioning," *Wessex Poems*, 1898)

Darwin himself found it difficult to adjust to a universe without meaning, and he retained residual hopes that evolution might in the end work for the good of living beings and community: that "the vigorous, the healthy, and the happy survive and multiply" (1859: Ch. 3). Cultural narratives, even now, strive to resist the randomness of events.

> Imagine a soap opera. If Michelle from *EastEnders* sees a man going into a shop and we see her seeing him, you know that is significant. You know that in a couple of weeks he's going to nick a baby or something. I'd always thought life was like that, that somewhere along the line everything would tie in. Falling out of the window made me realize that nothing was going to tie in, there was no magical thread running through life. It's all random. But once you realize that, it's quite good. (Cocker 1998: 16)

It is unusual for chance to be left to its own devices; instead, its presence lends itself to new forms of control. As the historian Ian Hacking has argued persuasively, the autonomous laws of chance took the place of determinism during the course of the nineteenth century. The greater the level of *in*determinism, the greater the opportunities for human agency and control. There was a parallel development in human self-perception. A model of normal people replaced human nature. The word "normal" has long served for both description and evaluation, but its use to mean usual or typical emerged in the nineteenth century, in the context of physiology. The notion of the normal presents itself as a blurring of "is" and "ought" (Hacking 1990: 160–9); a huge space had opened up for new theories and forms of social control.

Galton and Huxley

The uses made of Darwin's ideas by Sir Francis Galton, his cousin, and by Thomas Huxley, his arch-popularizer (as Adrian Desmond has demonstrated so well), testify to the diverse ends to which Darwin's ideas might be applied. Galton fathered eugenics, a class-based application of evolutionary discourses which aimed to regulate population by altering the balance of class in society. For Galton, who coined the term "eugenics" in 1883, Darwin's exposition of natural, sexual, and artificial selection provided justification for human selection; he claimed that eugenics was practical Darwinism, and set out to see "what the theory of heredity, of variations and the principle of natural selection mean when applied to Man" (Pearson 1914–30, II: 86; see also Chapter 2 of this volume). Those who opposed eugenics would be able to find counter-arguments in the same theory. Darwin himself was ambivalent. In *The Descent*, drawing on ideas of "artificial selection," Darwin declared that man might:

> by selection, do something not only for the bodily constitution and frame of his offspring, but for their intellectual and moral qualities. Both sexes ought to refrain from marriage if in any marked degree inferior in body or mind; but such hopes are Utopian and will never be even partially realized until the laws of inheritance are thoroughly known. All do good service who aid towards this end. (1871: II, 403)

However, he followed the most eugenic passage in *The Descent* – "excepting in the case of man himself, hardly anyone is so ignorant as to allow his worst animals to breed" – with an emphatic refutation of eugenic principles on the grounds that "the noblest part of our nature" would be lost if 'we were intentionally to neglect the poor and helpless' (a strategy of negative eugenics) (1871: I, 168, 169). Spencer opposed any social interference with evolutionary process, while Galton believed that state intervention, such as the state regulation of marriages, through the introduction of a eugenic health certificate, would speed up "progress." The ultimate aim of both was the attainment of a future society in which the egos of individuals would merge in the interests of the whole; an idea which would become a central tenet of eugenics.

Thomas Huxley, by contrast, saw human nature, given the slowness of evolutionary change, as more or less fixed; for him, improvements were to be sought in the environment. He questioned the "unfortunate ambiguity of the phrase 'survival of the fittest,'" remarking: "I sometimes wonder whether people, who talk so freely about extirpating the unfit, ever dispassionately consider their own history" (1894: 80).

Spencer and Galton hoped for a change in human nature; Huxley in human conditions. The camps map onto the nature–nurture divide (Galton had coined this oppositional pair of terms). The debates over the respective strengths of nature and nurture raged. Within the scientific community, the German biologist August Weismann (1834–1914) challenged Lamarckianism in the 1880s. In an experiment which involved cutting the tails off mice over a number of generations, he argued that acquired characteristics could not be inherited, for the tails returned to the mice of subsequent generations. While Lamarckians could argue that only those characteristics which were useful to the organism were inherited, the experiments did prove that mice deprived of their tails still carried the complete germ plasm for this characteristic, and that, therefore, Lamarckianism rested on a theory of soft heredity. Weismann advanced the idea of two sorts of cell, somatic, and germ cells (see Bowler 1983: 251). What was crucial about Weismann's theory was the idea that "germ plasm" was completely isolated from the body of the organism that carries it, and which it simply passes through; an organism could, under this law, only pass on to the next generation what it received from its parents. Excluding the somatic cells from any role in heredity, Weismann's theory of germ plasm effectively wrote the role of the environment out of evolutionary narrative. Hereditarian theories lend themselves to the right, and to social unfreedom, positing that people are intrinsically unequal in their inherent characteristics, and undermining the importance of environmental or social change in bringing about individual development.

The Life Sciences in Fiction

Biology was vital to nineteenth-century fiction (see Beer, Levine, Ebbatson, Greenslade, Amigoni and Wallace, Morton), and the impact of Darwin's ideas outside the scientific community was immense. George Eliot's *The Mill on the Floss*, published in 1860, the year following *The Origin*, already shows a new interest in race and fitness. As Tom Tulliver shoots peas at a bluebottle the narrator observes that nature "had provided Tom and the peas for the speedy destruction of this weak individual." Mrs. Tulliver, exercised by Maggie's general waywardness, seeks genealogical distance from her daughter, declaring that "idiocy" "niver run i' my family, thank God, no more nor a brown skin as makes her look like a mulatter," thus linking dark skin with low intelligence. She wishes Maggie had *"our family skin"* (493, emphasis in original). Skin color signals kinship, a metonymic figuring of race. Pondering the difference between his offspring, Mr. Tulliver remarks: "that's the worst on't wi' the crossing o' breeds: you can never justly calkilate what'll come on't" (59). His words pick up on a contemporary and popular anti-evolutionary concern over the consequences of racial mix. In the words of one broadsheet writer: "As the races intermix / You can't be certain about the chicks" (Anon., *Dr. Darwin*, in Ritvo 1997: 130). Maggie's father is of darker stock than her mother, and Maggie takes after him. But Maggie's coloring serves as a metaphor both for her dissension from the accepted model of femininity, and also for her alienation from her social and natural environment. Despite the palpable presence of Darwinian ideas in her fiction, Eliot was resistant to grounding human life entirely in material process. She felt that *The Origin of Species* was fine, so far as it went, but that it left out the *mystery* of life: "to me the Development Theory and all other explanations of processes by which things came to be, produce a feeble impression compared with the mystery that lies under the processes" (1954–78: II, 227). In 1852, she had criticized Spencer's overly rigid theories; at "a proof-hunting expedition" at Kew, "if the flowers didn't correspond to the theories, we said, *tant pis pour les fleurs*" (1954–78: II, 40). In her fiction, Eliot drew on Darwinian ideas in order to express, rather than reduce, the complexities of life.

In *Middlemarch*, set at the time of the first Reform Bill (1832), when the politics of evolution were most radical, Lydgate longs for "the true order," searching for a primitive, unifying tissue of life. Interconnectedness threw hierarchies into question: Bichat

> first carried out the conception that living bodies, fundamentally considered, are not associations of organs which can be understood by studying them first apart, and then as it were federally; but must be regarded as consisting of certain primary webs or tissues, out of which the various organs – brain, heart, lungs, and so on – are compacted[; now it] was open to another mind to say, have not these structures some common basis from which they have all started."

The very nature of existence was open to enquiring minds. The natural historian had viewed society as a collection of individuals; now life and society were being radically redefined as dynamic processes; communities were organic entities comprising interdependent individuals; reality itself was shifting and indeterminate. Even Casaubon ("a great bladder for dried peas to rattle in!" (83)) begins to doubt the efficacy of the process of fixing, of pigeonholes, and for Mr Brooke they take on the randomness of the alphabet ("everything gets mixed in pigeon-holes: I never know whether a paper is in A or Z") (42)

Throughout his fiction, Hardy draws on the various shifts and developments within biology, broadening the franchise of creative possibility. He grouped himself "among the earliest acclaimers of *The Origin of Species*" (1928–30: 198) and, at the end of his life, listed as the thinkers most important to him "Darwin, Huxley, Spencer, Comte, Hume, Mill" (Weber 1965: 246–7). His notebooks record the assertion that "according to Zola the novel has passed out of the region of art into that of physiology and pathology" (Tilly 1883: 265), and 1890 in the *New Review* he argued:

> life being a physiological fact, its honest portrayal must be largely concerned with, for one thing, the relations between the sexes and the substitution for such catastrophes as favor the false coloring best expressed by the regulation finish that "they married and were happy ever after" of catastrophes upon the sexual relations as it is.

Hardy's narratives, in particular *Tess*, are punctuated with chance events, coincidences, roads not taken. With an appetite for alternative evolutionary accounts, Hardy "dipped" into Weismann (1928–30, I: 301), and drew upon his ideas in his fiction, but ultimately rejected this reductive hereditarian model. The Weismannian idea of germ plasm forms the basis for his poem "Heredity" and is refuted in "The Pedigree"; nonetheless, biological determinism reappears in his fiction, as he grappled with possible explanations for existence. Unlike many of his eugenic-minded contemporaries, Hardy would question the morality of the Spencerian dictum "survival of the fittest" (Arabella survives, in *Jude the Obscure*, but in what way is she fit? And, to complicate matters, her child is a morbid degenerate, suicidal and murderous, a product, *par excellence*, of Max Nordau's worst fears). In 1876 he copied into his notebooks a passage from Theodore Watts-Dunton: "science tells us that, in the struggle for life, the surviving organism is not necessarily that which is absolutely best in an ideal sense, though it must be that which is most in harmony with the surrounding conditions" (1985, I: 40).

Why was fiction so taken by developments within the life sciences? The twentieth century witnessed an increasing and increasingly alienating tendency toward specialization, culminating in the "Two Cultures" controversy of the 1950s and 1960s. By contrast, Victorian scientists and other sorts of people moved in the same circles and spoke a common language.

The life sciences were about life, and what could be more fitting material for artists, equally preoccupied by the meaning of life? The new biology was actively *appropriated* by writers and transformed; novelists did not passively "inherit" a theory of inheritance; they selectively *grafted* new ideas of natural and sexual selection onto old roots, or reworked them to meet new social and literary agendas (for further discussion of the relation between science and culture, see Cooter and Pumfrey 1994, Beer 1996, and Chapter 10 in this volume).

Sexual Selection

Darwin's *Descent of Man* made the origins of humankind explicit, and placed ideas of mating and heredity in the spotlight of scientific (and social) interest: "'sexual selection' – a subject which had always greatly interested me" (F. Darwin 1902: 46) – took up more than two-thirds of the whole. Thrust into the evolutionary scheme, sexual selection would not only account for mental and physical differences between the sexes but also emerge as "by far the most efficient cause" of "the differences in external appearance between the races of man" (1871: II, 385; see also Prichard 1813: 41–3). Sexual selection differed from natural selection (the survival of favored individuals in the struggle for life) in that it centered on successful breeding and was dependent, therefore, on the advantage which an individual had over others of the same sex and species solely in respect of acquiring a mate and reproducing. Sexual selection explained physical and mental differences between the sexes as advantageous in finding mates; Darwin also believed it to be the key cause of racial differentiation in humans. In *The Descent*, Darwin used sexual selection to explain why competition occurred not simply between but also within species. If natural selection was selection by nature, then sexual selection, highlighting the importance of sexual choice in the process of evolution, invested agency, and agency for change, in individuals. Blending biology, ethnology, and anthropology, Darwin was to cash in on the contemporary enthusiasm for biological explanations of culture. *The Descent* sold 4,500 copies within weeks of its publication, and was reprinted almost immediately (Desmond and Moore 1992: 579). Sex, and relations between the sexes, suddenly mattered to scientists. Darwin cited Schopenhauer, who argued that individuals ought to make sexual choices that would improve the health of the race: "the final aim of all love intrigues, be they comic or tragic, is really of more importance than all other ends in human life . . . it is not the weal or woe of any one individual, but that of the human race to come, which is here at stake" (Asher 1871: 323 in Darwin 1874: 586).

Biology and Sex Roles

During the social and sexual upheavals of the nineteenth century, the boundary between the sexes became fraught with new and anxious uncertainty and was policed with a vengeance. Difference as an organizing principle thrives where divisions are not obvious. For example, while Hardy introduced Christian Cantle the hermaphrodite into *The Return of the Native* (1878) Frederic Harrison, social reformer and friend of George Eliot, declared: "Women must choose to be either women or abortive men. They cannot be both women and men. When men and women are once started as competitors in the same fierce race, as rivals and opponents . . . . Woman will have disappeared" (1891: 451–2). And, in his play of 1894, *The New Woman*, Sydney Grundy voices the same fears: according to his character Colonel Sylvester, Enid Bethune, author of the fictitious *Man, the Betrayer – a Study of the Sexes*, believes that "girls should be boys, and maids should be young men." Throwing down *The Physiology of the Sexes*, the Colonel declares: "Oh, this eternal babble of the sexes! Why can't a woman be content to be a woman? What does she want to make a beastly man of herself for? . . . these people are a sex of their own . . . . They have invented a new gender. And to think my nephew's one of them!" For Sylvester, the "Advancement of Woman" is the flipside of "the Decay of Man" (Grundy 1894: I, 1).

Biological determinism would prove a powerful counter-narrative to the emerging freedoms of the *fin de siècle*. From the early nineteenth century onward a newly emergent biology allowed pronouncements on sex to be made with greater certainty, and femininity, with its apparent attendant traits – care, maternity, morality – was increasingly biologized. Popularized through Spencer's synthesizing project, the idea that social and biological superiority were marked by increasing specialization intensified sexual difference in the name of higher civilization.

Darwin, for example, in his discussion of the "difference in the mental powers of the two sexes" in *The Descent of Man*, moving outward from differences between bulls and cows, wild boars and sows, wrote:

> woman seems to differ from man in mental disposition, chiefly in her greater tenderness and less selfishness; and this holds good even with savages . . . .
> Woman, owing to her maternal instincts, displays these qualities towards

her fellow-creatures. Man is the rival of other men; he delights in competition, and this leads to ambition which passes too easily into selfishness. These latter qualities seem to be his natural and unfortunate birthright. (1871: II, 326)

That women were the bearers of moral biology sat neatly with the idea, ascendant in the nineteenth century, that sex for women was a duty, not a pleasure. Angus McLaren has charted the demise in the perceived relevance of female sexual pleasure in the act of procreation. In *Making Sex* Thomas Laqueur charts the same developments in the shift toward the biologizing of femininity, and Ornella Moscucci records an increasing emphasis on the function of the ovaries (a function discovered in 1826) as the search for the cause and proof of woman's otherness intensified (1990: 33). In the eighteenth century the most popular work on sexuality was *Aristotle's Masterpiece*, an anonymously authored compendium of information derived from Nicholas Culpeper, Albertus Magnus, and common folklore. Reprinted more times during the course of the century than any other medical text, *Aristotle's Masterpiece* urged not only that women were able to feel sexual pleasure, but also that it was indispensable for conception. These theories were upheld by the prevalent theory of the creation of new life – epigenesis (that all parts of a new creation developed sequentially). However, the emergence of preformation theories in the late seventeenth and early eighteenth centuries, both on the Continent and in England, attributed to woman a much more passive role than had the previous semence or two-seed theory. Preformation theories held that a miniature embryonic life was already in place within the mother, and embryonical development consisted only of growth, not creation. Although these were challenged in the later part of the eighteenth century by more sophisticated epigenetic views, there was no return to the two-seed theory. Instead, there was a general consensus that the new creation of life required two distinct building blocks. The stress on difference continued to underplay the role of pleasure in the woman's contribution. As part of this shift in emphasis, the sexually active woman of the seventeenth century was medicalized by the nineteenth as a passionless creature and there was increasingly open disagreement about whether femininity was constituted by purity or lust, tenderness or heartlessness.

In *Desperate Remedies* (1871), Hardy's anonymous tale of lesbian and heterosexual love which appeared in the same year as *The Descent*, he notes – and protests against – the shift from a one-sex to a two-sex model of sexual difference: "in spite of a fashion which pervades the whole community at the present day – the habit of exclaiming that woman is not undeveloped man, but diverse, the fact remains that, after all, women are Mankind, and that in many of the sentiments of life the difference of sex is but a difference of degree" (183). But the intensification of sexual difference persisted. In 1899 the social purist Ellice Hopkins wrote: "Let us be of good cheer. Sex is a very ancient institution, the slow evolution of hundreds of centuries, and is in no danger of being obliterated by the fashion of a day" (93). Likewise, for Sarah Grand, the popular New Woman novelist and social-purity feminist, biology was central to sex: "womanhood is a constitutional condition which cannot be altered" (1892). In *The Heavenly Twins* Evadne, with a glint in her eye, declared that in championing sexual reform she was not so much ""revo" – but "evolutionary"" (230). "Revolution" ill-fitted the pronatalist embrace of civic virtue. As mid-Victorian ideas of duty were given a biological basis, women became bearers of moral biology, agents of racial regeneration, and men, in turn, began to be perceived as agents of degeneration. (The idea that women are morally superior still obtains among some strands of social and/or feminist thought: see, for example, Morgan 1982; for a discussion of the relations between feminism and biology over the last two centuries, see Richardson 2000.) Motherhood was a moral responsibility; a woman's first act in expressing a gendered citizenship of contribution rather than political entitlement. It conferred nobility, prestige, and power. Hopkins concluded her tract "The Present Moral Crisis" with the words "to you, as to woman of old, it is given to save your own nation" (1886: 24). Eve's role in the Garden was being rewritten, as women reinvented themselves as moral horticulturists. In *Darwin's Plots*, Gillian Beer writes: "evolutionary theory implied a new myth of the past: instead of the garden at the beginning, there was the sea and the swamp. Instead of man, emptiness – or the empire of mollusks. There was no way back to a previous paradise: the primordial was comfortless" (127).

There was no way back; but through a new, improved, and sexually responsible Eve, there might be a way forward, a way of regaining paradise lost. Reversing the androcentric bias of Darwin's account of human sexual selection, which assigned to men the power of selection, social-purity feminists argued that women would make sexual choices that would improve the health of the nation. Eugenics, the "natural" solution to the "population question," was figured as kind and feminine. In the *Eugenics Review*, founded by the Eugenics Education Society in 1909, Mrs. Alec Tweedie declared, "it is to the women of the country we must look in this great eugenic movement"; "could anything be more philanthropic than to stamp out degeneracy?" (1912: 857; see also Chapter 2 in this volume).

Degeneration and Regeneration

"Are we Degenerating Physically?" asked the *Lancet* in 1888, as it warned of the ill effects of urban migration for "the physique of the inhabitants of these islands." While the threat here is perceived to be environmental, the causes of ill health were increasingly being held as biological. In the same year the *Atlantic Monthly* posited, and to a much wider readership, a biological basis for crime. Concern over Britain's position amidst growing international imperialist rivalry converged with fears about national health and the strength of the imperial race (see Chapters 2 and 9 in this volume). The birth rate was perceived to be declining (among the middle class) and national health saw no improvement in spite of the institutionalization of public health. The early reverses of the Boer War whipped up these fears – Britain looked to be housing an army of invalids. According to official army statistics that were revealed in 1903 in the *British Medical Journal*, of 679,703 men medically examined for enlistment between 1893 and 1902, 234,914 were rejected as medically unfit, or 34.6 percent of the total. Of those accepted, some 5,849 "broke down within three months of enlistment" and another 14,259 were discharged as invalids within two years ("National Health and Military Service," 202, in Wohl 1984: 332).

Degeneration was in the air. Max Nordau's *Degeneration*, translated into English in 1895, heightened anxieties (see Pick 1989: 25–6 for its contemporary reception). Nordau recorded: "the prevalent feeling is that of imminent perdition and extinction," accusing contemporary artists of manufacturing a climate of biological pessimism (1892: 3; see also Talbot 1898, Morel 1857). Henrik Ibsen was a prime target: "there is not a single trait in his personages, a single peculiarity of character, a single disease, that he does not trace to heredity" (Nordau 1892: 350). The term *fin de siècle* was itself born of a biologization of time; the human body, its energies sapped, its health failing, was everywhere. Nordau questioned the sense of such incessant anthropomorphism: "only the brain of a child or of a savage could form the clumsy idea that the century is a kind of living being, born like a beast or a man" (1892: 1); but his own text was itself degenerative; morbid; pessimistic; hysterical.

For some writers degeneration was something to be celebrated. Even those who appeared to be turning against nature, taking refuge in a self-enclosed aestheticism, were still grounding their fictions in the biological sciences. Most notably, J-K. Huysmans's *A Rebours* (1884), which Dorian Gray found "the strangest book that he had ever read," is grounded in physiology; the hero's history is biologically determined; a reworking of Edgar Allan Poe's "The Fall of the House of Usher," with the elements of Gothic terror which mingle with material disease ("It was, he said, a constitutional and a family evil" (Poe 1839: 143)) replaced by physiology: "The degeneration of this ancient house had clearly followed a regular course, with the men becoming progressively less manly; and over the last two hundred years, as if to complete the ruinous process, the Des Esseintes had taken to intermarrying among themselves, thus using up what little vigour they had left" (17). Des Esseintes (who knows his Darwin (Huysmans 1884: 164)) is well-versed in the language of biology: "it amused him to liken a horticulturalist's shop to a microcosm in which every social category and class was represented – poor, vulgar slum-flowers, the gilliflower" (Huysmans 1884: 96). The biologization of class that would intensify in the closing years of the century (see Richardson 1999/2000) already finds full-bodied expression in Huysmans's fiction. Unlike Huysmans, who delights in the artistic potential of degeneration, other male writers mapped cautionary tales onto their forays into the world of degeneration. The French naturalist, Zola, for example, points up the relentlessness of heredity, most notably in *Doctor Pascal: or, Life and Heredity* (1893), while in *The Time Machine* (1895), H. G. Wells depicted the descent of the urban working class into violent anarchy, and the ruling class into decadence and neurosis (see Pick 1989: 157–9). And in *Dracula* (1897), Bram Stoker's embodiment of contemporary fears, degeneration is represented, and *displaced* onto a foreign count who is finally conquered with a wooden stake. Nonetheless, the novel does not allay fears: contagion seeps through it; disease passes, invisibly, relentlessly, between bodies (see Pick 1989: 167–75). And, like the women that the state had sought to regulate in the second half on the nineteenth century, under the Contagious Diseases Acts, women in Dracula *spread* contagion: "nothing can be more dreadful than those awful women, who were, who are, waiting to suck my blood" (*Dracula*, ch. 4). Jonathan Harker recalls:

> I was afraid to raise my eyelids, but looked out and saw perfectly under the lashes. The girl went on her knees, and bent over me, simply gloating. There was a deliberate voluptuousness which was both thrilling and repulsive, and as she arched her neck she actually licked her lips like an animal, till I could see in the moonlight the moisture shining on the scarlet lips and on the red tongue as it lapped the white sharp teeth. Lower and lower went her head as the lips went below the range of my mouth and chin and seemed to fasten on my throat. (ch. 3)

A few years earlier, in contrast to this fearful, and wholly negative depiction of female sexuality, the feminist writer George Egerton had embraced a sexual freedom in "A Cross Line" (1893), perhaps her most famous story. This positive expression of sexual freedom is contained within a waking dream (literature was not yet able to take it beyond the realm of fantasy):

> she can see herself with parted lips and panting, rounded breasts, and a dancing devil in each glowing eye, sway voluptuously to the wild music that rises, now slow, now fast, now deliriously wild, seductive, intoxicating, with a human note of passion in its strain. She can feel the answering shiver of feeling that quivers up to her from the dense audience. (20)

Interestingly, despite their differences, both these depictions of female sexuality are intimately connected with contemporary ideas about empire and degeneration. For Stoker, female sexual desire signals the unrestraint that was leading to British self-contamination; for Egerton, unbridled female sexual desire would allow women to exercise their powers of selection to their full in sexual relations, and this would improve national stock. In the closing years of the nineteenth century popular engagement with biology became underpinned by a new, and overtly political, agenda. The Victorian novel had always been interested in successive generations of family, often taking the mechanism of legacy as the plot pivot, as is the case in, for example, *Jane Eyre* (1847), *Bleak House* (1852–3), and *Felix Holt* (1866). At the *fin de siècle* the novel was the obvious vehicle for exploring the implications of heredity for social and biological responsibilities – one of the most pressing questions of the decade. As New Woman novelists became increasingly taken up with regeneration, so romance was replaced by marriage as a mediator of genealogy. In a deft reversal of the male reason versus female intuition divide, several writers were arguing that female reason would put a stop to the racial disasters of masculine passion.

Symbols of the ugly ("diseased") and beautiful ("healthy") sustain social orders through biological narratives (see Gilman 1995). These narratives were coming into their own in the late 1800s and are exemplified in the work of novelist Grant Allen. In his treatise of 1877, *Physiological Aesthetics* (dedicated to Herbert Spencer), Allen set out his object as "to exhibit the purely physical origin of the sense of beauty, and its relativity to our nervous organization" (2). For Allen, beauty is joined to function. In an essay in *Mind*, he wrote there must be "such an intimate correspondence between the needs and tastes of each species, that the sight and voice of a healthy, normal, well-formed mate must have become intrinsically pleasing for its own sake, as well as indirectly for its associations," extrapolating from this:

> the heart and core of such a fixed hereditary taste for each species must consist in the appreciation of the pure and healthy typical specific form. The ugly for every kind, in its own eyes, must always be (in the main) the deformed, the aberrant, the weakly, the unnatural, the impotent. The beautiful for every kind must similarly be (in the main) the healthy, the normal the strong, the perfect, and the parentally sound. Were it ever otherwise – did any race or kind ever habitually prefer the morbid to the sound, that race or kind must be on the highroad to extinction. (1879: 92)

Following the same line of thought, Egerton argued that the hermeneutics of the body be made simplified and accessible, urging for a universal, fixed, and exacting standard of health, and an easy way of identifying the "unfit" (arguments which have not been absent from debates surrounding AIDS and public "awareness": see Buckley 1986, Fee and Fox 1992). In Egerton's epistolary novel of 1901, *Rosa Amorosa*, the eponymous heroine declares "the whole world of men and women would suddenly stand in nudity, the moral effect would be colossal" in a moment of seeming (and seemingly anarchic) sexual liberation, but the moment is followed by a vision of a totalitarian health regime:

> all *false* shame would die a summary death, and the exigencies of continuing the ordinary duties of life would compel people to cast all consideration of it aside. The common idea of beauty would be entirely revolutionized; the human face would lose its undue prominence and become a mere detail in a whole; straight, clean limbs and a *beautiful form be the only thing admirable*; disease and bodily blemishes the one right cause for shame, and, as a result, concealment. (1901: 83–93, my emphasis)

Drawing heavily on biological discourses, Egerton's fiction points up ways in which women might realize their roles as agents of regeneration. As an example of Egerton's collusion with the new sociomedical interest in heredity, her epigraph to "The Regeneration of Two" – "love is the supreme factor in the evolution of the world" (1894: 163) – inks love indelibly into the master narrative of evolution.

Egerton believed that the early imposition of strategic reading programs would prepare girls for their regenerative roles. We learn of the heroine of "The Heart of the Apple" that there was "not one novel, not one romance" in her library (1897: 183); instead she has "books on birds and beasts and fishes and plants" – books which would convey the facts of life without the fiction of romance; "the miracle of sex, underlying every natural law, its individual working in the propagation of the young, was no mystery to her, and consequently no subject for prurient musing." Likewise, the following year in *The Wheel of God*, Mary "had books, school books, on botany and zoology; and yet it was a sin to think of quite natural things if they touched on men and women" (1898: 44). Until novels could treat the facts of life with the same frank clarity as a zoological treatise it was best to steer clear of them. In *Margaret Dunmore: or A Socialist Home*, as Vera and Joe attend the return of Vera's childbearing strength, "the study of physiology was engaged in *au sérieux* by both. A class for instruction in this science had been organized under the roof of La Maison, and to it outsiders were made freely welcome" (1897: 127).

The life sciences seemed to many to hold the key to regeneration. Evadne, the heroine of Sarah Grand's sensational bestseller of 1893, *The Heavenly Twins*, bans the romantic novel from her reading, feasting instead on medical textbooks, which would impart the facts of life frankly and honestly. Among the books Evadne reads are the works of Galton, and Spencer (1893: 176). *The Heavenly Twins* sold 20,000 copies in Britain within a few weeks, and more than five times as many copies in the USA (Kersley 1983: 72–3). Even *Tess* was being used for sex education; Hardy reported that numerous mothers "tell me they are putting *Tess* into their daughters' hands to safeguard their future" (Hardy 1978–88, I: 255). Tess herself rebukes her mother: "Ladies know what to fend hands against, because they read novels that tell them of these tricks; but I never had the chance o" learning in that way, and you did not help me!" (1891: 131).

As Grand saw it, it was the duty of women to rewrite the novel and cure civilization of its love-madness; the transformation of the plot of the romance and the sentimental as a more effective solution to the reading problem than direct censorship. In the words of Hugh Stutfield: "with her head full of all the 'ologies and 'isms, with sex problems and heredity, and other gleanings from the surgery and the lecture-room, there is no space left for humour, and her novels are for the most part merely pamphlets, sermons, or treatises in disguise" (1895: 837).

Reviewing *The Heavenly Twins* in *The Yellow Book*, Arthur Waugh asked: "what has [Sarah Grand] told us that we did not all know, or could not learn from medical manuals? And what impression has she left us over and above the memory of her unpalatable details?" (1894: 218). Interestingly, George Eliot had also been taken to task by male critics for putting too much science into her novels; Henry James, for one, complained that

"*Middlemarch* is too often an echo of Messrs. Darwin and Huxley."

Grand opened *The Heavenly Twins* with these words from Darwin: "I am inclined to agree with Francis Galton in believing that education and environment produce only a small effect on the mind of anyone, and that most of our qualities are innate" (1893: 1). In its study of the interchangeable qualities of twins, the novel has much in common with Galton's ongoing work on twins, which led him to conclude "a surprisingly small margin seemed to be left to the effects of circumstances and education, and to the exercise of what we are accustomed to call 'free-will'" (1882; see also Galton Papers 122). Sarah Grand was a staunch supporter of eugenic ideas. In 1896 she wrote in a letter to John Blackwood:

> I think further that it is in the action of woman in this particular matter, i.e. in regard to the improvement of the race, – that the one hope lies of saving our present civilization from the extinction which has overtaken the civilization of all previous peoples; and all I write is for the purpose of spreading this opinion and opening up these subjects to discussion.

Discussing the female franchise in an interview she gave in the same year, Grand declared:

> women are the proper people to decide on matters of population. Men have not managed to regulate either the population or the social question at all satisfactorily, and it would be well to give us a chance of trying what we can do. We could do much if we had the suffrage; the want of electoral power cripples our efforts.

She added that she hoped the marriage of certain men would soon be a criminal offence, and called publicly for the need for a "certificate of health" before a marriage could take place (Tooley 1896: 168). The following year, in her bestseller *The Beth Book*, Beth declares medical help for the "unfit" an unwelcome endeavor to hinder Nature's good work:

> Nature decrees the survival of the fittest; you exercise your skill to preserve the unfittest, and stop there – at the beginning of your responsibilities, as it seems to me. Let the unfit who are with us live, and save them from suffering where you can, by all means; but take pains to prevent the appearance of any more of them. By the reproduction of the unfit, the strength, the beauty, the morality of the race is undermined, and with them its best chances of happiness. (1897: 442)

Beth's diatribe is the fullest but by no means an unusual exposition in

Grand's work of negative eugenics as an act of *kindness* – a way of making the fit happy and the unfit extinct. As a further illustration of the extent to which eugenic ideas were being explored and promoted in fiction, Ménie Muriel Dowie, in her controversial novel of 1895, *Gallia*, charts Gallia Hamesthwaite's choice of a eugenically fit partner in preference to a dysgenic partner (Dark Essex): "people will see the folly of curing all sorts of ailments that should not have been created, and then they will start at the right end, they will make better people" (129).

The debates between the hereditarians and the environmentalists intensified in the last years of the nineteenth century. While Galton and his following were arguing for eugenic health certificates, and endorsing the elimination of the "unfit," Huxley was urging battle with nature, and, more precisely, with the nature which resided within each of us: primal impulses and instincts. The Russian anarchist and scientist Peter Kropotkin (1842–1921) was urging a third way; arguing that a basis for morality was to be found in nature, and that cooperation was just as necessary to the evolutionary scheme as struggle. In fiction, the humanitarian New Woman writer Mona Caird interrogated the hereditarian position, exposing the bias of biology and reclaiming the importance of environment and culture in shaping individuals (see Richardson 2001, 2002). She pursued the same line of argument as Huxley, arguing that nature was at best "primitive impulse and law, unmodified by human intelligence or moral development" (1894: 231). Human civilization and nature were at odds. The "primitive" mind was set against its transformed version in the social self.

At the close of the century, Sigmund Freud would give more precise formulation to the idea of internalized conflict, developing a new science of oppositions and submerged complexes and pointing up the unconscious determinants of actions (see Chapter 6 in this volume). Such ideas were not new to nineteenth-century conceptions of human nature. Passion and reason had warred in the novels of Charlotte and Emily Brontë and, more recently, Stevenson had given sustained expression to the divided self in *The Strange Case of Dr. Jekyll and Mr. Hyde* (1886). Psychology, which been developing apace over the course of the century (see Rylance 2000, Shuttleworth 1996), was too engaged with philosophical questions about the mind to subscribe to any theory of total hereditary determination of behavior and, as the hereditarians and environmentalists reached stalemate, psychoanalysis emerged as a new explanatory model, a means of resisting a biology that threatened to sweep all before it. Nonetheless, biology was crucial to the late Victorian and Edwardian quest to understand what it is to be human, and biological explanations would be increasingly debated and pursued in the new century, culminating, at its close, in the Human Genome Project.

References and Further Reading

Unpublished Manuscripts

Darwin, Charles (February 18, 1863). Letter to Huxley. Thomas Huxley Papers, Imperial College of Science and Technology, London.
Francis Galton's data and notes on the effects of nature and nurture on the physical and mental characteristics of twins assembled between 1874 and 1876, Galton Papers 122.
Galton, Francis. "Questions about Twins." 122/1B. Galton Archive, University College London.
Grand, Sarah (December 5, 1892). Letter to John Blackwood. Letters of Frances Elizabeth McFall [Sarah Grand], National Library of Scotland.
Thomas Huxley Papers. Imperial College of Science and Technology, London.

Published Works

Allen, Grant. 1877. *Physiological Aesthetics*. London: Henry S. King & Co.
——. 1879. Aesthetic Evolution in Man. *Mind* 4: 301–16.
——. 1889. *Falling in Love, with other Essays on More Exact Branches of Science*. London: Smith, Elder, & Co.
Amigoni, David and Wallace, Jeff, eds., 1995. *Charles Darwin's The Origin of Species*. Manchester: Manchester University Press.
Are we Degenerating Physically? 1888. *Lancet*: 1076–7, 1257.
Asher, David. 1871. Schopenhauer and Darwinism. *Journal of Anthropology*.
Beer, Gillian. 1983. *Darwin's Plots: Evolutionary Narrative in Darwin, George Eliot and Nineteenth-Century Fiction*. London: Routledge & Kegan Paul.
——. 1996. Translation or Transformation: The Relation of Literature and Science. In *Open Fields: Science in Cultural Encounter*, pp. 173–95. Oxford: Oxford University Press.
Bergson, Henri. 1911. *Creative Evolution*. London and New York: Macmillan.
Bowler, Peter. 1983. *Evolution: The History of an Idea*. Berkeley and Los Angeles: University of California Press.
Brooke, John Hedley. 1991. *Science and Religion: Some Historical Perspectives*. Cambridge: Cambridge University Press.
Browne, Janet. 1995. *Charles Darwin: Voyaging*. London: Jonathan Cape.
Buckley, William F. 1986. Identify all the Carriers. *New York Times* (March 18): 27A.
Burrow, John. 1966. *Evolution and Society: A Study in Victorian Social Theory*. Cam-

bridge: Cambridge University Press.

Caird, Mona. 1894. Phases of Human Development, pp. 37–51, 162–79; reprinted in *The Morality of Marriage*. In Ann Heilmann, *The Late Victorian Marriage Debate: A Collection of Key New Woman Texts* I, London and New York: Routledge (with Thoemmes Press), 1998.

Clapperton, Jane Hume. 1888. *Margaret Dunmore or A Socialist Home*. London: Swan Sonnenschein, Lowrey & Co.

Cocker, Jarvis. 1998. *In His Own Words*. Ed. Michael Heatley. London and New York: Omnibus Press.

Comte, Auguste. [1853] 1974. *Positive Philosophy*. Trans. Harriet Martineau. New York: AMS Press.

Cooter, Roger and Pumfrey, Stephen. 1994. The History of Science Popularization. *History of Science* 32: 48–249.

Crook, Paul. 1994. *Darwinism, War and History: The Debate over the Biology of War from the "Origin of Species" to the First World War*. Cambridge: Cambridge University Press.

Darwin, Charles. [1859] 1985. *The Origin of Species, or the Preservation of Favoured Races in the Struggle for Life*. Harmondsworth: Penguin.

——. 1868. *The Variation of Animals and Plants under Domestication*, 2 vols. London: John Murray.

——. [1871] 1981. *The Descent of Man, and Selection in Relation to Sex*. Chichester: Princeton University Press; 2nd ed. 1874. London: John Murray.

——. [1872] 1965. *The Expression of the Emotions in Man and Animals*. Chicago and London: University of Chicago Press.

——. 1985–91. *Correspondence of Charles Darwin*, 7 vols. Ed. D. Burkhardt and S. Smith. Cambridge and New York: Cambridge University Press.

Darwin, Francis. [1902] 1995. *The Life of Charles Darwin*. London: Senate.

Desmond, Adrian. [1994] 1997. *Huxley*. Harmondsworth: Penguin.

Desmond, Adrian and James Moore. 1992. *Darwin*. Harmondsworth: Penguin.

Dickens, Charles. [1852–3] 1994. *Bleak House*. London: Everyman.

Dowie, Ménie Muriel. [1895] 1995. *Gallia*. London, J. M. Dent.

Ebbatson, Roger. 1982. *The Evolutionary Self: Hardy, Forster, Lawrence*. Brighton: Harvester Press.

Egerton, George [1893] 1993. A Cross Line. In *Keynotes and Discords*. London: Virago.

——. [1894] 1993. The Regeneration of Two. In *Keynotes and Discords*. London: Virago.

——. 1897. The Heart of the Apple. In *Symphonies*. London and New York: John Lane.

——. 1898. *The Wheel of God*. London: Grant Richards.

——. 1901. *Rosa Amorosa, The Love Letters of a Woman*. London: Grant Richards.

Eliot, George. [1860] 1985. *The Mill on the Floss*. Harmondsworth: Penguin.

——. [1871] 1985. *Middlemarch*. Harmondsworth: Penguin.

———. 1954–78. *George Eliot Letters*, 9 vols. Ed. George S. Haight. New Haven: Yale University Press.

Marx, Karl and Friedrich Engels. 1868. *Selected Works in One Volume*. London: Lawrence & Wishart.

Fee, Elizabeth and Daniel M. Fox, eds. 1992. *Aids, the Making of a Chronic Disease*. Berkeley: University of California Press.

Foucault, Michel. [1966] 1970. *The Order of Things*. London: Tavistock.

Galton, Francis. 1882. The Anthropometric Laboratory. *Fortnightly Review* 37: 332–3.

———. 1883. *Inquiries into the Human Faculty and its Development*. London: Macmillan.

Gilman, Sander. 1995. *Health and Illness: Images of Difference*. London: Reaktion Books.

Gosse, Edmund. [1907] 1983. *Father and Son: A Study of Two Temperaments*. Harmondsworth: Penguin.

Grand, Sarah. [1893] 1992. *The Heavenly Twins*. Michigan: Ann Arbor.

———. [1896] 1907. Letter to Professor Viëter, December 15. In Ernst Foerster, *Die Frauenfrage in den Romanen Englischer Schriftstellerinnen der Gegenwart*, pp. 55–8. Marburg: N. G. Elwersche Verlagsbuchhandlung.

———. [1897] 1994. *The Beth Book, Being a Study from the Life of Elizabeth Caldwell Maclure, A Woman of Genius*. Bristol: Thoemmes Press.

Greenslade, William. 1994. *Degeneration, Culture and the Novel 1880–1940*. Cambridge: Cambridge University Press.

Grundy, Sydney. [1894] 1998. *The New Woman: An Original Comedy in Four Acts*. Oxford: Oxford University Press.

Hacking, Ian. 1990. *The Taming of Chance*. Cambridge: Cambridge University Press.

Hardy, Thomas. [1871] 1998. *Desperate Remedies*. Harmondsworth: Penguin.

———. [1887] 1986. *The Woodlanders*. Harmondsworth: Penguin.

———. [1891] 1986. *Tess of the D'Urbervilles*. Harmondsworth: Penguin.

———. [1928–30] 1994. *The Life of Thomas Hardy*, 2 vols. (published under Florence Hardy). London: Studio Editions.

———. 1978–88. *The Collected Letters of Thomas Hardy*. Ed. Richard L. Purdy and Michael Millgate. Oxford: Clarendon Press.

———. 1985. *The Literary Notebooks of Thomas Hardy*. 2 vols. Ed. Lennart A. Björk. London and Basingstoke: Macmillan.

———. 1990. *The Complete Poems of Thomas Hardy*. Ed. James Gibson. London: Macmillan.

—— et al. 1890. Candour in English Fiction. *New Review* 2: 15–21.

Harrison, Frederic. 1891. The Emancipation of Women. *Fortnightly Review* 56: 451–2.

Heschel, Abraham Joshua. 1965. *Who is Man?* Stanford: Stanford University Press.

Hopkins, Ellice. 1886. "The Present Moral Crisis." London: Hatchards.

———. 1899. *The Power of Womanhood, or, Mothers and Sons: A Book for Parents and Those in Loco Parentis*. London: Wells Gardner, Darton & Co.

Huxley, T. H. [1864] 1906. Darwin on the Origin of Species. In *Man's Place in*

Nature and Other Essays. London: J. M. Dent.

——. [1894] 1989. *Evolution and Ethics* (including "Prolegomena"). Ed. James Paradis and George C. Williams. Princeton: Princeton University Press.

Huysman, J-K. [1884] 1959. *A Rebours*. Penguin: Harmondsworth.

James, Henry. 1873. Review of T. S. Eliot, *Middlemarch*. *Galaxy* (March): 424–8.

Jones, Greta. 1980. *Social Darwinism and English Thought: The Interaction between Biological and Social Theory*. Brighton: Harvester.

Kersley, Gillian. 1983. *Darling Madame: Sarah Grand & Devoted Friend*. London: Virago.

Kropotkin, Peter. [1902] 1998. *Mutual Aid: A Factor of Evolution*. London: Freedom Press.

Lamarck, Jean-Baptiste de. 1809. *Philosophie zoologique*. Paris.

Lankester, E. R. 1880. *Degeneration: A Chapter in Darwinism*. London: Macmillan.

Laqueur, Thomas. 1990. *Making Sex: Body and Gender from the Greeks to Freud*. Cambridge, MA and London: Harvard University Press.

Levine, George. [1988] 1991. *Darwin and the Novelists: Patterns of Science in Victorian Fiction*. Chicago and London: Chicago University Press.

Marx, Karl and Friedrich Engels. 1968. *Selected Works in One Volume*. London: Lawrence & Wishart.

McLaren, Angus. 1985. The Pleasures of Procreation: Traditional and Biomedical Theories of Conception. In W. F. Bynum and Roy Porter, eds., *William Hunter and the Eighteenth-Century Medical World*, pp. 323–41. Cambridge: Cambridge University Press.

Meller, Helen, ed. 1979. *The Ideal City*. Leicester: Leicester University Press.

Morel, Bénédict Austin. 1857. *Traité des dégénérescences physiques, intellectuelles et morales de l'espèce humaine*. Paris: n.p.

Morgan, Robin. 1982. Feminism is the Key to our Survival and Transformation. In *The Anatomy of Freedom: Feminism, Physics and Global Politics*. Oxford: Martin Robertson.

Morton, Peter. 1984. *The Vital Science: Beyond the Literary Imagination 1860–1900*. London: George Allen & Unwin.

Moscucci, Ornella. 1990. *The Science of Woman, Gynaecology and Gender in England 1800–1929*. Cambridge: Cambridge University Press.

National Health and Military Service. 1903. *British Medical Journal* (July 25).

Nordau, Max. [1892] 1993. *Degeneration*. Lincoln, NE and London: University of Nebraska Press.

Oldroyd, D. R. [1980] 1983. *Darwinian Impacts: An Introduction to the Darwinian Revolution*. Milton Keynes: Open University Press.

Owen, Richard. 1858. On the Characters, Principles of Division, and Primary Groups of the Class Mammalia. *Journal of the Proceedings of the Linnean Society* 2: 1–37.

Pearson, Karl. 1914–30. *The Life, Letters and Labours of Francis Galton*, 3 vols. Cambridge: Cambridge University Press.

Pick, Daniel. 1989. *Faces of Degeneration: A European Disorder, c1848– c1918*. Cambridge: Cambridge University Press.

Pickering, Mary Auguste. 1993. *Comte: An Intellectural Biography*. Cambridge: Cambridge University Press.

Poe, Edgar Allan. [1839] 1967. The Fall of the House of Usher. In *The Fall of the House of Usher and Other Writings*. Harmondsworth: Penguin.

Porter, Dorothy. 1991. "Enemies of the Race": Biologism, Environmentalism, and Public Health in Edwardian England. *Victorian Studies* 34: 159–78.

———. 1997. *Social Medicine and Medical Sociology in the Twentieth Century*. Amsterdam: Rodopi.

Porter, Theodore M. 1990. Natural Science and Social Theory. In R. C. Olby et al., eds., *Companion to the History of Modern Science*, pp. 1024–44. London: Routledge.

Prichard, James Cowles. [1813] 1973. *Researches into the Physical History of Man*. Ed. George W. Stocking, Jr. Chicago and London: University of Chicago Press.

Richardson, Angelique. 1999/2000. The Eugenization of Love: Sarah Grand and the Morality of Genealogy. *Victorian Studies* 42: 227–55.

———. 2000. Biology and Feminism. *Critical Quarterly* 42: 35–63.

———. 2001. "People talk a lot of Nonsense about Heredity": Mona Caird and Anti-Eugenic Feminism. In *The New Woman in Fiction and in Fact: Fin-de-Siècle Feminisms*, pp. 183–211. New York and Basingstoke. Palgrave.

———. 2002. *Love and Eugenics: Science, Fiction, and the New Woman*. Oxford: Oxford University Press.

Ritvo, Harriet. 1997. *The Platypus and the Mermaid and Other Figments of the Classifying Imagination*. Cambridge, MA: Harvard University Press.

Rowold, Katharina, ed. 1996. *Gender and Science: Nineteenth-Century Debates on the Female Mind and Body*. Bristol: Thoemmes Press.

Russett, Cynthia Eagle. [1989] 1991. *Sexual Science: The Victorian Construction of Womanhood*. Cambridge, MA and London: Harvard University Press.

Rylance, Rick. 2000. *Victorian Psychology and British Culture 1850–1880*. Oxford: Oxford University Press.

Schiebinger, Londa. 1993. *Nature's Body, Sexual Politics and the Making of Modern Science*. London: Pandora.

Showalter, Elaine. 1990. *Sexual Anarchy: Gender and Culture at the Fin de Siècle*. London: Virago.

Shuttleworth, Sally. 1996. *Charlotte Brontë and Victorian Psychology*. Cambridge: Cambridge University Press.

Smith, Roger. 1997. *Human Sciences*. London: Fontana.

Spencer, Herbert. 1860. The Social Organism. *Westminster Review* 73: 90–121.

———. 1864. Principles of Biology. London.

———. 1972. *Herbert Spencer on Social Evolution: Selected Writings*. Ed. John David Yeadon Peel. Chicago: Chicago University Press.

Stoker, Bram. [1897] 1983. *Dracula*. Oxford: Oxford University Press.

Stutfield, Hugh. 1895. Tommyrotics. *Blackwood's Magazine*: 833–45.

Talbot, Eugene S. 1898. *Degeneracy, its Causes, Signs and Results*. London: Walter Scott.

Tilly, Arthur. 1883. The New School of Fiction. *National Review* 1.

Tooley, Sarah A. 1896. The Woman Question: An Interview with Madame Sarah Grand. *Humanitarian* 8: 161–9.

Tweedie, Mrs. Alec. 1912. Eugenics. *Eugenics Review* 9.

Waugh, Arthur. 1894. Reticence in Literature. *Yellow Book* 1: 201–19.

Weber, Carl J. [1940] 1965. *Hardy of Wessex: His Life and Literary Career*. New York: Columbia University Press.

Wilde, Oscar. [1905] 1954. *De Profundis*. Harmondsworth: Penguin.

Wohl, Anthony S. 1984. *Endangered Lives: Public Health in Victorian Britain*. London: Methuen.

2

Eugenics: "They should certainly be killed"

David Bradshaw

Hitler's Taint

"Eugenics," one recent study begins. "For the denizens of our planet, it would be difficult to find a more controversial concept . . .":

> [I]t gained its pejorative meanings after World War II, when the Anglo-American community associated any study of the "wellborn" or genetic manipulation with the horrors of Nazism. In societies built on notions of equality, justice, and equal opportunity, many eugenical studies were considered to be inextricably tied to racist notions of biological determinism or ethnic cleansing. (Hasian 1997: 1)

Over the past thirty years or so, these "pejorative meanings" have helped drive a sizeable wedge through the reputations of Eliot, Yeats, Lawrence, Huxley, Shaw, Wells, and other modern writers of a eugenicist cast of mind. Yet if John Carey's *The Intellectuals and the Masses* (1992) is the most vigorous excoriation of attitudes which were to find monstrous realization in the racial policies of the Nazis, and Donald Childs's *Modernism and Eugenics* (2001) the most compendious assessment to date of the attraction which an ideology now deemed repugnant held for writers who found it anything but repellent, Diane Paul has cautioned that:

> We will fail to understand the appeal of eugenics to so many people with such divergent interests, training, and political orientations if we start with the assumption that it was patently absurd. We may find the wide

enthusiasm for eugenics shocking, but it reflected scientific and social beliefs that our great-grandparents found satisfying and reasonable. (1995: 21)

Indeed, just about every construction of race, class, and human value which we now find "shocking" was regarded not only as "satisfying and reasonable" during the modernist epoch, but imperative to national survival and a prerequisite of future success. And sociopolitical programs which now sound jarringly ruthless and invasive were once thought to be compassionate and progressive.

The "appeal of eugenics" was by no means confined to the Anglo-Saxon world. From around 1890 onwards, eugenics movements grew up in more than thirty countries as far apart as Iceland and New Zealand, Mexico and the Soviet Union:

> In some places eugenics was dominated by experimental biologists, in others by animal breeders, physicians, pediatricians, psychiatrists, anthropologists, demographers or public health officials. In some places it was predominantly Lamarckian, in others Mendelian . . . a report on the International Commission of Eugenics published in 1924 in *Eugenical News* listed fifteen full members: Argentina, Belgium, Cuba, Czechoslovakia, Denmark, France, Germany, Great Britain, Italy, Netherlands, Norway, Russia, Sweden, Switzerland and the United States. In addition, seven other countries were eligible for cooperation: Brazil, Canada, Colombia, Mexico, Venezuela, Australia and New Zealand. (Adams 1990: 5)

But while the vogue for eugenics was far-reaching, in no country did it generate such a devoted following (prior to its embrace by the Nazi regime) as in the United States:

> For example, eugenics became part of the college curriculum; the number of colleges and universities offering courses in eugenics increased from forty-four in 1914 to three hundred and seventy-six in 1928 . . . . And eugenists played an important role in the enactment of America's most ambitious program of biological engineering, the National Origins Act of 1924, which imposed immigration quotas based squarely on eugenists' ideas of Nordic racial superiority and non-Aryan racial inferiority. (Cravens 1978: 53)

It is small wonder that the biggest single influence on German eugenics in the years leading up to World War II was American eugenics (Kühl 1994, Paul 1995: 84–5), and when the Eugenic Sterilization Law came into force in Germany on January 1, 1934 it simply marked, in one sense, the high point of many years' close collaboration and mutual admiration between American and German eugenists.

Far from plunging eugenics into immediate disrepute, the Nazi legislators had merely followed a trend: compulsory sterilization never got near the statute books in Britain in the 1930s (despite the best efforts of a small rump of diehard hereditarians), but by 1934 "sterilization laws had already been enacted in thirty American states, as well as a number of other countries, including Denmark, Finland, Sweden, Norway, Iceland, Switzerland and Canada" (Childs 2001: 15). "Within three years, German authorities had sterilized some two hundred and twenty-five thousand people, almost ten times the number so treated in the previous thirty years in America" (Kevles 1985: 117), and eugenics would soon reach its ghastly *terminus ad quem* in Hitler's death camps, but to conceive of it as a purely totalitarian phenomenon is to seriously misapprehend its origins, character, and the diversity of its following. For example, "*Erbkrank* [Hereditary Defective], a Nazi race propaganda movie . . . was also used by the American eugenics movement for informing high school students about the need to sterilize mentally handicapped people" (Kühl 1994: vii).

The Ultimate Future of These Islands

Plato advocates selective breeding to secure the public good in the fifth book of the *Republic,* but in the late nineteenth century this line of thinking suddenly gained urgent and unprecedented favor among the British intelligentsia. In the wash of the *Origin of Species,* with "social Darwinists insist[ing] that biology was destiny, at least for the unfit, and that a broad spectrum of socially deleterious traits, ranging from 'pauperism' to mental illness, resulted from heredity" (Kevles 1985: 20); with the advent of Weismann's germ plasm doctrine in 1883, which proposed that heredity was based upon the transfer, from generation to generation, of a substance with a definite molecular constitution (see Chapter 1 in this volume); and with the dissemination of Mendel's work in 1900, the eugenics movement coalesced around the writings of Darwin's cousin, Sir Francis Galton (1822–1911). In *Hereditary Genius* (1869) and other publications Galton had propounded the idea that the mental, moral, and temperamental characteristics of human beings were wholly determined by heredity. He coined the term "eugenics" in his *Inquiries into Human Faculty* (1883) and in 1909 defined the field as "the study of agencies under social control which may improve or impair the racial qualities of future generations" (quoted in Paul 1995: 3). Catering for a more specialist audience, the biometric school of eugenics evolved in parallel from 1895 onwards, when Galton's protégé, Karl Pearson, opened his Biometric Laboratory at University College, London, and began to develop the application of statistical methods to biological investigations. That the biometricians were permanently embroiled in controversy with the Mendelian geneticists "over the physiology or mechanism of heredity" served only to further "alert the learned scientific world to eugenic considerations" (Soloway 1990: 28).

The writings of Galton and other eugenists attracted a great deal of interest, both within and beyond the scientific community, not only because of a pervasive feeling that "the racial qualities of *future* generations" were worth striving for, but also because many believed that the "racial qualities" of the current population were rapidly deteriorating. As William Greenslade puts it:

> there was a paradox to be explained, and it was, in simple terms, the growing sense in the last decades of the century of a lack of synchrony between the rhetoric of progress, the confident prediction by the apostles of *laissez-faire* of ever increasing prosperity and wealth, and the facts on the ground, the evidence in front of people's eyes, of poverty and degradation at the heart of ever richer empires. (1994: 15)

The specter of degeneration shades many late nineteenth- and early twentieth-century texts, not least Conrad's *Heart of Darkness* (1902), in which the frame narrator repeatedly tugs the reader's gaze back from the luminous offing to the monstrous gloom hanging over imperial London. Moreover, in the same year that the phenomenally efficient Kurtz and other aspects of Conrad's novella received the attention of reviewers, the spectacular inefficiency of Britain in general, and her far from imperious performance in the Boer War (1899–1902) in particular, were subjected to the gravest scrutiny. In a single week in December 1899, for example, Boer guerrillas had defeated the supposedly peerless British Army three times, prompting a period of deep and anxious inquiry into national ineptitude which only intensified once the war had ended (Searle 1971). "It was difficult not to wonder," Richard Soloway has written, "if a country forced to spend three years and £250 million to defeat a handful of unorganized farmers had the right to call itself the greatest power on earth" (1990: 2). A subsequent report revealed, among other things, that over forty percent of recruits from Manchester had been declared unfit for military service (Paul 1995: 7) and by "1904 many English social workers, politicians, and philanthropists believed that the nation was in state of emergency requiring some rational program of 'efficiency,' and they were unwilling to allow the paupers and casual workers of their nation to languish and reproduce themselves endlessly in workhouses, jails, inebriate homes, and other institutions" (Hasian 1997: 113). Some eugenists, such as R. R. Rentoul, were convinced that the British "race" was almost on its last legs. "Day by day, hour by hour, and year after year we add diseased humanity – the children begotten by the diseased, idiots, imbeciles, epileptics, the insane," Rentoul wrote in 1906, the same year in which the Galton Laboratory for the Study of National Eugenics opened in London. "Does any one contend that such a scheme of pollution works for race culture?," Rentoul asked. "Rather, I contend, that it works for race suicide" (quoted in Childs 2001: 2; see Chapters 1 and 9 in this volume).

If the "people of the abyss" haunted bourgeois and intellectual alike just as powerfully at the beginning of the twentieth century as they had in the middle of the nineteenth, an alarming change was taking place in British fertility patterns which was providing even greater cause for concern.

> By the time of Queen Victoria's death in 1901 it was . . . becoming apparent that her subjects were reproducing themselves at markedly lower rates than in earlier generations. The high figures of 35 and 36 per 1,000 persisting throughout much of her long reign had begun to diminish steadily in the 1880s, and by the opening of the new century had fallen to 28.5, a decline of more than 21 percent. (Soloway 1990: 4)

This fall in the birthrate was all the more worrying in view of the steadily increasing population of Germany, but what really disturbed the governing classes and gave eugenics a hugely enhanced profile was that the decline in British fertility "was much more pronounced among the better-educated, economically successful middle and upper classes than among the poorer or lower classes of society" (Soloway 1990: 10). Eugenists, therefore, proposed "two at times overlapping approaches: 'positive eugenics,' which aimed to foster more prolific breeding among the socially meritorious, and 'negative eugenics,' which intended to encourage the socially disadvantaged to breed less – or, better yet, not at all" (Kevles 1985: 85).

Eugenics gained numerous adherents in the Edwardian period as trepidation about the likely consequences of the differential decline in fertility grew more intense. "Indeed, the fall in the birthrate was the catalyst that transformed eugenics from a relatively obscure, neo-Darwinist, statistically based science into an organized propagandist movement and, more important, into a credible biological way of explaining social, economic, political and cultural change readily comprehensible to the educated public" (Soloway 1990: 18). One of the most prominent spokesmen for the new creed was the leading socialist theorist Sidney Webb, who wrote in a Fabian Tract of 1907:

> In Great Britain at this moment, when half, or perhaps two-thirds, of all the married people are regulating their families, children are being freely born to the Irish Roman Catholics and the Polish, Russian and German Jews, on the one hand, and to the thriftless and irresponsible – largely the casual labourers and the other denizens of the one-roomed tenements of our great cities – on the other. Twenty-five per cent of our parents, as Professor Karl Pearson keeps warning us, is producing 50 per cent of the next generation. This can hardly result in anything but national deterioration; or, as an alternative, in this country gradually falling to the Irish and the Jews. Finally, there are signs that even these races are becoming influenced. The ultimate future of these islands may be to the Chinese! (1907: 16–17).

While Sinophobia and even race in general (unlike class) were never dominant themes within the British eugenics movement (though see Stone 2002: 94–114), Webb's dread of being swamped by Asian hordes (personified for the burgeoning reading public in the bloodcurdling mien and inexhaustible malice of Dr. Fu Manchu, first let loose on the world by "Sax Rohmer" in 1912), was not uncommon.

The Eugenics Education Society

By the time the Eugenics Education Society (EES; it operated under this name until 1926; between that year and 1989 it was called the Eugenics Society; since then it has been known as the Galton Institute) came into being in 1907, the ideology of eugenics had already infiltrated more or less every aspect of intellectual and public life in Britain, but such was the evangelical fervor with which the EES took up its "task of defending society from the multiplication within it of the residuum of degenerate, unemployable and feckless" (Jones 1998: 16) types and encouraging the better stocks to reproduce themselves more numerously, that nothing could deflect it from its mission. The first Chairman of the EES was "the unfortunately named Dr Slaughter" (Searle 1976: 92), while the Secretary of the Cambridge University branch was the more apt and steady-sounding "Mr

Stock" (Searle 1976: 93). "You would be amused to hear how general is now the use of your Eugenics!," Pearson exclaimed in a 1907 letter to Galton. "I hear most respectable middle-class matrons saying if children are weakly, 'Ah, that was not a eugenical marriage!'" (quoted in Hasian 1997: 30).

When Robert Baden-Powell launched his Boy Scout movement the following year (1908) it was partly as a result of his own anxieties about racial degeneration. Michael Rosenthal has noted how two of the most vociferous eugenists of the Edwardian era, Pearson and Caleb Williams Saleeby, were great admirers of Baden-Powell. Saleeby, indeed, saw him not only as an educator, but "the greatest educator of our time," and regarded the Scouts as a prime agency for combating the forces of national decline, declaring:

> If national eugenics is ever to be achieved in Great Britain it will come through the Boy Scouts and the Girl Guides, who almost alone, of all our young people, are being made ready, by "training in citizenship, character discipline, and patriotism", for education for parenthood, which must be the beginning of national eugenics. (Quoted in Rosenthal 1986: 159)

Saleeby, a temperance campaigner, and, in 1924, founder and chairman of the Sunlight League (Searle 1976: 117), typified the British eugenics movement's progressive core: freethinking and eugenical thinking invariably went hand in hand.

The EES never boasted a large membership, but it contained a host of influential figures among its ranks. "Almost the entire biological establishment joined the EES, and many of the most distinguished geneticists took an active part in its day-to-day work. The Darwin family were present in numbers" (Searle 1976: 11–12). Well-known politicians who were members of the EES included the sometime Prime Minister A. J. Balfour, the future Prime Minister Neville Chamberlain and the future Home Secretary Sir William Joynson-Hicks. Other members included the economist John Maynard Keynes, the psychologists Cyril Burt and William M. McDougall, the political theorist and economist Harold Laski, and the humanist and historian Goldsworthy Lowes Dickinson. Winston Churchill, Alexander Graham Bell, and Charles W. Eliot, former President of Harvard, were not members of the EES, but they were all sponsoring vice-presidents of the First International Eugenics Congress in 1912, held in London and organized by the EES (Kevles 1985: 63), while Bertrand Russell, F. C. S. Schiller, and Bernard Bosanquet were three philosophers of note who promoted eugenics with unbending conviction. Overall, as Searle and others have emphasized:

> eugenics, with its air of scientific authority, appealed to the "progressive mind" as well as to people of conservative disposition. Socialists, reforming Liberals, fighters for women's rights, advocates of sexual liberation: all could find in eugenics much with which they agreed . . . . It was certainly quite *logical* to view eugenics and social reform as complementary rather than as antagonistic creeds . . . . Yet, in its institutional form, the eugenics that triumphed had a decidedly conservative hue. Most official pronouncements, though allegedly non-partisan, exude a mistrust of progressive liberalism and a horror of socialism. (Searle 1998: 26–7)

In Searle's view, one of the main reasons for this was because the man who was President of the EES from 1911 to 1928, Major Leonard Darwin, author of *The Need for Eugenic Reform* (1926), was an arch-conservative.

Underlining the wide appeal of eugenics, Lesley Hall has pointed out that there were various "uses made of eugenic concepts by specific women when talking about motherhood, health, and women's place and role within society generally" (Hall 1998: 36–7; see also Chapter 1 of this volume), while Hasian goes even further, arguing that "women were among the prime social actors assuring that eugenics was more than a name for racist or statist hereditarian beliefs" (Hasian 1997: 73). Hall notes that the EES member and birth control reformer Marie Stopes, in *Radiant Motherhood* (1920), "made a passionate plea for legislation to enable the sterilisation of the 'hopelessly rotten and racially diseased', claiming that these 'would be the first to be thankful for the escape such legislation would offer from the wretchedness entailed not only on their offspring but on themselves'" (1998: 40). Another high-profile woman member of the EES was Lady Ottoline Morrell (Farrell 1985: 214), chatelaine of Garsington. Indeed, as Kevles reveals, "half the membership of the British eugenics society consisted of women, and so did about a quarter of its officers. In the United States women played an insignificant role in the national society but a prominent one in local groups. In both countries, women constituted a large part of the eugenic audience" (1985: 64). Naomi Mitchison was elected a Fellow of the EES in 1925, and even the Nazis' unholy zeal for compulsory sterilization did not deter "[t]he extreme left-wing feminist Stella Browne" from joining the Society as late as 1938; her membership did not lapse until 1942 (Hall 1998: 40–1).

Yet it was a sign of how far the Eugenics Society had by then broadened its horizons that in the same year, 1942, Robert Graves published a poem in the *Eugenics Review* which Galton would have read with bafflement:

The Eugenist

Come, human dogs, interfertilitate –
Blackfellow and white lord, brown, yellow and red!
Accept the challenge of the lately bred
Newfoundland terrier with the dachshund gait.

Breed me gigantic pigmies, meek-eyed Scots,
Phlegmatic Irish, perfume-hating Poles,
Poker-faced, toothy, pigtailed Hottentots,
And Germans with no envy in their souls.

Graves's poem is hardly sanitized of racial prejudice, but the Eugenics Society would have viewed its celebration of hybridity and its invocation of new kinds of ethnicity as unprintable anathema only a few years earlier.

Sweeney Erect

"The Eugenist" is one of the last vestiges of modernism's engrossment with breeding; forty years previously interest in eugenics had been so passionate in advanced circles that it took on the status of a secular religion. In *Anticipations* (1901), for example, H. G. Wells predicted that a "merciful obliteration of weak and silly and pointless things" (quoted in Childs 2001: 10) would one day be the norm, whereas Shaw promoted positive eugenics in *Man and Superman* (1903) and urged as late as 1933 that: "Extermination must be put on a scientific basis if it is ever to be carried out humanely . . . as well as thoroughly . . . . [If] we desire a certain type of civilization and culture, we must exterminate the sort of people who do not fit in" (Preface to *On the Rocks*, quoted in Childs 2001: 9). In his address to the EES in 1910, much to the annoyance of its senior officers, Shaw had come out "in support of lethal chambers and free love" (Searle 1998: 23), just as five years earlier Wells had observed that "the way of Nature has always been to slay the hindmost, and there is still no other way, unless we can prevent those who would become the hindmost being born" (quoted in Paul 1995: 75). "If I had my way," D. H. Lawrence wrote in a similar vein in 1908:

I would build a lethal chamber as big as the Crystal Palace, with a military band playing softly, and a Cinematograph working brightly; then I'd go out in the back streets and main streets and bring them in, all the sick, the halt, and the maimed; I would lead them gently, and they would smile me a weary thanks; and the band would softly bubble out the "Hallelujah Chorus." (Lawrence 1979: 81)

Lawrence has been pilloried for these remarks – and understandably so – but if we relocate them in their precise historical context it is clear that while his words are shocking to our ears they would not have upset many Edwardian progressives. To gloss Lawrence's comments (which he made in a private letter) in this way does not make them any more palatable, of course, but it does underline how much the complexion of social reform has changed over the past hundred years. In the heyday of eugenics, for example, Havelock Ellis's argument in support of birth control typified the interventionist approach to the so-called "social problem groups" which many progressives favored: "The superficially sympathetic man flings a coin to a beggar; the more deeply sympathetic man builds an almshouse for him so that he need no longer beg; but perhaps the most radically sympathetic of all is the man who arranges that the beggar shall not be born" (quoted in Kevles 1985: 90).

Lawrence's last novel, *Lady Chatterley's Lover* (1928), is among other things the culmination of his lifelong espousal of hereditarian eugenics, and this was to have been made even clearer in a sentence which did not make it into the published text. In the course of outlining his prerequisites for social renewal in Chapter 15, Mellors was to have added "An' let the insane and the deadly sick be put to sleep" (Lawrence 1993: 430) directly after informing Connie Chatterley that his followers will not be allowed to "have many children, because the world is overcrowded" (Lawrence 1993: 220). And even though this eagerness to annihilate the unfit was not reflected in the mainstream eugenics movement, which tended to play down talk of "lethal chambers" and "Extermination" and confined itself to campaigning for the incarceration and sterilization of "defectives," few eugenists, regardless of their politics, would have dismissed the standpoint of Wells, Shaw, Lawrence, and Mellors as entirely unconscionable.

The prolific popular novelist Eden Phillpotts (1862–1960) was a member of the EES (Farrell 1995: 227), while the less profuse and defiantly less readable Marianne Moore's "poems and essays, and her reading notes from the late teens and early twenties especially," it has been argued, "evince not only a direct knowledge of and involvement with genetics and eugenics, but a deliberate adaptation of the conceptual foundations of these sciences to language and writing" (Kadlec 1994: 23). The imprint of eugenics is even more noticeable in the early poetry of T. S. Eliot, much of which, in the words of Juan Leon, "reads like the transcript of a eugenicist's nightmare. Eliot's early work portrays atavisms, nervous debilitations, epileptic seizures, phthisic decay, and the atrophy of arms and legs" (1988: 169).

In a review Eliot wrote in 1918 for the *International Journal of Ethics* he drew attention to the "'exceptional importance' . . . of a series of articles by Professor McBride [*sic*] entitled 'Study of Heredity'." A passage Eliot selects from one of the articles is particularly intriguing (he is quoting MacBride):

> In all cases where large numbers of a given species of animals are raised under somewhat artificial conditions a certain number of monsters will be produced, apparently owing to a disturbance of the germ-cells in their growing and ripening. This is true both of insects raised on banana peel and of human beings raised in a large city. (Quoted in Crawford 1987: 68)

Robert Crawford has proposed that this passage "is certainly important for the disturbed sexuality of *The Waste Land* and of those monsters Sweeney and Tiresias" (1987: 69), and it is likely that he is more correct than he appears to have realized. E. W. MacBride (1866–1940), Professor of Zoology at Imperial College, London, was the exponent of "a Lamarckian version of eugenics based solely on race" (Bowler 1993: 83). Arthur Koestler once dubbed him "the Irishman with a heart of gold," but as Bowler explains, "if Koestler delved a little further into MacBride's career":

> he would have discovered that his subject was an Ulster Protestant who despised the Irish as an inferior race and who joined the eugenics movement in Britain to campaign for their compulsory sterilization. MacBride's extremism made him an embarrassment to the Eugenics Society. He later wrote a letter to the *Times* praising Hitler's policies in Germany. (Bowler 1993: 83–4)

Given MacBride's loathing of the Irish, it is all the more arresting that the unmistakably Irish Sweeney (a name of galloglass origin, ironically denoting "pleasant") figures so recurrently and menacingly in the poetry of a man who was so "exceptional[ly]" taken with MacBride's work on heredity.

Eliot's fears about the prolific fertility of the dysgenic city-dweller are evident in many of his poems. For example, when he writes in "Preludes":

> One thinks of all the hands
> That are raising dingy shades
> In a thousand furnished rooms

Eliot's phrasing encourages the reader to bring to mind "furnished rooms" inhabited not by impoverished single occupants but heaving congestively with the social residuum. But it is undoubtedly in *The Waste Land* that Eliot's anxieties about the differential birthrate are most glaringly on view, especially the second section of the poem, which juxtaposes barren opulence with the unchecked fecundity of proletarian life. The cloying excess of the opening scene of "A Game of Chess," with its iconography of mythical dalliance and desire, its allusive folds and verbal exorbitance, serves only to lay bare the inappetent neurotics whose attempts at intercourse fail within it. Lil, on the other hand, is already worn out with childbirth – she has five children and has terminated another – and at thirty-one looks "so antique." Chivvied by her coarse-minded friend, whose undisguised lust for her recently demobbed husband contrasts with the "strange *synthetic* perfumes" which emanate from the affluent woman, Lil personifies the case for negative eugenics. The friend's innuendoes and Eliot's porcine imagery savor of the uninhibited copulation which, he implies, has recommenced with a vengeance in the postwar world. In his own reading of *The Waste Land*, Childs is prepared to go much further, arguing persuasively that not just "A Game of Chess" but the poem as a whole is deeply concerned with such issues as prostitution, depopulation, and "biological regression" (2001: 143).

Aldous Huxley was another writer who brooded on the problem of "social degeneration" or "the multiplication of inferior types at the expense of the superior," as he put it in *Proper Studies* (1927). In an article of the same year Huxley wrote:

> In the future we envisage, eugenics will be practised in order to improve the human breed, and the instincts will not be ruthlessly repressed, but, as far as possible, sublimated to express themselves in socially harmless ways. Education will not be the same for all individuals. Children of different types will receive different training. Society will be organised as a hierarchy of mental quality and the form of government will be aristocratic in the literal sense of the word – that is to say, the best will rule. (Bradshaw 1994: xiii–xiv)

If this sounds like a prototype of *Brave New World*, it is because when Huxley wrote the novel he was uncertain in his own mind whether he was writing a satire, a dystopia, or a utopia (Bradshaw 1994: xii–xix). Yet when he called for the state use of eugenics in a radio broadcast in January 1932, the month in which *Brave New World* was published, his words contained not even the slightest hint of irony (Bradshaw 1994: 112–13).

But Huxley's most strident eugenicist statement was made two years later in an article entitled "What is Happening to Our Population." Citing the eugenic "sterilisation of defectives" in "more than half the states" of the USA, Alberta, Switzerland, and Nazi Germany as models to be emulated rather than spurned, Huxley outlined the situation in England and Wales (as he understood it):

> there are now eight mental deficients for every four or five that there were a quarter of a century ago.
>
> *If conditions remain what they are now, and if the present tendency continues unchecked, we may look forward in a century or two to a time when a quarter of the population of these islands will consist of half-wits. What a curiously squalid and humiliating conclusion to English history!*
>
> What is the remedy for the present deplorable state of affairs? It consists, obviously, in encouraging the normal and super-normal members of the population to have larger families and in preventing the sub-normal from having any families at all. (Bradshaw 1994: 150–1; emphasis in original)

The Catholic Church was the most vigorous opponent of eugenics in Britain and it was one of its most prominent spokesmen, G. K. Chesterton, author of *Eugenics and Other Evils* (1922), who hit back at Huxley: "A good many things have been compulsory in Germany since the beginning of the year; and I shall be surprised if Mr Aldous Huxley approves of them" (quoted in Bradshaw 1995: 167). Elsewhere, Chesterton attacked eugenics as "one of the most ancient follies of the earth" (quoted in Searle 1976: 3).

The 1930s: Yeats among the Reformists

Chesterton's response to "What is Happening to Our Population" was typical of the increasingly hostile press that eugenics received in Britain in the 1930s. By then, even Eliot had become critical of the tendency of eugenics "to take the place of religion":

> Now eugenics, we must all agree, has already done a great deal for our material well-being: it has helped to provide us with a number of perfect animals and plants for various purposes, it has made wheat grow in climates where no wheat grew before, and so forth. Furthermore, it will have, we

hope, when more highly developed, much to teach us about the breeding of human beings. It can help us to deal better with those unfortunate members of the community who ought not to breed at all. But I think the hopes of some eugenists have been set too high, and some have advocated what many of us regard as very dubious short cuts to the improvement of the race. (1932: 446)

Eliot, by now a devout Christian, goes on to hold that since we have no idea what a "perfect human being" is we should not attempt to breed one, while a more fleeting indication of the growing infamy of eugenics is the appearance in Dorothy L. Sayers's *Gaudy Night* (1935) of an unsympathetic American woman, Sadie Schuster-Slatt, "a dark, determined woman with large spectacles and rigidly groomed hair" (1935: 31), whose vocation has "something to do with the sterilisation of the unfit, and the encouragement of matrimony among the intelligentsia" (1935: 33). Nor was it only in the 1930s that literary opponents of eugenics made themselves heard. Stephen Dedalus is dismissive of eugenics in *A Portrait of the Artist as a Young Man* (1914–15), while in Sinclair Lewis's 1925 novel *Arrowsmith*, "the Eugenic Family at the Iowa fair is exposed as the criminal 'Holton gang'; the parents turn out to be unmarried, and one of their five purported children suffers an epileptic fit during a health demonstration" (Paul 1995: 11). Nevertheless, up until the early 1930s the champions of eugenics consistently outnumbered its opponents, whereas from the mid-1930s onwards there were many indications that eugenics had lost both its appeal and credibility in Britain.

Which makes it all the more significant that W. B. Yeats became a member of the Eugenics Society as late as November 1936 (Bradshaw 1992: 192). Leonard Darwin had "struggle[d] to preserve [the Eugenics Society] as a selective, pro-natalist propagandist agency, dedicated to encouraging the 'eugenically fit' to have more children" (Soloway 1998: 53), but under the socialist C. P. Blacker, General Secretary of the Eugenics Society from 1931 to 1952, the organization moved emphatically to the left. Soloway has described Blacker as "the aggressive architect of a reform eugenics that focused on negative or restrictive policies, primarily birth control, taking into account the need to weigh more accurately the interaction between heredity and environment as it affected the qualitative reproduction of people in all classes" (Soloway 1998: 54), and he was untiring in his efforts to keep the image of the Eugenics Society clean as opposition to the Nazis' eugenics policies mounted during the 1930s: in 1935 Blacker even tried to change the name of the organization to "The Institute for Family

Relations" (Soloway 1998: 71–2). But he was fighting a losing battle and the eugenics movement in Britain had now entered a period of steep decline. "Not only did the term evoke new Nazi-inspired images of racial tyranny, but to socialists it [now] meant class prejudice and bigotry; to Catholics . . . false and pernicious doctrine, and to many others, including influential scientists on the left, a joke" (Soloway 1998: 72).

Yeats's eugenics, on the other hand, were strictly hereditarian, elitist, and deadly serious. In the last two chapters of *Modernism and Eugenics* Childs examines "Yeats's earliest acquaintance with eugenics from the turn of the century" (2001: 170) and demonstrates convincingly that Allan Estlake's study of *The Oneida Community* (1900), with its description of J. H. Noyes's introduction of "stirpiculture" in the 1860s, and Auguste Forel's *The Sexual Question* (1905; English translation 1908), had a major impact on texts such as *The Speckled Bird, On Baile's Strand*, and *The King's Threshold*. Furthermore, poems of Yeats's middle period, such as "Upon a House Shaken by the Land Agitation," testify to the continuing vitality of eugenicist thought in his work throughout his writing life.

In the late 1930s, however, eugenicist issues began to dominate Yeats's work. He worries about the differential birthrate, for instance, in "A Bronze Head," while "Under Ben Bulben" contains a eugenicist decree:

> Irish poets learn your trade
> Sing whatever is well made,
> Scorn the sort now growing up
> All out of shape from toe to top,
> Their unremembering hearts and heads
> Base-born products of base beds.

In "Three Songs to One Burden" Yeats imagines that if "Crazy Jane" could "put off old age / And ranting time renew" she would introduce the usual positive and negative measures to improve Ireland's racial stock. She would, in other words: "Throw likely couples into bed / And knock the others down." Other late poems which are explicitly eugenicist in theme are "The Gyres," "The Statues," and "The Old Stone Cross," while Yeats's last major prose work, *On the Boiler*, is the culmination of his intense interest in the field from 1936 onwards. As *On the Boiler* took final shape, Yeats mused luridly on his eugenic utopia: "Centuries of bloodshed may [be] the only means of setting in all places of authority 'the best born of the best'" (quoted in Bradshaw 1992: 208).

Tainted Woolf?

In *Vita and Virginia*, Suzanne Raitt begins her chapter on "'Moral Eugenics': The Working-Class Fiction of Vita Sackville-West" with the observation that "Sackville-West's political and class allegiances have always been a stumbling block for her feminist admirers" (Raitt 1993: 41). She goes on to assert that Sackville-West `was already profoundly, and publicly, reactionary, by the time Woolf met her . . . . The woman with whom Woolf fell in love was, among other things, an unashamed eugenicist, and her extensive knowledge of the subject shapes the narrative of, and the assumptions behind, two of her earliest popular novels, *Heritage* (1919) and *The Dragon in Shallow Waters* (1921)" (Raitt 1993: 41). It is one of the chief contentions of Childs's recent book that there is every reason why Virginia Woolf's "admirers" should feel equally uncomfortable. Childs's subtitle is "Woolf, Eliot, Yeats, and the Culture of Degeneration," and even though the word "eugenics" only appears once in Woolf's entire *oeuvre*, Childs argues that there is a good deal to suggest that she was deeply tainted by the hereditarian thinking of her era. But what distinguishes Woolf's engagement with eugenics from that of Sackville-West, Eliot and Yeats, surely, is her irony? Woolf invariably subverts the hereditarianism which the other three accept as foundational, and it is this fundamentally playful element in Woolf's writings which seems to have eluded Childs.

Before turning to Woolf's fiction, there is one passage in her diary which has caused considerable consternation and which is not remotely ironic. On January 9, 1915 Woolf and her husband went for a stroll by the River Thames between Richmond and Kingston:

> On the towpath we met & had to pass a long line of imbeciles. The first was a very tall young man, just queer enough to look at twice, but no more; the second shuffled, & looked aside; & then one realised that every one in that long line was a miserable ineffective shuffling idiotic creature, with no forehead, or no chin, & an imbecile grin, or a wild suspicious stare. It was perfectly horrible. They should certainly be killed. (Woolf 1983: 13)

Childs characterizes Woolf's conclusion, quite rightly, as "a most negative eugenics" (2001: 23), while other readers have been more damning. Yet although Woolf's remarks are offensive to our way of thinking, if we read her words in their appropriate historical context, we can see that there is nothing particularly extreme about them. The same month that she took her walk by the Thames Woolf "'declared herself a Fabian'" (Lee 1996:

348), and in the Fabian, progressive circles in which she and Leonard moved her attitude to the mentally handicapped would have been viewed as sound rather than callous, entirely consistent with Havelock Ellis's "radically sympathetic" solution to the problem of the unfit.

In his chapter entitled "Virginia Woolf's Hereditary Taint" Childs (2001: 22–37) documents just how closely Woolf was surrounded by eugenists and eugenicist thought throughout her life, before going on to state that "the issues raised by eugenics were so important to Woolf as to force their way not just into her diary . . . but also into one of her most important novels, *Mrs. Dalloway* (1925)" (2001: 24). I would argue, conversely, that in *Night and Day* and *Mrs. Dalloway*, Woolf *satirizes* the hereditarian mindset as part of her more general opposition to patriarchy.

If Sackville-West's novels are "grounded in eugenic theory and the work of Francis Galton in particular" (Raitt 1993: 90), and if "Galton is cited in *Heritage*" (Raitt 1993: 51–2) and Sackville-West "consulted" his work on heredity for her biography of Joan of Arc (Raitt 1993: 121), Woolf deals with this eminent Victorian in a more Stracheyan manner in *Night and Day*. "Denham had accused Katharine Hilbery of belonging to one of the most distinguished families in England," the third chapter of Woolf's second novel begins:

> and if any one will take the trouble to consult Mr Galton's "Hereditary Genius," he will find that this assertion is not far from the truth. The Alardyces, the Hilberys, the Millingtons, and the Otways seem to prove that the intellect is a possession which can be tossed from one member of a certain group to another almost indefinitely, and with apparent certainty that the brilliant gift will be safely caught and held by nine out of ten of the privileged race. (1994: 24)

Galton was a friend of Woolf's father, Leslie Stephen, and we know she read *Hereditary Genius* in 1905, but although, at the end of *Night and Day*, Cassandra Otway looks set to marry William Rodney, a scion of "the oldest family in Devonshire" (50), when, against the wishes of her father, Katharine selects Denham (a man, ironically, who knows "as much about breeding bulldogs as any man in England," and who is also "an authority upon the science of Heraldry" (102), yet whose own family is "commonplace, unshapely, lacking in charm" (308)), she makes her escape from the hereditarian prison-house of the governing elite. Katherine cannot "live up to [her] ancestors" (8), but she can begin to live without them.

Similarly, when Denham and Mary Datchet bring to mind the Houses of Parliament and Whitehall at the beginning of Chapter 18, we read that "both belonged to the class which is conscious of having lost its birthright in these great structures . . . . They agreed in thinking that nature has not been generous in the endowment of our councillors" (178). Their opinion is backed up in two ways: William Rodney, a man by no means over-endowed with good sense, is employed in one of the "Government of-fices" in Whitehall (402), while Sir Francis Otway is apparently incapable of winning at whist, let alone running an outpost of Empire (160). Above all, the Otways are a typically half-educated distinguished family (like Woolf's own): intelligence (or at least education) has not been "passed on" straightforwardly, but has been distributed according to gender. In an equally mischievous manner, Woolf highlights Mrs. Hilbery's lack of he-reditary literary genius (she simply cannot bring shape to her life of her distinguished poet father, Richard Alardyce) and by allowing Katharine – who is said to look "wonderfully like [her] grandfather" (1994: 259) – absolutely no interest in literature at all. What *Night and Day* "prove[s]" is that "the intellect is [not] a possession which can be tossed from one mem-ber of a certain group to another almost indefinitely, and with apparent certainty that the brilliant gift will be safely caught and held." It shows the heads of distinguished families as inconsequential dullards and their daugh-ters as drudges desperate for education and freedom.

"Close attention to the role of eugenics in *Mrs Dalloway*," Childs con-tends, "reveals the extent to which Woolf accepted eugenics, regarding it as a literally unremarkable response to certain problems in the modern world" (2001: 24–5). Childs also claims that "it is by no means clear that [Woolf] criticizes eugenics itself" (2001: 38), but as I have shown else-where, it is almost certainly more clear than he allows. For instance, Lady Bruton's scheme "for emigrating young people of both sexes born of re-spectable parents and setting them up with a fair prospect of doing well in Canada" (Woolf 2000: 92) keys into a contemporary controversy about the alleged poor quality of British emigrants to that country which re-ceived press coverage in the early 1920s. A distinguished Canadian eugenist, Charles Clarke, traveled to London in May 1923 to plead for "'the intro-duction to Canada of the best Nordic types'" and *The Times* backed him up, insisting on the absolute necessity of preventing "weak or degenerate, and therefore potentially immoral types" from emigrating (quoted in Woolf 2000: xxv–xxvii). Once Lady Bruton's Canadian scheme is contextualized, Childs's assertion that "the object of Woolf's disdain is not the eugenical project itself, but rather the ineffectualness of Lady Bruton's enthusiasm" (2001: 41) looks less secure. Furthermore, Woolf ironizes Lady Bruton's project in such a way as to make it unequivocal that she disapproves of it.

Lady Bruton, we are told, has "lost her sense of proportion" about Canada and can think of nothing else – a sure sign of mental disturbance in the eyes of Sir William Bradshaw, for whom "health is proportion" (84) and a lack of it grounds for confinement in an asylum.

A little further on, Childs turns his attention to this striking description of Elizabeth Dalloway: "Was it that some Mongol had been wrecked on the coast of Norfolk . . . had mixed with the Dalloway ladies, perhaps, a hundred years ago? For the Dalloways, in general, were fair-haired; blue-eyed; Elizabeth, on the contrary, was dark; had Chinese eyes in a pale face; an Oriental mystery" (Woolf 2000: 104). Childs reads this "passage . . . as a freighted allusion to mongolism – a mysterious condition (today known as Down's Syndrome) that Woolf indirectly invokes as a figure for her eugenical anxieties about her own fertility" (2001: 50). He may be correct, but it seems much more likely that Woolf's main purpose here is to undermine Richard Dalloway's preoccupation with family purity and inherited ability. Dalloway is obsessed with Lady Bruton's pedigree, just as Sir William Bradshaw thinks all mental problems boil down to the matter of good or bad blood, but the novel forcefully opposes such a black and white view of life. In her description of Elizabeth, Woolf evokes F. G. Crookshank's "widely noted book *The Mongol in Our Midst*" (Kevles 1985: 160). Published in 1924, while Woolf was at work on *Mrs. Dalloway*, Crookshank maintained that Down's Syndrome could be "a vestige of man's evolutionary past, and that some Mongol blood no doubt flowed in the veins of many Europeans" (Kevles 1985: 160). "While it would be going much too far to suggest that Woolf envisages Elizabeth as a Down's Syndrome case," I have argued, "it is possible that she may have had at least something of Crookshank's recessive nuance of 'Mongol' in mind when she conceived the appearance of the Dalloways' offspring, and, if so, Woolf's point is surely that, *pace* Bradshaw and Dalloway, pure breeding is pure tosh" (Woolf 2000: xxxii). Earlier in his book Childs posits that Woolf, like Eliot and Yeats, "extends the imperial sway of the scientific discourse of the body into . . . the realm of the imagination" (2001: 14), but in *Mrs. Dalloway*, *Night and Day*, and her work in general, surely, it is Woolf's *rejection* of "imperial" ideologies (whether those of the state or the masculinist scientific community of her day) which brings a characteristic edge to her fiction?

Conclusion

Sir William Bradshaw, with his patriotic determination to immure Britain's "lunatics," prohibit childbirth, and make it "impossible for the unfit to propagate their views" (Woolf 2000: 84), embodies the conservative wing of the British eugenics movement, but in its origins, and looked at as a whole, eugenics in Britain:

> was in many ways radical and forward-looking. It was based on the new, dynamic science of evolution and was defined by equally new mathematical techniques that became the foundations of modern statistics. Finally, it placed its faith and found its disciples in a new, so-called aristocracy of talent whose pretensions to replace the old were supported not by tradition, custom, or violent revolution but by coefficients of correlation, deviations, regression, frequency curves, and, with the rediscovery in 1900 of Gregor Mendel's remarkable experiments, by the selective arrangement of genes as well. (Soloway 1990: 27)

While is easy for us to deplore eugenics and to feel abhorrence for what it degenerated into under the Nazis, it is important not to lose sight of its "radical and forward-looking" origins and its largely progressive constituency, especially in the 1930s.

Pauline Mazumdar is not the only commentator to have suggested that

> the decline of the eugenics movement in Britain is one aspect of the postwar change in *mentalité* that some contemporary sociologists saw as the "end of ideology" – the perceived growth of egalitarianism that followed the establishment of the Welfare State and the final break up of the Poor Law. The movement in its original form did not long survive the disappearance of the pauper class as an administrative category. (1991: 6)

This historical development, coupled with the moral enormity of the Holocaust, explains why eugenicist thought became almost literally unthinkable after 1945. But in the last twenty years of the nineteenth century and the first three decades of the twentieth, eugenicist ideas were all the rage, and there have been a number of signs in recent years that the term may have begun to shed its Hitlerian taint and that eugenics, especially in the realm of medical technology (Lynn 2001), may once again become not only thinkable, but seductive.

David Bradshaw

References and Further Reading

Adams, Mark B. 1990. *The Wellborn Science: Eugenics in Germany, France, Brazil, and Russia.* New York and Oxford: Oxford University Press.

Bowler, Peter J. 1993. *Biology and Social Thought 1850–1914.* Berkeley Papers in the History of Science, 15. Berkeley, California: Office for History of Science and Technology, University of California at Berkeley.

Bradshaw, David. 1992. The Eugenics Movement in the 1930s and the Emergence of *"On the Boiler."* In Deirdre Toomey, ed., *Yeats and Women* [*Yeats Annual* 9: A Special Number]: 189–215.

——, ed. 1994. *The Hidden Huxley: Contempt and Compassion for the Masses 1920–36.* London: Faber & Faber. (Published in the USA as Aldous Huxley, *Between the Wars: Essays and Letters.* Ed. David Bradshaw. Chicago: Ivan R. Dee, 1994.)

——. 1995. Huxley's Slump: Planning, Eugenics, and the "Ultimate Need" of Stability. In John Batchelor, ed., *The Art of Literary Biography,* pp. 151–71. Oxford: Clarendon Press.

Childs, Donald J. 2001. *Modernism and Eugenics: Woolf, Eliot, Yeats and the Culture of Degeneration.* Cambridge: Cambridge University Press.

Cravens, Hamilton. 1978. *The Triumph of Evolution: American Scientists and the Heredity–Evolution Controversy 1900–1941.* Philadelphia: University of Pennsylvania Press.

Crawford, Robert. 1987. *The Savage and the City in the Work of T. S. Eliot.* Oxford: Clarendon Press.

Eliot, T. S. 1932. The Search for Moral Sanction. *Listener* 7/168 (March 30): 445–6, 480.

Farrell, Lyndsay Andrew. 1985. *The Origins and Growth of the English Eugenics Movement 1865–1925.* Ed. Charles Rosenberg. The History of Hereditarian Thought, No. 10. New York and London: Garland.

Graves, Robert. 1942. The Eugenist. *Eugenics Review* 34/3 (October): 84.

Greenslade, William. 1994. *Degeneration, Culture and the Novel 1880–1940.* Cambridge: Cambridge University Press.

Hall, Lesley A. 1998. Women, Feminism and Eugenics. In Peel, ed., *Essays in the History of Eugenics,* pp. 36–51.

Hasian, Marouf Harif, Jr. 1997. *The Rhetoric of Eugenics in Anglo-American Thought.* Athens and London: University of Georgia Press.

Jones, Greta. 1998. Theoretical Foundations of Eugenics. In Peel, ed., *Essays in the History of Eugenics,* pp. 1–19.

Kadlec, David. 1994. Marianne Moore, Immigration, and Eugenics. *Modernism/Modernity* 1/2 (April): 21–49.

Kevles, Daniel J. 1985. *In the Name of Eugenics: Genetics and the Uses of Human Heredity.* New York: Alfred A. Knopf.

Kühl, Stefan. 1994. *The Nazi Connection: Eugenics, American Racism, and German National Socialism.* New York and Oxford: Oxford University Press.

Lawrence, D. H. 1979. *The Letters of D. H. Lawrence,* Vol. I: September 1901–May

1913. Ed. James T. Boulton. Cambridge: Cambridge University Press.

——. 1993. *Lady Chatterley's Lover*. Ed. Michael Squires. Cambridge: Cambridge University Press.

Lee, Hermione. 1996. *Virginia Woolf*. London: Chatto & Windus.

Leon, Juan. 1988. Meeting Mr Eugenides: T. S. Eliot and the Eugenic Anxiety. *Yeats Eliot Review* 9/4 (Summer–Fall): 169–77.

Lynn, Richard. 2001. *Eugenics: A Reassessment*. London: Praeger International.

Mazumdar, Pauline M. H. 1991. *Eugenics, Human Genetics and Human Failings: The Eugenics Society, its Sources and its Critics in Britain*. London: Routledge.

Paul, Diane B. 1995. *Controlling Human Heredity 1865 to the Present*. Atlantic Highlands, NJ: Humanities Press.

Peel, Robert A., ed. 1998. *Essays in the History of Eugenics: Proceedings of a Conference Organised by the Galton Institute, London 1997*. London: Galton Institute.

Raitt, Suzanne. 1993. *Vita and Virginia: The Work and Friendship of V. Sackville-West and Virginia Woolf*. Oxford: Clarendon Press.

Rosenthal, Michael. 1986. *The Character Factory: Baden-Powell and the Origins of the Boy Scout Movement*. London: Collins.

Sayers, Dorothy L. 1935. *Gaudy Night*. London: Victor Gollancz.

Searle, G. R. 1971. *The Quest for National Efficiency: A Study in British Politics and Political Thought, 1899–1914*. Oxford: Basil Blackwell.

——. 1976. *Eugenics and Politics in Britain 1900–1914*. Science in History, No. 3. Leyden: Noordhoff International Publishing.

——. 1998. Eugenics: The Early Years. In Peel, ed., *Essays in the History of Eugenics*, pp. 20–35.

Soloway, Richard A. 1990. *Demography and Degeneration: Eugenics and the Declining Birthrate in Twentieth-Century Britain*. Chapel Hill and London: University of North Carolina Press.

——. 1998. From Mainline to Reform Eugenics: Leonard Darwin and C. P. Blacker. In Peel, ed., *Essays in the History of Eugenics*, pp. 52–80.

Stone, Dan. 2002. *Breeding Superman: Nietzsche, Race and Eugenics in Edwardian and Interwar Britain*. Liverpool: Liverpool University Press.

Webb, Sidney. 1907. *The Decline in the Birth-Rate*. Fabian Tract No.131. London: Fabian Society.

Woolf, Virginia. 1983. *The Diary of Virginia Woolf*, Vol. I: 1915–1919. Ed. Anne Olivier Bell. London: Hogarth Press.

——. 1994. *Night and Day*. Shakespeare Head Edition, Ed. J. H. Stape. Oxford: Blackwell.

——. 2000. *Mrs. Dalloway*. Oxford World's Classics series. Ed. David Bradshaw. Oxford: Oxford University Press.

3

Nietzscheanism: "The Superman and the all-too-human"

Michael Bell

One day my name will be associated with the memory of something tremen-
dous – a crisis without equal on earth . . . . I am no man, I am dynamite. –
Yet for all that, there is nothing in me of a founder of religion – . . . I want no
"believers."

Nietzsche, Ecce Homo

The iconoclastic German philosopher, Friedrich Nietzsche (1844–1900),
had an immense vogue in both the early and the latter decades of the
twentieth century. In the Anglophone world, these two phases are divided by the mid-century impact above all of Walter Kaufmann, whose
translations, editions, and commentaries created for Nietzsche a wide and
informed readership. In some respects, the most recent phase enables a
better understanding of the earlier one, and of the literary developments
commonly grouped under the term "modernism," with which Nietzsche's
thought was closely entwined.

The direct impact of Nietzsche in the modernist decades, however, is a
complex question. He acquired notoriety as a name and reputation before
making an informed impact on the most serious and creative minds of the
time. In particular, his reception suffered from lurid misrepresentation in
Max Nordau's *Degeneration* (translated into English in 1895), which was
the first widespread source of information about him for many Anglophone
readers. Although Nordau's intemperate attack on almost the whole of
contemporary avant-garde culture as a form of degeneration was widely

dismissed, Nietzsche was seen as his associate rather than one of his victims.

Nietzsche's *oeuvre* was substantively produced in an intensive period between 1872 and 1888, before his lapse into permanent insanity, and his most significant relation to modern Anglophone literature is not as an influence but as having articulated discursively and in advance the complex of themes and the composite worldview that can be deduced from a large part of modernist writing. His radical cultural critique with its interrelated conceptions of aesthetics, art, history, language, morals, myth, science, and the end of metaphysics, found a variety of literary parallels in the modernist generation without these simply depending on his example. Moreover, insofar as Nietzsche had become a vogue, and was associated, often reductively, with iconoclastic ideas and attitudes, it was precisely the most Nietzschean writers who needed to distance themselves from him. In some cases, it is clear that the distancing, whether knowingly or not, is really from the popular conception of Nietzsche rather than from Nietzschean thought itself.

Furthermore, the immediate reception of Nietzsche, which focused on key ideas such as the "overman," "the will to power," and "eternal recurrence," tended to treat these Nietzschean themes as doctrines. There is a useful parallel in the early reception of Dostoevsky, including Nietzsche's own reading of him. He was likewise thought of as offering doctrinal, even dogmatic, solutions and analyses. In fact, unknown to anyone in the West, and to virtually no one even in Russia at the time, Mikhail Bakhtin was already arguing in the early 1920s the directly opposite interpretation: that Dostoevsky's power as a novelist lay in subjecting such doctrinal material to constant and radical dramatic testing. Bakhtin's actual influence in the West came in the latter decades of the twentieth century contemporaneously with a comparable change in the perception of Nietzsche. The "new" Nietzsche is likewise no longer read for doctrinal guidance in individual living, and still less in politics. Few would wish to follow such practical advice as might be deduced from some of his views on education, Jews, women, or social authority, although with all these bracketed out he still remains a uniquely fertile and compelling analyst of modernity. He is rather read for his extraordinarily agile and subtle awareness of the metaphoricity of thought, of the relativity of truth, and the self-serving delusions of conviction. This is likewise his most significant affinity with modernism, which also attacked systematic and idealist thought partly by meditating on its own medium at the levels of both literary genre and language itself.

The recent shift in emphasis casts a further retrospective light on the nature of the early reception by suggesting how Nietzsche's writings reveal their readers. Apart from problematizing the very notion of doctrine, or of a systematic body of thought, his power now seems to lie much more in the diagnostic and deconstructive critique of cultural forms than in political or social solutions. The need for some critical bracketing arises with many important thinkers, but in Nietzsche's case it is peculiarly invited as part of the internal dynamic of reading him. He freely contradicted himself and expressed contempt for the desire to acquire disciples, imaging it, in *Twilight of the Idols,* as merely adding zeros to a cipher, so that the truly Nietzschean response would be to stand apart even from Nietzsche himself. This means that the very notion of Nietzscheanism, although a cultural fact, is oxymoronic, if not self-contradictory. A truly Nietzschean relation to Nietzsche might echo his own powerfully agonistic identifications with Christ and Socrates while the most apparent adoption of his thought in the period tends to reflect, even more than with most thinkers, the preoccupations and attitudes of his followers. The same revelatory value may apply equally to those who reject him, as Bertrand Russell effectively did in his *History of Western Philosophy* (1946). Just as Nietzsche showed how much the world exists to human beings as interpretation, so he exists to an unusual and proper degree in the interpretations of his readers. Whereas Swift spoke of satire as a glass in which the reader sees everyone's face but his own, in Nietzsche there is a legitimate sense in which readers define themselves by what they find in him. Above all, whether accepted or rejected, he became an epochal symbol so that many who saw radical change, and fateful opportunity, in the experience of modernity were inclined to find in him echoes of their own enthusiasms and fears; some of which are not very savory.

A final caveat around the question of reception is that, although the immediate disciples of Nietzsche mostly knew German, and were often engaged in translating him, the English versions of his work emerged slowly and not in what would now be thought the ideal order of significance. He was probably best known, for example, as the author of the highly prophetic *Thus Spake Zarathustra,* while *The Birth of Tragedy,* his most weighty and influential work in relation to literature and aesthetics, was not translated into English until 1909. Although virtually all the elements which made up his thought had precedent in previous thinkers and artists, he gave them a unique configuration, tone, and urgency. In effect, he rethought all human values in naturalistic, biological, and evolutionary (instead of transcendental) terms and focused these wide-ranging perceptions in memorably summative formulae such as Zarathustra's pronouncement, both tragic and liberating, that "God is dead." He believed he had accomplished a "Copernican turn" in the realm of morals, and one might add in aesthetics too. For that reason it was difficult to assimilate single elements in isolation from the altered perspective of the whole, and a work like *Zarathustra*, without the more sustained argumentation of, say, *The Genealogy of Morals*, might seem merely rhapsodical. Furthermore, his preference for aphorism, a form which does not accommodate mediocrity, could nonetheless leave him peculiarly vulnerable to reductive reading. Sophisticated and vulgar implications lie in dangerous proximity.

This partly explains his minimal impact within the anglophone philosophical academy. His radical attack on metaphysics was closely tied to the German idealist tradition as developed through Kant, Hegel, and Schopenhauer, and he was at first hardly perceived as a philosopher at all in the sense of contributing to the academic discipline. The Edinburgh Professor Seth Pringle-Pattison wrote two dismissive articles in 1897–8, which were reprinted in book form (1902). One of the few professional philosophers to take an interest was F. C. S. Schiller, who remained fairly dismissive of him until just before World War I, while George Santayana wrote a hostile study, *Egotism in German Philosophy* (1916), in which he was given a culminating and representative role. In an essay reviewing the newly completed multi-volume English translation, however, Schiller distinguishes Nietzsche's serious interest from his vulgar notoriety, such as the association of his thought with insanity, and suggests that it lay in the two spheres of morality and knowledge (1913: 148–67). Although he had made more of a stir in the realm of morals his most influential impact would prove to be epistemological. This was not only a shrewdly prescient, but coolheaded, assessment and the essay as a whole might be seen either as a British domestication of Nietzsche or as an index of how the world had moved on since his early writings. For with the impact the new turn-of-the-century physics, as mediated through books like Karl Pearson's *The Grammar of Science* (1892), it was no longer shocking to acknowledge that our "truth" is human. As the most influential modernist writers were about to produce their most significant work, Nietzsche had become assimilable to modern thought even while maintaining his iconoclastic notoriety. This helps to indicate how the Nietzsche of the propagandists may be distinguished from his presence in some central writers of the period.

An English translation of Nietzsche's works was begun under the editorship of a Glasgow professor, Alexander Tille, but the publisher was unable to continue beyond the first three volumes (1896–7), of which

Tille's own version of *Zarathustra* was the first. The project of a complete translation was taken over by Oscar Levy, who translated some volumes himself, between 1909 and 1913. Levy was a doctor with the financial means to devote himself to making Nietzsche known in the English-speaking world which, he argued, was the crucial audience to convince both because of the political and economic power of Britain at the time and because English culture, pragmatic to the point of anti-intellectualism, had naturally the least affinity with Nietzsche's thought. For the British to absorb Nietzsche would be a significant cultural turn. At the same time, he saw Britain as a possibly fruitful location of Nietzschean values because, despite superficial reforms, it had, in his view, successfully resisted democratization. Levy's promotion of Nietzsche, in other words, was politically tendentious and his polemical endorsement of Nietzsche's contempt for English intellectual culture may have further undermined his advocacy.

Levy is a striking example of Gertrud Petzgold's observation that Nietzsche was taken up in Britain by journalistic enthusiasts rather than scholars or professional philosophers (1929: 136–7) and, given the later uses to which Nietzsche would be put, it is ironical that many of his principal early sponsors should be Jews. Nietzsche's apparently antisemitic remarks, like his comments on women, are often about the cultural construction, and self-construction, of these categories and they sit uneasily between the open antisemitism of the period and a late twentieth-century cultural critique. Levy was equally ambivalent from the other side. As an assimilated Jew he adopted some of the common accounts of the Jewish character; perhaps with a measure of preemptive self-critique. His introduction to a 1913 translation of Arthur Gobineau's *The Renaissance*, for example, lauds, in a Nietzschean spirit, the premodern toughness of Renaissance character, and Levy devotes most of its space to applauding the racial theory for which Gobineau was most well known. Just as the great figures of the Renaissance represented a culture that had not yet suffered modern degeneration, so Levy distinguishes between the modern Jew and the heroic race of the Old Testament. He likewise endorses Gobineau's hostility to democracy and dismisses de Toqueville's criticisms of him in this regard. The questions of race and gender sit on the faultline of Nietzsche's thought between nineteenth-century biological causality and a modern deconstruction of these categories as cultural formations. While Levy picks up both aspects in a reductive spirit, the great clue both to Nietzsche's enduring impact and to his ambiguous reception in the shorter term, lies in the powerful tension in him between the biologism of his own period and his anticipation of the radically deconstructive analysis which was to be fully developed only in the later twentieth century.

An early attempt to spread Nietzschean thought was a pamphlet-sized journal, *The Eagle and the Serpent* (*E & S*), which appeared from 1898 to 1903, edited by J. B. Burnhill (Erwin McCall). Its principal thrust was to argue the case for "egotism" against "altruism" as a social virtue. To some extent this recalls the scandal of Bernard Mandeville's early eighteenth-century argument in *The Fable of the Bees* that "private vices" may be "public virtues." One difference was that although literary and philosophical circles resisted Mandeville's analysis the serious underlying point was gradually, if rather unconsciously, assimilated into mainstream economic thought in the form of Adam Smith's "invisible hand." The new arguments for egoism, by contrast, were taken up by literary writers against the principal drift of the culture and the precise meaning of these terms for those who espoused them needs to be understood in the historical context. The magazine's writers appealed to a tradition of thought which they claimed was enunciated in Nietzsche, Emerson, Stirner, Thoreau, Goethe, Whitman, Humbolt, Spencer, and Ibsen, and the opening number placed side by side a series of strikingly similar aphorisms from Nietzsche and Emerson. As far back as George Meredith's *The Egoist* (1877) in the British context, the pressure of the Victorian ethic of abnegation had been challenged by the legitimate demands of the ego. As Meredith's novel also presaged, this was an especially urgent theme for women, as is reflected in the change of title of the important modernist journal the *The New Freewoman* in 1914 to the *Egoist*. But it was a more general theme central to several writers of the modernist decades and its significance for the magazine is suggested by the ironic title of Robert Tressell's posthumous *The Ragged-Trousered Philanthropists* (1914). Tressell's novel about the hard lives of a group of house painters sees their economic exploitation as a form of philanthropy directed toward the rich. Likewise, for Burnhill and his collaborators, the general acceptance of an ethic of altruism helped sustain an unjust social order: "As a basis for social policy altruism is a lie whose utility is strictly limited to schemes of exploitation" (*E & S* No. 1: 3). Responding to the editor's request for readers' comments, Thomas Common pointed out that Nietzsche's attitude to social progressivism would be incompatible with the magazine's democratic purposes. The editor's reply is instructive in showing how different streams of thought can be merged in surprising ways: those committed to the project of the magazine fully realized Nietzsche's hostility to democracy but valued him as the great philosopher of egotism. And Alfred R. Wallace pointed out that Nietzschean elitism would properly require a political and social equality from which truly outstanding ability and *virtu* could emerge. All these points were to be repeated by other commentators in the following decades. The quotation above could easily have come from another regular correspondent, George Bernard Shaw, who was drawn to clarify his own position on Nietzsche: Shaw rejected Nietzsche's views on specific topics such as music and socialism while respecting his iconoclastic wit and much of his underlying diagnostic insight. Indeed, in his Preface to *Man and Superman* (1901), he was to argue that the lamentable experience of "Proletarian Democracy" makes it important to evolve through selective breeding a new human type for a "Democracy of Supermen" (see Chapter 2 of this volume).

Starting two years before the Levy edition, the other principal locus of the dissemination of Nietzchean thought was the journal the *New Age*, which was taken over by Alfred R. Orage in 1907 to become an important forum for the generation of literary modernists. As the title suggests, the journal sought to alert readers to new developments and to understand modernity in a critical yet affirmative spirit. Orage's own introduction, *Nietzsche in Outline and Aphorism*, also appeared in 1907. Along with some of the modernists, Orage had a mystical side to him and saw Nietzsche partly through his own desire to transcend the present conception of the human and it is important, once again, to understand how certain themes were perceived at the time. For later readers, one of the most disturbing aspects of the Nietzschean proselytizers is their hostility to democracy drawing on his "aristocratic" individualism as a primary support. The *New Age* of 1909 included a supplement magazine on the House of Lords whose powers were to be curtailed in 1911. From the antidemocratic standpoint, the Lords were argued to be more independent than the Commons because they were not obliged to satisfy voters. For these writers, as for Shaw in the passage just quoted, democracy meant not so much government by the people as something more like populist rule. The fearful suspicion of democracy, in other words, is a period concern that runs more widely than the Nietzscheans or the *New Age*, or even right-wing thought, and it should be remembered that universal male suffrage was still new in Britain, the Commons had a long-standing history of corruption, and in the light of later twentieth-century developments, such as the popular press, the effects of a commercially driven and politically motivated stultification were not unreasonably feared. Later history has also created an apparently sharp division between fascism as opposed to democracy, or to socialism, but without the benefit of hindsight these movements were much more ambiguous. Hitler's party was to be called National Socialist, while

Stalin's Russia enacted a grotesque parody of socialism. Once again, if one concentrates on the foundational exploitation by these regimes of populist *ressentiment*, rather than their theoretical ideology, the antidemocratic suspicion of the early part of the century may seem less simply objectionable to later readers and might even be seen as prophetic.

Nonetheless, the quality of antidemocratic analysis and rhetoric was often sweeping and reactionary, as in Levy's argument in *The Revival of Aristocracy* (1906) that the French Revolution resulted from a failure of nerve in the aristocracy; a failure which must now be recuperated. Again, although the historical generalization may be wild, the sense of imminent catastrophe, to be captured most memorably in Yeats's "The Second Coming," was widely felt even in the prewar years. The Futurists put the most positive inflection on the potential of modernity, while others feared it, but the sense of radical and imminent change was widespread. Apparently metaphysical conceptions of history are always likely to reflect immediate historical concerns. Britain now had serious economic rivals in Germany and the USA. The new German state had been founded in 1870, just about the time of Nietzsche's first major publications. The high Victorian respect for German thought, in Carlyle, George Eliot, and G. H. Lewes, had given way in journalistic and often academic circles to a nationalistic hostility which was decisively intensified, and apparently vindicated, by the outbreak of World War I. Lawrence, in dedicating *The Rainbow* (1915) to his German sister-in-law, had to drop his original intention of using Gothic script. Nietzsche was so associated with the German national spirit and the motif of power that the war was even referred to journalistically as the "Anglo-Nietzschean war." The Nietzscheans of the *New Age* were obliged to show that Nietzsche meant something quite different by his emphasis on power and was actually hostile to the modern Bismarckian state. Unfortunately, the very sophistication and shifting relativity of Nietzsche, which should have removed him from vulgar reductions, also prevented him being entirely free from such interpretation. Most importantly, as will be seen, Nietzsche anticipated a serious and central concern of a number of modern writers with the nature and meaning of power but the early proselytizers, with their one-sided antidemocratic zeal, were not in a good position to argue this even if they had grasped it.

Another translator for the Levy edition, for example, and a regular contributor to the *New Age*, was Anthony Ludovici, an aesthetician at the University of London, who produced several proselytizing books based on lecture series. In *Nietzsche and Art* (1911) he emphasized Nietzsche's aesthetic thought but not so much for its central metaphysical claim that the aesthetic is the fundamental activity of man. The full metaphysical force of the aesthetic for Nietzsche only gradually became evident and Ludovici rather picks up the modernist emphasis, as developed for example in Wilhelm Worringer's *Abstraction and Empathy* (1908), in which great art is often, and perhaps necessarily, incompatible with realism. These forms, however, were politically loaded for Ludovici. He saw realism not just as the inferior but as the democratic form. His admiration of ancient Egyptian art for its hieratic transcendence of realism would find echoes in Lawrence and Yeats, who were also hostile to aspects of modern democracy, and this raises a larger question about the impact of Nietzsche. In an embattled summary of the Nietzschean movement in Britain, which formed Levy's introduction to the final volume of his edition, he claimed that it was the artists, rather than philosophers, who had truly absorbed Nietzsche and, as we look back on the modernist period, this is perhaps even more true than Levy realized, for the major modernist writers had absorbed the Nietzschean spirit or recognitions independently before having their own thought focused by him. Indeed, Nietzsche's most radical claims for the metaphysical significance of the aesthetic might not be comprehensible without the examples of such writers as Joyce and Yeats. But this does not mean they got these insights or convictions from Nietzsche, or that an affinity with one aspect of his thought implies an acceptance of the whole, and even where they did take in Nietzschean thought it was often mediated through other sources.

The French critic, Remy de Gourmont, for example, was a possible mediator of Nietzschean thought for Eliot and Pound, who did not take to Nietzsche directly. The sexologist, Havelock Ellis, wrote several thoughtful and informed essays on Nietzsche. Thomas Common's *Nietzsche as Critic, Philosopher, Poet and Prophet* (1901) was a compilation of extracts in which Common's introduction stresses Nietzsche's honesty as crucial to his thought. This suggests a more literary than philosophical power in his thinking and is reminiscent of T. S. Eliot's comment on Blake's "naked" independence of vision as "terrifying," even while deprecating his lack of an appropriate tradition (1951: 319–20). Blake himself was something of a Nietzschean before his time and his increasing reputation by the end of the nineteenth century was part of the broad current in which Nietzsche could gain proper appreciation. From a variety of sources, including Nietzsche's own direct sources such as Schopenhauer, this generation of writers found many essential points of affinity with him which were not always recognized, or were distorted by the need to distance themselves from the popular Nietzscheanism of their day. For this reason one has to consult their works rather than their explicit comments on him, and the works will often rehearse the ambivalences and anxieties of the Nietzschean legacy as much as its confident affirmations and rejections. Yeats, Joyce and Lawrence, for example, absorbed Nietzsche positively, although this would not readily be deduced from the explicit comments of the last two.

In 1902, Yeats received from the New York lawyer and artistic patron of the modernists, John Quinn, several Nietzsche texts, including Thomas Commons's volume, and read him absorbedly over the next few years, although Roy Foster believes he already had some inkling of Nietzsche's thought in the late 1890s (1999: 213, 584). Either way, the independent evolution of Yeats's thought is best articulated in Nietzschean terms: Nietzsche provides the philosophical fulcrum on which his *oeuvre* turns. If Yeats may be said to have had two careers, one as a nineteenth-century and one as a twentieth-century poet, there are underlying continuities by which the latter is a transposition rather than a rejection of the former. The early Yeats was strongly influenced by the aestheticism associated with Walter Pater, just as Nietzsche was by the different aestheticism of Arthur Schopenhauer. But between the early *The Birth of Tragedy* (1872) and the late *Twilight of the Idols* (1888), Nietzsche's view of Schopenhauer changed almost to the point of inversion, although this too was rather an assimilation and transposition of Schopenhauer's metaphysic than a rejection of it. The early Nietzsche was deeply impressed by Schopenhauer's melancholy metaphysic of the Will, whereby the only escape from the blind process of nature was through religious abnegation or aesthetic transcendence. On this model art stands in opposition to life. In his later account of the aesthetic, by contrast, he rejects Schopenhauer's quietism and abnegation for he now sees art as the paradigm of life's celebration of itself. Kant's formula of "purposiveness without purpose," which can be taken in a separatist sense, is now a reflection of man's place in a post-theological world: all human activity is the conscious affirmation of purposiveness without purpose. Whereas in *The Birth of Tragedy* man was imaged in the humiliating posture of the soldiers painted on a canvas depicting a battle, in *Twilight of the Idols* man seeks no metaphysical remove through the aesthetic but is enjoined to affirm his fate joyously as if enacting his role in history as a mythic drama.

The recognition that myth is not an alternative to historical consciousness but a deeper apprehension of it is consonant with the comments on myth in *The Birth of Tragedy* and is powerfully articulated in the early essay, one of the *Untimely Meditations* (1872), "On the Advantages and Disadvantages of History for Life." Nietzsche proposes a myth*opoeic*, rather than mythic, reading of history in that myth is not for him a static, timeless transcendence but a constant creation from within history. Myth focuses what history cannot of itself explain or encompass: while human values are historically conditioned they cannot be a mere arbitrary product of history. Such a myth*making* conception can be seen in Yeats's treatment of immediate historical violence and moral complexity in "Easter 1916." The title juxtaposes a mythic and an historical reference whose interactions are worked out with subtle precision in the structure of the poem as summed up in the refrain: "a terrible beauty is born." Not long after this Yeats began to work on the historico-mythic scheme of *A Vision,* which presented history as a series of vast cycles whereby successive civilizations rise and decline. How much Nietzsche may have influenced this, along with so much other material, is hard to say although almost contemporaneously, and without Yeats's apparent knowledge, Oswald Spengler, a frank disciple of Nietzsche, had produced his pessimistic postwar cyclic theory of history, *The Decline of the West* (1918). The most overtly Nietzschean of Yeats's poems is the very late "Lapis Lazuli," which contemplates the rise and fall of historical civilizations, including the contemporary one, with an aesthetically achieved affirmation of "tragic joy." Yeats was perhaps able to acknowledge Nietzsche more positively because of his frank use of his own personality as the mythopoeic center of his poetic *oeuvre*; and if his self-affirmation left no room for discipleship, this was deeply Nietzschean in itself.

Joyce's use of Nietzsche exemplifies most clearly the philosopher's relation of anticipation rather than influence to the major modern writers. Joseph Valente has argued the influence case by noting how for "Nietzsche and Joyce the road to *amor fati* led through the epistemological pass of perspectivism" (1987–8: 89). This neatly catches what they share but we may ask to what extent Joyce's ironic play with cultural forms is applied to Nietzsche himself. As Richard Ellmann notes, the young Joyce, in his iconoclastic mode, could draw on him to expound "a neo-paganism that glorified licentiousness, selfishness and pitilessness and denounced gratitude and other 'domestic virtues'," yet at heart "Joyce can scarcely have been a Nietzschean any more than he was socialist" (1982: 000). Indeed, Joyce's references to Nietzsche in *Ulysses* come most notably from the superficial joker, Mulligan, while the ultimately central figure, Leopold Bloom, is rather the epitome of the domestic. Such local and attitudinal differences do not gainsay Valente's fundamental metaphysical point, indeed they rather reinforce it, but his argument for influence only adduces analogy and, most importantly, he does not weigh the competing impact of

Flaubert, who is the nearest thing to being Joyce's acknowledged master. Nietzsche and Flaubert approached similar themes with opposite attitudes. Both meditated satirically on the condition of educated modern man as what Nietzsche, in "The Uses and Disadvantages of History," called a "wandering encyclopaedia." As moderns, we are stuffed with knowledge but, like an encyclopedia, we have no overall narrative or wisdom to impart. Although Joyce the novelist promoted a self-myth no less monumental than that of the poet Yeats, his Flaubertian concern for authorial impersonality signaled a fundamental metaphysical relativism in the book if not in the writer. Whereas Yeats was an agnostic fascinated by belief, Joyce was brought up in a culture of belief and he therefore privileged the multiplicity of perspectives; a position as far from simple rejection as it is from simple commitment. Joyce inflected Flaubert's satiric method into a comedic vision, and achieved a Nietzschean metaphysical posture by Flaubertian means. Flaubert's romantic nihilism and Nietzsche's tragic affirmation are the opposite attitudinal poles on which the Joycean universe turns, "macro- and microcosm, upon the void."

To express it in this way brings out Joyce's different inflection from Yeats's of a fundamental Nietzchean posture. Nietzsche's essay on history criticizes the nineteenth-century tendency to understand life questions historically and suggests that "historical" understanding has to be leavened with different modes of being in time. We need some tincture of "unhistorical" naivety in order to act decisively and effectively. We also need the rarer capacity for "superhistorical" detachment from the assumptions and urgencies of our contemporary world. Although the Chinese sages of "Lapis Lazuli" seem able almost regularly to enjoy this superhistorical vision, Yeats no more than Nietzsche sees it as a possible, or desirable, posture in which to exist permanently. As has been suggested, Yeats's emphasis is much more on myth*making* out of the complex of experience in time, and the aesthetic or visionary perfection of Byzantium is strictly an impossible ideal in his visionary/historical system. By contrast, Joyce's *Ulysses* and *Finnegans Wake* privilege the transhistorical mythic dimension already existing in the archaic structures. This is not turning from history. It is rather that, precisely because it is fraught with history, a work like *Ulysses* affirms the need to see the experience simultaneously under a superhistorical sign. Joyce's use of myth gives a firm structure to his relativity. By the same token, however, the very fact that his elusiveness at the level of belief is so "Nietzschean" makes it difficult to attribute it in any direct or exclusive way to Nietzsche.

Although D. H. Lawrence, by contrast, was a writer of overt conviction, his relation to Nietzsche is just as elusive in its own way. The moment of his encounter with Nietzsche's works in Croydon public library in 1909 is recorded by Jessie Chambers but, like Joyce and Yeats, he was already forming the relevant aspects of his own worldview. Furthermore, Lawrence had an agonistic relation to the writers who most deeply influenced him so that his references to them tend to be apparently the most hostile, and hostility itself can be a form of influence. The resulting complex can be seen most clearly in *Women in Love* (1920). Through the figure of Rupert Birkin, Lawrence criticizes the "will to power" associated with the industrial magnate, Gerald Crich, who has been educated in Germany and has brought technical modernization to the family mines. Gerald, even though he initially reminds Ursula Brangwen of "Dionysus," is gradually revealed to be a figure of inner emotional vacuity and nihilism whose exertion of social and economic power arises from a compensatory need. But despite Gerald's Nietzschean overtones, this critique is itself thoroughly Nietzschean and it is Birkin who is the truly Nietzschean character. In Gerald, Lawrence is critiquing only the popular conception of Nietzscheanism. It could be that this apparent confusion was quite conscious on Lawrence's part because the reductive popular conception was the significant cultural fact, but it is more likely that Lawrence had himself imbibed the common view and was now unaware of those aspects of Nietzschean thought which, because they were so consonant with his own thinking, he had simply assimilated as his own.

As for Yeats, too, the theme of power, with distinctly Nietzschean significances, was immensely important to Lawrence. All three saw the two millennia of Christian culture as having given rise to an embarrassment about power, and a cult of humility and abnegation, which was in fact a more cunning and damaging form of power whereby the externally weak are able, without risk to themselves, to dominate the naturally strong. The modern secular legacy of this is democracy. In Nietzsche, this analysis stays at a level of cultural generality, with a great power of suggestive insight which a reader may bring to bear on a wide range of experience without any immediately prescriptive consequences. Indeed, as with much Nietzschean thought, such as his "attacks" on logic and grammar, it is a Copernican shift in consciousness which may have no immediately visible impact on the world or behavior. Just as the sun still appears to rise and human life depends on the felt stability of the earth, so the recognition that the discourse of "truth" depends on "a mobile army of metaphors" does not mean that reason and language are not to be used. It has long been noticed that Nietzsche's thought does not engage closely with the sphere of association, with the common or garden necessities of social and political activity. It is less clear what should be made of this observation. It can be seen as a radical critique of his thought or as simply stating one of its necessary conditions. Likewise, it is hard to say to what extent this was an instinctive and intelligent tact on his part, an aspect of the power of his thought, or whether it was an accident of biographical circumstances. Thomas Common suggested his thought was "esoteric," not in Orage's or Yeats's sense of the "mystical," but in the sense that it could not be understood without gross misapprehension at any broader level of dissemination. Yeats, however, whose longevity brought him to the fascist era, and who had by then become a public figure with political as well as literary cultural associations, did cash in such ruminations literalistically as in his sympathy for the Irish blueshirts. There was a dangerous mixture of the highly speculative and the immediately political. By contrast, Lawrence the novelist, while sharing the wide-ranging historico-cultural speculations of Nietzsche and Yeats, was thoroughly concerned with the sphere of association, with the internal dynamics of human relationships of all kinds. He first learned about the truths and falsities of power in his own family: the struggle between his parents was a microcosm of social class, gender, and religion, and his great work arises from his inward and critical understanding of these forces. At the same time, he retained something of the larger Nietzschean conception that the culture suffered from a failure to acknowledge the motif of power, in both the personal and political spheres, so that some of his later works, such as *The Plumed Serpent* (1926), imagine the Yeatsian/Spenglerian demise of white European culture being effected not just by an internal decline but by a voluntary act, the willed revival of a pre-Christian world. Yet even here, "imagine" is the operative word. Despite the absurdities and extremities of his Mexican novel, it was still a thought experiment, a deeply Nietzschean form, in which Lawrence retained, particularly though his heroine, Kate Leslie, something of his novelistic skepticism in testing, rather than simply expounding, this possibility. Afterwards, he explicitly rejected the political power motif and turned to *Lady Chatterley's Lover* (1928) as a model of apolitical tenderness, and to the ancient Etruscans, in *Etruscan Places* (1932), as a model of early Italian culture whose subtle sense of touch was overrun by the Roman spirit of power even then undergoing a grotesquely parodic revival under Mussolini.

If Yeats, Joyce, and Lawrence were variously, if not always overtly, sympathetic to Nietzsche, Ezra Pound and T. S. Eliot seem more genuinely indifferent or hostile. Kathryne V. Lindberg, however, makes a strong case for seeing Pound as Nietzschean in his affinities and possibly by indirect influence. She argues that Pound has been too much understood, partly through the influential account of Hugh Kenner, as assimilated to Eliot's organic notion of tradition, whereas she sees him has offering a more atomistic view of the past and a disruptive conception of the present. She claims, also, that his term *Paideuma*, borrowed from the anthropologist Leo Frobenius, is derived in turn from Nietzsche's disciple, Oswald Spengler. Pound is perhaps the most elusive case for determining influence because his mixture of eclectic information, wide-ranging speculation, and literalistic conviction is peculiarly elusive in itself. Perhaps the nub of the matter lies in his understanding of the nature of language.

Nietzsche's remarks on language were not immediately so influential since the initial emphasis in his reception fell on doctrine rather than medium, and some of the relevant writings were fragmentary materials not published in his lifetime and not well known until later, yet he had given memorable expression to what has come to be called the "linguistic turn." In an early piece, "On Truth and Lie in an Extra-Moral Sense," he spoke of "truth" as a "mobile army of metaphors" and showed language to be an autotelic system of significances before being a description of the world. The human world is largely a creation of language rather than the other way round. This awareness grew stronger over the twentieth century with several, sometimes reductive, and mutually uncomprehending, implications among which we may distinguish the "poetic" and the "ideological." Pound and Eliot, though close, straddle the watershed between these possibilities. The former conception has been most notably espoused by Martin Heidegger, for whom language was the creative matrix by which new forms of experience come into being. Poetry is the highest, or the archetypal, use of language and its function is not, in the first instance, referential. This view, in privileging the autotelic power and unpredictability of language, tends to be agnostic concerning the direct relation of language to the world. The other view, by contrast, assumes that if language forms the human world, then it has complete control over it, or is coterminous with it. If your language is sloppy and inaccurate, emotionally as well as intellectually, so is your reality. Pound and Eliot seemed to share such a hygienic view of language and culture at the time of their early association but their underlying conceptions, and practices, were really quite different. Pound was frequently closer to the view underlying late twentieth-century ideological critique. For him, the relation between reality and cultural form had a literalistic immediacy often justifying dogmatic prescriptiveness. Eliot, although as a critic concerned with correctness of belief, tended when writing about his own poetry to stress the mystery of the creative process as coming from unknown sources. *Four Quartets* is a consummate example of the creative function of language as articulated by the later Heidegger, and Eliot's turn to religious belief took him well away from Nietzsche as well as from Pound. Between them, Pound and Eliot suggest the incipient fracturing of the Nietzschean recognition into its separate possibilities.

The anglophone writer who has been commonly credited with the most direct Nietzschean influence and sponsorship is George Bernard Shaw. But he came to Nietzsche through Ibsen and Wagner, and he perhaps illustrates in reverse the principle that the truest influence is likely to be the most thoroughly assimilated and therefore the least apparent. Although his play *Man and Superman* (1901) certainly had a verbal influence in changing the common translation of *(Übermensch* from "overman" to "superman," there seems no reason to doubt his claim that he had formed his own convictions before encountering some of them in Nietzsche. More importantly, his overt use of Nietzschean ideas is in a Shavian spirit. Whatever his personal convictions, Shaw's artistic relation to ideas was as motifs for rhetorical development in an operatic spirit, and sometimes on a near-Wagnerian scale. He is an inverted image of Nietzsche. Nietzsche, who despised profundity, and warned against moralism, was always weighty and serious even in his jests, whereas Shaw, who engaged great social and moral questions, communicated relatively little weight of experience. It is hard to believe he could be significantly imbued with Nietzschean spirit.

The point can be extended to modern theatre more generally. For while Shaw's rhetoric was part of a broader modern movement in theatre which recovered specifically theatrical values, much of the most innovative modern theatre, while sharing Nietzsche's turn from naturalism as argued in *The Birth of Tragedy*, sought a highly conscious effect on the audience serving a moral or social critique. Only at this thematic level did Ibsen's radical critique of the bourgeois social order provide a point of commonality with both Nietzsche and Shaw; just as Strindberg warmed to Nietzsche's misogynistic interpretation of modern decadence. But if *The Birth of Tragedy* was not a primary model for a modern non-operatic theatre, Nietzsche was part of the cultural matrix from which Yeats produced his hieratic and mythopoeic theatre in conscious opposition to realism and immediate social critique. And his more general sense of tragedy as breaking down the dykes between individuals to reach a primordial and universal level of the psyche is consonant with Nietzsche's conception.

71

This points to the larger theme of the "hero" in the period. Despite their immense mutual difference, both Shaw and Yeats were drawn to see salvation in the hero, and recognized a modern, or future, ideal in the Nietzschean superman. Eric Bentley has traced the political aftermath of such attitudes in *The Cult of the Superman* (1957). Yet the superman in Nietzsche is already a complex figure who exerts a spontaneous and personal, rather than a desired or institutionalized, authority; and he would not wish for followers. In this respect he points to a larger ambivalence about heroism in the period. Although the superman was frequently associated with the assertion of elite power, and with political leadership, Nietzsche's conception was so internalized as potentially to reverse such implications. Hence it is Birkin, the least conventionally heroic character, who is the most Nietzschean figure in *Women in Love*. *Ulysses*, largely composed during World War I, reversed the traditional meaning of the literary "mock heroic," above all in the "Cyclops" episode, to mock the anachronistic stupidities of heroism itself.

This brief survey of the British context concludes by noting the reception of Nietzsche in America, France, and Germany. Following Nietzsche's polemical praise of French culture in criticizing the Germans, the British Nietzscheans appealed to the French awareness of Nietzsche as a supposedly humiliating contrast to British indifference although, as Douglas Smith argues, the first really substantial French study was Charles Andler's multivolume *Nietzsche: Sa vie et sa pensée* (1920–31). The French first assimilated Nietzsche partly through the Symbolist movement and the Wagner vogue, but tended to read him initially as a biographical case and then increasingly, after the turn of the century, as representative of the German spirit. The principal American exponent was H. L. Mencken who, like Shaw, assimilated him to his own persona of iconoclastic gadfly. In Germany, by contrast, most serious philosophers and cultural commentators felt the need to come to terms with Nietzsche, Heidegger being the most notable philosophical example.

Perhaps the most striking literary instance in Germany is Thomas Mann, who was initially imbued with the romantic pessimism of Schopenhauer mediated through a Nietzschean interpretation of the internal contradictions of culture. As a scion of this German tradition, he was not initially sympathetic to the progressive and democratic values associated with the French and Anglo-American worlds and even as, over the course of his long writing life, he became more politically progressive he did not abandon his Nietzschean formation but differentiated its elements internally so as to set Nietzsche contra Nietzsche. Two works which especially depend on this internal Nietzschean agon are the tetralogy *Joseph and his Brothers* (1933–43) and *Doctor Faustus* (1947). With the Joseph sequence Mann, like other modernists before him, turned consciously to myth in a Nietzschean spirit not as a flight from civilized reason but as its proper culmination. As he put it in a related lecture on Freud, with the Joseph theme in mind: "the mythic is indeed, in the life of humanity, an early and primitive step, but in the life of the individual a late and mature one" (1947: 63). His Old Testament characters live out their existences as consciously created or discovered destinies, repeating and modifying the experience of their ancestors, and leading the human to its highest potential. Their *amor fati* is far from abandonment to fate, and the psychological expansion of the biblical narrative transposes it into a modern key. In a related piece, "Voyage with *Don Quixote*," ostensibly written on a journey away from Nazi Europe in 1934, Mann ends with a highly ambivalent dream vision of Don Quixote with Nietzsche's features. At one level, this gives the mad Nietzsche an iconically inaugural position in the twentieth century's phase of modernity comparable to Don Quixote in an earlier foundational epoch. More subtly, though, it points to the way Mann, in the Joseph sequence, actually accommodates Nietzsche's mythopoeic relativism to the humane purposes he sees in Don Quixote's creator, Cervantes. Likewise, in his final major treatment of these themes, Mann's German artist, Leverkuhn, clearly based on Nietzsche among others, is presented in tragic contrast to Goethe's optimistic inflections of the Faust legend. Yet once again, the dangers of Nietzschean extremity are contained homeopathically by the responsibility of a post-theological, Nietzchean relativism. Mann's agonistic struggle with Nietzsche is self-conscious and exemplary for reasons to do with his specifically German tradition and history, yet it brings to the fore, as does the late twentieth-century resurgence of interest in Nietzsche, the way his mode of thought, rather than any particular doctrines or attitudes, mapped out for habitation some of the inescapable conditions of modernity.

References and Further Reading

Andler, Charles. 1920–31. *Nietzsche: Sa vie et sa pensée* [*Nietzsche: his Life and Thought*]. Paris: Bossard.

Bell, Michael. 1997. *Literature, Modernism and Myth: Belief and Responsibility in the Twentieth Century*. Cambridge: Cambridge University Press.

Bentley, Eric. 1957. *The Cult of the Superman*. London: Robert Hale.

Bohlmann, Otto. 1982. *Yeats and Nietzsche: an Exploration of Major Nietzschean Echoes in the Writings of W. B. Yeats*. London: Macmillan.

Common, Thomas. 1901. *Nietzsche as Critic, Philosopher, Poet and Prophet*. London: Grant Richards.

Eliot, T. S. 1951. *Selected Essays*. London: Faber.

Ellis, Havelock. 1932. *Views and Reviews 1884–1932*. London: Desmond Harmsworth.

Ellmann, Richard. [1959] 1982. *James Joyce*. New York and London: Oxford University Press.

Foster, John Burt. 1981. *Heirs to Dionysus*. Princeton: Princeton University Press.

Foster, Roy. 1999. *W. B. Yeats: A Life. Vol. I: The Apprentice Mage*. New York and Oxford: Oxford University Press.

Gobineau, Arthur. 1913. *The Renaissance*. London: Constable.

Kaufmann, Walter. 1974. *Nietzsche: Philosopher, Psychologist, Antichrist*. Princeton: Princeton University Press.

Lindberg, Kathryne V. 1987. *Reading Pound Reading: Modernism after Nietzsche*. Oxford: Oxford University Press.

Ludovici, Anthony. 1910. *Nietzsche: His Life and Works* London: Constable

——. 1911. *Nietzsche and Art*. London: Constable.

Mann, Thomas. 1947. *Essays of Three Decades*. London: Secker & Warburg.

Milton, Colin. 1987. *Lawrence and Nietzsche*. Aberdeen: Aberdeen University Press.

Orage, Alfred R. 1906. *Friedrich Nietzsche: The Dionysian Spirit of the Age*. London: Foulis.

Petzgold, Gertrud. 1929. Nietzsche in English-Amerikanischer Beurteilung bis zum Ausgang des Weltkrieges [Anglo-American Assessment of Nietzsche up to the Outbreak of the World War]. *Anglia* 53: 134–218.

Pringle-Pattison, Seth. 1902. *Man's Place in the Cosmos*. London and Edinburgh: Blackwood.

Pütz, Manfred, ed. 1995. *Nietzsche in American Literature and Thought*. Columbia, SC: Camden House.

Schiller, F. C. S. 1913. The Philosophy of Friedrich Nietzsche. *Quarterly Review* 218: 148–67.

Smith, Douglas. 1996. *Transvaluations: Nietzsche in France 1872–1972*. Oxford: Oxford University Press.

Thatcher, David S. 1970. Nietzsche in England 1890–1914. Dissertation, University of Toronto.

Valente, Joseph. 1987–8. Beyond Truth and Freedom: The New Faith of Joyce and Nietzsche. *James Joyce Quarterly* 25: 87–103.

4

Anthropology: "The latest form of evening entertainment"

Jeremy MacClancy

The protagonist is worried. His friend's leg is gangrenous and they are high in the Andes. They ride slowly in the direction of a distant hospital. Within two hours they meet, by chance, an English doctor who is also, by chance, an anthropologist. After amputating the leg he talks:

> "Savage societies are simply civilized societies with the lid off. We can learn to understand them fairly easily. And when we've learnt to understand savages, we've learnt, as we discover, to understand the civilized. And that's not all. Savages are usually hostile and suspicious. The anthropologist has got to learn to overcome that hostility and suspicion. And when he's learnt that, he's learnt the whole secret of politics."
>
> "Which is . . .?"
>
> "That if you treat other people well, they'll treat you well."
>
> "You're a bit optimistic, aren't you?"
>
> "No. In the long run," said (*the now one-legged*) Mark impatiently, "we shall all be dead. What about the short run?"
>
> "You've got to take a risk."
>
> "But Europeans aren't like your Sunday-school savages. It'll be an enormous risk."
>
> "Possibly. But always smaller than the risk you run by treating people badly and goading them into a war. Besides, they're not worse than savages. They've just been badly handled – need a bit of anthropology, that's all."
> (Huxley 1936: 581)

Most of our themes are already here: the value of cross-cultural comparison to illuminate our understanding of Western ways; the potential of anthropology to help heal the ills of Western society; the anthropologist as itinerant intellectual, able to straddle worlds and bring back reports from the other side. All that is missing is the capacity of anthropology to expand our sense of cultural diversity.

By the 1930s anthropology had become an accepted part of life for broad sections of the British public, a relatively common topic for gay conversation by the lighthearted and a source for rumination by the more seriously inclined. For Huxley (the quote is from *Eyeless in Gaza* 1936), it was quite plausible that his isolated protagonist might meet a thinking doctor spouting his own, idiosyncratic version of the discipline. His readers would not be disoriented but entertained; maybe even educated.

In this essay I wish to explore how and why, in the last decades of the nineteenth century and the first ones of the twentieth, anthropology rose from almost nothing to this level of widespread popularity. I wish also to examine the diversity of ways anthropological ideas, exempla, models, and approaches were appropriated and exploited by modernist novelists and painters during this period. The ways they used this material were strikingly diverse, for not all were as optimistic as Huxley about the therapeutic value of the discipline. Only some had so kindly a vision of other ways of life.

Anthropologists

In Britain an anthropology recognizable as such to modern practitioners arose in the mid-nineteenth century as a belated consequence of the anti-slavery movement. From the beginning, its supporters were keen to promote their subject broadly. The Ethnological Society of London, founded in 1844, made its sole object the promotion and diffusion of ethnological knowledge. It held both special meetings, where "popular" topics were discussed, and ordinary meetings, at which "scientific" subjects were debated in more technical terms. The Society amalgamated with another learned body in 1869 to form the Anthropological Institute. Its leaders came from dissenting middle-class families, upheld liberal, humanitarian, and utilitarian ideals, and maintained the utopian belief that the sustained efforts of education and science would result in a better society. Evolutionists *avant la lettre*, they were happy to espouse Darwinism when *The Origin of the Species* was later published. All the members of this fledgling

Institute were, however, gentlemen amateurs or professionals engaged in other areas of scholarly or scientific activity. None of them regarded themselves exclusively as "anthropologists" but as intellectuals who occasionally studied anthropological themes. Those whom we may regard as the first true anthropological professionals only emerged in the last decades of the century, from the small group of full-time paid curators entrusted with the care of ethnographic collections.

Some anthropologists of this general period, from the mid-Victorian to the close of the Edwardian eras, classified their work as either "technical" or "popular," but the distinction between these categories was usually negligible. Though some of their writings might assume more knowledge on the readers' part than others, almost everything they wrote could be understood by any informed person of their time. Several anthropologists of this period were particularly skillful at spreading the word, mainly because they wrote well, wrote and reviewed for a variety of major periodicals, produced popular books, and lectured widely. They were virtually obliged to do all this if they wished to keep the subject alive as the government, despite repeated appeals, refused to fund anthropological endeavors.

These successful anthropologists were able to sell so many books and to fill lecture-halls so easily because, above all, they contributed to one of the great public debates of their time: the status and practical consequences of evolutionary theory. For instance, Edward Tylor, who held a personal chair at Oxford and was praised for his "convincing method of exposition" and the clarity of his writing, propounded that social difference was not due to biology (i.e., "race") but to culture, and that all societies on earth were progressing, albeit at different rates, through the same general processes of evolutionary development. Australian Aboriginals were usually placed at the bottom of this evolutionary ladder; northwestern Europeans were always at its top. Tylor proclaimed anthropology a "reformer's science" which could be employed, among other ways, to identify illiberal survivals fit only for elimination. Though his immediate influence was so great that some even called anthropology "Mr Tylor's science," his subsequent reputation has since been completely overshadowed by that of his illustrious successor, Sir James G. Frazer.

Frazer remains today the most famous, and certainly the most financially successful, of all British anthropologists ever. His books are still in print and his influence astonishingly widespread. His ideas have made themselves felt in almost every area of the humanities and the social sciences as well as within literature. Indeed, Lionel Trilling, writing of *The Golden Bough*, once claimed that "perhaps no book has had so decisive an effect upon modern literature as Frazer's". By the 1920s it had become essential reading for anyone with claims to an education or a critical attitude to life; hundreds wrote to its author thanking him for opening their eyes and changing their lives. Even by 1910 R. R. Marrett, an Oxford anthropologist, was able to complain how fashionable Frazer and his peers had made the subject:

> To show that Anthropology is becoming popular is, perhaps, superfluous. The fact is almost painfully borne in upon anyone who has allowed his anthropological leanings to become known to the world. Every headmaster would nowadays have you down to lecture to his boys. A provincial town will muster in hundreds to hear you discourse on totems and taboos. At the most old-fashioned of our Universities the youth of the nation delight in comparing the habits of primitive man with their own. In short, Anthropology is the latest form of evening entertainment. (Marrett 1910: 299)

Part of the reason for Frazer's remarkable success was his ability to convey his views, without distorting them, in a language free of technical jargon and obscure expression. Preferring eloquent elegy to clumsily formulated dogma, he did not present his arguments in a doctrinaire manner, but skillfully blended modesty of statement with a grand literary style, one sprung with biblical and Latinate rhythms. The weighty result he leavened with irony, humor, and an artful, sustained use of concrete imagery. Frazer, in other words, was not trying to batter his readers with the power of bald logic, but to persuade them with the appeal of his rhetoric. As the record of his sales shows, if he did not always manage to win over his enormous audience, at the very least they were prepared to read his words. In the 1910s alone over 35,000 copies were printed of *each* of the twelve volumes of the third edition of *The Golden Bough* (1890–1915).

The custom which initially stung his interest was one from classical antiquity, from the temple of Aricia southeast of Rome. There, in a sacred grove dedicated to Diana, a man could only assume its priesthood by first plucking the "golden bough" and then killing the incumbent. Of course, once the deed was done, the slayer had to live with the knowledge he would in turn and time be slain by his own successor. He laid bare his plan for the book in a letter to his publisher:

> By an application of the Comparative Method I believe I can make it probable that the priest represented the god of the grove and that his slaughter was regarded as the death of the god. This raises the question of a widespread custom of killing men and animals regarded as divine. I have col-

lected many examples of this custom and proposed a new explanation of it. The Golden Bough, I believe I can show, was the mistletoe, and the whole legend can, I think be brought into connexion, on the one hand with the Druidical reverence for the mistletoe, and on the other with the Norse legend of the Balder. Of the exact way in which I connect the Golden Bough with the Priest of Aricia I shall only say that in explaining it I am led to propose a new explanation of the meaning of totemism. This is the bare outline of the book which, whatever may be thought of its theories, will be found to contain a very large store of very curious customs, many of which may be new even to professed anthropologists. The resemblance of the savage customs and ideas to the fundamental doctrines of Christianity is striking. But I make no reference to this parallelism, leaving my readers to draw their own conclusions, one way or the other. (Letter 11, viii, 1889 to George Macmillan, Macmillan Archive, British Museum; quoted in Stocking 1996: 138–9

Frazer has here summarized many of his main aims and methods: the concerns with divine kingship; rebirth through slaughter; vegetative symbolism; the extremely delicate handling of otherwise disturbing parallels; the explanation of one rite, symbol or myth by comparative analogy with a similar cultural facet from anywhere on the globe; a keen awareness of his need to win, and keep, a public. Magic and religion, no matter how seemingly "primitive," were to be seen as logical in process, though based on faulty reasoning. His comparativism he underpinned with a thoroughgoing intellectualism: he imputed the reasoning of indigenes when performing any kind of rite or custom and tried to persuade readers of his explanations by their inherent plausibility. E. E. Evans-Pritchard, the great British anthropologist of the 1950s and 1960s, termed this intellectualist manner of imputation and overstress on the role of deliberate reasoning as an "If-I-were-a-horse" style of explanation.

Frazer's accomplishment was a complex one, for his sprawling yet ultimately unified work achieves multiple aims. First and foremost, *The Golden Bough* is an astonishingly broad compendium of both ethnographic and folkloric data, held together by his version of "the Comparative Method". Secondly, his trawl through this data is presented as a voyage of discovery, the sprawling text framed by a narrative of travel and exploration. Thirdly, in a highly indirect manner, *The Golden Bough* addressed many of the central issues of its time: questions about the status of religion, the value of empire and industry, the role of the classical past, as well as the nature of the domestic and the sexual, the rural and the urban. Fourthly, by an encyclopedic display of supposedly primitive customs, Frazer demonstrated how far civilized humans had come. Yet, by providing much harsh evidence of contemporary barbarity both abroad and at home, he at the same time tempered any blind faith in progress.

Frazer at times worked together with his academic contemporaries in what was known as the "ritualist school" of anthropologically informed classicists, led by Jane Harrison, F. M. Cornford and Gilbert Murray. To Frazer, following Tylor, myths were post hoc rationalizations, used to explain rituals whose original meaning had been long forgotten. Harrison extended this idea by applying evolutionist approaches to classical material. She argued that myth arose out of rite, and not vice versa; that it was "the spoken correlative of the acted rite"; that it was not anything else or of any other origin. She underpinned these ideas with her developmental conception of rites dying out while myths continued in religion, literature, and art. As an ancient rite over time became ever more misunderstood, the associated myth, freed from its origin, could become attached to historical events or people, or come to be used as a scientific or etiological explanation of nature. Over the course of the 1910s she and her colleagues extended the application of these ideas to all branches of the arts in the classical world.

By the 1920s, however, all this kind of anthropology was rapidly becoming obsolete within academia; evolutionism, though still popular, was coming under increasing attack. Frazer was gaining critics as well as fans. One anthropologist described his technique of "chopping up" cultures, taking bits from a variety of ethnographic sources and then putting them together in the literary form of a workable, living whole as Frankensteinian in nature. A key catalyst of this change was a Polish expatriate, Bronislaw Malinowski, who in 1918 had returned to London after several years living on an island off Papua New Guinea. A tireless and skilled promoter of both himself and the discipline, Malinowski soon persuaded his students of the value of a self-defined modern form of exclusively *social* anthropology, one marked off from historically related endeavors. His key innovation was the necessity of "fieldwork," of intensive "participant-observation" for a prolonged period living with the people being studied. From now on, no self-respecting or respected anthropologist could leave collection of data to others, whether learned missionary or perspicacious colonial officer, nor could they "cut and paste" information culled from many different societies. Instead they had to concentrate on studying cultures one by one, as unities in themselves. In the process Malinowski helped engender the successful image of "the anthropologist as hero," as plucky intellectual not scared of going into the bush for the sake of coming home with the data. This attractive image of bold anthropologists going where no highbrows had pussyfooted before helped secure the popularity of the discipline for new generations of the educated public.

Malinowski also helped change the dominant literary style of anthropology. Frazer and his peers had tried in their writings to establish a closeness between themselves and their readers. In contrast, Malinowski and his students wished to bracket off their ethnography as a professionally distinct form of intellectual exercise. By using their experience of fieldwork as a legitimating device, they created simultaneously a distance between themselves and their readers, and a closeness between themselves and the societies they studied. Tylor, Frazer, and others of their general period spoke as though from their armchairs, to people who were in a similar position. Malinowski and his colleagues spoke as though from the village hut, to people who had never been in a similar position. Yet the number of anthropologists was still so low that those of the interwar generation, like their predecessors, had to write their books with both academic and non-academic audiences in mind. To that extent the functionalist ethnographies of the 1920s and 1930s may be regarded as works of "popular" (i.e., relatively non-technical) anthropology.

On his return from his Trobriand Island fieldwork, the then unknown anthropologist had tried to establish his reputation – and make a little money – by writing a readable book acceptable to a commercial publisher. Malinowski toyed with calling it "Kula: South Sea Enterprise and Adventure" or "Kula: a South Sea Adventure," before deciding on the far more catchy and marketable *Argonauts of the Western Pacific*. Despite his avowed concern to write a new kind of ethnography, the continuities with Frazer (who supplied its foreword) are still plain: the classical allusion in the title, the framing of the work as a voyage of discovery, his concern to describe local life with "vividness and colour." Soon afterwards, Malinowski attempted to revise Freud, by using the evidence of his Trobriand material to question the supposed universality of the Oedipus complex. Though orthodox Freudians summarily rebuffed his challenge to their position, his controversial endeavor ensured his views would become slogans of progressive morality and education. Thanks to such tactics Malinowski helped enable a vision of anthropology as an integral part of the British interwar avant-garde.

Primitivisms, Myths

Both these terms are so very usefully vague that I leave to others the usually sterile task of defining either. Instead I wish to sketch the ways key modernist writers have used anthropological writings for ends which commentators have marked as "primitivist" or "mythopoeic."

To start, let us look at long-held images of "the primitive" (here referring to non-Western, pre-industrial peoples and their ways of life). It seems that from the earliest explorations of Africa and the Americas, tales of indigenous customs and attitudes excited a complex reaction in Westerners: on the one hand, fear and horror at their supposed licentiousness, heathenism and violence; on the other, interest blending into admiration for their communal life and apparent ability to live in harmony with nature. These mirror-images of the "ignoble" and "noble savage" are of course primarily Western constructions which tell us far, far more about contemporary Western concerns than about the ways indigenes actually led their lives. For those keen to denounce the ignoble, deployment of the "primitive" was primarily a way to underline, laud, and legitimate their conception of civilization. Fundamentalist preachers, missionaries, and colonial apologists were among the more common exploiters of this strategy. In contrast, for those happy to praise contented indigenes lounging in Arcadia, contemplation of the "primitive" was a lever for questioning the dominant Western values of the day. These eulogists sought inspiration, or confirmation of the need for social, political, and personal transformation in the striking image of indigenes who seemed to have found their own paradise on earth.

The key modernist writers on whom I wish to concentrate would have rejected this simple-minded dichotomy. They did not denigrate indigenous difference in an ignorant fashion, but nor did they succumb to seductive visions of an Eden elsewhere on earth. Some of them, deeply unhappy with the decadent state of European civilization at the turn of the century, propounded the destruction, or at least the necessarily radical revitalization of the West. At the same time, they extolled a complex primitivism, one enticing yet savage, illuminating yet dark.

Conrad's *Heart of Darkness* (serialized 1899; published 1902) is an exemplar of this style. It is as much *fin du globe* as *fin de siècle*, with Kurtz as the ivory-trader gone native to wildly destructive effect. To Conrad, Europe is a museum of moribund values, and Africa horrific yet vital, a home of the primitive, providing a means of access to "the essential." In a worldview which chimes with those of evolutionist anthropologists, Conrad portrays sailing up the Congo as a voyage into our own prehistory, with the jungle able to awaken "forgotten and brutal instincts, … the memory of gratified and monstrous passions." Kurtz had had the courage to voyage much further up that track than his narrator, the stolid, unimaginative Marlow, would have ever dared to go. By venturing so far Kurtz throws off the moral hollowness suffered by his European contemporaries and comes close to achieving a sort of moral emancipation, though he dies before the process is complete. His final cry is critically ambivalent. Is "The horror! The horror!" he shrieks a deathbed recognition of the evil that going bush revealed, or a final spit in the face of a degenerate self-styled "civilization"? Conrad leaves the matter vague. He has Kurtz's Russian disciple state that the trader had experienced "both the diabolic love and the unearthly hate of the mysteries (he) had penetrated," while he leaves the otherwise upright Marlow on the verge of recognizing the heroic dimensions of Kurtz's endeavors: the gains he had made, the costs he had paid by escaping into primitivist excess.

D. H. Lawrence's view of "the primitive" sustains much of the same ambivalences. This was especially so during the first years of World War I, when he was writing *The Rainbow* and *Women in Love*. To him, very different indigenous ways of life both enchant and appal, both seduce and threaten. Disgusted with the decay of the West, he turns to Africa as one of the few remaining places where savagery retains its ancient life-taking, life-giving power. An overdeveloped European civilization had, by its nature, excluded its products from so much; it was only on a still dark continent, where the forces of disease and death were yet rampant, that people could continue to tap into great sources of vitality. For this pessimistic Lawrence the last hope for the West and the self lay in a liberating release achieved through a destructive rebirth grounded in savagery.

Many of Lawrence's ideas about the "primitive" and myth were confirmed and boosted by his enthusiastic readings of Frazer and the ritualists. As he wrote to Bertrand Russell in December 1915:

> I have been reading Frazer's *Golden Bough* and *Totemism and Exogamy*. Now I am convinced of what I believed when I was about twenty – that there is another seat of consciousness than the brain and the nervous system. . . . There is the blood-consciousness, with the sexual connection, holding the same relation as the eye, in seeing, holds to the mental consciousness. One lives, knows, and has one's being in the blood, without any reference to nerves and brain. This is one half of life, belonging to the darkness. And the tragedy of this our life, and of your life, is that the mental and nerve consciousness exerts a tyranny over the blood-consciousness, and that your will has gone completely over to the mental consciousness, and is engaged in the destruction of your blood-being or blood-consciousness, the final liberating of the one, which is only death in result. (Zytaruk and Bolton 1981: 469)

This mode of blood-being, whose feelings were "always true," was preeminent among indigenes. Michael Bell finds evidence of this primitive mode of feeling pervasive in *The Rainbow*. At points throughout the book, he argues, Lawrence succeeds in portraying certain characters' intuitively animistic sensibility, their sense of unity with the natural world. Lawrence's main means of achieving these effects are the slight extension of the meaning of words, so imparting a special aura to much of the text, and the investing of simple domestic scenes with ritualistic significance.

By the time he wrote *The Plumed Serpent* in the mid-1920s, sex had become not the point but a means to an end: the boundary-dissolving participation in larger, cosmic unities, what Marianna Torgovnick, following Freud, calls "the oceanic experience." Once again "primitives," this time Pueblo Indians, hold the key to attainment of a transcendental state, of quiescence, beyond words. These natives do not divide, partition off and judge the world but partake, in an unmediated manner, in an essential "Being-ness." However, his desire for their collective ineffable is undercut by a fear that nature, of which they are a part, is vast, alive, and all too able to swallow an individuating presence such as his own. For Lawrence, then, one could approach the primitive but not dive too far without paying the consequence.

By this stage Lawrence's "primitive" was almost exclusively a projection of his own concerns, relatively unfettered by readings of the ritualists. The case of T. S. Eliot is an almost complete contrast. Eliot was so well-read in anthropology he would review key French texts within a year of their appearance. He was able to cite, accurately, Lévy-Bruhl and Rivers, Durkheim and Harrison, Cailliet and Frazer. Lucien Lévy-Bruhl was a particular influence, with his "law of participation": indigenes were supposed to exhibit a "prelogical mentality" because they were capable of not recognizing divisions between the physical and the supernatural, the human and the nonhuman. According to Lévy-Bruhl, natives did not separate the sacred from the profane but regarded the two as parts of a seamless whole. Though he was criticized by academic contemporaries for the racist implications of "prelogicality" and though he himself later repudiated the idea, Eliot continued to use it, for his own purposes.

For Eliot, an early modern "dissociation of sensibility" had caused artists to separate the aesthetic from the practical, the poetic and mystical from the quotidian. Twentieth-century poets had to overcome this division and to cultivate prelogicality. They needed to be like "witch doctors" or other indigenous performers, who used prelogical and ritualistic methods to elicit communal pleasures from those watching them. Poets had to work their word-magic on their audiences. They were at their bardic best as public entertainers, maintaining "primitive" forms of art and performance where they relied on spontaneous interaction between actor and audience. Thus Eliot's later shift from poet to verse dramatist may be regarded as not so much a major change of literary mode, but rather a move into a more effective way of achieving the same end: awakening prelogicality.

Eliot defined this "primitive" prelogical instinct as:

> The feeling for syllable and rhythm, penetrating far below the conscious levels of thought and feeling, invigorating every word: sinking to the most primitive and forgotten, returning to the origin and bringing something back, seeking the beginning and the end. It works through meanings, certainly, or not without meanings in the ordinary sense, and fuses the old and the obliterated and the trite, and the current, and the new and surprising, the most ancient and civilized mentality. (Eliot 1933: 111)

Poets bridged the primitive and the civilized by an inherently mystical process of banging syllable and rhythm together. This acoustic forging of poetry he saw in starkly primitivist, evolutionist terms: "Poetry begins, I dare say, with a savage beating a drum in a jungle, and it retains that essential of percussion and rhythm; hyperbolically one might say that the poet is *older* than other human beings" (Eliot 1933: 148). Eliot, stimulated by the work of the ritualists, argued that the origin of drama was primitive ritual, and the essence of ritual was rhythm. Without that rhythm a performer could work no magic on his audience. An arrhythmic poet-shaman would have no clothes.

Poets, like primitives, relied on not just rhythm but metaphor as well, for what was metaphor but a magical process of making two unlikes like? According to Marc Manganaro, Eliot was here relying on another idea of Lévy-Bruhl's: that the word can hold a prelogical, mystical power. If this be the case, then wordsmiths – whether modern poets or native magicians – wield considerable power. By the deft arranging of words they can call on mystical forces in order to effect change among humans. Given this prelogic where words and spirituality are intrinsically connected, the power to name becomes a key attribute of both shamans and poets, a literal source of their authority. Lévy-Bruhl's emphasis on the power of the word also led him to stress indigenes' reverence for the language of rituals, where the meaning of what was said was of much, much lesser import than the efficacy of uttering the words. And Eliot valued Lévy-Bruhl precisely because he did not try to explain rituals away but concentrated on the study of mentality and the efficacious processes of ritual performance instead.

As Manganaro argues, Eliot's poet was modeled on Lévy-Bruhl's medicine-man: "a figure who unites social power and transcendence . . . because his channelling of mystical participations is instrumental to the social formations and maintenance of the tribe" (1986: 415). On this vision poets used primitive means for civilized, but conservative ends. As influential upholders of orthodoxy, they acted as powerful participants in society. As self-elected spokespersons, one might say they pretended to constitute a government of the tongue.

It was *The Waste Land* and its notes which first brought *The Golden Bough* to the attention of so many lovers of literature. But it seems it was Yeats who first realized the literary potential of Frazer's vade-mecum to myth. Yeats's reading and use of Frazer became a key stimulus both to much of his poetry and to his evolving vision of humans' place in the world. In his own words, "*The Golden Bough* has made Christianity look modern and fragmentary." To replace the creed in which he had been reared, Yeats drew on comparative mythology, theosophy, occult mysticism, and astrology. He wanted to "reconstruct" (more accurately, invent) the supposedly common, age-old matrix of cosmological experiences which preceded Christianity. This matrix included visions, spiritual experiences, the presence of the miraculous (i.e., the interruption of supernatural forces into ordinary life), and the evocation of collective memory through the power of symbolism. Within this scheme spirits still inhabited sacred places within the landscape, while the modern performance of ritual magic or the staging of séances held the promise of reviving and reintegrating sections of his matrical world, a world where everything, ultimately, was stitched together in a grand, cosmic unity.

Frazer's compendia provided Yeats's poetry and projects with greater comparative scope and historical depth, and helped enable his more universalist generalizations. The profusion of examples he supplied strengthened Yeats's conviction in the maintenance of continuity amidst constant change over the course of eons. *The Golden Bough* also gave him a storehouse of compelling images (e.g., the scapegoat, the king, the prophet, the priest, the magician) and actions (e.g., sacrifice, initiation, incarnation) as well as narratives capable of arousing powerful emotion. Furthermore, since Yeats believed in the power of the word or the symbol to evoke an otherwise almost inaccessible reality then, according to John Vickery, *The Golden Bough* offered him "another perspective on the magical power of language to create a world of concrete immediacy." Following this line of thought, poetry had the enchanting potency to revive the forgotten, make the past present, and the unconscious conscious.

For Yeats, however, Frazer was more a facilitator than an innovator. The poet was already well-versed in folklore before he encountered *The Golden Bough* and, unlike Frazer, actually conducted fieldwork, whether collecting folk beliefs in the west of Ireland or participating in Soho séances. Moreover, Yeats's approach was syncretic rather than comparative and he cleaved to a cyclical, not a linear, theory of history. Denying the myth of "progress," he strove for the revival of magic, whose validity would be scientifically confirmed, he believed, by spiritualism.

An integral part of many of Yeats's projects were their potentially nationalist dimension and an integral part of that dimension was its exploitation of folklore. For Yeats, transcribing folk tales from locals was not just a rare remaining opportunity to record the traces, among a European people, of primitive beliefs in spirits and the efficacy of magic. It was also of national cultural significance, as this material, appropriately deployed, could feed a nationalist myth. Through the hidden power of such a myth, a cultural renewal could be brought about, so invigorating a spiritual renaissance. On this reading, anthropology and cognate disciplines had essential roles to play in one's encounter with oneself, one's nation, and even the cosmos.

Perhaps the wildest of all the modernist interpreters of the anthropological message was Robert Graves, whose deeply idiosyncratic approach can be seen to be as magical in style as the material he discusses. A man so learned in the subject he can justly be called an amateur anthropologist, Graves had read deeply in the work of the Cambridge ritualists and of W. H. R. Rivers, an anthropologist and doctor who helped introduce Freud to the English public and was a personal friend of the poet. Indeed the central tenets of Graves's conception of poetry are essentially quasi-anthropological, though of a rather peculiar bent. In *The White Goddess* he explicitly stated his belief in a universal primordial matriarchy which was overturned by the agents of a patriarchal system. The goddess of passion and fertility was ousted by a god of reason. This change led humans to ignore the world of nature and its seasonal rituals, and to emerge from prehistory and myth into historical time. To Graves, this loss is the predicament poets must overcome, by striving to reconnect with the goddess, "the true Muse," and with the original idiom of poetry, myth. Though the White Goddess is as dangerous as she is attractive, as able to kill as to vivify, it is the duty of a poet to worship her.

Graves thought the poetic impulse arose from conflict, whether caused by psychic factors or external ones impinging on the self. He claimed that when a poet was unable to resolve a conflict logically, he hypnotized himself as witch doctors, "his ancestors in poetry," had done. In this trancelike state, similar to that of a "waking dream," all inhibitions were lost, all defenses lowered, and words were able to exercise their full magical power. Committed poets had to cultivate this state of self-hypnotism if they wished to produce "true poems." By means such as these Graves wished to rediscover and expose the magical principles underlying poetry, otherwise lost since the fall of the goddess. For him magic, like love, was an essential component of the imaginative life, disbelief in either diminishing the quality of one's life experience.

Graves made an exceptionally detailed study of *The Golden Bough* because it chimed so well with beliefs he already held: for instance in seeing the world of magic and fairies as identical with those of children and of poets. Frazer's works both bolstered Graves's ideas and helped him extend them much further: for instance, the mythic resonances of individuals' actions; the use of comparative mythology to create metamyths; the futility of religious dogmatism, since Christianity was but a transformation of Judaism which was but a transformation of paganism, whose ghosts continued to harass and terrify Jews and Christians. Yet Graves's theories were much more elaborate than Frazer's and thus, to a disbeliever, that bit much more contrived. Also, the poet was no respecting student of the man, as he was quite prepared at times to satirize Frazer's approach, in comic poems about seemingly bizarre customs. Furthermore, he was very ready to contradict the anthropologist on anthropological matters. Frazer is quite clear that the presence of matrilineality (the tracing of descent through female lines) does not imply matriarchy. In fact there is no ethnographic evidence whatsoever to support Graves's fiction about universal (or even widespread) worship of a goddess, white, brown, purple, or any other color. But Graves's mind was soon set; for much of the time, he merely used anthropology as an intellectual springboard on which to bounce his own ideas. In the 1950s, when in Oxford as Professor of Poetry, the leading British anthropologists of the day tried to discuss the subject with him but quickly realized he was only interested in expounding, not listening. Perhaps Graves's goddess, an archetypal figure, chameleonic in her variety of forms, a mistress of metamorphosis, is best viewed as "an extended metaphor for the vicissitudes and exaltation that come to man from the external world of nature and society and from the internal world of his own metabolism and psyche" (Vickery 1972: x). Because as anthropology, strictly understood, she's a nonsense.

Given these comments it is ironic that in *The Long Week-End*, the social history of interwar Britain he wrote in 1939 with Alan Hodge, Graves, who knew he could be a prig at times, chose to act the severe schoolmaster admonishing modern anthropologists, especially Malinowski, whose works include *The Sexual Life of Savages*:

> Sometimes they were such poor scientists that they became very friendly with their subjects of study. The true scientist was not supposed to fraternise with his guinea-pig, for fear that he might influence its emotional behaviour. And sometimes they could not disguise their bawdy relish in the sex habits of primitives, and their reports were published rather as refined erotic reading than as stern works of research. (Graves and Hodge 1940: 92)

As the quotation suggests, the more ethnographically focused studies of Malinowski and his students had rather different effects to the works of earlier anthropologists. They might have stretched the cross-cultural horizons of their literary contemporaries but none, deliberately, provided a grand Frazer-like vision of past and present humanity. It is true that Huxley spent four pages of *Eyeless in Gaza* discussing the ideas of the American Ruth Benedict's bestselling *Patterns of Culture*. But this excursus on the congruence of certain kinds of culture and the personalities they produced is best viewed as yet another intellectual contribution to an already well-stocked novel of ideas. It is also true that sections of Auden's *The Orators* rely on an understanding of the anthropologist John Layard's elision of epilepsy and Melanesian shape-shifters. However, this key but recondite source was unknown to most of Auden's admirably persevering readers. It is because of examples such as these (I could go on) that, if we wish to seek evidence of the critical influence of any post-Frazerian anthropology upon modernism, we need to turn our attention to the Paris of the 1920s.

Realisms, Anthropologies

Famously, it was Picasso and his peers who made aesthetes revalue the artistic accomplishments of supposed savages. Their use of indigenous figures for their own artistic ends is all too well known; Picasso's *Les Demoiselles d'Avignon* is the exemplary icon of this revolutionary time, with its imposition of African masks and "Oceanic" colors on the faces of three of the prostitutes. It is also common knowledge that these founders of artistic modernism were curious about native artifacts only to the extent they could inspire or confirm their visual experiments. Ethnography held no interest for them. Once again it is Picasso who is the exemplar. His Olympian ignorance of the origin of these objects is notorious.

Exceptions to this rule were very few, and the most noteworthy of these was the Russian exile Wassily Kandinsky. A trained anthropologist who had conducted fieldwork in a remote corner of the Russian Empire, Kandinsky wanted to create a syncretic worldview as a way for faith to endure during the dark cataclysms of modern Western times. Ethnographic materials were to be exploited for therapeutic purposes: cultural healing and regeneration. To that end, he made discriminating use in his paintings of the entire iconography of Arctic shamanic lore, from Lapland to Siberia. At the same time he came to see the figure of the shaman himself as representing the artist on his quest for a universal legend which could dovetail with modernity. If the shamanic ideal was to restore social harmony for his own group, Kandinsky would strive to do the same, through ethnographico-artistic means, for the sake of Western culture.

Petrine Archer-Straw has written of the negrophilic craze that enlivened Paris in the 1920s where the avant-garde's fashion for "blackness" furthered their desire to outrage, their sense of a sterilizing Western over-development justifying their indulgence in the "spiritual" vitality of Africans. But whether in dance, dress, décor, music, or other modes of cultural production, this was less a misencounter with the "Other" than the old racism in bright new garb, even when illuminated by ethnography. For our purposes, the most interesting group here is also the most curious and the most anthropologically educated: the loose band of wayward Surrealists typified by Georges Bataille and Michel Leiris.

These learned dissidents promoted a hardcore primitivism concerned with sexual deviance, fetishism, magic, and ritual violence. Sternly dedicated to *épater les bourgeois*, these Surrealists wished to critique "civilized" norms in a radical manner. Their key joint production was the journal *Documents*, which mixed articles on ethnography and archaeology with commentary on contemporary art and music. Bataille was editor and Leiris a frequent contributor. Both had studied under the great French anthropologist of those decades, Marcel Mauss. Bataille celebrated human baseness, regarding human orifices and bodily functions as far more significant than cerebral activity. Inverting the usual cultural priorities, he saw cannibalism and sadomasochism as means to validate the human condition. Bataille was also a leading member of the quasi-initiatory society Acéphale, committed to the headless commemoration of viscerality, and planned secretly to stage a voluntary human sacrifice in a Paris square. As Archer-Straw observes, the interests of Bataille and his cohort "might be more aptly called 'sousrealist': a term that better situates their dissident thinking in a sort of abstracted hell somewhere beneath mainstream surrealism."

Bataille and Leiris kept the subversive edge of *Documents* sharp by deploying a cultural relativism meant to undercut bourgeois values and to replace them with non-European alternatives. They wanted to do away with the old certainties. Leiris, for instance, wanted to see the Western duality of mind and body destroyed by whatever means of "mysticism, madness, adventure, poetry, eroticism." Both wished their readers to cast away their inhibitions and frolic in the sordid, the occult, and the darkly primitive. For them, black culture had a savage potency worthy of nurture, not denigration. Leiris's most extended early encounter with African ways was as secretary-archvist of the 1931 Mission Dakar-Dijbouti. His famed *L'Afrique fantôme,* an open-ended "diary" of his impressions on the expedition, details his erotic obsessions, his reveling in dirt and filth, the course of his bowel movements as well as of his dreams. A fieldworker much of his own making, he gives Dada-like lists of data and describes an Ethiopian *zâr* sacrifice, performed for him, tasting the animal's blood and having its entrails coiled around his brow. Though Leiris was the only Surrealist to make a living from anthropology, he maintained an ambiguous distance from both. André Breton's movement, albeit revolutionary in tone, was too constricted for his tastes while, as a rigorous subjectivist, it was easy for him to undercut the claimed objectivism of orthodox ethnography. Compared to Malinowski's ideal of the anthropologist as dedicated would-be scientist in the bush, Leiris preferred to present himself as militant rogue tempted to go bush.

The Surrealism imported to London was of a much politer kind than that of Bataille or Leiris. The key group here was a band of British poets and artists, headed by Charles Madge and Humphrey Jennings, who joined forces with a popularizing anthropologist, Tom Harrisson, to form Mass-Observation. Its central aim was social therapy, which they hoped might help to bring about social change. Its central method was the production of ethnography of the people by the people for the people. Through the collation of "mass-reports" by a mass of observers about key and minor moments in the life of the country, they hoped to perceive the leading "collective images" of society and to lay bare its social unconscious. Their most significant publication was their first: *May 12th, 1937.* An edited collection of reports taken on the day of George VI's coronation, it revealed the diversity of public responses to the event, in the words of the participants themselves. Thus theirs was not just a democratic surrealism, but a demotic one as well, giving voice to the people, in the people's own tongue. Its editors, Madge and Jennings, wished to underline the poetry of everyday speech and, in their more inspired moments, to dissolve the distinctions between poetry and science. They also provided a diversity of indexes, so enabling the interested to read the text in a plurality of ways and undercutting any authoritativeness attributed to the editors' ordering. Though Mass-Observation won great literary and public interest, the pragmatic and overbearing Harrisson ensured that the work of Mass-Observation soon turned almost exclusively pop-anthropological. The promise of an ethnographic surrealism was abandoned. Professional anthropologists, at first in favor of the movement, did not lament the demise of this potentially destabilizing competitor.

There is, however, a final twist to this tale of the meetings between anthropology and Surrealism. For the Oxford anthropologist Rodney Needham has mischievously suggested that Claude Lévi-Strauss, participant in the wartime New York circle of exiled Surrealists, should be regarded not as the famed proponent of structuralism but as the greatest Surrealist of them all. Trying to account for Lévi-Strauss's indisputable popular success, Needham argues his work is best viewed as an essentially Surrealist enterprise since it "can evoke a response liberated from the confinements of exactitude, logic and scholarly responsibility." The source of his appeal for the public does not lie in his academic ability but

> Must be sought in the idiosyncrasies of Lévi-Strauss himself: the "poetic" quality in his writing; his very obscurities can be seen as enigmatic and hence profound; there are intimations of great mysteries, refractions of perennial insights, echoes of oracular utterances. His vision is hermetical, and his writings have prospered because they promise to reveal what is hidden, the occult factors by which human experience is shaped. (Needham 1984: 393)

Needham's comment is a deft reminder that anthropology, for all the pretensions of some of its practitioners, can be as much one of the humanities as one of the social studies, as much an art as a purported science. One of the points of this essay has been to underline that there is no singular anthropology, with its own tidy definition, but a kaleidoscope of possible anthropologies, different patterns appearing with each turn. The same is true of primitivism and the analysis of myth. It is not just that the work of anthropologists can be used in different ways by different factions or generations of writers, rather that anthropologists are always also writers and some writers also anthropologists. Misleading then to score a sharp divide between the two and trace the supposed interconnections between them. Best to acknowledge the ambiguities and the overlaps, and to tease out their consequences. For there will be new anthropologies, new primitivisms, new myths.

References and Further Reading

Archer-Straw, Petrine. 2000. *Negrophilia. Avant-Garde Paris and Black Culture in the 1920s.* London: Thames & Hudson.

Barkan, E. and Bush, R., eds. 1995. *Prehistories of the Future. The Primitivist Project and the Culture of Modernism.* Stanford: Stanford University Press.

Bell, Michael. 1972. *Primitivism.* London: Methuen.

——. 1997. *Literature, Modernism and Myth. Belief and Responsibility in the Twentieth Century.* Cambridge: Cambridge University Press.

Eliot, T. S. 1933. *The Use of Poetry and the Use of Criticism. Studies in the Relation of Criticism to Poetry in England.* Cambridge, MA: Harvard University Press.

Fraser, Robert, ed. 1990. *Sir James Frazer and the Literary Imagination.* London: Macmillan.

Graves, R. and Hodge, A. 1940. *The Long Week-End. A Social History of Great Britain 1918–1939.* London: Faber.

Harmon, William. 1976. T. S. Eliot, Anthropologist and Primitive. *American Anthropologist* 78: 797–811.

Huxley, A. 1936. *Eyeless in Gaza.* London: Chatto & Windus.

Hyman, Stanley Edgar. 1958. The Ritual View of Myth and the Mythic. In T. A. Sebeok, ed., *Myth: A Symposium,* pp. 84–94. Bloomington: Indiana University Press.

Lawrence, D. H. 1981. *The Letters of D. H. Lawrence,* Vol. II: June 1913–October 1916. Eds. George J. Zytaruk and James T. Boulton. Cambridge: Cambridge University Press.

MacClancy, Jeremy. 1986. Unconventional Character and Disciplinary Convention. John Layard, Jungian and Anthropologist. In G. W. Stocking, ed., *Malinowski, Rivers, Benedict and Others. Essays in Culture and Personality,* History of Anthropology 4, pp. 50–71. Madison: University of Wisconsin Press.

——. 1995. Brief Encounter: The Meeting, in Mass Observation, of British Surrealism and Popular Anthropology. *Journal of the Royal Anthropological Institute* 1 (n.s.): 495–512.

——. 1996. Popularizing Anthropology. In J. MacClancy and C. McDonaugh, eds., *Popularizing Anthropology,* pp. 1–57. London: Routledge.

Manganaro, Marc. 1986. "Beating a Drum in the Jungle." T. S. Eliot on the Artist as "Primitive". *Modern Languages Quarterly* 47: 393–421.

——, ed. 1990. *Modernist Anthropology. From Fieldwork to Text.* Princeton: Princeton University Press.

——. 1992. *Myth, Rhetoric and the Voice of Authority. A Critique of Frazer, Eliot, Frye and Campbell.* New Haven: Yale University Press.

Marrett, R. R. 1910. The Present State of Anthropology. *The Athenaeum* 4298 (March 12): 299–300.

Needham, R. 1984. The Birth of the Meaningful (review of C. Lévi-Strauss, *Le regard éloigné*). *Times Literary Supplement* (April 13), p. 393.

Ruthven, K. K. 1968. The Savage God: Conrad and Lawrence. *Critical Quarterly* X: 39–54.

Stocking, G. W. 1987. *Victorian Anthropology*. New York: Free Press

——. 1996. *After Tylor. British Social Anthropology 1888–1951*. London: Athlone.

Street, Bryan. 1975. *The Savage in Literature*. London: Routledge & Kegan Paul.

Torgovnick, Marianna. 1990. *Gone Primitive. Savage Intellects, Modern Lives*. Chicago: University of Chicago Press.

——. 1998. *Primitive Passions. Men, Women, and the Quest for Ecstasy*. Chicago: University of Chicago Press.

Vickery, John B. 1972. *Robert Graves and the White Goddess*. Lincoln: University of Nebraska Press.

——. 1972. *The Literary Impact of the Golden Bough*. Princeton: Princeton University Press.

Weiss, Peg. 1995. *Kandinsky and Old Russia. The Artist as Ethnographer and Shaman*. New Haven: Yale University Press.

5

Bergsonism: "Time out of mind"

Mary Ann Gillies

In 1943, two years after Henri Bergson's death, Ben-Ami Scharfstein commented that "As Henri Bergson became the most famous philosopher in the world, he was welcomed with hosannas, and he was roundly damned" (1943: 3). One might be tempted to accuse Scharfstein of hyperbole, for the Frenchman's name is not as well known today as are the names of some of his contemporaries such as Bertrand Russell or William James. Yet it is a fact that Bergson did excite just this sort of reaction during the early years of the twentieth century, when his ideas were debated by readers and audiences as diverse as professional philosophers and society matrons. However, Bergson's philosophy seemed to disappear in the middle years of the twentieth century, particularly in the Anglo-American world, so that by the 1980s Scharfstein's description could well be dismissed as exaggeration. Nevertheless, from an early-twenty-first-century vantage-point, one could argue, as many have begun to, that Bergson's ideas did play important roles in formulations of a variety of philosophical, cultural, and scientific theories and practices throughout the twentieth century. In this essay, I will argue that Bergson's ideas were crucial to the emergence of modernism as a significant cultural movement in the early twentieth century. Furthermore, I will suggest that his ideas have continued to underpin the debates in several, seemingly diverse, disciplines.

In order to convey what it was that made Bergson and his theories so captivating to audiences in the early twentieth century, I will first place Bergson on the cultural stage, emphasizing the importance of his public presentations of his ideas and their dissemination through the popular media as well as professional journals. Having set the scene, so to speak, I will then turn to his key ideas – time, memory, creative evolution, intuition, and his aesthetics – illustrating the ways in which they served as foundations for modernist culture. In each of these sections, I will look at not only what Bergson's ideas were, but also at how authors and artists employed them. Finally, I will turn briefly to a discussion of Bergson's continuing presence in postmodern culture. Here I want to make the case that the return to Bergson's theories – notably in the work of Gilles Deleuze – substantiates the argument that Bergson plays a central role in the creation of modernism, for postmodernism, much as its theoreticians and practitioners claim otherwise, is firmly rooted in the experiments of modernism. Because of the complexity of Bergson's theories, I have chosen to present them in this manner, one that Bergson would have found inimical to his insistence that his theories constitute an organic whole. However, Bergson understood that such schematization was a necessary condition of intellectual life, one he himself practiced in his lectures and his writings.

Bergson the *Mondain*

Marguerite Bistis suggests that Bergson "belonged to a particular type of French academic whom Terry Clark has aptly named 'the *mondain*' and whose defining characteristic is a profound rapport with the educated public." She goes on to define the *mondain* as individuals who

> act as "arbiters of the goût public" shaping the intellectual outlook and sensibility of their times. They tend to produce academic bestsellers which make them into celebrities on a par with politicians, writers and actors. Like the institution with which they are usually but not always affiliated, they occupy the liminal space between the professional world of academe and the nonprofessional world of general culture. (1996: 391)

This definition well captures the place that Bergson occupied not only in France but also throughout Europe and America in the first two decades of the twentieth century. His lectures at the Collège de France were wildly popular, and he played a prominent role in French intellectual life. Indeed, Robert Grogin claims, with justification, that

> Amid all the intellectual controversies before the First World War in France, none was more intense or bitter than the disputes ignited by the philosophy of Henri Bergson. . . . As the most charismatic intellectual figure of his day,

he was able to communicate his attack on the mechanistic principles of nineteenth-century thought to a public which was increasingly attracted to his lectures. (1988: ix)

In Britain, where the tradition of the public intellectual was less well established than in France, Bergson's popularity was also impressive. The period 1909–11 saw over two hundred articles published on Bergson in English journals, newspapers, and books. These ranged from philosophical treatises on his work – like those presented by his major British critic Bertrand Russell and one of his strongest supporters, A. D. Lindsay – to pieces in leading newspapers aimed at capturing the essence of Bergson's enormous popularity. This burst of interest in Bergson is only partially explained by the renewed interest in European culture and thought that is characteristic of the Edwardian age. Three specific factors entered into this blossoming of Bergson's philosophy in Britain around 1910–12.

The first important element is the widespread availability of English translations of Bergson's central works. *Time and Free Will* became available in 1910, *Creative Evolution* and *Matter and Memory* in 1911, and *Introduction to Metaphysics*, Bergson's most accessible work, in 1912. While many would have read Bergson's texts in the original French, the translations provided his philosophy with a wider English audience. Reviews of the books were found in most major philosophical journals, but they were also found in journals such as the *Lancet* and other more mainstream publications such as the *Athenaeum*, the *Saturday Review* and the *Nation*.

The second element is found in Bergson's visits to England in 1911. At Oxford on May 26 and 27 he received an honorary degree and lectured at the Examination Schools to an audience of more than three hundred. At Birmingham on May 29, he gave the Huxley Lecture. In October, he gave four public lectures at University College London. Contemporary testimony indicates that the lectures were successful social events as well as intellectual exchanges. A notice in *The Times* for October 20 reads "No further applications for tickets can be entertained for the forthcoming lectures at University College by M. Henry [sic] Bergson. Persons to whom tickets have already been allotted and who find themselves unable to use them are requested to return them immediately to the secretary of the University College, in order that they may be re-allotted." And members of the "very large audience" which assembled for the four lectures included the "French Ambassador, M. de Fleuria, the First Secretary of the French Embassy, and Dr. Sadler, Vice-Chancellor of Leeds University." The audience for the final lecture is described as "fill[ing] to overflowing" the theater with "Professor Dawes-Hicks, Chairman of the Board of Philosophical Studies . . . in the chair" and "the French Ambassador, the First Secretary of the French Embassy, and Sir Francis and Lady Younghusband" present. It is noted that "this was Sir Francis's first appearance since his accident" and this lends the air of a society event to the lectures. Bergson lectured in French and *The Times* records that "Professor Bergson . . . was loudly cheered on rising" and that his lectures were greeted with "Loud Cheers."

These very popular lectures worked to reinforce the impact of the translations. Bergson lectured in Oxford on the nature of change and how our perspectives on change may resolve philosophical problems – this is based on his central thesis about the nature of time that was first articulated in *Time and Free Will*. At Birmingham, the lecture dealt with consciousness and life and their relationship. He examined evolution, the duality of mind and body, and the limitations of science and philosophy. This is the underpinning of both *Creative Evolution* and *Matter and Memory*. The London lectures dealt with "the Nature of the Soul" and examined how the actions of the mind operate on the body and how they should be represented. He rebutted scientific and philosophic oppositions to his opinion. These lectures amplified the essence of Bergsonian teachings from all his major works. Of the three series of lectures, the London ones are most accessible to a lay reader – the summaries of them in *The Times* are fairly easy to follow – and they reached an audience well beyond the crowded lecture theatre because of the *Times*'s extensive coverage. The combined impact of the lectures and translations of his work served to place Bergson near the forefront of the European invasion of England around 1910–11, but they alone do not account for the popularity he enjoyed at this time.

At the risk of oversimplification, it seems likely that Bergson's popularity stems from the ways in which he engaged with the dominant issues of the day. His was a voice raised in many debates about the nature of life – both in a scientific sense and a philosophical/spiritual one. He articulated the fears of the time – that new discoveries in science degraded the position of humans as central forces in the world – and he offered solutions to many vexatious questions. And he did this in a very public forum; his lectures were open to whoever wished to attend them. His approach to intellectual life was one of inclusion, rather than the more typical exclusion brought about because of the ever-increasing specialization of academia. His appeal to those who were actively involved in intellectual and aesthetic pursuits was great, but so was his appeal to the many who aspired to greater intellectual awareness but who had neither the training nor the time to acquire it. So Bergson occupied in Britain the same position as in France: he was a *mondain*. It is from this position that his ideas were disseminated widely, finding places in philosophical, literary, and even scientific and political debates.

Bergson's Theories

Many of Bergson's critics point to his enduring debt to the French spiritualist philosophers prominent in the Academy in the mid-nineteenth century and others have detected a very strong Romantic strand in his work, likely the influence of German Romanticism. There is no denying that spiritualist ideas – particularly the central concern about the place of free will in a determinist world – are important in Bergson's philosophy. Indeed, it may be possible to ascribe much of Bergson's initial popularity to the fact that he was seen as assuming the spiritualist mantle once worn by Felix Ravaisson, Jules Lachelier, Maine de Biran, and Emile Boutroux. His debt to Romanticism is chiefly found in his insistence on adopting an organic view of life, but he differs from most Romantics in denying a central, or indeed any, place to a transcendental or ideal force. But how much Bergson's initial engagement with the ideas of the spiritualists or the Romantics determined the subsequent course of his own philosophy is moot, for although he does embrace their insistence that the inner life is important, he also shows his independence from them in other aspects of his complex philosophy. To argue that Bergson was simply the successor to these nineteenth-century thinkers and that he did little but frame the standard spiritualist ideas in terms that were appealing to a twentieth-century audience disillusioned with the rationalist, determinist society of the Third Republic is to present a corrupt account of both his academic training and his work.

Bergson's initial training was in physics and mathematics; in fact, he won prizes in mathematics as a student and his first publication was a solution to a mathematical problem. Like most young intellectuals in the post-Darwinian era, he was forced to confront the disconcerting discoveries of natural science and his most famous work, *Creative Evolution*, clearly demonstrates his wide knowledge of contemporary evolutionary theories and their scientific bases. Furthermore, throughout his life, he maintained an interest in the sciences and he was as well-read in contemporary scientific literature as he was in philosophy. His work reflects this lifelong interest in both the spiritual and the physical realms. Critics often dismiss Bergson's statements about the necessity of understanding both spiritual and physical worlds, citing them as proof of the contradictions inherent in his philosophy. Yet remarks such as those found in the introduction to *Matter and Memory* indicate a willingness to accept the findings of rational, physical science coupled with an insistence that there are facets of life that are less amenable to these types of analyses, but which are nonetheless crucial for a full understanding of what it is to be human. He says that

> This book affirms the reality of spirit and the reality of matter, and tries to determine the relation of the one to the other by the study of a definite example, memory. It is, then, frankly dualistic. But, on the other hand, it deals with body and mind in such a way as, we hope, to lessen greatly, if not overcome, the theoretical difficulties which have always beset dualism, and which cause it, though suggested by the immediate verdict of consciousness and adopted common sense, to be held in small honour among philosophers. (1911b: xi)

His express aim in this book, as in all of his work, is not to exile rationalist thought or determinism in favor of an equally one-dimensional and exclusive spiritualist tradition. Rather, he wanted to find a way of wedding the two and thereby allowing philosophy, and other intellectual endeavors, to mirror what the ordinary individual's common sense said: that the world consists of physical and spiritual aspects that necessarily work in concert to define human beings and their existence.

It is this deceptively modest aim that forms the fundamental basis of Bergson's philosophy. It runs through each of his major works where he tackles different philosophical problems using the same basic theoretical precept: that life is dual, both matter and spirit being essential, and that true understanding of life's phenomena can only be grasped by accepting this fundamental duality. Yet the duality is one that Bergson doesn't seek to resolve, as did Hegel, for instance; Bergson insisted upon the importance of holding both simultaneously, arguing that the tension of the apparent opposites was the necessary condition of existence. I would contend that it is this duality that, in part, accounts for not only his spectacular public success, but also for the unusually varied nature of his many adherents. Many different, often very opposed, groups claimed Bergson as their own for each found in his work something that permitted them to defend their own position. For example, the art historian Mark Antliff notes that Bergsonism played a seminal role "in shaping the art and politics of the Fauvist, Cubist, and Futurist movements" (1999: 6). But each movement utilized different aspects of Bergson's theories to justify their artistic theories and practices. As many critics have noted, the positions taken were perhaps possible only through a conscious misreading of Bergson's ideas; nonetheless, his thought permeated the era's culture. His concepts were so thoroughly assimilated that today it is commonplace to think of the memory as self-reflexive or time as consisting of both lived experience and externally quantified experience. These are the ideas that modernists relied on in their drive to create new artistic modes.

Time

Few concepts so preoccupied the twentieth century as time. Whether it was Einstein's radical challenge to centuries-old notions about how we measure time or Cubist representations of figures in motion, such as Marcel Duchamps's "Nude Descending a Staircase," how time is analyzed or represented was a cornerstone of modernist culture. Bergson's theories about time were widely known and debated, and because of their radical challenge to traditional temporal concepts, they were central to the reconfigurations of culture carried out by modernists. He first presented his ideas about time in *Time and Free Will* (the original French text, titled *Essai sur les données immédiates de la conscience*, was published in 1889). He elaborated on them in later works, but the basic ideas were in the public domain at the turn of the century, and thus they were well placed for use by those about to challenge the status quo.

In *Time and Free Will*, Bergson argues that time has become spatialized and that this is the source of our failure to apprehend the true nature of existence. According to Bergson, "by introducing space into our perception of duration, [we corrupt] at its very source our feeling of outer and inner change, of movement, and of freedom" (1913b: 74). Bergson insists that when time is no longer spatialized, it may be possible to become aware of life's true nature. He says that

> There are . . . two possible conceptions of time, the one free from all alloy, the other surreptitiously bringing in the idea of space. Pure duration [*durée*] is the form which the succession of our conscious states assumes when our ego lets itself *live*, when it refrains from separating its present state from its former states . . . . it need not be entirely absorbed in the passing sensation or idea; for then, on the contrary, it would no longer *endure*. Nor need it forget its former states: it is enough that, in recalling these states, it does not set them alongside another, but forms both the past and the present states into an organic whole, as happens when we recall the notes of a tune, melting, so to speak, into one another. (1913b: 100; emphasis in original)

The two times here are both essential to Bergson's discussion, but *durée* is the one that most occupies his attention.

Durée is internal time, the time of active living; it cannot be applied to the world outside the self because the individual cannot perceive *durée* unless it is cut into segments and thus spatialized. Bergson defines *durée* throughout his first work, but the best description of it is found in Chapter II, where he writes that "duration properly so called has no moments which are identical or external to one another, being essentially heterogeneous, continuous, and with no analogy to number" (1913b: 120). Real time simply is: no moment is ever recoverable; no moment is ever perceived as external to the living of it until after it has been experienced. Bergson's view of time removes the external standard and replaces it with what the internal sense of time reveals – that real time is that in which people live and it is qualitative, not quantitative in nature.

It is easy to see why many people call Bergson's time theories relativistic. The privileging of *durée* seems to indicate that Bergson viewed all existence as a continual free-flowing flux in which no states were ever permanent and no states ever recurred. This is only half the story, however. In the Bergsonian construction of reality, though real living goes on in the indivisible realm of *durée*, this world is broken into segments in order to explain, analyze, and even understand the nature of experience. The conscious reconstruction of our experiences distorts them, but this distortion is inevitable because of the impossibility of ever halting the flow of *durée* and because of the equally inevitable human need to violate this flow in order to assert our will over the natural environment.

While many of Bergson's contemporaries failed to grasp that his argument was not that *durée* alone accounted for how time worked, his ideas did resonate strongly within intellectual and artistic circles. Bergson's reconfiguration of time was particularly attractive because it provided artists and authors with a theory that corresponded with their own need to find a new mode of representing experience. What they created has been well documented and discussed, but it is worthwhile to illustrate briefly how Bergson's temporal notions were used in the transformation of literature.

Stream of consciousness, perhaps the characteristic formal innovation in modernist prose, clearly demonstrates Bergsonian concepts of time. Virginia Woolf described the writer's process of rendering the stream of consciousness memorably when she wrote: "Let us record the atoms as they fall upon the mind in the order in which they fall, let us trace the pattern, however disconnected and incoherent in appearance, which each sight or incident scores upon the consciousness" (1984: 150). Her novels, along with those of Marcel Proust, James Joyce, Dorothy Richardson, and William Faulkner, to name four of the most prominent practitioners of stream of consciousness, present such moments in a manner that has been characterized by many critics as Bergsonian. Certainly, these writers privilege the experience of being over the analysis of it; and just as clearly, the formal innovations they adopt to convey this experience privilege being over a consciously stylized representation of being.

Yet the mere act of recording the "atoms as they fall upon the mind" renders static the dynamic moments of life that the atoms represent. This paradox evident in stream of consciousness as a method of conveying lived experience was anticipated by Bergson. The act of writing necessarily spatializes experience, as Bergson noted when he said about language that "the word with the well-defined outlines, the rough and ready word, which stores up the stable, common, and consequently impersonal element in the impressions of mankind, overwhelms or at least covers over the delicate and fugitive impressions of our individual consciousness." He continues, saying that writers "ought to express themselves in precise words; but these words, as soon as they were formed, would turn against the sensation which gave birth to them, and invented to show that the sensation is unstable, they would impose on it their own stability" (1913b: 131–2). Language cannot capture the flux of life because it relies on analyzing, organizing, and spatializing experiences so that they might be communicated to others. Language, however, is one tool that approximately conveys experiences to others. In this sense, Bergson believed that short of intuitive interaction, language was the best means of communication available and it was incumbent upon us, and especially on writers, to use language as effectively as possible. To illustrate this he said:

> Now, if some bold novelist, tearing aside the cleverly woven curtain of our conventional ego, shows us under this appearance of logic [in language] a fundamental absurdity, under the juxtaposition of simple states an infinite permeation of a thousand impressions which have already ceased to exist the instant they are named, we commend him for having known us better than we know ourselves. (1913b: 133)

Such a command of language is what the stream-of-consciousness writers aimed to achieve and it is not hard to imagine Bergson commending them for "tearing aside" the conventional novel forms in order to render consciousness in a new manner.

Memory

Bergson's treatise on memory – *Matter and Memory* (the French text was initially published in 1896 and was titled *Matière et mémoire*) – continued to develop his dualistic rendering of existence, but it added significant new concepts to the debate. Of most importance to his lasting influence in modernist culture were his ideas about memory – what constituted it and how it functioned – and his theory about the self.

Bergson asserted, much like Descartes, that there are two types of memory: voluntary memory (cerebral memory) and involuntary memory (pure recollection). Unlike Descartes, Bergson maintained that every sensation an individual experiences is retained by one of the two memories. Cerebral memory is tied to the body, for it is the repository of habitual actions. Motor functions which have been learned by dint of long practice are stored in habit memory, and are liable to recall when the will is deliberately exerted to bring them forward to consciousness's attention and for use. Involuntary memory records all the perceptions of past experience, but unlike habit memory, these perceptions cannot always be called forward. The more useful the perception stored in involuntary memory is to the present moment, the more likely it is that it will be spontaneously recalled. It is evident that Bergson's two memories are not equal in stature; involuntary memory is privileged over voluntary memory, although both are necessary for a proper functioning memory system.

It is memory that permits the existence of consciousness. In turn, consciousness is discussed in terms of the concept of the self. The self is a real entity that experiences continuous growth by reabsorbing and reinscribing the whole of its experiences and perceptions at any single moment. Each moment it presents a new "whole" self to the world, but paradoxically this "new" self is a compilation of "old" selves. The self cannot exist without memory, for the self is in fact memory. Bergson best addresses the issue of what the self is in *An Introduction to Metaphysics* (first published in French in 1903 as "Introduction à la métaphysique" in *Revue de métaphysique et de morale*). Here he says:

> There is, beneath these sharply cut crystals and this frozen surface [self], a continuous flux which is not comparable to any flux I have ever seen. There is a succession of states, each of which announces that which follows and contains that which precedes it. They can, properly speaking, only be said to form multiple states when I have already passed them and turn back to observe their track. Whilst I was experiencing them they were so solidly

organized, so profoundly animated with a common life, that I could not have said where another commenced. In reality no one of them begins or ends, but all extend into each other. (1913a: 9–10)

The self consists of a solidified upper layer, a crust, which is the apparently stable whole person that is projected to the external world. It is this projection which allows one to function in the world, but it is also true that this self is atrophied and effectively dead because it ceases to be mobile. The real living being consists of the many interpenetrating and constantly mobile selves that exist below the surface of the solidified crust. The link between the two layers of self is primarily memory. In their own ways each of the two layers of self are important for an individual's wholeness.

Here again Bergson's common philosophical method of mediating between two apparently contradictory views is evident. On the one hand, he is in agreement with contemporary psychoanalysts such as Freud who maintain that the tumultuous inner world provides the true essence of the self, yet he also upholds previous theorists' contentions that it is the surface layer that deserves the title of self since it presents a stable and coherent personality to the world. By embracing both points of view, Bergson creates a third view that, because of its combination of the other two views, was very attractive to his contemporaries.

His concepts of memory and self were particularly appealing to writers who were grappling with new notions of consciousness. For example, T. S. Eliot's continuing interest in the nature of individual existence – consciousness – prompts him to make a full exploration of it in *The Waste Land*. This poem is a tapestry of different consciousnesses: Marie, Madame Sosostris, the hyacinth girl, the typist, the young man carbuncular, the Phoenician Sailor, the currant seller, the merchant, and a host of others. How to deal with these many personae is problematic. If one allows that Eliot's "Notes" to the poem provide pertinent information about it, then his note on Tiresias helps explain how involuntary memory is used to establish a link between all the disparate consciousnesses in the poem. Eliot wrote:

Tiresias, although a mere spectator and not indeed a 'character', is yet the most important personage in the poem, uniting all the rest. Just as the one-eyed merchant, seller of currants melts into the Phoenician Sailor, and the latter is not wholly distinct from Ferdinand Prince of Naples, so all the women are one woman, and the two sexes meet in Tiresias. What Tiresias *sees*, in fact, is the substance of the poem. (1969: 78; emphasis in original)

This description of Tiresias' position as the poem's all-encompassing consciousness has long provided a point of difficulty. However, Bergson's ideas may bring us closer to Eliot's meaning. In Bergsonian terms, Tiresias assumes the role of the poem's central self because it is his superficial social self who provides the stability necessary to relate the poem. Since all the characters in the poem "meet in Tiresias," then in Bergsonian terms they are all layers of Tiresias' self, merging and interpenetrating throughout the poem. The many other voices that vie for prominence provide the subject matter of the poem just as the layers of self which exist below the social self are ultimately responsible for its shape. The tension which Bergson and Eliot see as existing due to the collision of the various aspects of self provides a dynamic element in the poem, while placing these aspects within a superficially stable self (Tiresias) gives the poem a semblance of stability. The complexity of Tiresias' role is, therefore, within the bounds of what Eliot stated in his note to the poem itself.

Other modernists also found Bergson's concepts of memory and self appealing. Collage, as a technique, is very much dependent on memory and perception for it requires the viewer to make connections between the various components of the artwork. Stream of consciousness is predicated on the existence of a self whose consciousness we follow. The works of Joyce and Faulkner, in particular, challenge the notion of a singular self, replacing it with a multiplicity of selves that is very Bergsonian.

Creative Evolution

Many of his contemporaries considered Bergson's *Creative Evolution* (first published in French as *L'Evolution créatrice* in 1907) as his most important work. In it he argues that living occurs in a temporal plane and that reconstruction or representation of that living occurs in a spatial one, but he insists that the totality of human life is explained by the interaction of the two. He suggests that an understanding of how individual organisms develop over time would permit a fuller understanding of how the universe as a whole operates. And he develops the concept of the *élan vital* to account for evolutionary change. He defines it as the

> *original impetus* of life, passing from one generation of germs to the following generation of germs through the developed organisms which bridge the interval between generations. This impetus, sustained right along the lines of evolution among which it gets divided, is the fundamental cause of varia-

tions, at least those that are regularly passed on, that accumulate and create new species. (1928: 92; emphasis in original)

This force exists both in global terms – all living organisms are subject to the push of the *élan vital* – and on individual terms – each organism has its own *élan vital* which accounts for its evolution. Bergson's creative evolution counters the prevailing neo-Darwinian mechanism which said that adaptation is purely an organism's response to external stimuli, and it also opposes neo-Lamarckian finalism because it does not argue that the adaptations occur in order that the organism reach some state of evolutionary perfection.

Equally important as the *élan vital* to Bergson's evolutionary theory was his concept of intuition. By intuition, Bergson meant "instinct that has become disinterested, self-conscious, capable of reflecting upon its object and of enlarging it indefinitely" (1928: 186). Intuition, "by the sympathetic communication which it establishes between us and the rest of the living, by the expansion of our consciousness which it brings about, . . . introduces us into life's domain, which is reciprocal interpenetration, endlessly continued creation" (1928: 187). But intelligence cannot be dispensed with, for it is "from intelligence that has come the push that has made [intuition] rise to the point it has reached" (1928: 187). Together these two permit a fuller understanding not only of objects external to the individual, but also of the inner world, for when we turn our gaze inward, we intuitively enter into an understanding with ourself and then employ our intelligence to explain what intuition has revealed. Intuition becomes the means by which we may apprehend the essence, the organic wholeness, of other organisms and ourselves. Together, *élan vital* and intuition create an alternative approach to understanding the nature of life – the one describing how life evolves and the other how we can experience objects outside ourselves.

Bergson's evolutionary theories fit into the tradition of early twentieth-century vitalism that had been renewed by developments in nineteenth-century science. However, his vitalism was controversial, prompting many of his contemporaries to attack his ideas with great force. As Paul Douglass and Frederick Burwick point out, the prewar moment when Bergson's *Creative Evolution* became the center of debate "was a period of rant and rhetoric, during which Bergson was called a phony and a fake by many who had adopted aspects of his philosophical method – like Maritain, Russell, Jung, and Santayana." They go on to suggest that "Santayana accused Bergson of stirring the 'winds of doctrine'" and that "he helped to fire a new mode of Western thought – one which required sacrificial figures. Bergson became the scapegoat" (1992: 2) and his vitalist theories became a prime target. They claim that "the damnation of Bergson suggests a disturbing possibility: that his work is a repressed content of modern thought" (1992: 7).

This claim is borne out by the way in which Bergson's vitalism inserts itself into twentieth-century thought, for unlike his notions of time or memory, there are few examples of the *élan vital* or intuition being used directly by artists. Rather, it is the organic wholeness explicit in Bergson's creative evolution that provides a foundation for Modernist experimentation. It provides them with justification for insisting that the form of an artwork must be considered as essential as its content; indeed, that the two are an inseparable organic whole in which both function to achieve the desired effect. Furthermore, modernism takes as one of its central aesthetic tenets the notion that the artist must continually create the absolutely new work; they must constantly counter the tendency of the materials of art to become lifeless. Imagism, for instance, can be viewed in a different light if we recognize the extent to which it embraces Bergsonian concepts as articulated in *Creative Evolution*. Ezra Pound's description of how an image works on the reader of an Imagist poem is remarkably Bergsonian, especially given Pound's stated opposition to Bergson's theories. Pound wrote that "An 'Image' is that which presents an intellectual and emotional complex in an instant of time" and he said that it "is the presentation of such a 'complex' instantaneously which gives that sense of sudden liberation; that sense of freedom from time limits and space limits; that sense of sudden growth, which we experience in the presence of the greatest works of art" (1954: 4). The immediate, intuitive interaction with the image, the instant of time in which this interaction takes place, the spontaneous growth that implies the presence of the *élan vital*, and the freedom from normal limits imposed by a deterministic framing of the image, all have direct counterparts in Bergson's creative evolution.

Aesthetics

Bergson did not write a work devoted exclusively to aesthetics, but his aesthetic theory nonetheless permeates his works on other subjects. Arthur Szathmary, one of Bergson's most perceptive commentators, provides a useful insight into Bergson's approach to art when he says that "Bergson conceives of art, not as an expression superimposed upon the more vital aspects of experience, but as the finest rendition of experience itself" (1937: 50). For Bergson, all aspects of life are aesthetic because art is not found simply in static objects. Art is an experience of life which may be reconstructed in an object but whose meaning is released when the object's perceiver penetrates to its living elements. Szathmary comments on the continuity between Bergson's general philosophic concepts and his aesthetic notions in a telling manner:

> By the expansion of the term "aesthetic", Bergson suggests a criticism of all esoteric and mythological interpretations of art; he points to the immediate approach through sensory discrimination. More than this, he suggests that the lesser experiences – our everyday contact with natural objects – may be "aesthesized" and "heightened". (1937: 54)

Art becomes much more than a finished poem, painting, or symphonic score; for Bergson art is the experience of these things. The real art lies behind the object (or deep within it). In aesthetic experience and through aesthetic experience both artist and audience are joined in a common activity – the rediscovery of the emotions, perceptions, and impressions that prompted the fashioning of art. In simple terms, what Bergson says occurs is the understanding of the object (through intuition), the re-creation of the object according to the perceiver's experience of it, and the final assimilation of the object by the perceiver so that the object ceases to be part of the external world and becomes an intimate part of the perceiver's inner world. Thus the experience of art is a highly personal one in which the ultimate end is the appropriation of the art object into the perceiver's private world.

We can easily see how other Bergsonian concepts support this aesthetic. Intuition, for example, supplies a means through which one can enter the art object in order to experience its organic wholeness. Memory becomes crucial to the reconstruction of the experience and perceptions that the artist uses to fashion the art object and that are reexperienced by the observer. And notions of the self as multiple interpenetrating entities existing below a superficially stable surface provide a template for understanding the multiple experiences and perceptions lurking beneath the surface of an apparently stable art object. Bergson's aesthetic resists closure, and instead embraces multiplicity in terms of both the experiences and interpretations of art. Though modernist aesthetics are heterogeneous rather than homogeneous and thus it is impossible to claim a single aesthetic that describes all modernist art, I will hazard a few generalizations about modernist art that illustrate its Bergsonian undertones.

First, modernists were concerned with the formal qualities of their art, and they questioned the nature of the forms they used. For example, writers focused on *how* language functioned in poetry or prose. They refused to accept that it held any absolute meaning in itself; by questioning traditional uses of it, and by stretching it to the limits of intelligibility (and beyond), modernists shifted the emphasis away from "content" to "form." John Middleton Murry suggests just this when he talks about the nature of language and the writer's struggles to make it vital again. He says, "Every work of enduring literature is not so much a triumph of language as a victory over language: a sudden injection of life-giving perceptions into a vocabulary that is, but for the energy of the creative writer, perpetually on the verge of exhaustion" (1960: 85).

Second, as we saw with the Imagists, form was an organic whole, to be intuitively apprehended by the perceiver who then made the object his or her own. Mark Antliff suggests this was also an aesthetic concern of painters when he says of Matisse's work that it relied on Bergson's theories for its aesthetic foundation. Indeed, Antliff says that Matisse developed

> three interrelated aesthetic strategies: a disavowal of Euclidean space in favour of a Bergsonian notion of extensity; an absorption of the frame within the "organic" parameters of the painting itself; and the rhythmic structuring of the canvas with a view to initiating a reopening of aesthetic closure.

He also says "that reopening was premised on a Bergsonian conception of the interrelation of artist to sitter, and beholder to the finished work of art"(Mullarkey 1999: 186).

Third, the social, moral or didactic function of art was replaced by the belief that art need not concern itself with anything other than the impressions of life that the artist recreated. This life need not be the material, external world of things; in fact, the focus shifted to the internal world of self, where the dynamic, fluid nature of experience was thought to be more truly accessible. Stream-of-consciousness fiction rests on just such an aesthetic. While all of these ideas have counterparts of one sort or another in previous artistic traditions it is the way that the ideas are abstracted and altered to meld together into an unusual amalgam that brings about the art characteristic of this period. Bergson's influence here is clear.

Bergson and Postmodernism

Leszek Kolakowski has suggested that in the post-World War II world, "Bergson has survived only as a dead classic. Even in France interest in his work is only residual" (1985: 1–2). But this orthodox view of Bergson has encountered increasing opposition from thinkers in a wide variety of fields and the continuing presence of Bergsonian ideas in postmodern culture has been noted by a growing number of critics. Perhaps the most well-known postmodern proponent of Bergsonian thought is Gilles Deleuze, himself a *mondain* in the tradition of Bergson. His 1968 book on Bergson – *Bergsonism* – reinserted Bergsonian ideas into a new context, one that was very much engaged in attacking the ideas and aesthetics of modernism. While Kolakowski dismisses Deleuze's work as making for "interesting but difficult reading" (1985: 111) and others suggest that Deleuze twists Bergsonian concepts to fit his poststructuralist agenda, he nonetheless brought Bergsonian ideas back into the spotlight. As Paul Douglass suggests, Deleuze "has re-imagined Bergson as a precursor of the 'post-structuralist turn': philosophy turning its own powers back upon itself, reflecting upon its own flaws, gaps, and limitations – philosophy as an act of self-consciousness" (1992: 377). Deleuze finds in Bergson's philosophy concepts and language that permit him to explore the idea of "coexistent multiplicities" and the "becomings of which multiplicities are made up" (1998: 8). He explores multiplicity throughout his diverse body of work; for example, using Bergsonian concepts to articulate a semiology of cinema in *Cinema 1* and *Cinema 2* and also to develop his theory of the rhizome in *A Thousand Plateaus*. While Foucault's assertion that this "century might perhaps one day come to be known as 'Deleuzian'" (1992: 368) may be as hyperbolic as Scharfstein's comments about Bergson, there is no denying the central place that Deleuze occupies in postmodern culture. The fact that Bergson's ideas occupy such a prominent place in Deleuze's thought surely must be seen as a powerful refutation to the orthodox view that Bergson is a "dead classic."

Deleuze is not the only postmodern to have adopted or incorporated Bergsonian ideas into his work. Jure Gantar, for instance, traces the connections between Bergson's comic theory (articulated in *Laughter*, first published in France as *Le Rire* in 1900) and chaos theory. He concludes that

> There appear to be no major discrepancies between [Bergson's] ideas in *Le Rire* and the corresponding postulates of chaos theory. While this may partly

be so because Favre and his co-authors at least implicitly see Bergson as their philosophical kin, Bergson's ideas lend themselves just as well to Ilya Prigogine's concept of 'order produced by fluctuations' and Patrick O'Neill's investigations off the comedy of entropy. (1999: 54–5)

Richard Lehan briefly discusses Bergson's place in postmodern philosophy; he suggests that "If Bergson positions himself in the discourse of postmodern phenomenology, his presence in what has been called systems philosophy is even more keenly felt" (1992: 327). He concludes that "The systems philosophers had to go through Bergson to arrive at different conclusions. Thus, on the highest plane of debate today in physics and biology, Bergson is still very much part of the discourse" (1992: 328). Milic Capek has made a powerful case for Bergson's continuing place in twentieth-century physics in his book *Bergson and Modern Physics*. Douglass and Burwick's collection of essays establishes convincingly the importance of Bergson's vitalist ideas to disciplines as diverse as biology, physics, and poststructuralist philosophy. The self-reflexive nature of art – it is as much about the individual experiencing it as it is about the art itself – is commonly understood as a marker of postmodern art. The roots of this aesthetic, as we have seen, can be found in Bergsonian ideas about the self, memory, intuition, and perception. Looking at these various manifestations of Bergsonian philosophy, it seems likely that Bergsonism does function as Douglass and Burwick suggest – as the repressed content of not only modern thought but also of postmodern thinking.

Conclusion

The last two decades of the twentieth century witnessed a renewed interrogation of all facets of modernist culture. The 1980s, in particular, witnessed a reassessment of modernist aesthetics. The work of Sanford Schwartz, Michael Levenson, and Ricardo Quinones, to name just three of the important reinterpreters, transformed the way that we talked about the literature and art of the early twentieth century. All three of these critics explored Bergson's role in the development of modernism, thereby following Deleuze's lead of reinserting Bergson into critical debate. It is also notable that several books on Bergson and various national literatures have appeared since the early 1980s – Paul Douglass and Tom Quirk's books consider Bergson and American literature, Mary Ann Gillies discusses Bergson and British modernism, and Hillary Fink looks at Bergson and Russian modernism. Mark Antliff's book on Bergson and Cubism extends recent discussion into the realm of twentieth-century avant-garde art. And Robert Grogin's study of the Bergsonian phenomenon in France provides us with a much-needed reassessment of Bergson's cultural significance in his own country. This renewed interest in a philosopher may puzzle many who study philosophy today, for as Kolakowski suggests, "today's philosophers, both in their research and in their teaching, are almost entirely indifferent to [Bergson's] legacy" (1985: 2). However, I believe it is evident from not only the rekindled interest in Bergson, but also the enormous interest of the thinkers, writers and artists of his own day, that Bergson stands as one of the intellectual giants of the twentieth century. As John Mullarkey says, "At the threshold of the twentieth century, [Bergson] reset the agenda of philosophy and its relationship with science, art and even life itself" (1999: 1). At the beginning of the twenty-first century, it seems appropriate that the renewed interest in Bergson reveals that he still occupies a central place in the construction of postmodern culture, albeit one that, just as was the case a century earlier, often goes unacknowledged by those who borrow his ideas and make them part of their own work.

References and Further Reading

Ansell-Pearson, Keith and Mullarkey, John, eds. 2002. *Key Writings: Henri Bergson.* New York: Continuum.

Antliff, Mark. 1993. *Inventing Bergson.* Princeton: Princeton University Press.

——. 1999. The Rhythm of Duration: Bergson and the Art of Matisse. In John Mullarkey, ed., *The New Bergson*, pp. 184–208. Manchester: Manchester University Press.

Bergson, Henri. 1911a. *Laughter: An Essay on the Meaning of the Comic.* Trans. Cloudesley Brereton and Fred Rothwell. London: Macmillan.

——. 1911b. *Matter and Memory.* Trans. Nancy Margaret Paul and W. Scott Palmer. London: George Allen & Unwin.

——. 1913a. *An Introduction to Metaphysics.* Trans. T. E. Hulme. London: Macmillan.

——. 1913b. *Time and Free Will.* Trans. F. L. Pogson. New York: Harper & Row.

——. 1928. *Creative Evolution.* Trans. Arthur Mitchell. London: Macmillan.

Bistis, Marguerite. 1996. Managing Bergson's Crowd: Professionalism and the *Mondain* at the Collège de France. *Historical Reflections/Réflexions Historiques* 22/2 (Spring): 389–406.

Burwick, Frederick and Douglass, Paul, eds. 1992. *The Crisis of Modernism.* Cambridge, Cambridge University Press.

Čapek, Miliĉ. 1971. *Bergson and Modern Physics: A Reinterpretation and Re-evaluation.* Dordrecht: Reidel.

Deleuze, Gilles. 1988. *Bergsonism.* Trans. Hugh Tomlinson and Barbara Habberjam. New York: Zone Books.

——. 1986. *Cinema 1: The Movement Image.* Trans. Hugh Tomlinson and Barbara Habberjam. Minneapolis, University of Minnesota Press.

——. 1989. *Cinema 2: The Time Image.* Trans. Hugh Tomlinson and Robert Galeta. Minneapolis: University of Minnesota Press.

—— and Guattari, Félix. 1987. *A Thousand Plateaus: Capitalism and Schizophrenia.* Trans. Brian Massumi. London: Athlone Press.

Douglass, Paul. 1986. *Bergson, Eliot, & American Literature.* Lexington: University Press of Kentucky.

——. 1992. Deleuze's Bergson: Bergson Redux. In Frederick Burwick and Paul Douglass, eds., *The Crisis of Modernism,* pp. 368–88. Cambridge: Cambridge University Press.

Eliot, T. S. 1969. *The Complete Poems and Plays of T. S. Eliot.* London: Faber & Faber.

Fink, Hilary L. 1999. *Bergson and Russian Modernism 1900–1930.* Evanston, IL: Northwestern University Press.

Gantar, Jure. 1999. The Case of the Falling Man: Bergson and Chaos Theory. *Mosaic* 32/2 (June): 43–58.

Gillies, Mary Ann. 1996. *Henri Bergson and British Modernism.* Montreal and Kingston: McGill-Queen's University Press.

Grogin, R. C. 1988. *The Bergsonian Controversy in France 1900–1914.* Calgary: University of Calgary Press.

Gunter, P. A. Y. 1974. *Henri Bergson: A Bibliography.* Bowling Green, OH: Philosophy Documentation Center.

Kolakowski, Leszek. 1985. *Bergson* Oxford: Oxford University Press.

Lehan, Richard. 1992. Bergson and the Discourse of the Moderns. In Frederick Burwick and Paul Douglass, eds., *The Crisis in Modernism,* pp. 306–29. Cambridge: Cambridge University Press.

Levenson, Michael. 1984. *A Genealogy of Modernism: A Study of English Literary Doctrine 1908–1922.* Cambridge: Cambridge University Press.

Moore, F. C. 1996. T. *Bergson: Thinking Backwards.* Cambridge: Cambridge University Press.

Mullarkey, John, ed. 1999. *The New Bergson.* Manchester: Manchester University Press.

Murry, John Middleton. 1960. *The Problem of Style.* London: Oxford University Press.

Pound, Ezra. 1954. A Retrospect. In T. S. Eliot, ed., *Literary Essays of Ezra Pound,* pp. 3–14. London: Faber & Faber.

Quinones, Ricardo. 1985. *Mapping Literary Modernism.* Princeton: Princeton University Press.

Quirk, Tom. 1990. *Bergson and American Culture.* Chapel Hill: University of North Carolina Press.

Scharfstein, Ben-Ami. 1943. *Roots of Bergson's Philosophy*. New York: Columbia University Press.

Schwartz, Sanford. 1985. *The Matrix of Modernism: Pound, Eliot and Early Twentieth Century Thought*. Princeton: Princeton University Press.

Szathmary, Arthur. 1937. *The Aesthetic Theory of Henri Bergson*. Cambridge, MA: Harvard University Press.

Woolf, Virginia. 1984. Modern Fiction. In *The Common Reader I*, pp. 146–54. London: Hogarth Press.

6

Psychoanalysis in Britain: "The rituals of destruction"

Stephen Frosh

One of the claims one might make about the relationship between psychoanalysis and modernism is that each is a beast of the other. That is, psychoanalysis, at least in its pre-World War II form, is an emblematic modernist discipline; conversely, modernist perceptions of subjectivity, individuality, memory and sociality are all deeply entwined with a psychoanalytic sensitivity. This two-way traffic seems not to have been perceived as such by many psychoanalytic practitioners of the time. Freud himself had virtually nothing to say about the modernist credentials of his creation, only wishing to subsume it under the banner of "science" (e.g., Freud 1933). That this is a classic modernist move is part of the point. From the other side, debate about the relevance and believability of psychoanalytic claims, particularly concerning the existence and nature of the unconscious, are significant points of concern for modernist philosophers and literary intellectuals; in this chapter, some of the intersections between psychoanalysis and "Bloomsbury" will be highlighted as exemplary in this respect. What I will suggest, focusing on the internal dynamics of psychoanalysis in Britain between the wars, is that the extraordinary tumult produced in the modernist consciousness by the devastating destructiveness enacted in World War I, and by the storm-clouds of fascism as they cohered throughout the period, are reflected in the concerns of psychoanalysis at this time. In particular, the coming of the Kleinians, with their insistence on the passionate irrationality of the human

116

condition and on the management of destructiveness, not only offered a language in which this destructiveness could be thought about, but also a vision of creativity as reparation which itself is beautifully attuned to the modernist impulse to make something good out of chaos.

The Emergence of Psychoanalysis in the Context of Modernism

Rationality, irrationality

In the course of developing an argument that psychoanalysis, particularly in its contemporary Kleinian variety, is a (or the) "last modernism," Michael Rustin comments: "Psychoanalysis came late in the historical succession of projects of rational enlightenment .... Psychoanalysis sought to extend the domain of reason to the sphere of the emotions, and of the residues of irrationality which were not readily comprehensible within rationalistic categories" (1999: 106). This idea, that modernism deals with the extension of reason and that psychoanalysis partakes of this same agenda, is a central one in making the link. Understanding the modernist impulse as "a movement which sought to understand, and develop new languages and cultural forms to represent the intractable obstacles which remained to human freedom and the powers of reason" (1999: 108), Rustin sees psychoanalysis as the modernist project which undertook to bring science to bear on the regions of the mind which were "a hitherto undiscovered territory" (1999: 105). Indeed, one might extend this by saying that psychoanalysis came in as a modernist weapon trained against precisely those areas of the mind which threaten to undermine the rationalist project, those recalcitrant irrationalities which keep popping up to wreck all the best-laid plans. What is the unconscious if not an attack on reason? Or at least a major circumscription of what reason can do? Gellner, drawing attention to the way the unconscious always undermines claims to knowledge – is always subversive and tricky – sees psychoanalysis generally as characterized by "conditional realism." This means that it proposes that

> the mind *can* know objects it is concerned with, by means of contact with them, but that it does not necessarily or always succeed in doing so. It fails to do so because it chooses (unconsciously) to deceive itself. The Unconscious is a kind of systematic interference, which hampers full and proper contact between the mind and its object, and thereby prevents effective knowledge. (1985: 82–3)

Thus, what psychoanalysis deals with is nature *inside*, as difficult to manage as those external forces which science has gradually but incompletely tamed, and just as significant for the project of expelling irrationality from the conditions of human existence. What always distinguished the Freudian unconscious, from the first moment of its theoretical inception, was its *dynamic* character. Something lives at the heart of the human subject, outside the realms of normal egoic control, something not-I (that is, not *das Ich*, the ego, but more an *it, das Es*), but nevertheless *present*, active, pushing for expression, motivating, causal. It is a force of disruption (sexual, destructive) and (crucially for Rustin's link with modernism) recalcitrant, resistive. The task of psychoanalysis is to control this something, to channel its energy into personally and socially useful ends. Famously, Freud puts this precisely in cultural terms: psychoanalysis seeks, therapeutically and philosophically, "to strengthen the ego, to make it more independent of the superego, to widen its field of perception and enlarge its organisation, so that it can appropriate fresh portions of the id. Where id was, there ego shall be: it is a work of culture – not unlike the draining of the Zuider Zee" (1933: 112). The sea, inchoate, unplumbably deep, is to be channeled, its energy made useful for human endeavor. This is no easy task, but then modernism never proposes ease: "Modernism was a movement of emancipation because of the idea that reason had to engage with a universe always resistant to its understanding, and to its control" (Rustin 1999: 107). Similarly, psychoanalysis deals with the obstacles to reason within the psyche – that is, with the real fifth column sabotaging the rationalist project, with its dependence on clarity of mind.

Femininity and colonization of the hysteric

This rationalist project of modernism, with its science–nature opposition and the search for mastery of a resistive other, is wrapped around a highly gendered structure in which what is central is the idea of the male master placing order on feminine chaos – that is, mind conquering the body. Freud, too, was clearly immersed in this, from his deep study of (his own) dreams in *The Interpretation of Dreams* (1900), a "dark continent" to match that of the woman, right through to his discussion, in *Moses and Monotheism* (1939), of the cultural advantages of masculinity over femininity: "But this turning from the mother to the father points in addition to a victory of intellectuality over sensuality – that is, an advance in civilisation, since maternity is proved by the evidence of the senses while paternity is a hypothesis, based on an inference and a premise" (1939: 361). So, the woman is to be passed on from, a necessary stage perhaps, like being born, but too messy to leave as the final point in culture. As such, psychoanalysis is echoed by many modernist projects, with their clean lines and muscular assertions of what is real and true.

However, just as the assertion that modernism is univocally misogynist would be a misreading of what is in fact a complex pattern of ambiguities and ambivalence around the feminine, so psychoanalysis too expresses both sides of the rationality–irrationality tension. Once again, this might actually be one of its modernist features: that it aspires to conquering the irrational but in so doing gives it voice, so widening the scope for facing conflict and contradiction, and thence for deepening human experience. Toril Moi expresses this well in reminding us of the origins of psychoanalysis in Freud's examination of a "female malady," hysteria.

> Psychoanalysis is born in the encounter between the hysterical woman and the positivist man of science . . . . It is in this reversal of the traditional roles of subject and object, of speaker and listener, that Freud more or less unwittingly opens the way for a new understanding of human knowledge. But the psychoanalytical situation is shot through with paradoxes and difficulty. For if Freud's (and Breuer's) act of listening represents an effort to *include* the irrational discourse of femininity in the realm of science, it also embodies their hope of *extending* their own rational understanding of psychic phenomena. *Grasping* the logic of the unconscious they want to make it accessible to reason. (1989: 196–7)

In this account, Freud allows the woman hysteric to speak, creating a space in "science" for the voice of the irrational. This reverses the conventional male/female division: the hysteric speaks, Freud listens, reflects her speech back to her, makes it visible and meaningful. What she says is not mad any more, it makes sense, it is worthy of respect. At its most radical, this approach deconstructs the ready-made polarities of traditional western thought; now it is no longer clear that truth equals rationality, that meaning equals sense. But the other side of this is that Freud acts as the one who tames this irrational speech, making it rational, explaining it and taking it over. He quotes the woman, only to know better. This, too, is present in psychoanalysis: interpreting everything, it can make it all dry as dust, reduce its poetry to the logical formulations of an unconscious "explained." Moi says about this ambiguity:

> When the colonising impulse gains the upper hand, psychoanalysis runs the risk of obliterating the language of the irrational and the unconscious,

> repressing the threatening presence of the feminine in the process . . . . But there is also in [Freud's] texts a will to let the madwoman speak, to consider *her* discourse as one ruled by its own logic, to accept the logic of another scene. (1989: 197)

Both-and rather than either-or, this would be in contemporary postmodern thought; psychoanalysis as both rationalist *and* irrationalist, controlling master and receptive other. In Freud's time, the time to 1939, the former was always the aspiration: take hold of this thing, the unconscious, the feminine, and make it speak – precisely so that it could have said its piece and need no longer whisper scandalously and perversely in the night. However, even in Freud's time there was plenty of evidence of people (including Freud) falling in love with the whisper, recognizing something in this non-sense which could be a resource for deepening modern experience. Freud himself at times celebrated Eros, but gradually became enthralled much more by destructiveness, a tendency which Klein brought most forcefully to the British scene. Others, however, used the unconscious to discover a poetic free from the dominion of old masters. For example, Chisholm (1992), exploring the poet H. D.'s relationship with psychoanalysis, draws attention to the way H. D. portrays Freud (with whom she had a brief analysis and about whom she wrote exquisitely in *Tribute to Freud* [H. D.1948]) as a humanist rather than a scientist, someone in contact with an arena for creativity which leaves the "classic," male modernists behind.

> What Freud gave H. D., what she especially attributes to his genius and daring, is access to the universal myths of (pre) history through her own symptomatic dream symbols . . . . He helped affirm her own sense of *spiritus mundi*, which modernist male poets plundered as an exclusively male domain. Their access to this treasure-source of symbols, primarily through recovery and translation of masculinist mythos/logos, was not her access, not her way of reading the palimpsest of the Western mind . . . . Instead of having to turn exclusively to the "tradition" of male-dominated literary history to compose her modernist text, H. D. discovers, through Freud and the medium of her own symptomatic mind/body processes, an other realm for semiotic excavation and translation. (Chisholm 1992: 17)

Thus, the woman writer finds in Freud a muse which honors and respects the messy, rhythmic, and mythological foundations of an artistic temperament. Thoughtfulness rather than emotional acting-out prevails in Freud, but this is not only the focused, instrumental, and limiting thought of the rationalist conqueror. It is also, *at the same time*, the poetic thought of the one who can allow his mind to wander, can perceive and let be. Interestingly, it is this receptive, think-about-everything state of mind which remains the aspiration of most psychoanalytic psychotherapists in the British tradition. Bion (1962) called it "reverie" and emphasized its maternal rather than paternal origins, the therapist/mother's capacity to hold whatever comes her way. "Analyzing" may be a "male function," as Guntrip (1968: 360) stereotypically puts it, but it is "based on the female function of intuitively knowing." More to the point, struggling with something can be a way of recognizing its existence – as Jacob (and Freud) proved to the angel.

Depth and revolution

What is perhaps neglected up to this point in this account of the parallels between modernism's approach to reason and that of psychoanalysis, is the degree to which the rationality/irrationality tension was an utterly explosive one throughout the period. Berman says it best: "[Modernity] pours us all into a maelstrom of perpetual disintegration and renewal, of struggle and contradiction, of ambiguity and anguish. To be modern is to be part of a universe in which, as Marx said, 'all that is solid melts into air'" (1982: 15). Modernism is about change: at its most literal, modernism is always the most recent theorization and representation of experience, of necessity a critical engagement with what has come before – with the traditional or premodern situation. Modernism is, therefore, always about the present, but it dramatizes an awareness that the present is a temporary state, that modernity continues to update itself, that each new modern movement stands in a critical relationship to that which has gone before. Hence, as Eagleton points out, the "typically modernist images of the vortex and the abyss, 'vertical' irruptions into temporality within which forces swirl restlessly in an eclipse of linear time" (1986: 139). Modernism is not about a stable state, but about the possibility for complete change – for both reconstruction and personal, cultural, and political revolution. And modernism is *critical:* its awareness of the tragedies of modern existence arises from an image of people and of society as containing possibilities for development, which can be nurtured or squashed. Its criticism, therefore, can be scathing, as in the most powerful modernist images and texts; but it is also based on the premise that alternatives can be envisioned, that there could be a state of being which is not so exploitative, degenerate, alienated, or destructive. Modernism is, in this sense, a product of modernity, but one which, even as its products are appropriated into the "high art" and commodity fetishism so characteristic of late capitalism (Eagleton 1986), protests at the gap between what is and what might be.

The parallels here, between the maelstrom of modernity and that of the early psychoanalytic movement, are very compelling. The classic Freudian patients were hysterics and obsessional neurotics – people with relatively clearly differentiated symptoms who might be understood to be suffering from too much repression. These people were not mad; they functioned on the ordinary human level which requires recognition of reality and the ability to form relationships with others. On the whole, they could manage this, but at an exaggerated cost. Like everyone else, their toleration of the demands of society required renunciation of certain inner demands, pressures for sexual and aggressive satisfaction which, if acted upon, would lead to the devastation of their social relationships and hence their selves. These inner demands, these "drives," were theorized by Freud as basic, the fundamental inherited forces underlying all personality and motivation. Such a theory was, as many post-Freudian commentators have explained, rooted in some now discredited assumptions of nineteenth-century physics. But it was also rooted in Freud's experience of his patients' psychology, in the compulsiveness with which they sought out hurts, in their sense of being controlled by passions the nature of which they could barely perceive, let alone accept. The drive model may be outdated scientifically, but it remains a common personal metaphor; what Freud felt, listening and struggling with his bourgeois neurotics, was their sense of the forceful flow of their inner desires as they began to burst the dams.

In this they expressed a common cultural concern, but the problem for these patients was that their underlying fixations and desires created unbearable anxieties, particularly centering on the destruction of self-control and of the ego-integrity which lies behind it. The cliché of the dam bursting was one by which millions lived their lives; the consequence of the resulting flood would be the overcoming of intellect by emotion, masculine order by feminine anarchy, rationality by irrationality, reason by desire. Order and control: this is the language of the ego; according to Freud, it is also the essential bulwark against disintegration. Imposing order on the chaos of the unconscious is the task of civilization and the individual project of all who live within it, including psychoanalysts: hence the Zuider Zee simile mentioned above. It is this struggle, the struggle to maintain order in the face of threatening chaos, that in the Freudian view characterizes the life of the individual in society.

Freud's patients were no different from non-neurotics in adhering to the metaphor of the dam, but for them it was just that bit nearer bursting – their desires were that much nearer flooding through. These classic neurotic patients were the base upon which psychoanalytic theory was formulated; they have dominated cultural images of analysis from the start, as well as dictating the therapeutic techniques employed. In particular, switching away from the laborious metaphor of the dam, they embody the characteristic modern image of tension between surface and depth, between appearance and the forces which lie beneath. For Freud, examination of the discourse of his patients revealed that there is a real turbulence of truth behind all ostensible acts, and that this truth – this set of underlying meanings – can make sense of what seems senseless and mad. Moreover, excavation of the truth, uncovering of the unconscious forces that "really" govern behavior, is a *therapeutic* task: it overturns the specious falsities of the everyday world, which is held together only through compromise and at a terrible cost to psychic health. So the undercover life of the unconscious is dangerous: its forces and formations pressing for expression constantly undermine the precarious relations between the self and the world. But it is also the source of truth, and it offers a possibility of change.

The notion that there is some interpretive depth reality which is more true than surface appearances is central to traditional psychoanalysis just as it is crucial to modernist views of creativity and resistance – and just as it is opposed to the celebration of seduction that characterizes much postmodernist criticism. It can also be detected in Freudian-based analyses of the sociopolitical situation. Here, the surface-depth model led first to Freud's *Civilisation and its Discontents* (1930), which emphasized the perpetual contradiction between personal desires and social necessity, with the attendant restrictions on full human happiness. For Freud, the most that can be hoped for is that individuals will learn to tolerate reality, and that reality will be sufficiently tolerable to allow moderate amelioration of pain. "It is impossible," Freud writes, "to overlook the extent to which civilisation is built upon a renunciation of instinct, how much it presupposes precisely the non-satisfaction . . . of powerful instincts" (1930: 286). Underlying psychological stability are unmet desires; social stability, too, is built on the renunciation of instinctual impulses. Hence the connection between the advent of psychoanalysis and the many modernist images (in art, literature, music, and politics – paradigmatically in Russia) of revolution, of what is underneath breaking through and overturning the established order. Freudian psychoanalysis spoke fully to this, and offered a route through, a way of thinking about how such elemental forces might be expressed without wiping out everything in their way.

The British Scene

Psychoanalysis in Europe had been produced largely by marginals – Jews, mainly, on the outside of an antisemitic society, scathingly perceptive about its foibles and menace, and capable of looking sideways at received wisdoms, seeing something new. Their search for truth was precisely that of the modernists who "identified themselves as enemies of conventional forms of expression and representation, which they saw as obstacles to human freedom and authenticity" (Rustin 1999: 109). These iconoclastic Jews, emancipated but not allowed to be unequivocally part of society, were willing to speak of the darkness at the troubled heart of bourgeois consciousness. In Britain, very oddly, there was a strikingly different trajectory: a non-Jewish (at times, antisemitic) psychoanalysis evolved, quite haughty and aristocratic, bowled along by a certain mode of feminism but mainly characterized by the artistic Freud who so affected H. D. – although the institutional, clinical Freud is perhaps the one which has survived the best (Hinshelwood 1998). Abel notes, "The characterization of psychoanalysis as a literary rather than a scientific discourse became a leitmotif in England; radically divided between medical and humanist sectors in their evaluation of Freudian theory, British reviewers reached consensus on the imaginative status of the Freudian text" (1989: 15). How this happened, and what it might have meant, is worthy of some attention.

Origins of psychoanalysis in Britain

In a rather tendentious account of the history of psychoanalysis in Britain, emphasizing the "independence" of the British group from the start, Rayner comments:

> Freud's ideas, with scientific methodology modulating the perception of emotionality and the psychodynamics of the unconscious born of romanticism and idealism, must have intrigued and disturbed the empirical, pragmatic-minded British intelligentsia . . . . Even so, those who committed themselves to psychoanalysis in Britain at the start were almost pure English, Welsh or Scots. Their backgrounds were middle class, mercantile and

professional, with some from the gentry. Many had deeply Protestant religious backgrounds, some were scientific, others literary and artistic. (1991: 8)

It is indeed striking that Freudian psychoanalysis, a scion of German romanticism and Jewish emancipation (some would even argue, Jewish tradition and mysticism – see Bakan 1958, Roith 1987, Frosh 2001), should find a receptive audience amongst the "almost pure English, Welsh or Scots," although the situation is redeemed somewhat by the large number of women and mavericks amongst those first attracted to psychoanalysis, as well as by recognition of the weed-clearing undertaken by British sexologists such as Havelock Ellis. (Ellis himself seems to have seen Freud first as a follower and then as a rival, although Hinshelwood [1995: 139] credits him with spreading knowledge of psychoanalysis throughout British professional culture through his "diligent reviewing [of psychoanalysis] in the medical and psychiatric journals.") There had been some response to even the first publications on psychoanalysis, with positive reviews of, and commentaries on, Breuer and Freud's (1895) *Studies on Hysteria* published in the prestigious journal, *Brain* (Kohon 1986). In addition, the Society for Psychical Research, in which Joan Riviere's uncle, Arthur Verall, was a significant figure, created interest in Freud's work in the early years of the twentieth century, particularly amongst Cambridge-based intellectuals, partly because of the apparent similarity between its own concern with trance states and spiritualism and the Freudian account of hysteria. Frederic Myers, one of the founders of the Society, reviewed *Studies on Hysteria* for its *Proceedings* in 1897 and Freud himself became a corresponding member in 1912 (Hinshelwood 1995). In 1916, the Medical section of the Society was integrated into the British Psychological Society (BPS) with the formation of the BPS's Medical Section, a bastion of psychodynamic thinking for decades thereafter. There was also considerable interest in psychoanalysis within the medical schools in London even prior to World War I (although there was also strong opposition, reflected particularly strongly in the British Medical Association) and even more so after the war, when the experience of various experiments in dealing with trauma and shell-shock (for example, that of W. H. R. Rivers at Craiglockhart in Edinburgh) could be processed (Hinshelwood 1998).

However, it was the apparently limitless energy of Ernest Jones, conservative and radical at once, that mobilized psychoanalytic energies in Britain, and specifically in London. He met Freud in 1908 at the First Psycho-Analytical Congress in Salzburg and thereafter was an unswerving

advocate of psychoanalysis, and a swerving one of Freud. In 1913, return-
ing from a scandal-induced exile in Canada, Jones was briefly analyzed by
Ferenczi and then formed the London Psycho-Analytical Society, with fif-
teen initial members. By 1919, the Freud–Jung split had infiltrated this
group in the person of David Eder (who later became a more orthodox
Freudian again); to retain psychoanalytic purity, Jones then dissolved the
London Society and formed the British Psycho-Analytical Society, incorporating along the way members of James Glover's Medico-Psychological
Clinic in Brunswick Square, which had originally been founded by two
strong suffragette doctors, Jessie Murray and Julia Turner, and had flourished as a treatment center during the war but had fallen into debt and
schism thereafter (Hinshelwood 1998). The importance of this, as
Appignanesi and Forrester note, was that "The immigration into the Society of those already experienced practitioners, imbued with the high ideals of philanthropy, feminism and socialism, in part explains why the British
Society had so many lay women members from early on" (1992: 353).
This sowed the seeds for the spirited discussions both of feminine sexuality and of "lay" (i.e., nonmedical) analysis which permeated the British
Society's life in the 1920s. Interestingly on this last point, Jones advocated
a view of psychoanalysis as a branch of medicine, against Freud's own
vision (Freud 1926, Kohon 1986). Nevertheless, the British Society not
only tolerated but respected and supported lay analysts from the start (by
the late 1920s, the British Society had the highest proportion of lay members – 40 percent – anywhere in the world), the culmination of this being
that neither of the two colossi of the British scene, Melanie Klein and
Anna Freud, were doctors – and both, of course, were women.

Some extraordinarily talented individuals joined the British Society in
its early years: for example, Joan Riviere, James and Edward Glover, Susan
Isaacs, John Rickman, Sylvia Payne, James and Alix Strachey, and Ella
Sharpe (Kohon 1986). They established a culture of high criticism, mixed
with an empiricist interest in the grounded practice of psychoanalysis,
with a particular focus on child development. Kohon notes that some of
the earliest papers presented at the British Society marked this characteristic concern: "'The Psychology of the New-born Infant' by Forsyth was,
according to the 'Minutes', the first paper discussed (15 May 1919). This
was followed by 'Note-taking and reporting of Psycho-Analytic cases',
presented by Barbara Low, emphasizing the British preoccupation with
the immediacy of the clinical situation (12 June 1919)" (Kohon 1986:
27). They also created a receptive climate for the coming of the Kleinians,
a point I shall return to below. But another noticeable element in the

early group was how "artistic" so many of its members and hangers-on were; that is, how many of them came from an intellectual elite which, particularly through "Bloomsbury," was central in the development of twentieth-century British modernist culture. (Kohon comments, possibly acidly but certainly crudely and reductively, "The fact that so many psychoanalysts came from this particular background led to the acceptance of people with a certain degree of psychological disturbance, but who could be of 'outstanding personality'" [1986: 7].) Hinshelwood, in his account of the permeation of Freudian thought into British culture, notes the remarkable breadth of references to Freud in the period to 1918 – that is, before the founding of the British Society – and lists "seven points of access into British cultural life in the 25 years or so after 1893. Though greatly misunderstood at times, there were aspects of psychoanalysis which were telling for a number of people with different and often conflicting interests" (1995: 135).

These cultural sites include the Society for Psychical Research, interest in the psychoanalytic theory of sexuality in support of radical attitudes toward sexual freedom, and the attraction of some progressive educationalists to Freud's outline of child development. Hinshelwood argues both that this wide interest from numerous quarters contributed to the success of the Freudian implantation, and also that it was in the clinical and institutional domain that psychoanalysis had its most substantial and long-lasting effect. Thus the formation of the British Society, the training of analysts, links with the Tavistock Clinic (founded in 1920, but disparaged by Jones for its eclecticism) and the institutionalization of professional practices are what have carried psychoanalysis forward. Be that as it may, looking back at the British environment of the 1920s, what is impressive is not so much the professional scene, though this did develop apace and received substantial recognition (for instance, three government ministers attended the British Psychoanalytic Society's anniversary banquet in 1939 – Hinshelwood 1998), but rather the fervent interpenetration of psychoanalysis with a certain strand of British literary culture, that of the heightened interwar consciousness of the Bloomsbury set. Through them, psychoanalysis became a cultural tool, as Freud had always wished it to be, provoking reconsiderations of language, gender, and memory, and of course of the relationships between external "reality" and what has come to be called (through Kleinian influence) the "internal world."

The literary Freud – Bloomsbury

Appignanesi and Forrester sum up the situation admirably:

> The rapid dissemination of Freud's ideas in the English-speaking world after the First World War, the depth with which they took hold, owed much to the manner in which Freud was reimagined in English. And this manner – in its seductiveness, its liveliness, erudition, refinement, lucidity and wit- is as thoroughly Bloomsbury as Virginia Woolf herself, whose works, after all, bear the imprint of the same publisher as the *Collected Works* – the first attempt systematically to order Freud's writings in English. (1992: 352)

What is misleading in this quotation is the implication that Virginia Woolf herself was involved in the promulgation of psychoanalysis, when in fact (as Appignanesi and Forrester point out elsewhere) she was openly hostile to it, at least as an adjunct to literature, if not so much as an approach to understanding character. As Stonebridge points out, Woolf seems to have thought of her own writing as sometimes paralleling the psychoanalytic therapeutic process: writing of *To the Lighthouse*, she said, "I suppose that I did for myself what psycho-analysts do for their patients. I expressed some very long felt and deeply felt emotion. And in expressing it I explained it and laid it to rest" (1998: 63). Perhaps this relates to the reason Woolf would not countenance psychoanalytic treatment for her own psychological distress; in the version given by Alix Strachey, this was because of the fear (which Strachey endorsed) that psychoanalysis might endanger Woolf's creativity, that is, that unpicking her madness might destroy her work (Appignanesi and Forrester 1992, Abel 1989).

While Woolf's antagonism to psychoanalysis was shared by some other Bloomsbury characters, for example Roger Fry and Cive Bell (Stonebridge 1998), for many others it was central. The Woolfs published Freud in English through their Hogarth Press, an activity given the highest priority by the British Society and by Jones himself. Abel calls the publication of four volumes of Freud's *Collected Works* in 1924–5 "the turning point in the dissemination of psychoanalytic theory in England" (1989: 1) and goes on to note that Virginia Woolf "avoided opening the books, which she consistently represents as objects to be handled rather than as texts," making them sound like *phobic* objects for her, a genuine threat. Adrian and Karin Stephen, Virginia Woolf's brother and sister-in-law, became psychoanalysts and housed the first series of lectures Melanie Klein gave in London in 1925 (Woolf was writing *To the Lighthouse* at the time). James and Alix Strachey were both analyzed by Freud in 1920 and went on to dominate

•

the translation of Freud's work into English, as well as (through Alix's enthusiasm and interpretive brilliance) to open the door for Klein. Joan Riviere, a stunning intellect in her own right, was analyzed first (disastrously) by Jones, then (compellingly) by Freud, who seems to have used her as the model for his reformulated structural model of the mind, in *The Ego and the Id* (1923; Appignanesi. and Forrester 1992: 358). Riviere, as well as being translation editor of the *International Journal of Psycho-Analysis* until 1937, also made crucial contributions both to the gender debates of the period and to the development of Kleinian thinking. On the former issue, her 1929 paper, "Womanliness as a Masquerade," has provided one of the most fertile grounds for the development of an imaginative psychoanalysis of sexual difference, and has successfully negotiated the advent of postmodernism through its terrific playfulness around performance and mirroring. What is a woman? For Riviere, in her life as well as her writing (Sayers 2000), as intellectual woman, it is pretence: "The reader may now ask how I define womanliness or where I draw the line between genuine womanliness and the "masquerade." My suggestion is not, however, that there is any such difference; whether radical or superficial, they are the same thing" (Riviere 1929: 94).

This concern with gender is no accident in the interwar modernist context. The sexual politics of the time, with a more open sexual freedom side by side with the blossoming of women as social agents, called into question the received wisdom of masculine dominance in the cultural sphere – a wisdom which Freud strongly shared. Quite suddenly, for example through anthropological debates on matriarchal societies as well as literary means, and in the wake of the devastation produced by and amongst men in World War I, femininity asserted itself openly and flamboyantly. Freud himself, despite the polemical nature of some of his pronouncements, recognized the provisional nature of his understanding of femininity, and early on some major psychoanalysts (e.g., Jones, Horney, Deutsch, Klein, Lampl de Groot) were willing to risk this as an arena for dissension from his views. The characteristic feature of this opposition was to deny Freud's idea that femininity develops through a growing awareness of lack and absence in comparison with men, an account which places at the center of the female mind a desire to be male. Although Freud was correct in thinking that the first love-object of both sexes is the mother, this does not mean that girls are in fact "little men," as Freud would have it; neither does his correct observation of the existence of penis envy mean that girls are necessarily different from boys in their ideas about loss and threats to their personality. Jones (1927), for example, suggested that children of either sex can feel threatened with the extinction of their sexuality; he proposed that castration anxiety is part of this wider, non-gender-specific anxiety, which he called *aphanisis*. Horney and Klein emphasized the pre-Oedipal role of the mother in determining sexual development and saw this as originary even of the Oedipus complex. Thus, Horney (1926) claimed that the notion that there is only one genital, the penis, which one either has or lacks is in fact a defense against the overwhelming power of the mother; further, she irreverently suggested that Freud's account of femininity is fixed at the level of the four-year-old boy who cannot bear to envision the reality of a girl's separate sexuality, but must defend himself by disparagement of her possibilities. This fixation, she held, prevented Freud from recognizing the specificity of female development and hence producing an adequate psychology of women. Jones (1935), correctly recognizing the importance of all this, took up the issue of female sexuality as his own contribution in a series of "exchange lectures" between London and Vienna in the 1930s, which were supposed to help the two centers, by then rivalrous over Kleinianism, understand each other better.

Riviere's idea of womanliness as masquerade is in some respects aligned with Freud in this debate, but what is most striking is its revelation of the struggle of womanhood to find a place for itself in culture, to feel real or whole. It is this poetic invocation of the struggle which has had such a lasting influence and which reflects the concerns of other, patently feminist, women of the period. Virginia Woolf, again, gave it its most powerfully expressive voice; while rejecting the paternal figure invoked by Freud, she was also, as Abel points out, much closer to the maternal-fixated imagery employed by Klein and her devotees: "By questioning the paternal genealogies prescribed by nineteenth century fictional conventions and reinscribed by Freud, Woolf's novels of the 1920s parallel the narratives Melanie Klein was formulating simultaneously and anticipate the more radical revisions that emerged in psychoanalysis over the next half century" (1989: 3). More generally, Abel claims, "Woolf's relationship to psychoanalysis was not monolithic: many of her objections to Freudian theory do not apply to the discourse launched by Klein, which de-emphasizes sexuality, values the aesthetic, and, perhaps most importantly, calls into question the prevailing hierarchy of gender" (1989: 19). We are moving here right into the heart of the turmoil that Britain provoked: from Freud to Klein, from father to mother, from drive to object, from past to present, from sexuality to destructiveness. Once Klein arrived, nothing was the same again.

Kleinians

Klein first came to London to give a series of lectures at the Stephens' Bloomsbury house in 1925, a trip organized as a result of Alix Strachey's enthusiasm. Strachey, like many early British psychoanalysts, had gone to Berlin to be analyzed, in her case by Abraham, Klein's analyst. Hearing Klein present her work on psychoanalysis with children, Alix Strachey seems to have been impressed by her unequivocal brutality: "Strachey felt that Klein saw children as they really were, was hard-nosed about them and thus was able to help them" (Schwartz 1999: 212). Klein's six lectures in London, assiduously tuned by Alix Strachey, seem to have fed into the mixture of interest in child development and observation characteristic of British empiricism, the desolate sense of tragedy and destruction conse-quent on World War I and its aftermath (discussed below), and the British Society's (or perhaps Ernest Jones's) ambition to become distinct from the Viennese, to create its own psychoanalytic position. In any event, Klein was soon ensconced in London, analyzing Jones's children and his wife and very actively participating in the life of the Society, including assaults on Anna Freud's work in 1927 which incensed Sigmund Freud and which opened the rocky road that ended, after the Freud's arrival in London in the late 1930s, in open conflict. What was all this about? A deep dispute about the nature of the infant, the place of phantasy, the unconscious function of the mother, and – most of all – the centrality of destructive-ness.

The extraordinary viciousness of the Kleinian world has few counter-parts anywhere, except perhaps in external reality. Here, famously, is Joan Riviere, fully Kleinian by the mid-1930s:

> Limbs shall trample, kick and hit; lips, fingers and hands shall suck, twist, pinch; teeth shall bite, gnaw, mangle and cut; mouth shall devour, swallow and "kill" (annihilate), eyes kill by a look, pierce and penetrate; breath and mouth hurt by noise, as the child's own sensitive ears have experienced. One may suppose that before an infant is many months old it will not only *feel* itself performing these actions, but will have some kind of *ideas* of doing so. All these sadistic activities in phantasy are felt not only to expel the dan-ger from the self but to transfer it into the object (projection). (1936: 407)

Right from the start, Klein's work focused on the conflictual and complex phantasy life of children, uncovering brutalities and hates which fully put paid to any idealized notion of childhood innocence. What Freud had started with the notion of infantile sexuality was fully developed by Klein to por-

131

tray infancy as characterized by an inner battle in which good (love) could only precariously triumph over bad (hate), and was always on the edge of destruction. Even though her notions of paranoid–schizoid splitting and envy were not fully worked out until the 1940s and 1950s (e.g., Klein 1957), from early in her psychoanalytic career, analyzing the play of young children in the same way as others analyzed adults, Klein emphasized the brutality and punitiveness of the infantile psyche and addressed the need for the analyst to pay it due heed. In contrast to Anna Freud, who argued the necessity for a careful nurturing of the treatment alliance and placed value on the "educative" potential of psychoanalysis, Klein was unstinting in her assertion that analysis is about revelation of the deepest layers of the mind – that only thus could the terrors of unconscious impulses be faced and overcome. "Analysis is not in itself a gentle method: it cannot spare the patient *any suffering* and this applies equally to children" (1927: 344). Riviere was even clearer: "analysis . . . is not concerned with the real world, nor with the child's or the adult's adaptation to the real world, nor with sickness or health, nor virtue or vice. It is concerned simply and solely with the imaginings of the childish mind, the phantasised pleasures and the dreaded retributions"(1927: 377). The Oedipus complex and super-ego formation, dated by Freud as at about the fifth year of life, are brought right forward by Klein, so the infantile super-ego becomes "pre-Oedipal," there in the obscure prehistory of the human subject, the period which Freud largely forgot. The intensity of this is overwhelming: the biting, needy, hating, desiring infant is an exploding cannon of emotional turmoil. In the mid-1930s, Klein added a further gloss to this with a major innovation which, according to Segal (1979) amongst others, marked the real beginning of a Kleinian "school." This was the introduction of the concept of the depressive position, adumbrated in her 1935 paper, "A Contribution to the Psychogenesis of Manic-Depressive States." This is a profoundly integrative concept, in which what is stressed is the complexity of the process whereby an infant puts together her or his feelings of love and hate and owns them both. The depressive position is constituted by the movement from feelings of rage to those of loss, carried along by a recognition of the reality of ambivalence and the necessity, as well as possibility, of making something reparative out of the fissiparous impulses toward destruction. Taking hold of hate, recognizing its existence, ameliorating it through the containment which a benevolent environment (such as the analyst) can offer, owning one's destructiveness, creatively repairing the damage one has done to self and other – these are now the tendencies and aspirations of the Kleinian psyche. Abel comments, thinking of Virginia

Woolf, "For Kleinians, culture, opposed not as (paternal) law to instinct but as creativity to inner chaos, emerges from the impulse to make reparation to the mother" (1989: 11).

The context for all this in post-World-War-I culture is self-evident, and in many ways was shared by Freud with his announcement of the Death Drive in *Beyond the Pleasure Principle* and his acerbic cultural commentary in *Civilisation and its Discontents* (1920, 1930). Schwartz summarizes:

> The psychoanalysts of Europe were responding to the same events as was everyone else. Theory in psychoanalysis, in its own way, had to cope with turmoil, uncertainty and death. Melanie Klein's vision of the child's inner world was as situated in the uncertainties and brutalities of the aftermath of the First World War as was the literature, the movies and the architecture. (1999: 199)

For the British, too, the concern with tragedy and the fragmentation of the past was overwhelming. By the mid- to late 1920s, the nature of World War I was very well known and its devastating consequences had been felt across an entire generation. Everything had changed and had to change. *The Waste Land* (1922), despite or perhaps alongside its misogyny and reactionary class bias, grabbed hold of this feeling and represented it with appalling precision, in a manner congruent with Freud's later versions of psychoanalysis and especially with the fascination with destructiveness which was Klein's specific contribution. Ellman, in a marvelous examination of the poem's "abjection" (a concept taken from Kristeva 1983, itself inspired in part by Klein), comments on the wiping out of a history which then returns, plaguing the text, like the return of the repressed which in Freud is the prototype of death: "Whereas Freud discovers the death drive in the compulsion to repeat, *The Waste Land* stages it in the compulsion to citation" (1990: 188). Biographically,

> written in the aftermath of the First World War, and in the midst of a disastrous marriage, the poem has so much to forget: madness, feminism, sexuality, the slaughtered millions, and the rattle of its own exhausted idioms. Yet . . . *The Waste Land* works like an obsessive ceremonial, because it re-inscribes the horrors it is trying to repress. For Freud argues that obsessive rituals repeat the very acts that they are thought to neutralize: the ritual, he says, is ostensibly a protection against the prohibited act; "but *actually*. . . a repetition of it". (1990: 179–80)

The "waste" in *The Waste Land* is what constantly returns, the living dead; the ghosts and fragments, of people and particularly of writing. Obsessed by death, both literature and psychoanalysis have to ask what it is in the modern consciousness that can create such vicious fragmentation, such a violent spell.

> The speaker of *The Waste Land* also stages his own death when he conjures up the writings of the dead, sacrificing voice and face to their ventriloquy. In this sense he resembles the child in *Beyond the Pleasure Principle*, who stages his extinction in the mirror. Freud compares his grandchild to the victims of shell-shock, who relive their terrors in their dreams, repeating death as if it were desire. This is the game *The Waste Land* plays, and the nightmare that it cannot lay to rest, as it stages the ritual of its own destruction. (Ellman 1990: 198)

"Limbs shall trample, kick and hit," writes Riviere (1936), and Klein (1932) describes a vast range of destructive impulses in the young child, for example (p.128) "an early stage of development which is governed by the child's aggressive trends against its mother's body and in which its predominant wish is to rob her body of its contents and destroy it." *The Waste Land*, too, "stages the ritual of its own destruction," as did, in World War I, the whole of European society. Not surprising, then, that Klein should be attractive in Britain and that the growth of fascism and Nazism in the 1930s should simply augment that attraction, as explanations had to be sought for the continued eruption of the bestial tumor out of the body of the modern world.

Conclusion

Psychoanalysis both fed into and off the British modernist scene before 1939. Dependent upon its artistic and literary commentators as much as its professional practitioners, it took off both as a mode of therapy and as a cultural form, the "climate of opinion" of Auden's famous reference (1966). By the time the Freuds arrived in 1938, and notwithstanding the battle with the Kleinians which they entered into within the British Psycho-Analytic Society, psychoanalysis had planted deep roots in the country and the words of Freud, beautifully translated, were read throughout the English-speaking world. For British culture, especially literary culture, the advent of psychoanalysis was the discovery of an intellectual system, a methodology, and a vocabulary that could parallel the literary imagination and give it greater depth. Indeed, part of Virginia Woolf's opposition seems to have been due to an appreciation of its claims as a rival to imaginative literature, although she also clearly (and in the light of some psychoanalytic approaches to literature, correctly) objected to its reduction of characters to "cases" (Abel 1989: 17).

Most significantly, the models of psychic activity produced first by Freud and then by Klein were very well attuned to the concerns of interwar modernism in particular. They began with the vortex and the eruptive, disruptive capacities of the underworld – revolutionary mass, occluded rhythms, surreptitious discourses, repressed desires – and proceeded to the phantasmagoric confusions of infantile rage. From Freud to Klein went the trajectory, from paternal to maternal and masculine to feminine, from the detective task of piecing together the past to the intense emotion of the immediate, psychophysical encounter of self and other, from the discovery of the sexual impulse to that of death. Psychoanalysis, mediated and transformed in London, expressed, coded, and theorized the deeply traumatized consciousness that lived, suspended unhappily between relentless devastation and the rise of fascism. A kind of coda perhaps, to the hope that a sweet reason would prevail: after this time, no one could deny the irrational its due.

References and Further Reading

Abel, E. 1989. *Virginia Woolf and the Fictions of Psychoanalysis*. Chicago: University of Chicago Press.
Appignanesi, L. and Forrester, J. 1992. *Freud's Women*. London: Weidenfeld & Nicolson.
Auden, W. H. 1966. In Memory of Sigmund Freud. In *Collected Shorter Poems*, pp. 166–70. London: Faber & Faber.
Bakan, D. 1958 [1990]. *Sigmund Freud and the Jewish Mystical Tradition*. London: Free Association Books.
Berman, M. 1982. *All That is Solid Melts into Air*. London: Verso.
Bion, W. 1962. *Learning from Experience*. London: Maresfield.
Chisholm, D. 1992. *H. D.'s Freudian Poetics: Psychoanalysis in Translation*. Ithaca: Cornell University Press.
Eagleton, T. 1986. *Against the Grain*. London: Verso.
Eliot, T. S. 1922 [1940]. The Waste Land. In *The Waste Land and Other Poems*. London: Faber.
Ellman, M. 1990. Eliot's Abjection, In J. Fletcher and A. Benjamin, eds., *Abjection, Melancholia and Love: The Work of Julia Kristeva*, pp. 179–99. London: Routledge.
Freud, S. 1920 [1984]. *Beyond the Pleasure Principle*. Harmondsworth: Penguin.

——. 1923 [1984]. *The Ego and the Id*. Harmondsworth: Penguin.

——. 1926 [1962]. The Question of Lay Analysis. In S. Freud, *Two Short Accounts of Psychoanalysis*, pp. 89–170. Harmondsworth: Penguin.

——. 1930 [1985]. *Civilization and its Discontents*. Harmondsworth: Penguin.

——. 1933 [1973]. *New Introductory Lectures on Psychoanalysis*. Harmondsworth: Penguin

——. 1939 [1985]. *Moses and Monotheism*. Harmondsworth: Penguin.

Frosh, S. 2001. Freud and Jewish Dreaming. *Psychoanalysis and History* 3: 18–27.

Gellner, E. 1985. *The Psychoanalytic Movement*. London: Paladin.

Guntrip, H. 1968. *Schizoid Phenomena, Object Relations and the Self*. London: Hogarth Press.

H. D. 1948 [1985]. *Tribute to Freud*. Manchester: Carcanet.

Hinshelwood, R. 1995. Psychoanalysis in Britain: Points of Cultural Access, 1893–1918. *International Journal of Psycho-Analysis* 76: 135–51.

——. 1998. The Organizing of Psychoanalysis in Britain. *Psychoanalysis and History* 1: 87–102.

Horney, K. 1926. Flight from Womanhood. *International Journal of Psychoanalysis* 7: 324–39.

Jones, E. 1927. The Early Development of Female Sexuality. *International Journal of Psychoanalysis* 8: 459–72.

——. 1935. Early Female Sexuality. *International Journal of Psycho–Analysis* 16: 263–73.

Klein, M. 1927. Symposium on Child Analysis. *International Journal of Psycho-Analysis* 8: 339–70.

——. 1932. *The Psycho-Analysis of Children*. London: Hogarth Press.

——. 1935. A Contribution to the Psychogenesis of Manic-Depressive States. *International Journal of Psycho-Analysis* 16: 145–74.

——. 1957 [1975]. Envy and Gratitude. In M. Klein, *Envy and Gratitude and Other Works*, pp. 176–235. New York: Delta.

Kohon, G. 1986. Notes on the History of the Psychoanalytic Movement in Great Britain. In G. Kohon, ed., *The British School of Psychoanalysis*, pp. 15–51. London: Free Association Books.

Kristeva, J. 1983. Freud and Love. In T. Moi, ed., *The Kristeva Reader*, pp. 238–71. Oxford: Blackwell, 1986.

Meisel, Perry and Kendrick, Walter. 1986. *Bloomsbury/Freud: The Letters of James and Alix Strachey, 1924–1925*. London: Chatto & Windus.

Moi, T. 1989. Patriarchal Thought and the Drive for Knowledge. In T. Brennan, ed., *Between Feminism and Psychoanalysis*, pp. 189–205. London: Routledge.

Rayner, E. 1991. *The Independent Mind in British Psychoanalysis*. London: Free Association Books.

Riviere, J. 1927. Symposium on Child Analysis. *International Journal of Psycho-Analysis* 8: 370–7.

——. 1929. Womanliness as a Masquerade. *International Journal of Psycho-Analysis*

10: 303–13.

——. 1936. On the Genesis of Psychical Conflict in Earliest Infancy. *International Journal of Psycho-Analysis* 17: 395–422.

Roith, E. 1987. *The Riddle of Freud*. London: Tavistock.

Rustin, M. 1999. Psychoanalysis: The Last Modernism? In D. Bell, ed., *Psychoanalysis and Culture*, pp. 105–21. London: Duckworth.

Sayers, J. 2000. *Kleinians*. Cambridge: Polity.

Schwartz, J. 1999. *Cassandra's Daughter: A History of Psychoanalysis in Europe and America*. Harmondsworth: Allen Lane.

Segal, H. 1979. *Klein*. Glasgow: Fontana.

Stonebridge, L. 1998. *The Destructive Element: British Psychoanalysis and Modernism*. Basingstoke and London: Macmillan.

7

Language: "History is a nightmare from which I am trying to awake"

April McMahon

Modernism and Modern Linguistics

It is perhaps both inevitable and appropriate for this essay on language to begin by considering the meaning of the word "modern," at least in the context of its even more problematic relative, "modernism." Kermode (1968: 27) argues that "modern" implies "a serious relationship with the past . . . that requires criticism and indeed radical re-imagining"; and this interpretation provides an entirely appropriate framework for the development of linguistics during the period from 1880 to 1939. In the work of two of the best-known linguists of the early twentieth century, Ferdinand de Saussure in Europe and Leonard Bloomfield in the United States, we find an acknowledgment of the value of their late nineteenth-century predecessors, along with Kermode's "criticism and indeed radical re-imagining." The contributions of these two linguists in particular lead to the development of an awareness of linguistic complexity (and especially in Saussure's case, of a framework within which to place and understand that complexity) which goes beyond the assumptions of orderliness characterizing much linguistic work in the previous generation. The "serious relationship with the past" of Kermode's definition is also relevant in a slightly less direct sense, since the dominant school of late nineteenth-century linguistics had as its primary preoccupation the study of the linguistic past, and hence of language change. Saussure and Bloomfield, while not rejecting the study of history, place the focus of modern linguistics squarely on synchronic study, or the characterization and understanding of languages at a particular point in time, and on general principles of language which are intended to be universally relevant and independent of time; these overarching, theoretical concerns remain at the heart of modern linguistics.

The Neogrammarians

Linguistics has a long and intermittently distinguished history, and it is not at all appropriate to think of a fascination with language and an attempt to understand it as developing suddenly in the last quarter of the nineteenth century. However, it is quite clear that the study of language did take a great leap forward during this earliest part of the modernist period; and paradoxically, that leap forward resulted from a serious study of the linguistic past.

Towards the end of the nineteenth century, various intellectual strands were developing, in the study of language and elsewhere, which set the scene for the formalization of historical linguistics. The later Victorian period saw a great expansion of the historical sciences, with geology, archaeology, and evolutionary biology increasingly debated, and increasingly taken up by amateur naturalists. In more strictly linguistic terms, Sanskrit, the ancient religious and literary language of India, was discovered by European scholars. As Indian culture and history became a preoccupation of fashionable society, so linguistic scholars uncovered similarities between Sanskrit and the other classical languages, Latin and Greek. These affinities led to the hypothesis, now universally accepted, that these languages are related: they, and many present-day languages from Hindi to Russian, English to Armenian, and Italian to Welsh, are daughters or granddaughters of the unrecorded Proto-Indo-European, and their relationships can be shown in linguistic family trees. Such trees, based on those proposed for species by taxonomists like Linnaeus and developed further in an evolutionary context by Darwin and his followers, were introduced into linguistics by Schleicher in the 1860s in a rather literal fashion, with carefully drawn bark, leaves, and birds nesting in the branches; but in a more idealized and schematic form, they became commonplace as illustrations of claimed linguistic relationship. It is entirely natural that linguists should then seek ways of demonstrating these proposed relationships, and of reconstructing the unattested protolanguages which inhabited the higher reaches of the trees.

The development of the Comparative Method, still regarded by linguists as the 'gold standard' technique for establishing the relatedness of languages and for reconstructing their ancestral forms, predated the main activities of the Neogrammarians in the late nineteenth century, but provided a necessary context for their ideas. The key idea here is that we can identify regular correspondences of one sound in a particular language, with another, different sound in a related language, in a whole range of words where the meanings in the two languages are the same or similar: so, we might compare French *père, poisson, pied*, all with initial [p], with English *father, fish, foot*, all with initial [f]. These regular correspondences suggest that the daughter language sounds, which are now different, were once the same. Since Latin, the ancestor of French, has spellings that suggest [p] in the equivalent words, we can assume that the [p] forms are older and that some change has taken place in the history of English, or the branch of the family to which English belongs, so that we reconstruct *p for the beginnings of these words in Proto-Indo-European. Of course, this example is very limited – many more words, sounds, and languages would be used in a real case of Comparative Reconstruction – but it provides the bare bones of that sort of argument.

However, although these correspondences and comparisons were an accepted part of mid-nineteenth-century historical linguistics, there was relatively little emphasis on the actual changes by which a reconstructed sound like *p would become the [f] we find today in English (and German, for that matter). Typically, these changes were explained as part of a natural tendency toward decay in languages; this view of language as an organism, which eventually grows old and deteriorates, seems to have been one held by Schleicher, for instance. Alternatively, changes in language were ascribed to particular characteristics of speakers or their environments, so that race or climate might be held responsible. However, the gradual acceptance of evolutionary thinking in biology superseded this kind of development-and-decay model, as well as lengthening the time-frame involved, so that Latin, or Sanskrit, or Hebrew, or even Proto-Indo-European were no longer seen as likely candidates for the first language of mankind. These changes in perspective led to the Neogrammarians' concentration on the formulation of linguistic changes.

The Neogrammarians (or, to give them their contemporary German title, *Junggrammatiker*) were a group of historical linguists working mainly in Leipzig in the last quarter of the nineteenth century. They typically came from fairly standard philological backgrounds: Karl Brugmann and Hermann Osthoff were trained as classicists, while Hermann Paul's background was in the history of Germanic, for example. What they shared was a recognition that the Comparative Method could only be successfully and rigorously formulated if there was some understanding of how sound change worked. That is to say, it is all very well to claim that *p can turn into [f]; but how can we be sure that this is the more likely change, rather than *f becoming [p]? And why should we believe that all cases of *p are equally likely to become [f]? Moreover, why should any instances of *p change into anything else at all?

The Neogrammarians addressed these questions by conducting research in two very different directions. First, they produced general hypotheses about the way language and language change work; these provide a framework within which predictions can be made, and the most famous is the regularity hypothesis, part of Osthoff and Brugmann's "Neogrammarian manifesto" of 1878 (see Morpurgo Davies 1998), which states that sound change is regular and exceptionless. This sort of grand universal statement was very much part of the spirit of the age, mirroring the natural laws being proposed in the physical and biological sciences, and reflecting a sense that scientific enquiry demanded the recognition of principled limits on the way the world and its constituents operate. If we accept the regularity hypothesis, we will automatically assume that, if one case of *p changes to [f], absolutely all cases should follow suit: and moreover, if some do not, we must find out why. That is, we should try to identify something in the context which determines which cases change and which do not. In the example of *p and [f], there are indeed words which do not show a change – so Latin *spuo*, "spit," corresponds to Old English *spiwan*, not the nonexistent **sfiwan* we might expect. As it turns out, each unchanged [p] in English immediately follows a particular set of sounds, including [s], so that we can say *p changed into [f] except in a particular, specifiable set of contexts – as Karl Verner famously expressed it, "There must . . . exist a rule for the irregularities; the task is to find this rule" (1978: 36). This search for rules and regularities characterizes the Neogrammarian program, and put historical linguistics on a secure and scientific footing. Indeed, reconstruction is only possible if we do accept the regularity hypothesis: changes which are regular and which take place in a definable set of environments can be reversed to tell us the most likely ancestral form, whereas if change was sporadic or random, reversing its effects in this way would not be feasible.

However, expecting regularity and formulating laws still does not tell us which specific regular sound change we should expect to find, and the Neogrammarians recognized that the likelihood of particular changes could only be established by considering the characteristics of modern, present-day languages, to determine which sounds and structures were most common. Similarly, as comparison and reconstruction became more detailed, it became more important to show that the characteristics proposed for reconstructed systems like Proto-Indo-European were realistic: and again, this required a general knowledge of possible and likely linguistic patterns. The range of languages studied correspondingly became wider, with the Neogrammarians writing grammars of Armenian and Lithuanian, for example, alongside the Romance and Germanic languages. This increasing breadth was complemented by increasing depth, as the study of dialects began to develop: research by Ascoli, Wenker, Gilliéron, and others marks the beginning of dialectological documentation for Italian, German, and French.

Increasingly, this dialectological dimension brought the role of the individual into focus, with Hermann Paul the foremost of the Neogrammarians in developing elementary psychological explanations for sound change. This emphasis on the individual's use of language in turn foregrounds the role of variation in the speech community, which colors much immediately post-Neogrammarian work: Schuchardt, for example, was a pioneer in considering language mixing and the social meaning and relevance of language, and even embarked on a study of pidgins and creoles, which at the time were still seen as broken, incomplete versions of more sophisticated European languages. Schuchardt and Schmidt also developed the so-called wave model in opposition to the family tree: according to the wave model, contact and influence of geographically adjacent languages were at least as important as characteristics inherited from a common ancestor. Nonetheless, the Neogrammarians as a school were adamant in attributing present-day variation to historical causes. Again, they focused on apparent exceptions in the structure of modern languages, but again their main concern was to identify the underlying rules. For example, the normal means of marking the plural on English nouns is to add -*s*, giving *cats* from *cat*, *books* from *book*, and *aardvarks* from *aardvark*. However, there are some nouns with exceptional, irregular plurals, including *feet* (rather than **foots) from *foot*. The Neogrammarian approach in this sort of case would be to assume that the noun in question was once regular, and to identify the factors that made it become irregular: in this case, an early plural ending -*i* (which was subsequently lost) caused the stem vowel to change in the plural, but not in the singular, and the two then developed differently. Consequently, although observations of present-day languages are valuable, their explanation is necessarily historical, leading to Paul's famous assertion that the only truly scientific approach to language is historical.

Saussure

The Neogrammarian approach, however, contains an inbuilt contradiction: as Morpurgo Davies puts it,

> The upholders of the theory that modern languages were the best field of enquiry were in fact Indo-Europeanists or medievalists . . . . Moreover, the scholars who pleaded for a "systematic exploration of the general conditions of the life of language" . . . in fact spent most of their working life dealing with . . . minute problems of historical morphology or phonology. (1998: 237)

The time was clearly ripe for a return to the most general level of enquiry. The question of what language is, and what languages are, had not had to be asked in the earlier nineteenth century, when Schleicher's organic view saw each language as subject to a life-cycle culminating in decay and death. However, the new dominance of Darwinian thinking, the scientific, historical approach characteristic of the turn of the century, and the new recognition of contemporary complexity among the Neogrammarians and dialectologists demanded a revised answer, and a theoretical context for that answer. No single individual was more responsible for providing these than Ferdinand de Saussure.

Virginia Woolf tells us that "in or about December, 1910, human character changed" (1924: 320). While it is not possible to date the major change in perspective away from the study of linguistic change with quite this precision, it is impossible to overestimate the contribution of three series of lectures given in Geneva by Saussure in 1907, 1908–9, and 1910–11. Saussure might in some ways seem the least likely architect of this change, being himself steeped in the Neogrammarian tradition; moreover, he did not himself write up his lectures for publication, and it is remarkable that we have his work to consult at all. When Saussure died in 1913, two of his colleagues, recognizing the importance of his thinking, attempted to reconstruct his main arguments, working from the few documents Saussure himself had left, and the recollections and notes of students who had attended the lecture series: the resulting book, the *Cours de linguistique générale* or *Course in General Linguistics*, is therefore strictly speaking neither a single course, nor by Saussure. His contribution is therefore in some ways paradoxical, and as we shall see, it is also based on the recognition of paradoxes and oppositions.

Ferdinand de Saussure was born in 1857 – this, as Culler (1985: 13) points out, was one year later than Freud and one year earlier than Durkheim, and as we shall see, Saussure's work provides rather less tenuous links with psychology and sociology. Saussure began his university career in his home town of Geneva in 1875, intending to study physics and chemistry; however, he was already an accomplished learner of languages, both ancient and modern, and decided quite swiftly that his real interests lay here. After his first year at Geneva, he therefore moved to Leipzig, and spent the next four years between Leipzig and Berlin, studying Indo-European languages. It follows that he was in the heartland of Neogrammarian activity at the crucial time; and indeed, Saussure's first book, and the only one published in his lifetime, was a *tour de force* of Neogrammarian scholarship, involving the reconstruction of the sounds of Proto-Indo-European. This highly influential work featured Saussure's hypothesis of a group of sounds now commonly referred to as the laryngeals: these have no direct descendants in the modern Indo-European daughter languages, but have left indirect traces which Saussure used to hypothesize their earlier existence. This early linguistic detective work was only confirmed years after Saussure's death, when the decipherment of texts in the ancient Indo-European language Hittite showed a particular symbol consistently where Saussure had postulated one of the laryngeals. Although his conclusions were ahead of their time, his methods, based on the classic reconstructive techniques of the Neogrammarian school, were very strongly of it; and this rigorous and detailed example of historical linguistic scholarship was published in 1878 – when Saussure was twenty-one.

After this early and spectacular success, Saussure became a well-known exponent of Indo-European studies in Paris, but unexpectedly returned to a professorship in Geneva in 1891. Here, he published very little, turning gradually away from his historical research and the typical preoccupations of the age, and toward much more general, theoretical considerations. This refocusing occurred almost despite himself: Culler quotes a personal letter from 1894, in which Saussure notes that he would really much prefer to get back to his Indo-European vowels: "The utter inadequacy of current terminology, the need to reform it and, in order to do that, to demonstrate what sort of object language is, continually spoils my pleasure in philology, though I have no dearer wish than not to be made to think about the nature of language in general" (1985: 15).

Here, Saussure articulates as a somewhat frustrated individual, a paradox which was beginning to be felt by the Neogrammarians as a school. As Morpurgo Davies notes:

> dissatisfaction with the current state of affairs surfaces at this point in time and no doubt also there is a yearning for a serious discussion of more general problems: from this point of view Saussure's discontent is representative. There is also an increasing realization that some problems cannot be discussed within a purely historical (i.e. diachronic) framework. (1998: 325)

As we have seen, the main linguistic preoccupation of the Neogrammarian era was with historical issues; but it turns out that, to understand and appreciate those individual historical changes fully, we have to see how and where they fit into the greater scheme of things. A single piece of jigsaw puzzle can be an object of some interest – intriguing partial pictures can probably be made out from it, and its shape may be strange or pleasing. But there is no escaping the fact that this single piece does fit into an overall design, and make part of a larger pattern; and it is only by looking at the complete picture that we can see how the single pieces work together. Saussure, while apparently wishing to focus on his single pieces, nonetheless reluctantly made the first serious attempt to provide that overall framework.

Arguably, his first step here was to articulate the separation of the diachronic, or historical perspective, from the synchronic – and here we have the first of Saussure's famous oppositions or dichotomies. One might assume that if diachrony is history, synchrony must mean now: but in fact, the distinction is not between past and present, but between the study of the movement through time on the one hand, and the consideration of a single stage, a frozen moment in time, on the other. A synchronic study, that is, can involve the English or French or Quechua of October 2002; but it can equally involve the Old English of King Alfred, or the Norman French of 1066, or the Quechua spoken at the height of the Inca empire; or indeed, some other language, say Latin or Proto-Indo-European, which is no longer spoken except in the form of its highly diversified daughters. So long as we are considering a particular language at a particular stage in its history, we are practicing synchronic linguistics. One reason for Saussure's concentration on synchronic description was his recognition of the importance of the native speaker, and the native speaker's perspective and perceptions, in linguistic analysis: this shift away from the pronouncements of grammarians, and toward the question of what ordinary speakers know, also ushers in a greater concentration on the social aspects of language. Since, as Saussure reminds us, native speakers only very rarely have access to information about the history of their own languages, that historical information must also be secondary for linguists, and we must begin our task of describing and understanding language in the way that native speakers also do, by concentrating on the information available at a particular moment in time. Saussure's analogy here is to a game of chess: a spectator can come into a room during a game, and will be able to understand the state of play, and even predict the likely outcome, without knowing quite how the players have arrived at the present situation. If the newcomer was asked to take over from one of the existing players, her main requirement is to grasp the current relative positions of the pieces on the board: she might be interested in what decisions the earlier player has made, and hence in why the current situation has arisen, but strictly speaking she does not need to know this in order to continue the game, and it is not especially likely to affect the standard of her play to know, or not to know, the sequence of earlier moves.

This does not mean, however, that Saussure sees diachronic work as unimportant or uninteresting: recall that his own early work involved the reconstruction of aspects of the Proto-Indo-European sound system. Instead, he tells us that the synchronic and the diachronic interact, imagining history as a vertical axis, and the set of synchronic, contemporary systems as a horizontal one, which will inevitably intersect at a particular point. However, he argues very clearly and insistently that synchronic study has priority, and hence that we must establish the characteristics of the language at the point when a change begins, and at the later point when it ends, in order to produce a valid comparison and to understand how, and ultimately why, the change took place. Saussure is not devaluing diachronic work, but he is saying that synchronic description is necessary as a first step. Moreover, this takes us into even deeper, more theoretical waters: if we are to produce synchronic descriptions, and understand what a language is at a particular time, then we must also confront the more general problem of what language is.

Indeed, "Saussure's own view of the importance of his enterprise was that he posed the basic question of *what a language is*, and held it to be the fundamental responsibility of linguistics to provide an answer" (Anderson 1985: 18). Saussure's essential insight is that each language is a system (or strictly, a whole series of interacting systems), and that the identity and behavior of each element depends on its place in the system. Languages, more accurately, are systems of signs, where the sign is composed of two parts: the signifier, which is the linguistic part of the equation, and the signified, the meaning in the speaker's mind or in the world. So, the English word *cat*, in either its written form or as spoken [kat], forms one part of a sign; the word is usable because native speakers of English associate it with a particular meaning, or concept, in this case relating to a specific sort of animal. If an English speaker is shown a picture of a cat, or has that concept described, she will retrieve the word *cat*; and conversely, given the word and asked what it means, she will describe, or draw, or point to a convenient illustrative cat.

However, Saussure also points out that signs are essentially arbitrary: that is, the association between *cat* and the creature in question exists only by convention. Native speakers of English learn it that way; but there is no intrinsic connection between that string of letters or sounds, and that particular meaning. For one thing, if the link between signifier and signified was not arbitrary, there would be no differences between languages; and for another, the arbitrariness of the connection allows languages to change through time. Saussure above all people knew that change was a fact of linguistic life, and his doctrine of arbitrariness shows how the purely conventional connection between signified and signifier allows either to drift. Of course, there are odd examples where the link between signifier and signified is not arbitrary, but natural: the obvious example is onomatopoeia, for instance in imitative animal-noise words like *moo, meeow, woof,* and so on. Even here, the link is not an absolute one: objectively, there isn't that much difference between the noises cockerels make in English, French- and German-speaking communities, although they apparently say *cock-a-doodle-doo, cocorico*, and *kikeriki*, respectively.

The signifier–signified connection is also more complex than a simple choice, for each language, of what word to assign to what concept, since there is no given, agreed list of signifieds for which each language must find signifiers. Languages differ widely in the range of meanings they lexify, or provide words for, and this also changes over time. One of the best-known examples here concerns English, which typically has a word for an animal and a separate word for meat from that animal: hence, *sheep* goes with *mutton, pig* with *pork, cow* with *beef,* and so on. This is not the case for French, where *mouton, boeuf,* and so on signal both the sheep or cow, and the meat derived from it; but it was not true either of Old English. The distinction between the animal words and the meat words only developed in Middle English, as a result of influence from French: English, which David Crystal has described as "the great vacuum-cleaner of languages" on account of its prolific borrowing of vocabulary, hoovered up the words now used for meat, along with many others, from French following the Norman Conquest. Since the French-speaking aristocracy tended to see the meat rather than the animal, the more prestigious French loans were specialized for the table, and the native Germanic forms were restricted to the actual animals, the messier concern of the English-speaking peasantry.

The case of colors provides another example of cross-linguistic variation, since by no means all languages have separate words for the considerable spectrum of colors recognized in English or other European languages, with brown, blue, and red alongside magenta, burnt sienna and aquamarine, leaving aside the more abstruse concoctions of paint charts or make-up counters. At the opposite end of the scale, there are languages with words only for "black" and "white" (or more accurately, "darker" and "lighter"); others add "red"; and so it goes on, with color terms being added in a predictable and repeated order. However, the language-specific nature of this variation also means we must pay attention to the whole range of labeled colors in a given language in order to understand the meaning of any single color term. While we might initially consider "black" to be a universal and clear concept (there is, after all, a scientific definition of black and white, namely the absence of light and the combination of all frequencies of light in the spectrum respectively), it turns out to be no such thing. The signifier for "black" in a language where there are only "black" and "white" will correspond to a different signified than would be the case if "red" were labeled too, and this would be different again in a language like English, with a wealth of color terms. What this also means is that any individual learning a particular language will have to learn what the signifiers actually mean, by contrasting them with the other signifiers in the same semantic area. Culler (1985: 25) expresses this very clearly, noting that we cannot hope to teach a learner of English what *brown* means by showing him a large number of brown objects, then taking him into another room and asking him to identify only the brown objects from a large collection. The problem is that we have, as native speakers of English, arrived at our knowledge of what *brown* means by learning that it contrasts with all the other color terms which are not brown: rather than defining brownness intrinsically, as light at a particular frequency, we learn that brown is everything that is not black, white, purple, orange, green, and so on. This kind of extrinsic definition is highly characteristic of the structure of language, and shows the essentially systemic nature of linguistic signs.

What this also means is that difference is absolutely vital to understanding how languages work. Units of language gain their identity from their place in a system of other units, each of which is meaningfully distinct from all the others. *Brown* signals a particular, potentially shifting section of the color spectrum; and what really matters is not the specific characteristics that brown things share, but the fact that they can be distinguished from black ones, blue ones, and red ones. Saussure gives us an analogy to help us out with what is potentially a rather difficult concept. He asks us to consider the 8.25 Geneva to Paris train. This train has a particular position in the system – that is, in the set of trains which travel each day from Geneva to Paris, or indeed the larger system of trains which travel from Geneva to anywhere. What matters is not any specific characteristic of that physical train, because in fact there are likely to be different engines, carriages, and so on traveling from Geneva to Paris at 8.25 on any two different days. It doesn't even matter (at least for reasons of identification; it might matter to the grumbling passengers) whether the 8.25 leaves at 8.25 or not. A passenger might turn up at 8.25, catch a train from Geneva going to Paris, and be told that in fact it is not the 8.25, but the delayed 6.25 (the delayed 8.25 will leave at 10.25). Although this might sound surreal, the passenger will accept the argument (and not waste time looking for her seat reservation).

This issue of distinctness also has some bearing on the nature of the signifier. It would be tempting to identify the signifier with some actual utterance, which is physically real and measurable; but this does not seem to be Saussure's intention. We have already seen that the 8.25 Geneva to Paris train need not share the same physical characteristics each day, yet it can still be "the same" train. The same goes for language. If I say the word *cat* ten times, minute differences in airflow and in the configuration of my articulators will mean the ten resulting utterances will be minutely different too. If you say *cat* ten times, your ten utterances will also all be slightly different, and each will in turn be slightly more different from each of mine. Somehow, however, we recognize that each of us is repeating the same word. What this means is that humans can abstract away, in interpreting speech, from insignificant, low-level variation, as they identify which signifier is intended; and in turn, this means the signifier cannot be directly equated with any particular pronunciation, or occasion of speaking or writing. The signifier must be something more abstract, which can more plausibly be shared by different speakers.

We now arrive at Saussure's second major dichotomy, between *parole* and *langue*. *Parole* is the easy one: it means particular examples of linguistic behavior – actual, observable, recordable instances of speech or writing (or, anachronistically but importantly, signing). The fact that I pronounce an [r] at the end of *car*, while you may well not do so, is a fact of *parole*, as is the variation between different utterances of the same word. However, the fact that we recognize our rather different pronunciations as being the same word, or strictly the same signified, is to do with our shared resources as speakers of English, and hence is an aspect of *langue*. It follows that the more abstract system is part of *langue*, which Saussure considers to be the main concern of the linguist, an attitude which has remained central to theoretical linguistics into the Chomskyan era of the mid-twentieth century and beyond.

Of all Saussure's terms, *langue* is perhaps the most challenging to interpret. The definition included in the *Course* (13–14) sees *langue* as what each individual speaker learns, on the basis of what he or she hears in the linguistic environment: it is a "hoard deposited by the practice of speech in speakers who belong to the same community, a grammatical system which, to all intents and purposes, exists in the mind of each speaker." At the same time, however, Saussure tells us that *langue* is not complete in any single individual – only a collective consideration of all speakers of the language in question would provide us with a full, perfect picture of their *langue*. The complexity of this definition lies in the fact that *langue* seems to be simultaneously social (since it is shared by members of the same speech community) and individual (since it "exists in the mind of each speaker"). There are some problems here which persist into Chomsky's much later distinction of performance, or E-language, from competence, or I-language, to do with the question of whether two speakers of the same language can really be said to share the same internal system. Where, for instance, do accent differences fit in? I might very well want to say that my pronunciation of *car*, with an [r] at the end, is part of my system; and speakers of English who do not have a final consonant in this word will nonetheless accept my pronunciation as possible within the general envelope of "English." But does this mean that all the signifieds for "car" in all the minds of all the native speakers of English must be identical in form, so that somehow I get my pronunciation with the [r] from a more common Standard Southern British English version without (or alternatively, that Standard Southern British English speakers start out with a mental representation of *car* that has my [r] in it, and somehow lose it somewhere between the brain and the vocal tract)? There is a more substantial problem for Saussure himself, in that he seems to regard combining forms into larger units as necessarily part of *parole*, although clearly native speakers do acquire more abstract knowledge of the possible syntactic patterns for their language, which would seem to place aspects of syntax firmly in *langue*.

Despite these inclarities and points of debate, however, linguistics takes a significant step forward with Saussure's distinction of *langue* from *parole*, since this allows us to focus on the system, ignoring all the minute details of variation which might be crucial to a complete description of the language use of an individual, but which are simply distractions if we seek to understand the more general, shared patterns underlying that language use and unifying speakers of a single language despite their superficial differences. All this leads to another of Saussure's dichotomies, this time his assertion that language is crucially form, and not substance. By this, he means that the language, the underlying system learned and shared by different individuals, is an abstract system of signs which gain their identity from their differences, and hence from their place in that system. The system, that is, is relational. The precise substance, or actual shape which speakers give those elements on particular occasions of utterance, is not central to linguistic analysis, and indeed needs to be abstracted away to allow the linguist to focus on the essential, shared element of language.

However, recognizing this common, shared system, along with the central tenet of the arbitrariness of the sign, means Saussure's ideas are also necessarily social. If the sign is arbitrary, then meaning is achieved, and language use is made possible, if the members of a speech community tacitly agree to maintain a particular connection between the signifier and the signified. A particular *langue* at a particular synchronic stage is therefore a set of social conventions, which can themselves be studied. This also means that Saussure's work opens the door to the study of how and why departures from those conventions may arise, and hence to social causes of linguistic change. Paradoxically again, a focus on the synchronic can cast light on the diachronic.

This recognition of language as a social fact also relates Saussure to his contemporaries, Freud and Durkheim, and to modernism: as Culler (1985: 72) tells us, the contributions of all three men depend on the acceptance of a social reality, and all three "reverse the perspective which makes society the result of individual behaviour and insist that behaviour is made possible by collective social systems which individuals have assimilated, consciously or subconsciously." This change of perspective allows the development of psychoanalysis; of Durkheim's social milieu and the collective unconscious; and of a social, systemic approach to language. The recognition of such social norms, and our awareness of their existence and of their effects on the individual, is in turn surely central to the development of modernism.

Structuralism in the United States

Just as Saussure was profoundly influenced by his Neogrammarian predecessors, while simultaneously articulating a general discontent over their
concentration on diachrony and on specifics, so he in turn influenced the
subsequent development of linguistics. The locus of activity in linguistics
shifted, as the twentieth century moved on, from Europe to the United
States, where Saussure's systemic, structuralist approach was accepted but
developed for a new context, and a new set of problems. Leonard
Bloomfield, one of the key players in the development of American structuralism, was certainly aware of Saussure's contribution, and indeed, as
Matthews (1993: 6) reports, reviewed the second edition of the *Course in
General Linguistics* in 1923, considering it a "clear and rigorous demonstration of fundamental principles." Bloomfield continued, alluding to parallel developments of similar, structuralist thinking in North America, by
noting that "Most of what the author says has long been 'in the air', and
has been here and there fragmentarily expressed" (cited in Matthews 1993:
6). However, the specifics of the American situation led again to a revised
perspective and to new developments of Saussure's structuralist principles.

American scholars had been involved on the fringes of the
Neogrammarian movement, notably William Dwight Whitney, a Sanskritist
who studied in Berlin and taught at Yale; and as one might expect, much
of the work in American linguistics at the outset of our period involved
the comparison, classification and reconstruction of languages. The main
difference was not one of methodology, but of data: linguists in the New
World recognized that in the native languages of the Americas they were
dealing with a fascinating, unfamiliar resource – but also a diminishing
one, as speakers turned increasingly to the more recently arrived, socially
dominant Indo-European languages, and especially English. Two scholars
in particular are associated with this early phase of descriptivist linguistics
in North America, namely Franz Boas and Edward Sapir.

Boas was born in Germany and trained as a natural scientist, becoming
interested in the Eskimo peoples, whose culture and language he began to
study. Since most linguistics up to this point had focused on widely-spo-
ken European languages, which could be studied by consultation of grammars or by introspection, or on ancient languages like Latin, Greek, and
Sanskrit, for which only written data are available, there were few worked-
out methods for fieldwork in cases where an investigator wished to con-

struct a grammar for unwritten languages he did not himself speak. Boas consequently began to invent his own, and became involved with a large-scale program of documentation of Native American languages coordinated by the Bureau of Ethnology. Now a linguist, Boas moved to New York in 1896 and taught at Columbia until his death in 1942, training students as fieldworkers. One of his students was Edward Sapir, who had also been born in Germany, but whose parents emigrated to the United States when he was only five. Sapir began conducting fieldwork on Native American languages as a graduate student at Columbia, and headed the first major survey of native languages in Canada, later becoming a professor at Chicago and then Yale. His main concern was with connections of language and other cultural dimensions, and his perspective was more anthropological than methodological.

On the other hand, Leonard Bloomfield, a contemporary of Sapir, "was closely identified with the rise of a distinct professional field of linguistics" (Anderson 1985: 250). Bloomfield, like Saussure, did early work in historical linguistics, and spent 1913–14, when he was a postdoctoral researcher in his mid-twenties, working in Germany on Indo-European and specifically Sanskrit. He held several university posts teaching German, and began fieldwork on native American languages only in 1915–16. He combined an essentially structuralist view of language with a strong commitment to the currently fashionable behaviorist psychology, and wrote a highly-regarded textbook, *Language*, which was published in 1933 and strongly influenced the future direction of linguistics in the United States.

Despite their differing backgrounds, and the differing relationships they perceived between linguistics and other disciplines, Boas, Sapir, and Bloomfield all shared a common concern for the accurate description of native American languages. This means that, although they shared a number of assumptions with Saussure, their own structuralist approach to language was also innovative. Like Saussure, Boas, Sapir and Bloomfield were all linguistic historians, but they also developed a commitment to synchronic work as essential and primary. This shift toward a synchronic approach was particularly notable for Bloomfield, who comments, in a review of Sapir's 1922 book *Language*, that "we are coming to believe that restriction to historical work is unreasonable and, in the long run, methodologically impossible" (cited in Matthews 1993: 7). Again, this does not mean that Bloomfield himself ceased to regard historical issues as important – indeed, eleven of the twenty-eight chapters in Bloomfield (1933) were concerned with comparative and historical linguistics. However, he very clearly accepted Saussure's prioritization of synchronic work, producing, as Matthews (1993: 14) suggests, perhaps a more extreme reaction in his followers than he might have intended: "The consequence in practice, though it is hard to believe that it is one which Bloomfield would have welcomed, is that many leading theorists did not concern themselves with problems of history at all, and passed on to the next generation a view of linguistics either wholly or largely synchronic."

Bloomfield departed more radically from Saussure's tenets in the area of *langue* and *parole*. As we saw earlier, Saussure was particularly keen to stress the division of actual, observable language behavior, or *parole*, from *langue*, the language system of the speech community. The linguist's main concern was taken to be *langue*, since this allowed abstraction away from individual variation, and concentration on differentially defined linguistic units. Bloomfield, however, was profoundly influenced by behaviorist psychology, which regarded human behavior, including linguistic behavior, as a set of responses to stimuli from the outside world. This behaviorist stance emphasizes the physical at the cost of the psychological, and it is inevitable that Bloomfield would be uneasy with a largely psychological concept of the linguistic system, like Saussure's conception of *langue*. Bloomfield consequently regards linguistic units as essentially observable, and advocates a set of procedures for ascertaining the structure of a grammar which begins with the immediately perceptible level of sound, works up through the identification of meaningful units (morphology) and their combination into sentences (syntax), and only then attempts to discern meanings (semantics). Conversely, as we have seen, the central unit of Saussure's linguistic universe was the sign, which crucially involves meaning. It follows that, while Saussure's main concern was with the word, Bloomfield's attention shifted upward to the sentence; and from this develops the increasing concentration, in post-Bloomfieldian and then in Chomskyan linguistics, on syntactic structure.

The main novelty which Boas, Sapir, and Bloomfield brought to the elementary ideals of structuralism was their application to a whole series of languages which were far from the familiar, Indo-European type. The typical reaction of early investigators of native American languages, often travelers with an amateur interest in languages, or missionaries aiming at Bible translation, had been to interpret native American languages as barbaric jargons which fell sadly short of the ideal grammatical type represented by Latin and Greek, transcribing their sounds using the nearest English or French equivalent, and concerning themselves more with what these inadequate systems expressed about the speakers' equally primitive societies than with any serious, scientific attempt at description. Boas, Sapir,

Bloomfield, and their contemporaries, however, made a serious attempt to understand the structures of these languages in their own terms: and in this enterprise they were aided and encouraged by Saussure's ideas of arbitrariness and of the relational nature of the language system. Recall that each unit in a language belongs to a system, and is definable only in relation to all the other units in that same system; moreover, the units included in the system, both in terms of signifiers and signifieds, are wholly dependent on the language itself. What this means, as the early American structuralists point out, is that every language must be defined in its own terms. A native American language cannot be regarded as a variant of a type defined by Latin or Greek; its particular units and rules must be seen in their own right, and can in turn tell us more about what a possible language is, and how far languages can vary. This objective, descriptive approach is absolutely central to linguistic work now, but was revolutionary in the early years of the twentieth century. Some early structuralists took it to a logical extreme, claiming, as Joos (1957: 96) reports, that the radical differentiation of sounds and grammar found between Europe and the Americas meant "that languages could differ from each other without limit and in unpredictable ways." It is not clear how far this was a strongly held belief, and how far a methodological starting point, a kind of null hypothesis to be investigated and disproved. Either way, this view provided one motivation for the beginnings of a principled investigation of linguistic universals and a systematic study of typology, or possible language structures and their correlations across systems: these have been central to linguistic investigation and linguistic theory ever since.

Conclusion

How, then, do these developments within linguistics relate to the more general rise of modernism and modernist thought? Faulkner (1977: 1) suggests that "Modernism is part of the historical process by which the arts have dissociated themselves from nineteenth-century assumptions, which had come in the course of time to seem like dead conventions." As we have seen, although the Neogrammarians advanced linguistic study very considerably in the last quarter of the nineteenth century, fitting language into the classical Victorian paradigm of law-governed behavior and historical investigation, by the beginning of the twentieth century they were themselves expressing discontent with their own approach. Saussure articulates particularly clearly the need for synchronic description and a universal framework, along with a necessary consideration of the nature of language itself, and his work illustrates the typically modernist search for "a balance between pattern and experience" (Faulkner 1977: 12). Saussure and his followers are conscious of contradictions in language, and again, Saussure's own attempt to understand language through these contradictions, by identifying and using oppositions like those between *langue* and *parole*, signifier and signified, and synchrony versus diachrony, connect him, albeit unawares, to the wider modernist movement.

This connection is further developed by the work of the American structuralists, following Boas, Sapir, and Bloomfield in their emphasis on description of the wide variety of structures found in native American languages, and in their integration of Saussure's general framework with these novel and highly complex forms. Again, we find here a classically modernist opposition, in "the tension between the awareness of complexity and the commitment to unity" (Faulkner 1977: 12). However, although Saussure's general theory of language, Boas and Sapir's objective approach to the intricacies of native American languages, and Bloomfield's adaptations of structuralist tenets to the physicalist context of behaviorist psychology are all reactions to the linguistic complexities they perceived around them, they are not entirely new or revolutionary, but build on the contributions of their predecessors. Morpurgo Davies gives the specific example of "the realization that some of the actual questions to which historical linguists were seeking an answer ... had to be tackled synchronically – in the first instance at least. Saussure said it more sharply than anyone else and was listened to, but the last decades of the nineteenth century had prepared the ground" (1998: 325). More generally, she summarizes these connections and this continuity:

> Some of those in close contact with the neogrammarians went on to do what the neogrammarians had recommended, others went on to do what the neogrammarians had not done. It may not be chance that both Bloomfield and Saussure, who played such a role in the creation of linguistic structuralism, had passed through Leipzig. (1998: 269)

References and Further Reading

Anderson, Stephen R. 1985. *Phonology in the Twentieth Century*. Chicago: University of Chicago Press.
Bloomfield, Leonard. 1933. *Language*. New York: Holt.

Culler, Jonathan. 1985. *Saussure*, 2nd ed. London: Fontana.

Darnell, Regna. 1990. *Edward Sapir: Linguist, Anthropologist, Humanist*. Berkeley: University of California Press.

Faulkner, Peter, ed. 1977. *Modernism*. London: Routledge.

Fox, Anthony. 1993. *Linguistic Reconstruction*. Oxford: Oxford University Press.

Joos, Martin, ed. 1957. *Readings in Linguistics*. New York: American Council of Learned Societies.

Kermode, Frank. 1968. Modernisms. In Frank Kermode, ed., *Continuities*. London: Routledge & Kegan Paul.

Matthews, P. H. 1993. *Grammatical Theory in the United States from Bloomfield to Chomsky*. Cambridge: Cambridge University Press.

McMahon, April. 1994. *Understanding Language Change*. Cambridge: Cambridge University Press.

Morpurgo Davies, Anna. 1998. *Nineteenth-Century Linguistics*. Vol. IV of Giulio Lepschy, ed., *History of Linguistics*. London: Longman.

Robins, R.H. 1997. *A Short History of Linguistics*. 4th ed. London: Longman.

——. 1988. Leonard Bloomfield: The Man and the Man of Science. *Transactions of the Philological Society* 86: 63–87.

Sampson, Geoffrey. 1980. *Schools of Linguistics: Competition and Evolution*. London: Hutchinson.

Saussure, Ferdinand de. 1916. *Cours de linguistique générale*. Paris: Payot. (*Course in General Linguistics*. Trans. Christiane Baltaxe. London: Fontana, 1974.)

Verner, Karl. 1978. An Exception to Grimm's Law. In Philip Baldi and Ronald N. Werth, eds., *Readings in Historical Phonology*, pp. 32–63. University Park: University of Pennsylvania Press.

Woolf, Virginia. 1924. Mr. Bennett and Mrs. Brown. In Virginia Woolf, ed., *Collected Essays, Volume I*. London: Hogarth Press.

8

Technology: "Multiplied man"

Tim Armstrong

Ideas of modernity and of technology have, since the Enlightenment, been inextricably related. The control of nature and the rationalization of production and social process offered by technology, broadly considered as the instrumentalization of scientific knowledge, are central to the modern worldview and to modern capitalist society, as are versions of the self and body which conceive them as mechanisms which might be improved or better exploited. At the same time, modernity has produced a critique of technology, whether expressed in terms of the totality of the social order it demands, or in terms of its impact on the human subject or nature. This tradition of critique, sometimes nostalgic and often drawing on vitalist notions of the uniqueness of life-energies, is equally a part of modernity. Any account of modernism and technology must account not only for these opposed positions, but also for their instability: for the tendency of the "natural" to become mechanism, and of technology to become a form of life.

One of the defining characteristics of modernist thought in social science and the philosophy of history is its focus, in a post-Darwinian context, on technology as it relates to a range of issues: the process of civilization, the human body, communication, mass culture. Works in this tradition include Spengler's *Man and Technics* (English edition 1932), Lewis Mumford's *Technics and Civilization* (1934), Siegfried Giedion's *Mechanisation Takes Command* (1948) and Jacques Ellul's *The Technological Society* (originally published as *La Technique*, 1954), something of a synthesis in that it amalgamated a Weberian critique of rationalization with a history of mechanization. Heidegger's 1953 essay "The Question Concerning Technology" should perhaps also be included; as should psychoanalytic writings on technology and the body-image: Victor Tausk's 1919 paper on the "Influencing-Machine" and schizophrenia; Hanns Sachs's "The Delay of the Machine Age" (1933). If Walter Benjamin's "The Work of Art in the Age of Mechanical Reproduction" (1936) has been the most influential of these works in recent years, that is arguably because its focus on visual technologies and communication matches postmodern concerns. More characteristic of modern thought is the parallelism which places technological evolution alongside human evolution generally. This essay will accordingly stress the confluence of technology and evolutionary thought suggested by George Crile's popular *Man, an Adaptive Mechanism* (1916) – an interlocking whose complexity is produced by the fact that, as Samuel Butler had implied in *Erewhon* (1872), the development of technology provides both grounding metaphors for biological evolution (evolution is "like" the development of tools; technology is a form of cultural evolution), and a semi-autonomous sphere which might be seen as out of step with the human body (our technology has outpaced us or rendered human biological evolution meaningless).

What do we mean by technology? Analyses of the subject have usually distinguished between the tool, seen as an extension of the human body, and the freestanding and self-energizing machine typified by the giant dynamo at the Paris Exposition which Henry Adams saw, in 1900, as emblematic of the coming era. As we will see, literary celebrations of *techne* or making typically focus on the tool, whereas critiques of technology and the social order it involves refer to it as involving a scale which dwarfs the human. Subscribers to the first issues of the Harmondsworth *Popular Science* encyclopedia, published in parts in 1912, would have encountered a characteristically modern version of this distinction in discussions of how technology was "Making the World Anew" and "Magnifying Our Senses." The former article describes the huge powers unleashed by technological modernity, and the conquest of nature that will result; the latter chronicles "the enormous and sudden development of the senses of mankind in the last three hundred years," via the microscope, telescope, spectroscope, interferometer, seismograph, photograph, radio, and X-rays. These devices, a later writer insists, enable us to see "things as they are" rather than a world limited by the human perceptual apparatus: to capture the instant in which a bee's wing beats; to show microbes; to penetrate the body. Another aspect of the taxonomy of the field offered by the encyclopedia is also worth noting: it includes sections in each volume on "society" and "eugenics," suggesting the way in which the management of human relations might itself be seen as technological (see Chapter 2 of this volume).

A final preliminary point. It is important to recognize that the interface between writing and technology works in multiple ways. Technology impinges on thinking about making, perception, communication, and form; about modes of representation, production, and distribution (radio, cinema, tabloid newspapers); about social issues and the construction of the "human." To take one example, recent discussions of Virginia Woolf have explored modes of transport (airplane, motor car, bus), vision (telescope, film), and sound (telephone, gramophone). Formal issues predicated on the interpenetration of machines and writing include the relationship between gramophone, radio, and the chaotic voices of *The Waves* and *Between the Acts*; the way in which the "Time Passes" section of *To the Lighthouse* relates to the look-less looking of the camera and the impersonality of the microphone. Technology supplies metaphors for the operation of mind, even for the unconscious and desire (for example, the London Underground in Peter Walsh's reverie in *Mrs. Dalloway*). But we also have to note her politicized analysis of mass media: the role of the BBC in the General Strike reflected in *Three Guineas*; the propaganda of wartime subverted in the "chuffing" gramophone and megaphones of *Between the Acts*. Technology, then appears in Woolf's work as literal and metaphorized subject matter; as part of the organization of the society she describes; as constructing the self, and as an element of style and narrative.

Brave New Word

Victorian technology might be seen as typified by the static, massive, and even overloaded; a set of terms which find one terminus in the sinking of the *Titanic* in 1912. Technology at the turn of the century was defined by a different set of concerns: weightlessness; torque and flow; exchange and storage; the curved edge. The airplane and bicycle; the typewriter, telegraph, and radio – as Hillel Schwartz suggests, these find their correlatives in flowing new dance movements, gymnastics, looser clothing; even in more relaxed handwriting styles (though in each of these cases, we need to notice, the "natural" is a *technique* that needs to be taught). The elements incorporated by Robert Delaunay into various versions of his painting of "The Cardiff Team" (1922–3) illustrate these changes: a leaping rugby player; the Eiffel Tower and the great wheel erected on the Seine; Blériot's airplane; a huge commercial sign representative of new advertising techniques. To defy gravity, real or metaphorical, was one point of his paint-ing; another is the assemblage of these elements in itself, into what Deleuze and Guattari would much later call a "desiring machine," a series of con-nections, flows, and pleasures which reposition (and in some senses elimi-nate) the human subject.

The rhetoric of machine-age dynamism implicit in Delaunay's painting was pioneered by the Italian Futurists, whose celebration of speed and movement, the automobile and airplane, reflected a desire for modernity and for a momentum which would break through the established social order. Marinetti's first Manifesto of Futurism (1909) ends its opening sec-tion in seeming bathos as the huge automobile which he rides upends in a ditch, only for the author to be reborn from its "nourishing sludge." This traumatic rebirth is, incipiently, that prophesied in the "Multiplied Man" section of *War, The World's Only Hygiene* (1911–15), the creation of a trans-formed "man" who is "endowed with surprising organs: organs adapted to the needs of a world of ceaseless shocks." Marinetti produces an explicitly Lamarckian description of the machine as prosthetic extension, collapsing the distinction between the "vital" and the machine in order to expel the interiority which is the target of Futurist scorn:

> It is certain that if we grant the truth of Lamarck's transformational hypoth-esis we must admit that we look for the creation of a nonhuman type in whom moral suffering, goodness of heart, affection and love, those sole cor-rosive poisons of inexhaustible vital energy, sole interrupters of our power-ful bodily electricity, will be abolished.

This sets the keynote for much later discourse on the machine: a stress on transformation, exteriorization, and shock; Marinetti's Lamarckianism finds echoes in Remy de Gourmont, Pound, and others. Yet it is important to note the traces of idealism in Marinetti's writings: when he writes of "the day when man will be able to externalize his will and make it into a huge invisible arm," his model is the spiritualist séance; the "invisible arm" is an occult technology. In this respect it seems important that Marinetti's auto-mobile is attached to the death drive – that is, to a sense of the end of the human, and of a present moment that is freed from the drag of the past. Bergson, William James, and others had suggested that in our embodied experience the "moment" is always informed (contaminated, for Marinetti) by the past. Accordingly the catastrophic presentism of Futurism is ex-pressed through an identification with Bergson's object of attack: the time of the machine. (It is for related reasons that Futurism adopts the time-lapse photography of E-J. Marey in its "Photo-Dynamism.") Wyndham Lewis stressed in 1922 that *The present man in all of us is the machine,* arguing for a greater distance from the photographic "moment."

Alongside the regulation and abstraction of time critiqued by Bergson, technology implies a relation to the shape of time: on the one hand bound up with ideas of progress and development, on the other offering a conquest of time, insofar as time represents struggle and uncertainty. This paradox is apparent as early as Wells's *The Time Machine* (1895), but it is equally visible in the apocalyptic mode of the Futurists, or in the abolition of the historical past and imaginable future in the technological society of Orwell's *Nineteen-Eighty-Four* (1949). What Jacques Ellul described as the "autonomy" of technology – its tendency to develop independently of social logic – has been qualified by recent cultural analysis of science, but nevertheless the fantasy of autonomy represented a powerful attraction for those who sought a rupture with human temporality, human inertia, and the limitations of the self. For Marinetti, and also for Pound, who christened Mussolini an "artifex" and praised his ability to get things done, this had a political dimension: Fascism depicts the individual as a component in the massed ranks of a mechanized being exteriorizing, mesmerically, the will of the leader.

For other varieties of European modernism, particularly Constructivism and the Bauhaus, the machine served more general purposes: as a model for a utilitarian and anti-elitist art; as an emblem for a more "efficient" and functional artwork; as suggesting an "objectivity" of vision. The "Machine Art" exhibition at the Museum of Modern Art in New York in 1934 represented the triumph of this functionalism, its aesthetic realized in the exhibition poster depicting self-aligning ball bearings. The exhibition included gasoline pumps, safes, adding machines, and steel pans, as well as machine parts. As Lewis Mumford wrote, "expression through the machine implies the cognition of relatively new aesthetic terms: precision, calculation, flawlessness, simplicity, economy."

Modernist critics of literature were to take up some of these terms (notably the scientifically-minded I. A. Richards, who in 1919 likened himself to Wilbur Wright and five years later, in the opening of his *Principles of Literary Criticism,* declared that "A book is a machine to think with"). But in applying these ideas to literature, we are often on difficult ground, since the metaphoricity of such terms in relation to writing makes their application uncertain. Certainly the general stance which depicted the artist as maker, stressing *techne* over inspiration, was attractive to many modernists. For Ezra Pound in the era of Imagism, the "efficient" poem was "hard and clear," it avoided unnecessary words (especially adjectives and adverbs), and it aimed for a "concentration" which enabled an instantaneous reception which Pound often modeled on the electromagnetic impulse. But what, in formal terms, this amounted to is less clear; certainly not a celebration of technology itself; rather an abstraction founded on the sculpture of Brancusi and others, and (in Pound's Vorticism) a tendency, reinforced by the stress on the force field in modern physics, to layer plains of material against each other in assemblages which demand a sense of causality or linkage. (In a similar way, the Russian "Futurian" Khlebnikov had defined a "supersaga" as like a building "made up out of independent sections," each with its own logic; his poem *Zangezi* is "a stack of word planes.") Pound's later essay "Machine Art" (1927–30) develops his ideas further: Pound believes that it is in the moving parts of a modern machine, "where the energy is most concentrated," that the pressure uniting form and function is most marked. Hence, to look at the part is to study form, and beauty as indissoluble from form. One corollary is that Pound sees the moving part (especially the spare part), tied to a single function, as more beautiful than the assemblage: "one must sort out the essential parts from the parts that merely happen to be there and which keep an assemblage of machines in more or less fortuitous relation to each other" (1996: 69). Another is the fact that the evolved mechanical device is the production of many generations of improvement: "These single parts and the foci of their action have been made by thought over thought; by layer on layer of attention" (1996: 59). Both these comments suggest the aesthetics of the *Cantos*: the layering of historical attention; the tension between haphazard assemblage and a logic of connection; both also tease out some of the technological subtexts of evolutionary thinking.

For Wyndham Lewis, on the other hand, it is precisely this evolutionary history which differentiates the machine from art, as his comments in "What is Industrial Art?" (1935) suggest:

An ocean liner, or a large passenger-plane . . . is not a work of art, any more than a whale, or a vulture, is a work of art. When we speak of Machine Age art, we mean something that is "evolved" in the same way as members of the animal kingdom . . . . For the engineer is *not* an artist . . . . It is essential that we should make this distinction. If we do not, however much we may talk of the great "abstract" qualities inherent in the productions of the machine, we shall really be falling into the errors of naturalism – namely of confusing art with nature.

The critique of modernity in Lewis's later work involves a rejection of the progressive and abstract, equated with the unnecessary aesthetic "stream-lining" of everyday objects and even (in the case of Auden) poems. Marinetti's "multiplied" or hyper-evolved man involves a dangerous confusion for Lewis. Nevertheless, it was just this evolutionary, prosthetic imagination which informed much popular writing on technology in the period: H. G. Wells's *Anticipations* (1901); Arnold Bennett's *The Human Machine* (1908); the futurological studies published by Kegan Paul in the "Today and Tomorrow" series in the 1920s; and the work of a range of popular boosters of the new era: Gerald Stanley Lee, Charles W. Wood, Edwin Slosson, Edward Filene, Silas Bent, and others.

It is American writers who seem most at home with technologized aesthetics, unsurprisingly given that America emerged from World War I as the world's most powerful and technological economy. In Bryher's *West* (1925), one of the characters insists on driving a European visitor around Manhattan and across Brooklyn Bridge: "I want you to get the streets, the pulse of the machinery, the beauty, the barbaric splendor of it all." Her cry "Put your rebellion into finding a new form" is fundamental to modernism, offering *techne* as Oedipal drama. A similar fascination with the technologies of metropolitan life is visible in much twentieth-century American writing: in the steel and concrete structures of Carl Sandburg's *Chicago Poems* (1916) and Hart Crane's *The Bridge* (1930); in the crowded city of Jean Toomer's *Cane* (1923) and Dos Passos's *Manhattan Transfer* (1925); in the work of the American "precisionist" painters of the 1920s – Charles Demuth, for whom a grain elevator is the American "Classic Scene," Charles Scheeler, Joseph Stella, and others. As Stella later declared, "steel and electricity had created a new world."

If Stella, like Crane, renders this world with religious intensity, Sheeler's paintings apply a technological logic to representation: often based directly on photographs, they flatten their subjects into geometry. The poetic correlative is William Carlos Williams, whose links to the precisionists are visible in his fascination with the edge (the rose which "is obsolete" but which can nevertheless be remade, almost as a machined product); with advertising signs, automobiles. Williams's engagement with technology traverses many fields. His interest in the well-engineered poem is expressed most clearly in his introduction to *The Wedge* (1944):

> A poem is a small (or large) machine made of words. I mean there can be no part, as in any other machine, that is redundant.
>
> Prose may carry a load of ill-defined matters like a ship. But poetry is the

machine which drives it, pruned to a perfect economy. As in all machines its movement is intrinsic, undulant, a physical more that a literary character.

This is inflected by a particular desire to make the arts, in 1944, something other than escapist, "the war or part of it"; elsewhere Williams's definitions of poetry place far more stress on the wandering or distracted nature of art. But in poems like "Classic Scene" we can see his belief that the whole of modern life must be included in the poem, even a power plant, or the list of bore samples from wells included as part of the industrial archeology of *Paterson*. The "microscopic accuracy" (as one early critic put it) and impartiality of his looking has been linked to the technological medicine inaugurated by the American Flexner Report. However, like Pound, Williams often gains from the machine ideas of imaginative openness rather than a sense of closed systems and regulation: in the fugitive vistas seen from the doctor's car (the synchronicity of writing and driving is explored in Marinetti's writings, in Apollinaire's "The Little Car," in Jon Rodker's "To a Renault in the Country," in Woolf's "Evening over Sussex: Reflections in a Motor Car"). Williams even finds inspiration in the car crash of *The Great American Novel*. As in Pound's writings, an interest in technology coexists with a stress on the fluidity of the imagination, and a critique of industrial production and its culture; of "Minds beaten thin / by waste," as *Paterson II* puts it. This is a typical modernist ambivalence: *techne*, making or fabrication, is celebrated, as is the extension of human powers in the machine; but the totality of industrial civilization is nevertheless attacked as depersonalized and empty

More generally, we must also pay attention to the way technology in modernist texts often produces sudden, if ambivalent, pleasures and new possibilities – the arresting sight of the body's interior in the X-rays of Thomas Mann's *The Magic Mountain*; the pleasures of transport in *Ulysses*; the flux of telegrams in the work of Ford Madox Ford; the sudden and startling likening of the Unconscious to a cinema screen in Freud. That the mass-produced product is pleasurable is also, in an odd way, the implication of Marianne Moore's use of the stanza form as a visually regulated "grid," independent of syllabics, which is "stamped out" for each poem, but which nevertheless contains a variety of thought and observation within its formula, as if expressing the pleasurable surfaces of a commodity called (say) "The Pangolin."

Perhaps the best vehicle for such pleasures is the aircraft. Leaving the Victorian Thomas Hardy on the ground – he disliked "anything to do with the air," his wife said – we could imagine making a fictional–factual flight across the fields of literary modernism: taking off in an early glider with

Wells's *Tono Bungay* (1909); navigating the skyscrapers of Manhattan and parachuting into Harlem playing a saxophone with Herbert Julian, the "Black Eagle," in 1923; sign-writing in *Mrs. Dalloway* (1925); flying to Europe with Lindbergh in 1927, and so giving birth to new excesses of modern celebrity (and a Brecht cantata). Our flight might culminate in a pamphlet-drop with Auden's airman in *The Orators* (1932), followed by a bombing-run on a town in northern Spain in 1937: Guernica. The appeal of the airman to Fascism – Mussolini depicting himself as an aviator; Hitler descending to Nuremberg – is attributable not only to the modernity of the aircraft and the speed of the Blitzkrieg, but also to the distance and indifference epitomized by Yeats's pilot in "An Irish Airman Foresees His Death," and the obscure linking of flight and the death-drive – as, again, in Yeats's "Lapis Lazuli," with its bombs pitched out "Until the town lie beaten flat." The fascination with the aviator which is characteristic of Auden's work is also political, in the sense that the airman (partly, in *The Orators*, a version of T. E. Lawrence) represents a type of romantic personality who is at odds with the modern world. Auden's description of more warlike airmen a few years later in *In Time of War* declares that these bombers "will never see how flying / Is the creation of ideas they hate, / Nor how their own machines are always trying / To push through into life." More generally, the airborne view in Auden suggests a perspective from which human life becomes a series of cinematic views and maplike plottings of the body politic. To write "Consider this and in our time / As the hawk sees it or the helmeted airman" is to lay out before the viewer a swooping panorama, in which the landscape of Europe appears as a flux of general views and sudden detail indicative of a psychic state which Auden identified with the modern bourgeoisie, characterized in terms of distance and fugue. Such questions about the modern self turn us toward the modernist critique of technology.

Contaminated Critiques

When Carlyle, in 1829, described the changes in human society effected by the "Age of Machinery," he was careful to balance admiration of this new world with an insistence on study of "the primary, unmodified forces and energies of man, the mysterious springs of Love, and Fear, and Wonder, of Enthusiasm, Poetry, Religion." The mechanical and "vital" remain opposed. Carlyle's suspicion of the Machine Age was to deepen, to the point that he could, in 1850, describe "the universal Stygian quagmire of

British industrial life," bequeathing a set of terms taken up by many sub-sequent writers. For Yeats, Lawrence, Forster, and others, the technologi-cal, rationalist, and utilitarian worldview derived from Newton, Hobbes, and Locke was the enemy of art, and to be opposed by a return to the sources of life – to what Pound in his Preface to *The Natural Philosophy of Love* called the "horned gods." More generally, for the philosophical and sociological critique which descends from Marx and Weber to Ellul and Foucault, the culture of technology implies the loss of freedom, or the offering of freedoms which are regulated and illusory.

The Great War intensified such thinking, seen by many as rationalized slaughter, conducted according to what Daniel Pick describes as a remorse-less "logic of technology" (1993: 165), including not only gas, the machine gun, tank, Zeppelin, and bomber, but the new communication apparatus which could send tens of thousands of troops over the top at once. The technological war was an expression, for the Allies, of the aggressive mo-dernity of the German state. Henri Bergson, in *The Meaning of the War* (1915), attacked the "mechanical" Prussian spirit, its tendency to rigidity and au-tomatism. Technology seemed out of control, careering unstoppably like the mobilization railroad timetables which thrust both sides into war in 1914.

The political and economic order in which technology is implicated is the focus of attack here. In Kafka's "In the Penal Colony" (1920), E. E. Cummings's *The Enormous Room* (1922), Huxley's *Brave New World* (1932), Orwell's *Nineteen-Eighty-Four*, and elsewhere, technique is fundamental to the vision of a society based on surveillance and control – dystopic ver-sions of the "engineered" and rationalized society which the Soviet Union aspired to, and which many Western liberals (like Thorsten Veblen in *The Engineers and the Price System*, 1921) were happy to contemplate in the in-terwar period. In Huxley's novel, that technique centered on eugenics and on the science of work (bodies and minds scientifically matched to occupations), but could also include the repressive desublimation arranged by a state which engineers desire. At the end of Dos Passos's *Nineteen-nineteen* (1932), the military induction of the nameless "John Doe" is em-blematic of a culture of control, particularly as he is shortly to become another exploded, rotting body, cynically used in the Tomb of the Un-known Soldier:

> they weighed you, they measured you, looked for flat feet, squeezed your
> penis to see if you had clap, looked up your anus to see if you had piles,
> counted your teeth, made you cough, listened to your heart and lungs, made

> you read the letters on the card, charted your urine and your intelligence, gave you a service record for a future (imperishable soul) and an identification tag stamped with your serial number to hang around your neck, issued OD regulation equipment, a condiment can and a copy of the articles of war.

As here, one figure for the destructive effects of both military and industrial technology is the dismemberment and fragmentation of the human body. Upton Sinclair's *The Jungle* (1906) describes the Chicago meatworks as a war zone in which both animals and humans are shredded. A number of subsequent texts focus on the body and fate of the industrial laborer, from the silk workers of the Paterson Strike Pageant held in New York in 1913 to the stoker of Eugene O'Neill's play *The Hairy Ape* (1922), in which the actors are imprisoned in a posture-distorting set representing the bowels of a ship. Muriel Rukeyser's 1938 poetic sequence "The Book of the Dead" investigates the effects of silica mining in West Virginia, attacking the cover-up of the effects of silicosis on the part of mining companies with "statements," cut-up committee proceedings, cross-examination, individual stories, stock quotations – aligning the modernist poetic fragment with the wasted body and hacked-up land.

In Heidegger's "The Question Concerning Technology" (1953) another element is added to the critique described above: a sense that modern technological society freezes forms of knowledge into a dogmatic system abstracted from nature, occluding any understanding of Being (that is, *techne* replaces *poesis*). This argument can be related, on the one hand, to Bergson's insistence that it is the cinematographic analysis of the body and of time and its uniform capture of its flow which represent a rupture with the classical tradition in which time represents lived experience; in which moments may be charged with a meaning which informs a life (see Chapter 5 of this volume); and, on the other hand, to the implication that in the fully technological society (like that of *Brave New World*) history as a human process is eliminated, since every impulse is managed, every question about human needs and desires answered.

In such arguments as Heidegger's, and in much modern literature, the effect of technology on the ontology of the modern self is the central issue. In "The Metropolis and Mental Life" (1903), Georg Simmel describes the individual as "a mere cog in an enormous organization of things and powers which tear from his hand all progress, spirituality and value in order to transform them from their subjective form into the form of a purely objective life." This does more than metaphorically apply a mechanical vocabulary to social process; it depicts technological society as ultimately evacuating the subject, colonizing the waste spaces of the self for capital. As Theodor Adorno put it in *Minima Moralia* (written in 1946–7), "Even what differs from technology in man is now being incorporated into it as a kind of lubrication." Sinclair Lewis's novel *Babbitt* (1922) is perhaps the most thorough satire of technological enthusiasms in this sense, in that its hero is a self-deluded devotee of the "God of Progress" whose passion for American gadgetry and self-improvement techniques permeates every aspect of his life, rendering him a version of the programmable self described in the period by Operant Psychology. In Elmer Rice's play *The Adding Machine* (1921), even rebellion is seen as automatic.

The externalization of the self described by Simmel was exemplified for many by Hollywood film, which as early as Hugo Münsterberg's *The Photoplay* (1916) was seen as a commodification of inner experience. By the time Huxley depicted the state mass-culture industry as offering a surrogate, synaesthetic experience in *Brave New World*, the argument was familiar. Depictions of mass culture as a kind of influencing-machine were often gendered, with the realm of technologically mediated mass culture coded as feminine. In E. M. Forster's 1909 story "The Machine Stops" the central figure, Vashti, represents a decadent civilization subservient to the machine, gossiping with her friends via television, worshipping the Machine, and picking over the traces of a etiolated secondary culture from the underground cells to which humanity has retreated; it is her rebellious son who attempts to break through to the reality represented by the earth's surface. Eliot's anemic secretary in *The Waste Land* (1922), starting the gramophone with "automatic hand," is another version. Why are women portrayed as consumers of mass culture? One set of answers, clearly, lies in associations between women and leisure and in notions of feminine passivity and receptivity ultimately grounded in mesmeric psychology. But it is also a more general anxiety about the self and its boundaries that this complex reveals, with the "feminine" standing for the permeable body from which the "natural" may be evacuated in favor of the technological.

Anxiety about the permeability of the self is also visible in the weaker form of modernist critique, which states that technological modernity imposes impossible strains on the subject, producing overload, fatigue, or violent rupture. The hugely popular diagnosis of neurasthenia or nervous exhaustion, pioneered by the American physician George M. Beard in the 1860s, was applied by a range of writers to modern culture as a whole. The human body was seen as increasingly out of step, in terms of scale and speed, with the mechanical world. For Beard, the pace and recurrent "shocks" of the modern world – streetcars, electric light, telegraphy – was particularly exhausting for brain-workers. A similar set of ideas about technological trauma informed the diagnosis of "Railway Spine" in the 1860s and of shell-shock in World War I. The works of modernism are littered with neurasthenic, overtaxed bodies (Eliot's Prufrock, Proust's Marcel, James's Strether), as well as with shell-shock victims like those depicted in West's *The Return of the Soldier* (1918), Ford's *No More Parades* (1925), and Woolf's *Mrs. Dalloway*.

In a related line of dystopian thinking – epitomized by *The Time Machine* and "The Machine Stops" – the coming technological conquest of nature deprives the human race of its dynamism. Evolution requires struggle; technology substitutes for the human in that struggle. In extreme forms it is, to adapt Villiers de L'Isle-Adam's famous phrase, the machines who do the living for us. In popular adventure stories of the early twentieth century, like Owen Wister's *The Virginians* (1903) and John Buchan's *Greenmantle* (1916), the answer to this conundrum is a return to violent struggle, to frontier life – as indeed in Wells's tale, which has the Time Traveller beating off Morlocks with a club. (Much later, *Brave New World* contains a parody of this flight, suggesting its futility.)

Forms of anorexic refusal represent a parallel reaction to technological modernity and consumer society. In Kafka's "A Hunger Artist" (1922), in Bennett's *Riceyman Steps* (1923), in Orwell's *Coming Up for Air* (1939), and elsewhere, there is a refusal not simply of the burgeoning energies of modernity (related to food and fat in both these novels) but of its construction of a "distracted" self. At the turn of the century the problem of overload in relation to sensory input was considered by William James, Freud, and many other psychologists, and generalized as a crisis of *attention*: in the flux of mechanically produced images, sounds, and movements of the modern world, the role of consciousness is to filter or sample and render coherent this flux. F. Scott Fitzgerald's *Tender is the Night* (1934) presents an extreme example of that distraction: the central character Dick Diver is constantly described as half-attending, overwhelmed, or deadened by stimuli. More generally, it is arguably in this way that we can best understand the "stream of consciousness" of *Ulysses*: what is represented is not the meditations of a centered subject, but rather something closer to a telephone exchange through which various sensory messages distractedly flow.

But as the relation between "stream of consciousness" and distraction above might suggest, and as recent work on modernism has emphasized, much modernist critique of technology is compromised by the way in which the senses are, even where they are seen as the basis of a notionally "natural" or "authentic" experience, conceived as technologies which might be manipulated or corrected; the "natural," that is, is itself a matter of technique. The result is a version of that tension between thinking about the natural and the technological which Mark Seltzer describes in turn-of-the-century literature, and which appears, in the individual, as an uncertainty about authenticity: "Am I real, or a machine?" As Bruce Clarke demonstrates, vitalist thinking is as typically expressed in terms of tropes borrowed from thermodynamics and science: bodily electricity or telepathy; the "physiology of matter" which Lawrence insisted was his focus. Even horrified attacks on machine-age culture, like Sophie Treadwell's play *Machinal* (1929), Chaplin's film *Modern Times* (1936), or Kenneth Fearing's poem "Dirge" (1935) remain compelled by the energies – the mechanical rhythms and speech patterns – of the modern city. Chaplin's film is ultimately a celebration of the *pleasures* of mechanized human motion, like Busby Berkeley's films.

In a parallel way, the materials of technological mass culture give rise to a kitsch aesthetic which energizes critiques of the modern world. Eliot's description of mass-produced detritus in *The Waste Land* is one example; as in Duchamp's "Fountain," a relabeled urinal, technological culture is ironically aestheticized. For the Surrealists, this reclaiming of the discarded products of industry became programmatic, emblematic of the self's ability to explode the given order of things and explore the potentiality of areas of waste and freedom. Yet as we have already seen Adorno suggesting, it can be argued that the space of this exploration is itself opened up by Capital. Businessman Edward Filene, in his *Successful Living in this Machine Age* (1931), contested the idea that mass production "mechanizes and standardizes human life," insisting that on the contrary it offers choice, leisure, and a mobility which liberates the individual from class, localism, even nationalism. He was right to the extent that attacks on Taylorism, Fordism, and mass manipulation through film and advertising, like Upton Sinclair's *The Flivver King* (1937), Dos Passos's *The 42nd Parallel* (1930), and Huxley's *Brave New World*, tend to misrepresent Taylorism (the "science of work"), which sought to align the human body with technology while remaining aware of the *limits* of that alignment, thus opening up the space of "rest" or "leisure" which in some senses became the paradigmatic place of modernist activity. Which is to say that even in attempting to map the limits of technology, to work creatively with waste, fatigue, and resistance, the logic of modernist texts shares elements with Taylorism.

Finally, as suggested above, modernist attacks on technology often focus on its systematic nature, its creation of a surrogate world, rather than the tool as bodily extension. But an important exception is the robot, which serves as the image of a fully technological and exploitable body. Postmodern prophets of the cyborg body like Donna Haraway echo, in at least one sense, the modernist fascination with puppet-figures, visible in the theatrical work of the Futurists, the Surrealists, Meyerhold, Lewis, Yeats, Edward Gordon Craig, and others. For the modernist dramatist the puppet represents an actor freed from mediation and interiority, better able to represent the human by virtue of abstraction from the human. But in its other aspect as a version of the fully Taylorized body, the puppet-as-robot (the term "robot" comes, of course, from Capek's 1920 play *R.U.R.*) threatens to supplant the human, to link itself to alienation and (as Craig insisted) death. At least one modernist theory of why the ancient world did not develop technology (and hence, implicitly, a theory of modernity), the psychoanalyst Hanns Sachs's "The Delay of the Machine Age" (1936), founded itself on this uncanny supplanting. Sachs sees the modern self as less concerned with narcissistic defense; more willing to see itself imitated and duplicated by technology. But equally, as Freud's famous subject Judge Schreber demonstrated, technology readily links itself to paranoid thinking, to fantasies of control and the penetrated body which are the shadowy accompaniment of the synchronized ranks of the Fascist storm troopers.

The Recording Apparatus

The remainder of this essay deals with an aspect of technology which illustrates the argument about its reconfiguration of the human sensorium: technologies of storage and transmission. Such technologies, as Steven Kern argues, profoundly alter human perceptions of time and space, producing a world characterized by the instantaneous, the coordinated, the captured. Time ceases to be a local phenomenon, a socially specific flow, but instead is systematized by telegraphic or radio impulses and train timetables. Distance is eliminated by the telephone. Twentieth-century people can see photographs of themselves at birth; can hear the captured voices of Tennyson, dead grandparents, or absent lovers; can see recent events of world history which took place thousands of miles away. Other faculties, for example sexuality, are also affected: from early in the twentieth century, the cinemagoer could see representations of others making love, often impossibly perfect and technologically "finished" beings.

Moreover, technologies of reproduction and transmission bear a close relation to literature, to some extent encroaching on its function; to some extent providing fresh possibilities in terms of the conceptualization of representation (the "telegraphic" style, for example, which Hemingway claimed to derive from his journalism; the "camera eye" of Dos Passos, which is paradoxically the subjective mode of *U.S.A.*, but which nevertheless carries traces of the elegiac presentism of the camera). Gertrude Stein claimed that the endless repetition-with-slight-variation of her *The Making of Americans* (1925) was modeled on the jerking of film through the projector's gate – an effect which is naturalized in film, but which renders literary narrative a painful exercise in the interaction of attention and forgetting (in order to read Stein, the pressure of recollection is such that it is constantly necessary to forget, to cast behind). Stein creates a new form, the novel as time-lapse: "a history of every one must be a long one." As Mary Anne Doane has argued, the mechanisms of temporal storage proposed by Freud, Marey, and others are haunted by the desire to recapture lost time, including the physiological time lost in processing information; it is as if Stein were demanding that, like film, the novel make good all such losses.

It is on the issue of language that the new media exert the most significant impact. In a series of powerfully articulated discussions of the culture of technology, Friedrich Kittler has recently argued that the period around 1900 saw a technologically mediated shift in the conceptualization of discourse. Where a century earlier the Mother Tongue (whether maternal or mother nature) was the deep source of utterance divined in a vision by the male poet, by 1900 modern linguistics and psychophysics meant that language was, Kittler argues, more typically conceived as a depth-less stream of units produced by the human mechanism, dictated by a male author to a female secretary or a machine. That stream could be studied in terms of its tolerances, limits, pathologies; its tendency to degenerate into random production. This paradigm applied both to speech (studied in terms of memory, aphasia, alexia, etc.) and writing (studied in terms of automatic writing, typing speeds, etc.). The technological media, which process language in stylized forms, represent a series of devices which exploit discourse as encodable information in order to store and disseminate it.

As a dedicated Foucaultian, Kittler undoubtedly schematizes, stressing discursive shifts over the contingencies of history, and flattening important differences between philosophies of language in different modernisms. But we can certainly see forms of debate about the theories of discourse he propounds enacted in many modernist texts. Serenus Zeitblom, the narrator of Thomas Mann's *Doctor Faustus* (1947), moves in the space of a page, late in the novel, from a discussion of the fact that "The echo, the giving back of the human voice as nature-sound, and the revelation of it *as nature-sound,* is essentially a lament," to a consideration of how, in Mann's fictionalized version of the twelve-tone scale (which the composer Leverkühn describes as a technology of musical production), "melody and harmony are determined by the permutation of a fundamental five-note motif, the symbolic letters h, e, a, e, e-flat" (*sic:* the "h" here is another random signifier, a typographical mistake for what should be "b"). A similar debate between systematic/random and Orphic/feminine accounts of language is present in *Ulysses,* and is part of its experimentation with what Zeitblom calls "a sort of composing before composition" – the decision, say, to filter an account of a birth through a history of the English language; or hang a day in Dublin on a structural template involving the *Odyssey. Ulysses* is, as Hugh Kenner points out, a text irrevocably tied to the misprint: not only in its complex and disputed textual history, but in the insertion of deliberate typewriter transpositions, lines of botched newspaper type. Misprints tell the truth of the psyche, as Freud divined, and as suggested in Christina Stead's sprawling novel *The Man Who Loved Children* (1940), when Sam Pollit reads his daughter Evie's letter: "'Dead Dad,' he muttered and then shouted it with laughter. Then miserably he said, 'Dead Dad, it's almost telepathic: I bet little Smudge knows how her poor Dad really feels.'" (Late in the novel the "telepathic" words come back as a hidden truth, when the parricide Louie says of her mother "I think she's dead, Dad," and he can only echo "Dead, Dad, Dead Dad.")

In such instances, the dissonance between the human and technology, or the limits of the human apparatus considered as a machine for the processing of perceptions or discourse, is an important element in modernist aesthetics. Wyndham Lewis insisted that art is linked to the private "oddities" of the writer, "blind spots, omissions, colour-blindness . . . astigmatic distortions, and the rest of it" ("'Detachment' and the Fictionist," 1934). Automatic writing, widely practiced and referred to within modernism, plays on those limits, conceived as a playing with the limits of attention and control. This point is elaborated by Wallace Stevens in his 1936 lecture "The Irrational Element in Poetry":

> While there is nothing automatic about the poem, nevertheless it has an automatic aspect in the sense that it is what I wanted it to be without knowing before it was written what I wanted it to be . . . . If each of us is a biological mechanism, each poet is a poetic mechanism. To the extent that what he produces is mechanical: that is to say, beyond his power to change, it is irrational.

This is to suggest that the trace of the self considered as "mechanism" rather than as deep source might be fundamental to poetry. That is also implicit in Gertrude Stein's 1896 paper on "Normal Motor Automatism," written while she was still a young psychological researcher at Harvard, a blueprint for writing conceived in terms of the encounter of the writing self and the body considered as technology; as a device which, without a clear intentionality, observes itself as it produces discourse – a kind of literature Stein was later to label "Talking and listening all at once" ("How Writing is Written," 1935). In *The Use of Poetry and the Use of Criticism* (1933), T. S. Eliot described *The Waste Land* as "approaching the condition of automatic writing . . . not a vision but a motion terminating in an arrangement of words on paper," again suggesting that it is the throbbing of the "human engine" (as the poem describes it) which concerns the modern text – the noise of the body, of consciousness as process.

A particularly fascinating late modernist example is provided by *Finnegans Wake* (1939), which can be read as a kind of multimedia, demanding that the reader attend to different channels simultaneously, while also, James Theall argues, reimagining the human body as a barrage of electromagnetic devices: the mouth as a "vitaltone speaker," the brain as a "harmonic condenser enginium," sex as electric flux. Joyce even smuggles television (the "bairdboard") into a barroom scene. Descriptions of *Finnegans Wake* as "polyphonic" or "woven" texture thus barely begin to describe a text which is conceivable only as a technologized media, adapted to the expanded human sensorium of an age of tele-technology. One example is the use of "noise" in the text ("Cracklings cricked . . . . Morse nuisance noised"), that is, effects of uncertainty which are intrinsically related to the medium of transmission, and to contingent effects within the environment.

The function of technology as recording apparatus also affects literature in more general ways. "The Work of Art in the Age of Mechanical Reproducibility" (the more correct title of Walter Benjamin's famous 1936 essay) posits that the mass reproduction of the artwork has the effect of destroying that "aura" which represents both cultural capital and a depth associated with distance and reserve. For the literary text, this is an old argument, extending back as far as Caxton and manuscript culture. And as Adorno commented in his exchange with Benjamin, the technological dissemination of an individually crafted product – a symphony, Pound's *Cantos* – needs to be distinguished from forms of cultural production intrinsically linked to technological media: the tabloid newspaper, radio, television. Nevertheless Benjamin alerts us to the altered condition of modernist texts, within a discursive environment in which media increasingly reproduce reality, and force literature to confront the issue of representation and the specificity of literature. In *Discourse Networks*, Kittler argues that it is the mimetic function of writing which is usurped by the coming of technological storage: "Since December 28, 1895, there has been one infallible criterion for high literature: it cannot be filmed" (1990: 248) – by which he means that film has usurped both the realistic and the imaginary roles of literature, leaving it with "words as literal anti-nature," abandoning referentiality. This provides a powerful impulse in the modernist text: the Russian Futurist *Zaum* or Eliot's broken syllables in *The Waste Land* posit a word which refuses not only realism but mass readership, instead dwelling on the roots of language. A more literal version of this refusal is the importance of small-press publication for modernist writing, which represented, Lawrence Rainey has argued, an attempt to create a cultural space apart from (and in that sense conditioned by) mass-market publication (see Chapter 11 of this volume). The small-press book, appreciating even before it is published, carries the imprint of the human hand in its typography and binding, a regressive technology realized as cultural capital.

This essay has traversed a wide range of areas in its search for the traces of technology in modernism: celebrations of technology as extending human capacity, including the power of literature; critiques of industrial capitalism and mass culture; descriptions of the social "machine" as they relate to technology; consideration of the human body and language. The plurality of areas in which technology must be considered is a function of its omnipresence in modern life, its tendency to freely plug into contexts and generate new connections, linguistic or otherwise. We need to accept, that is to say, the challenge of seeing technology not simply as a matter of devices or even techniques, but as central to notions of the human – and to thinking itself. We have also seen technology likened to notions of evolution and progress, and also to the idea of evolution interrupted, overtaken by technology's semi-autonomy; or even to the fixity of death. Technology as anti-human, technology as fundamental to the human; technology as culture, technology as the destruction of culture – these are the contradictions which form the modern subject.

References and Further Reading

Adorno, T. and Horkheimer, M. [1947] 1979. *The Dialectic of Enlightenment*. Trans. John Cumming. London: Verso. (Original translation London: Allen Lane, 1973.)

Armstrong, T. 1998. *Modernism, Technology and the Body: A Cultural Study*. Cambridge: Cambridge University Press.

Benjamin, W. 1936 [1968]. The Work of Art in the Age of Mechanical Reproduction. In Hannah Arendt, ed., *Illuminations* Trans. Harry Zohn. New York: Harcourt, Brace.

Clarke, B. 1996. *Dora Marsden and Early Modernism: Gender, Individualism, Science*. Ann Arbor: University of Michigan Press.

Conrad, P. 1998. *Modern Times, Modern Places*. London: Thames & Hudson.

Crary, J. 1999. *Suspensions of Perception: Attention, Spectacle, and Modern Culture*. Cambridge, MA: MIT Press.

Danius, S. 2002. *The Senses of Modernism: Technology, Perception and Modernist Aesthetics*. Ithaca: Cornell University Press.

de Laurentis, T., Huyssen, A., and Woodward, K. eds., 1980. *The Technological Imagination: Theories and Fictions*. Madison: Coda Press.

Doane, M. A. 1996. Temporality, Storage, Legibility: Freud, Marey and the Cinema. *Critical Inquiry* 22: 313–43.

Forum for Modern Language Studies. 2001. Special Issue: *Literature and Technology* 37/2.

Hård, M. and A. Jamison, eds. 1998. *The Intellectual Appropriation of Technology: Discourses on Modernity, 1900–1939*. Cambridge, MA: MIT Press.

Kenner, H. 1987. *The Mechanic Muse*. New York: Oxford University Press.

Kern, S. 1983. *The Culture of Time and Space, 1880–1918*. Cambridge, MA: Harvard University Press.

Kittler, F. A. 1985 [1990]. *Discourse Networks 1800/1900*. Trans. Michael Metteer. Stanford: Stanford University Press.

——. 1999. *Gramophone, Film, Typewriter*. Trans. Geoffrey Winthrop-Young and Michael Wutz. Stanford: Stanford University Press.

Lutz, T. 1991. *American Nervousness, 1903*. Ithaca: Cornell University Press.

Marx, L. 1988. *The Pilot and the Passenger: Essays on Literature, Technology and Culture in the United States*. New York: Oxford University Press.

Mitcham, C. 1994. *Thinking Through Technology: The Path between Engineering and Philosophy*. Chicago: University of Chicago Press.

Nye, D. 1994. *The American Technological Sublime*. Cambridge, MA: MIT Press.

Pick, D. 1993. *War Machine: The Rationalization of Slaughter in the Modern Age*. New Haven: Yale University Press.

Pound, E. 1996. *Machine Art and Other Writings: The Lost Thought of the Italian Years*. Ed. Maria Luisa Ardizzone. Durham: Duke University Press.

Rabinbach, A. 1990. *The Human Motor: Energy, Fatigue, and the Origins of Modernity*. New York: Basic Books.

Schwartz, H. 1992. Torque: The New Kinaesthetic of the Twentieth Century. In Jonathan Crary and Stanford Kwinter, eds., *Incorporations* [*Zone* 6], pp. 71–126. New York: Urzone.

Seltzer, M. 1992. *Bodies and Machines*. New York: Routledge.

Steinman, L. M. 1987. *Made in America: Science, Technology and the American Modern-*

ist Poets. New Haven: Yale University Press.

Theall, D. F. 1997. *James Joyce's Techno-Poetics*. Toronto: University of Toronto Press.

Tichi, C. 1987. *Shifting Gears: Technology, Literature and Culture in Modernist America*. Chapel Hill: University of North Carolina Press.

9

The Concept of the State, 1880–1939: "The discredit of the State is a sign that it has done its work well"

Sarah Wilkinson

> "Stability," said the Controller, "stability. No civilization without social stability. No social stability without individual stability."
>
> Aldous Huxley, Brave New World *(1932)*

British political and constitutional stability in the late nineteenth and early twentieth century disguises the complexity of concepts of the state in circulation. This survey attempts to explore that complexity, albeit as a parasite on the wide and detailed research available on the subject. The British debate appears narrow when compared to the Continent in the same period, where the distinctions between political theories, such as those of Durkheim and Sorel, were much starker and far less capable of producing a pragmatic political consensus. In Britain, debates about the state resulted in legislation for a mixed economy and considerable centralized provision for the individual, by using taxation to extract the "social" value of wealth and then to use it for social purposes. The extension of the suffrage and the successful waging of a protracted European war also suggest stability rather than innovation in state functions. It is argued that although the parameters of debate were relatively narrow, and did not include influential Marxist or fascist groups until late in the period, there were multifarious distinctions within those parameters which were vehemently contested in both political and theoretical debate. To accompany this argument, we look in brief at the problem of "atmosphere" and the transmission of ideas between theorists, academics, and politicians which could inform legislation. In such a survey, as Collini has noted, a certain amount of patchworking must go on: the juxtaposition of quotations from different theorists without context to suggest the extent of their beliefs (1979: 10). All such references are given here with the knowledge of their limitations.

Our view of the development of the state is clouded to some extent by the knowledge of the formation of a welfare state in the post-1945 period. The apparent retraction of state functions after 1918 is often contrasted with the extensions of 1945, and World War II has been viewed as the catalyst for changes which had their roots in the late nineteenth century, and were retarded rather than advanced by the experience of World War I. The role of war as a test of state function was recognized during World War I, however, and the point was made by the Oxford philosopher Ernest Barker that when the state was working well, it was least popular and vice versa (1915: 121). The ability of the state to wage war and to defend its imperial possessions were growing preoccupations after the Boer War, and similar arguments about the health of British democracy were made in the face of the Nazi threat as were made about the health of the British population after the Boer campaign.

The threats to the effective functions of the state were insidious as well as external, and can be broadly defined as the claim to universal male and female suffrage, organized labor, and Irish nationalism. Settlements on these subjects were largely achieved within the progressive models of state development prevalent in the Edwardian period, with the exception of the Irish civil war. The scale and violence of suffrage and labor demonstrations before World War I suggest some resistance to the pace of the legislative development of state function. Yet the Pankhursts opposed the labor demonstrations which had coincided with their own and the suffragette movement largely supported the war effort. With Labour backing, the Liberal government responded with plans for a general franchise extension in August 1916, despite Asquith's previous opposition.

Terminology accentuates the impression of stability in state theory. The dual political and economic meanings which the terms "individualism" and "collectivism" have acquired can lead us to conflate the ethical end desired from political organization with the economic organization chosen to accompany it. Individualism and collectivism, often used as the philosophical pseudonyms of the political terms "liberalism" and "socialism," take the individual as the basic unit of social analysis but place him in different contexts, at one time alone, at another inexorably linked to his companions by something which may be mere voluntary association but which may be something less tangible, like the attachment of a cell to an organism. Some of the problems of distinguishing the bands of the spectrum of debate stem from the fact that "individualism" has acquired not only the economic sense inherent in free trade, but also the political and ethical sense of the moral nature of personality and self-fulfillment associated with liberalism. Whilst individualism can connote unrestrained competition and freedom, Michael Freeden has suggested that the political and ethical sense might more properly be called "individuality" (1978: 29–30). To meet these problems, Stefan Collini has suggested in his work on L. T. Hobhouse that historians can use individualism and collectivism to reflect the way that they were used by the theorists in question and to reflect the full range of their meaning (1979: 13). In this survey, we try to show both historiographical and historical usages.

This duality can also be seen in usage of the term "collectivism." It can encompass forms of economic organization, such as nationalization of essential industries, which place greater emphasis on the individual's role in the community and the interdependence of all the constituent parts of that community. It can also suggest the ethical end of improving the life of all the individuals in the community equally. This holistic view of society and the role of the state shared with some individualists the metaphor of the state as an "organism" from the biological language pilfered from evolutionary theorists. In some cases, the ethical emphasis on the common good became more important than the fate of the individual; in other interpretations, the individual, rather than the community or "state," remained the first unit of analysis. In both cases, the change of emphasis toward increased recognition of the community justified the label of collectivism over individualism. When the organic metaphor is taken to its extreme, the individual is replaced by the community itself as the basic unit of analysis, producing the type of state theory most associated with both Stalinist Russia and fascism.

Almost all of the ideas that will be outlined below were and are capable at some point in our period of being dubbed "liberal." Some could also be labeled "socialist." Freeden has condensed classical liberal tenets to a belief in the rationality of man as an individual, belief in the possibility of human progress, freedom, and concern for society as a whole rather than sectional interests. The meaning of "socialism" was equally as broad and fluid between 1880 and 1939. At the beginning of our period, the label denoted a broad movement to secure working-class representation and living standards, incorporating both radical and more moderate elements. Although the international socialist movement had some influence in Britain, it was the Liberal Party's enduring appeal to the working man which contained "socialism" within the existing system of representation. The fight for better working conditions and representation for the industrial worker was, therefore, contained largely within a capitalist framework. The eventual pact between the trade unions, the Labour Representation Committee, and the Liberal Party in the early 1900s demonstrated the extent to which socialism could be a non-revolutionary movement. Groups such as the Fabians fell within this non-revolutionary framework, whereas the Social Democratic Federation (SDF) formed in 1883, under Henry Hyndman, fell outside of it.

Although Beatrice Potter (she married Sidney Webb in 1892) declared herself a socialist in 1890 after observing the Fabians at work in the London dock strikes, she disassociated herself from the SDF's encouragement of a "catastrophic overturning of the existing order" (Mackenzie 1978: I, 68–9). The socialist interests of the Fabians themselves spanned study of Marx to interpretations of Ricardian political economy and were declared in their statement of purpose in 1887: "the general dissemination of knowledge as to the relation between the individual and society in its economic, ethical and political aspects" (Mackenzie 1978: I, 105). Insurrectionists such as Hyndman can thus be included under the broad banner of "socialism" but were in a minority compared to the pragmatic, moralistic, and non-revolutionary views of many Fabians and even of other members of the SDF. At the other end of our period, the socialist movement was much more broadly radicalized, encompassing both the middle ground of social reform occupied previously by the Liberal Party and a growing affiliation to international socialism. Many of the moderate reformers of the early part of the period became proponents of more radical communist views between the wars and, in the case of Beatrice and Sidney Webb, this transformation manifested itself as an overt commitment to Soviet communism.

The theorists examined here, however, perceived a much sharper contrast between individualism and collectivism than we have argued for with hindsight. A. D. Lindsay, of Balliol College, Oxford, wrote, in February 1914, "we are familiar with the fact that the latter half of the nineteenth century was marked by a change in political practice and thought from Individualism to Collectivism" (1914: 128). Lindsay's view was similar to the introduction to the second edition of A. V. Dicey's *Law and Public Opinion*, also published in 1914, which noted that "the current of opinion had for thirty or forty years been gradually running with more and more force in the direction of collectivism." Whether within the narrow debate suggested here or the wider debate which contemporary theorists perceived themselves to be in, Lindsay rightly identified considerable changes. During the first half of our period, roughly to the end of World War I, arguments centered on the economic implications of the relationship between state and individual for society's least privileged members. A shift occurred from a concept of the individual as a politically isolated agent towards his life within associations, which could mean family, trade, or state. This reflected a growing trend to define liberty not simply in terms of political freedoms such as suffrage and demonstration, but also in terms of the equalization of economic opportunity and safeguards against economic contingencies. On this analysis the individual was not an isolated economic agent, and the community or "social sphere" of his life played an equally important role in determining his economic life and the fulfillment of his individuality.

The achievement of this political and economic liberty through state as opposed to voluntary action, however, was facilitated by the loss of confidence in the self-regulation of the market caused by experiences of depression and long-term unemployment in the 1880s. Most state theorists arrived at the conclusion that greater state intervention in the economic sphere was necessary to help individuals achieve personal fulfillment, but they approached this conclusion from different philosophical directions, yet with the common metaphor of the society as an organism. The nature of the individual's political representation, whether on a local or national level, assumed much greater importance. National government as well as local traditions of self-government were recognized as having a role in the efficient promotion of moral and economic welfare. For some, this entailed a glorification of the state apparatus as a means of achieving efficiency and fairness. For others, such reliance implied the slavery of the masses and the subjugation of the individual.

Philosophy and Philanthropy

The basic metaphor of the organism used to describe the state and the questions asked about the relations between individual and state were common to most shades of theorist. Yet in 1915, this unity was obscured by what the Ernest Barker called the "current number of new 'isms' which had, in his opinion, the effect of making men feel that they lived in new and unstable days" (1915: 74–5). The first "ism" of our chronology is the British Idealist school, whose most prominent members were T. H. Green,

F. H. Bradley, Bernard Bosanquet, and D. G. Ritchie. Although chronologically prior, their work and influence ran in parallel to the new liberal movement which gained recognition slightly later. Their work focused on describing the personality of the state and its relations with individuals, which metaphor earned them the tag of neo-Hegelians. Hegelianism was identified by its critics as the triumph of the reified state over the individual, of the state as the universal will, from where the individual derived his place in society and whose ends the individual served. The British Idealists, however, explored rather than confirmed the Hegelian position. In *Principles of Political Obligation* (1915), T. H. Green emphasized the role of the individual over that of the state, claiming that the life of the nation had no real existence except as the life of the individuals composing the nation. Writing in the same collection of essays as Green, Bernard Bosanquet interpreted the reification of the state as the "universal will" to mean that the common mind existed in, but not outside of, the minds of all those who shared a common purpose.

The British Idealists also differed amongst themselves as to the extent of state activity which would endanger the self-reliance of the individual, drawing on J. S. Mill's maxims in *On Liberty* (1859) for balancing state action against individual education. In *Socialism and Natural Selection* (1895), Bosanquet acknowledged that the reality of the general will should not be extended to guarantee without protest the existence of all individuals, because this would be destructive of social life and fatal to character. The moral development of the individual was not incompatible with state intervention in his life, on this analysis, and could even be stimulated by state action up to a certain point. In 1876, F. H. Bradley had also stated this potential interdependence between state and individual in his essay "Ideal Morality," arguing that the realization of the "best self" as a moral duty comprised two components, the realization of a social and a nonsocial self.

The Idealist argument that the state, to whatever degree, could be involved in the moral self-development of the individual supposed a beneficial relationship between state and individual which had been denied by the natural rights theorist, Herbert Spencer, in the 1850s and 1860s. Spencer advocated that natural rights were a priori characteristics of the individual and that nature and spirit were unified. Natural selection determined the morality of an individual. Spencer denied that the individual derived any sense of self, position, or duty from the state. For him, as a result, most forms of legislation were encroachments upon liberty. As his close friend Beatrice Potter noted, he drew most of his conclusions by applying biological and evolutionary data to human social relations, and she doubted that social laws could really be deduced in this way but thought that they needed scientific investigation in their own right (Mackenzie 1978: I, 22). By the end of his career, Spencer had engaged with the urban problems revealed by social investigation, but had indicted state intervention in the processes of natural development as their cause. In contrast, the Idealists thought that society was, as David Boucher has described it, a "moral organism the cohesiveness of which is not mechanical or biological ... but instead depends upon the relation in which each person stands with every other" (1997: xx–xxi). They drew a more harmonious picture of social relations than Spencer, but the importance of self-realization and self-reliance to both increases the continuity of moral purpose rather than the disjuncture between the two.

The argument for continuity can be further supported by the way in which the Idealists themselves were influenced by evolutionary theory. The metaphor of evolution, applied to spirit or mind, was common in Idealist writing even if some of its scientific predicates were rejected. The Darwinist T. H. Huxley had rejected the unity of nature and spirit, suggesting that natural rights benefited the individual at the expense of society, whereas moral rights conferred obligations as well as benefits upon the individual. Fitness could not be an ethical condition because it was not inherent in the individual, it could be affected by external circumstances. Bosanquet rejected this proposition by arguing that the end aim of survival was not survival itself, as he considered Huxley to believe, but the type of survival created, which introduced a moral element, considering that not only the bare fact of survival, but the nature of the struggle in which survival has to be sought had to be examined. (See also Chapter 1 of this volume).

Most of the Idealists worked professionally in Oxford, but a growing number had dual lives in London, linked, like Bosanquet and his wife Helen, to the Charities Organization Society and its social work. Social and political theory increasingly moved to the site of empirical research in the 1880s and 1890s, and became more involved with pragmatic theories of state which dealt with the urgent social and economic situation in the modern industrialized metropolis under the umbrella label of the "New Liberalism." In the hands of L. T. Hobhouse, and, to a greater degree, J. A. Hobson, the actual relationship between the state and the individual was increasingly defined in economic rather than sovereign terms, but Collini points out that many theorists, including Hobhouse, still maintained that state action had an ethical, not a purely materialistic purpose (1979: 67, 73). Instead of the polarity of individual and state, however, a wider sphere in which both state and individual functioned was identified. Michael Freeden has pinpointed the awareness of the "social" as a concept in addition to that of the individual as the crucial break from the assumptions of classical liberal individualism (1978: 13). Within the "social" sphere, the question of the responsibility for the alleviation of social ills, or, more positively, the provision of social welfare, prompted debate on forms of taxation as means of redistributing wealth which was not created solely by the individual and the recognition of any responsibility by the wealthy toward the working classes which should be channeled through the state.

The conceptualization of a "social sphere" shows the growing marriage between external conditions and academic theory about the role of the state. In March 1886, Beatrice Potter wrote to Joseph Chamberlain explaining the difference between her two worlds: "When I leave London, and the peculiar conditions surrounding the working class there, I am lost in a sea of general principles and crotchets" (Mackenzie 1978: I, 53). The purely academic life which someone like F. H. Bradley had lived gave way in the early 1880s to an active philanthropy amongst intellectuals. Within voluntary bodies such as Toynbee Hall, the Charities Organization Society, and Charles Booth's social survey movement, figures as diverse as the Webbs and Bernard Bosanquet developed the sense that the scale of the poverty problem, in London at least, could not purely be the product of the individual's enterprise or lack of it, but had its causes in economic life which was beyond the control of the individual.

Perhaps the most important result of both charitable and investigative work was the sectionalization of the poverty problem by class. For some, the classes might still be qualitative and the language of the deserving and the undeserving poor took some considerable time to lapse. Accusations that poverty was to some extent the result of bad moral character appeared in both the majority and minority reports of the Royal Commission on the Poor Laws in 1909, which had been established in 1905 to investigate relief for the unemployed. Booth, the economist Alfred Marshall and William Beveridge all favored the removal of the unhelpable "residuum" of society to disciplinary labor colonies. Much social work, however, particularly that of Helen Bosanquet, was centered on trying to rescue and rehabilitate the residuum before their final descent into irretrievable pauperdom. Some investigators themselves perceived that moving among the poor had significant class implications, as an early contribution to the *Pall Mall Gazette* in 1886 by Beatrice Potter entitled "A Lady's View of the Unemployed" made plain (Mackenzie 1978: I, 50).

The class divisions between subject and investigator created the tension between the inclusion of the urban masses in economic and political life and the fear experienced by some of the power latent in the mass. Despite the ambivalence detectable in even the most left-leaning socialist, the sheer quantity and extremity of urban poverty made the working class the obvious target for future theorization about the relationship between the state and the individual. London's experience of seasonal and cyclical unemployment in the 1880s prompted a reassessment of the Ricardian trade cycle and suggested an economic phenomenon dependent more on national trade than individual enterprise. The mere identification of unemployment as a concept not controlled solely by character and personal morality was perhaps the greatest discovery of the investigative sociology centered on London. Jose Harris has dated the appearance of "unemployed" and "unemployment" as terms used by political economists to 1888, although many references had been made to it in the previous fifty years according to the literature used by the Webbs (1972: 4).

The medium by which the depth and darkness of the poverty abyss was illustrated was survey literature, based on a growing methodology for sociological study. The earliest example is perhaps Andrew Mearns's *The Bitter Cry of Outcast London: A Study into the Condition of the Abject Poor*, published in 1883. In the bibliography to *Problems of Poverty*, published in 1891, J. A. Hobson also mentioned Charles Booth's *Labour and Life of the People*, (1889; expanded as *Life and Labour of the People of London*, 17 vols., 1891–1902) and the Report of the Industrial Remuneration Committee. Hobson considered Booth's work to be of particular importance because it not only provided a wealth of factual information, "for the formation of sound opinion and the explosion of fallacies," but had also laid down the lines of a new branch of social study. The moral purpose of this new social study, in Hobson's opinion, was that men and women of "the more fortunate classes" felt that they had no right to be contented with the condition of the poor, "the demand that a life worth living shall be made possible for all, and that the knowledge, wealth and energy of a nation shall be rightly devoted to no other end than this, is the true measure of the moral growth of a civilized community." Similar sociological enterprises were published by Seebohm Rowntree in 1901 and Beatrice Potter on sweated labor in 1890, which work had formed the basis of her submissions to the House of Lords Committee on the subject in the previous year. Literary representations of London by George Gissing and H. G. Wells shared this preoccupation with the nether world of hidden London and the implications of the "quagmire of society" identified by Booth.

It was the definition of the community itself and its role, as Freeden has

argued, which became the defining characteristic of the philosophical debate surrounding social work in the East End of London in the 1880s and
1890s. The basis of the conceptualization of the "social" revisited the Idealists' territory of the community mind and also Mill's contention that part of
the individual's moral development should include responsibility toward
others. Hobhouse continued the debate as to whether this community "mind"
existed within or without the minds of the individuals of a community,
although he marked himself off clearly from the Idealist school in his attack
on Bosanquet in *The Metaphysical Theory of the State* (1918). He had previously contributed to the debate over the extent to which state action could
infringe the liberty of the individual in *The Labour Movement* (1893). Nonetheless, in the later book he adheres to Mill's defense of the need to safeguard free thought and discussion and restates that true liberty is found
when each man has the greatest possible opportunity for making the best of
himself. His statement of the "collective interest," as an extension of the
existence of the collective mind, also appears in *The Labour Movement*, where
he states that the decisions of a democratic community present the nearest
approach to a collective judgment of the social organism upon its collective
interests. That judgment on the fundamental conditions of social health
should then be enforced by collective authority. In *Liberalism* (1911),
Hobhouse was then able to argue that if the individual had certain rights,
inherent in society, agreed upon by the collective judgment, state action to
fulfill those rights could be justified. These rights had to contribute to the
moral aims of society, which might be equated, semantically, with "the common good."

New Liberalism, Legislation, and Atmosphere

Liberalism was published in 1911 after the battle for the implementation of
new liberal economic theory had already been won in Parliament, starting
with Asquith's differential income tax in 1907. The main party political
divide over the economic function of the state had been between free
trade (liberal) and protectionism (Conservative) in the period up to 1906.
This was superseded by the redistributive arguments of Hobson and
Hobhouse but continued to inform economic policy throughout the period. The first major contribution to the redefinition of the justifiable economic functions of the state was J. A. Hobson's *The Physiology of Industry*,
published in 1889. Freeden argues that Hobson was " by far the most original and penetrating of the new liberal theorists at the turn of the century,

one who deserves far greater credit as an outstanding social thinker with a much larger amount of influence than is generally realized." Hobson identified a balance between expenditure on consumption and capital goods as crucial to economic prosperity and saw the hoarding of capital by the wealthy as a major hindrance to the maintenance of this balance. He also identified two factors by which capital was created: personal and social. As the result of the social element contained in it, it was possible to interfere with some personal property for the common good. In practical terms, this took the form of redistributive direct taxation on both a graduated and differentiated basis. Hobson himself believed that he was in fact only codifying an existing state of affairs, writing,

> When it is said that "we are all socialists to-day", what is meant is that we are all engaged in the active promotion or approval of legislation which can only be explained as a gradual unconscious recognition of the existence of a social property in capital which it is held politic to secure for the public use. (1891: 195)

The main governmental response to the social work of the previous twenty years came, stimulated by the exigencies of the Boer War, in the establishment of the Royal Commission on the Poor Laws in 1905, which investigated relief for the unemployed. This became the vehicle for the Webbs, amongst others, to express their vision of a comprehensive state medical service, insurance, and pensions provision. The stimulus behind the Commission itself, however, merits closer attention. Fears about the degeneracy of the population, either caused by biological inheritance if you were a Spencerian, or by environment if you were a Webb, had been stimulated by the difficulty of raising an army fit enough to win the Boer War. The National Efficiency movement, whilst not strictly philosophical, nevertheless united interest in genetic biology with the reality of the fitness of the population (see Chapters 1 and 2 of this volume).

Divisions over the Boer War also split some important groups who were generally united on social policy. Close to the Liberal Imperialists on social terms through R. B. Haldane, Sidney Webb, for example, disagreed profoundly with their stance on the war. Jose Harris has pointed out that although characteristic of the period that members of rival political factions regularly dined together, gossiped together, and visited each other's houses (1993: 185), social homogeneity was not reflected in agreement on all areas of policy, though Beatrice Webb was anxious to cultivate these links to have a chance of influencing legislation. On October 1, 1901,

Beatrice recorded her fears that

> neither Rosebery nor Asquith mean to declare themselves in favor of our measure of collectivism. But they hold no views that are inconsistent with it .... The time will come when, if they are to be a political force they will have to "fill up" the political workers with some positive convictions. Then, we think, for the needful minimum of nourishment they will fall back on us. (Mackenzie 1978: II, 137)

The influence of intellectuals and philosophers was often achieved through the media, as well as by personal contact. Editors who published philosophical and social theory were often those with the widest span of political connections. It is unusual to find copious references in political biographies to contemporary theorists but much more common to find references to newspaper editors. H. W. Massingham, editor of the new liberal paper, the *Nation*, from 1907, had been close to the Webbs and George Bernard Shaw in the 1890s. He was also heavily involved in internal liberal politics between 1900 and 1916. Leonard Hobhouse, with much leader-writing experience from the *Manchester Guardian* under C. P. Scott, was taken on as political editor of the new London newspaper, *Tribune*, in 1905, despite thinking that he would be too socialistic for its proprietor. Other periodicals advertised the work of rather narrower groups. The Rainbow Circle, with its mixture of liberal and socialist thinkers, published its papers in the *Progressive Review*. The Circle also involved some political figures, namely R. B. Haldane, Ramsay MacDonald, and Herbert Samuel, alongside newspapermen such as A. G. Gardiner.

Where intellectuals and social philosophers did have links to politicians, the meeting of minds was not always complete or comprehensive beyond general principles. One of the potential pitfalls of describing an "atmosphere" is to claim its existence through the simple equation of a philosophical idea in currency with legislation which seems to match the broad outline of that philosophy. Presaged by Harcourt's death duties on landed estates in 1894, the social insurance legislation of 1909 was centrally funded from taxation. It provided old-age pensions to those over seventy on low incomes on a noncontributory basis and seems broadly to fit the new liberal and socialist theories about taxing "social" capital to provide social welfare.

Neat consonance, however, between new liberalism and legislation proved impossible. New Liberalism and its affiliated groups covered too wide a spectrum of belief for any such direct link to exist. Two potential architects of the pension scheme, the liberal William Beveridge and the Fabian Webbs, who had links to both new liberalism and to the social investigation movement of the 1880s and 1890s, had very different ideas about the form the legislation should take, and neither party actually shaped the resulting Act. Beveridge was impressed by the German scheme of compulsory insurance for pensions, in contrast to the Webbs, who favored a scheme which promoted better conduct by the recipients of the pension. More generally, Beveridge's biographer has shown that there is no evidence that Beveridge was influenced by Hobhouse's ideas, and that he explicitly rejected Hobson's under-consumptionist theories in his 1909 book, *Unemployment: A Problem of Industry* (Harris 1997: 167). His methods for alleviating unemployment did involve centralized governmental intervention in the economy but through labor exchanges and existing trade organizations rather than redistribution.

World War I

The sphere of the "social" appeared to have been established in the 1909 and 1911 pension and unemployment insurance legislation but World War I extended and bureaucratized it far beyond the scope of New Liberal or Labour theorization. On August 28, 1914, the Webbs dined with Earl Grey, Lloyd George, Haldane, and other Cabinet ministers. Beatrice Webb recorded in her diary that Lloyd George for one was prepared for the boldest measures to reestablish credit and to keep the population employed for the duration of the war. At the beginning of the month, she had been impressed that the Asquith government seemed to be playing a bold hand, being far more radically collectivist than she had hoped. Four years later, on December 8, 1918, she was considerably less optimistic and could report that a revolution was not going to come from the Haldane Committee on the machinery of government, nor from the senior civil service (Mackenzie 1978: III, 148).

After the 1918 election, Webb also lamented the passing of the Liberal Party, and the polarization of party politics between the Lloyd George–Conservative phalanx and the Labour Party, with its ideal of the "equalitarian state." Despite her pessimism about the progressiveness of the Lloyd George coalition, the crisis Britain was undergoing did demand some notion of renewal and reconstruction, which was given shape in the Reconstruction Committee of 1914 and later the Ministry for Reconstruction. Here was an opportunity for both intellectuals and politicians to set out a utopia, to redesign and to plan. Yet even with the rubicon of taxation for social welfare crossed, the state went out of vogue in 1918, perhaps as a result of the vilification of the Prussian state and the dangers of state idolatry which the war had laid open to view. Revulsion at the compulsive powers of the state under the Defence of the Realm Act, 1914 (DORA) and in the conscription debate even provoked the restatement of Spencerian objections to the state by new liberal thinkers such as Hobhouse. Most of these doubts had started earlier in the war. By 1916, in *Questions of War and Peace*, Hobhouse was desperately concerned that in the course of fighting a war to safeguard "a free and human civilization", Britain might become a militarist nation with conscription and tariff reform.

Much historiography examines the impact of World War I from the assumption that the growth of state intervention up to 1914 continued during the war and then radically retracted afterwards, with resulting disaster for the economy in the 1920s and 1930s. The extent of state intervention during the war was considerable, but David French has argued convincingly that this was the result of the nature of the war, rather than ideological hangovers from the Edwardian period. The enlargement of national state control of industry in May 1915, typified by the creation of the Ministry of Munitions, shows clearly the coincidence between the escalation of the war, as the result of Kitchener's raising of a mass army, and state intervention. The interpretation inspired by an article by the socialist R. H. Tawney in 1941 argues that the Asquith government and the coalition failed to develop a coherent theory of state controls of industry which could be continued after the war. In contrast, Peter Cline has pointed out that it was the sudden economic collapse of Germany in 1918 which reduced the need for continued controls and which coincided with the Ministry of Reconstruction's plans (Burk 1982: 157). The Ministry's Report of December 1918 identified its main areas of work as transitional economics, commerce and production, labor and industrial organization, rural development, and social development. Of these, the last category is perhaps most redolent of prewar reformulations of state functions whereas the first three were predominantly concerned with the situation created by the war. However, the wartime Ministries of Labour and Health survived the end of the war and provide some argument to suggest all the lessons of war collectivism had not been discarded.

There is a divergence between the role of social policy and economic controls during World War I caused by the constraints of planning without the certainty of decisive victory, and the specter of protracted economic warfare with Germany after a ceasefire. The state's role in industrial relations, however, was common to both economic and social policy and to ideas surrounding the organization of the state. The huge strike actions both immediately before and during the war demanded that attention be paid to the specific problems of individual industries as well as to the broader, theoretical picture. Perhaps the clearest indication of governmental reluctance to continue its intervention in industry in the postwar period came in the decontrol of mining in 1921, despite the Sankey Commission's recommendation that the industry should be nationalized. Raised again in 1925–6 and debated throughout the 1930s, nationalization became the chief extension of governmental function demanded after the war, but the strength of its appeal lay more in the practical relief of industrial action rather than in a socialist approach to economic problems.

However, there was no absence of left-wing theorization. Looking back on the period, G. D. H. Cole stated that it was the unity and interdependence of human life as the benchmark of planning implicit in the work of J. A. Hobson which had gone so far to justify social welfare legislation:

> The main question will be, not how are we to organise the machinery of government, but how are we to organise the entire economic and political life of the community, and of one community in relation to others. Politics and economics will cease to be thought about as mainly separate problems, and will present themselves as one and the same problem. (1932: 151)

Twelve years earlier, in *Social Theory* (1920), Cole had already disputed that social theory should revolve solely around the relationship between the individual and the state but should attempt to explain man's social relations in terms of his will, and, consequently, of his associations, of which the state was just one. The liberty of the individual expressed through associational self-government, above all, in industry, was the most coherent, non-revolutionary alternative to state socialism. Organization for war had itself thrown up some proto-syndicalist movements such as the Whitley Councils. These boards, comprising employers and employees in individual industries, had introduced state organization of wage controls in the public sector and survived the postwar period. The Reconstruction Report in December 1918 described these councils in the organic, interdependent language of new liberalism, enthusing about the "promise of a wide extension of those bodies and of future developments in the direction of an industrial policy based on joint responsibility and mutual understanding." Although guild socialism, stimulated by Ruskin's accounts of voluntary trade organizations in the Middle Ages, was a minority view in the trade union movement before the war, it had received some limited support from the Webbs and the Fabian movement in 1911–12. These "young men," Cole, Lansbury, and Mellor, were studiously ignored by Old Labour at the 1915 party congress and had alienated parts of the Fabian Society but became reconciled to the latter as the war progressed, and they found little support amongst the trade unions. This radical syndicalism, however, which Webb described as having taken the place of old-fashioned Marxism, became the mainstream of liberal and Labour opposition to the state in the postwar period.

Expansion of the Spectrum

The vision of an organic society adhered to by the New Liberals before the war continued to be debated during the 1920s. H. J. Laski, a political theorist who had spent considerable time in the United States and had held guild socialist views, preferred in *The Grammar of Politics* (1925) to restate society as a collection of individuals which emphasized the individual's right of participation in government as a means of achieving liberty. The problem of participation in government increasingly came to dominate writing about the state in the interwar period, alongside plans for how industry and government should be organized. The debate about the nature of political participation in Britain and industrial organization took place within the same broad framework of agreement as the earlier debates on the state and the individual had done. Rather than a debate amongst theorists, this movement aimed at producing a "national" consensus within the party political sphere, to which intellectuals and theorists could be drawn:

> We are divided in so far as we belong to one or other of the main political parties, but we are united in believing that nothing is at present more important than to reveal how wide is the measure of agreement that can be assembled on an immediate programme. At no time in British political history have so many minds been turned to the complete reorganisation of our social and economic life and to the promotion of a policy of economic reconciliation. (Cole 1935a: 309)

The forum for planning debate tended to take the form of think-tanks, exemplified by Political and Economic Planning (PEP) and the Next Five Years Group but also by the Liberal Summer School movement. The latter was largely responsible for the reinvigoration of the Liberal Party, after the wartime split, producing the pamphlet "Britain's Industrial Future" in 1928. Partly the result of evidence that the unmanaged postwar economy was failing and partly the result of European examples of political overmanagement, the planning movement in Britain combined some Keynesian economic theory with that of the New Liberals and shrouded it in the necessity to include the masses in government in some way. The planning movement was already under way before the fiscal crisis of 1931 and the launch of "A National Plan for Great Britain" by Gerald Barry's *Week-End Review* afforded it both force and urgency. The formation of the National Government after the collapse of MacDonald's second Labour administration in the summer of 1931 lent an extra edge to the "national" rhetoric in which these investigations of the coal, steel, and electricity industries were presented by PEP and the *Week-End Review.*

The *Plan for Britain*, published in book form in 1935, seemed to have achieved a marriage of theorists and politicians which denied the need for party structures to implement a broad shake-up of the organization of the state. In the industrial sphere, the *Plan for Britain* argued that the old dichotomy between individualism and socialism was no longer applicable, since Britain already had a mixed economy, comprising elements of both, and was likely to continue to do so. Amongst their recommendations was an expert Economic Advisory Board which would consult all sectors of industry, and various models for self-government which industries could chose to adopt. The social ills which the plan was supposed to cure mirrored to a large extent those which had concerned the New Liberals. Inequality of wealth, inequality of privilege and unequal distribution of production, capital, and labor all contributed, according to the *Plan*, to the "degree of poverty and misery at the lower end of the social scale which is an indictment both of our brains and of our hearts." Casting an eye down the list of signatories to the plan, this overlap should not surprise us unduly, since the list contains a good sample of the major Liberal, if not a fair sample of Labour, theorists of the previous forty years. Thus the names of Allen of Hurtwood, Norman Angell, H. A. L Fisher, J. A. Hobson, C. E. M. Joad, A. D. Lindsay, Gilbert Murray, and Seebohm Rowntree stood next to those of the young Conservative politicians Harold Macmillan and Robert Boothby, which in turn stood next to more radical names such as H. G. Wells and Eleanor Rathbone.

The call for national unity and for the rejection of extreme political alternatives to manage the crisis served to reinforce the idea of Britain as the home of individual liberties. Kingsley Martin, editor of the *New States-*

man, summarized this sentiment in a pamphlet from 1938:

> When people speak of England as the home of liberty, they refer to something very deep in the character of the British people and institutions – to a conception of fair play and toleration, and to that habit of reasonable compromise and common-sense in politics, which is the only alternative to violence and dictatorship. (1938: 31)

The celebration of "Englishness," redolent of Baldwin's 1924 speeches on national rather than class unity and the glory of rural Britain, was also a way in which political participation by the masses could be encouraged. The science of public opinion was a huge Anglo-American growth industry in the first half of the twentieth century. American theorists such as A. Lawrence Lowell, Harold Lasswell, and Harold Childs had close links to the British academic James Bryce and the polemicist Norman Angell. Even without a generally accepted theory of the relations between the public and the press, or of the usefulness of public opinion polling, the importance of the "man in the street" as a bulwark against dictatorship was not overlooked by political theorists or politicians. The importance of political education, in the eyes of many theorists, had to be matched by governmental willingness to lead the public. Lord Allen of Hurtwood considered in *Britain's Political Future* (1934) that the emergence of a new dark age of revolution or dictatorship could only be avoided if politicians insisted on interpreting democracy as following rather than leading opinion. The Next Five Years Group was also convinced that a political system was more surely founded upon a free and educated public opinion, democratically led, than upon any authoritative regime. If the public were to play such a significant role, the transmission of information to them and the gleaning of their opinions was crucial. The Gallup opinion polls and anthropological group Mass-Observation, headed by the Surrealist poet Charles Madge see Chapter 5 of this volume), pursued these goals in a comparable way to the New Liberal desire for social facts about poverty. Similar approaches to depicting "ordinary life" in a realistic way can also be seen in the documentary film movement inspired by John Grierson at the Post Office Film Unit.

Middle opinion, as Arthur Marwick has termed it, regarded the dichotomy of individualism and socialism as obsolete, and formed a sort of conservative popular front on this basis (1964: 285ff.). Although the sense that Britain had failed to recover from World War I and was equipped with political institutions designed for the nineteenth century was common across the political spectrum, the answer to the crisis of democracy of the 1930s also came in forms other than moderate planning. Alternative continental models provided by the dictator states in Europe expanded the parameters of British political theory, producing more pronounced collectivist arguments on the left and importing the language of "national reconstruction" on the right. In the latter case, the fear of constitutional revolution was still minimal, and planning was aimed to take place within a capitalist system. Oswald Mosley's political career commenced on the left wing of the planning movement, introducing proto-Keynesian theories of public works and government control of credit to the 1929 Labour government, before enshrining his ideas in the separate "New Party" in 1930. The failure of the New Party in the 1931 election, combined with Mosley's visits to Italy and political adventurism, resulted in Britain's only organized fascist party, the British Union of Fascists (BUF) in 1932. The ideology of the BUF translated the crisis of democracy into a fight to the death between communism and fascism as a means of solving the crisis.

Socialist planning, on the other hand, looked to the Soviet Union and its Five Year Plans for pragmatic models for regeneration. The work of G. D. H. Cole and Barbara Wootton advocated centralist economic planning on the Soviet model, but maintained the old progressive rather than the new revolutionary mode of transition. Although the British Communist Party had working-class strongholds in the mining districts of Wales and Scotland, it suffered poor election results throughout the 1930s. Yet the constant challenge of the Communist Party at municipal elections provided a more effective fourth-party influence than that of the BUF. The antifascist Popular Front movement announced by the Communist International in 1934 was more than an electoral ticket, however, and provided an attractive theoretical position for many intellectuals.

To return to our opening remarks, the relative stability of British institutions and the maintenance of democracy do detract from the extent of the challenges to state function which took place during this period. As Martin Pugh has suggested, the debate about the state was largely one between groups of moderates (1993: 288). Yet the scale and pace of change should not be underestimated, particularly in the spheres of social welfare provision and suffrage. Perhaps the most significant trend was the growing confidence that the state was the most efficient, if not always the most desirable, guardian of liberties. An emphasis on moral self-improvement lingered in much of the rhetoric which described the mass electorate but the mere fact of that electorate required large-scale administration at a national level, particularly after World War I. Yet the major shifts in theorization occurred in peacetime rather than during war, until the very end of our period, when planning for reconstruction during World War II formed the basis of the economic and welfare reforms which occurred thereafter. Otherwise, the need for pragmatic solutions to contemporary social problems prompted the bulk of the redefinitions that occurred. The emphasis on the individual in his social context informed both left- and right-wing theorization throughout the period and did not produce the cult of the state itself as an end, except in some models of efficiency on the extreme left of the Labour Party in the interwar period. The examples of dictatorship in Europe and the Soviet Union informed mainstream British debate, however, by reinforcing the idea of a "national" democratic solution to the economic exigencies of the aftermath of World War I. This same flavor of party political compromise which nonetheless took account of theoretical developments can be traced throughout our period, and is perhaps one explanation of Britain's beguiling state expansion.

References and Further Reading

Barker, E. 1915. The Discredited State. *Political Quarterly* 5: 101–21.

——, ed. 1915. *Political Thought from Herbert Spencer to the Present Day*. London: Home University Library.

Boucher, D., ed. 1997. *The British Idealists*. Cambridge: Cambridge University Press.

Cline, P. 1982. Winding down the War Economy: British Plans for Peacetime Recovery, 1916–19. In K. Burk, ed., *War and the State. The Transformation of British Government, 1914–1919*, pp. 157–78. London: Allen & Unwin.

Cole, G. D. H. 1932. *Modern Theories and Forms of Political Organization*. London: Gollancz.

——. 1935a. *Liberty and Democratic Leadership, The Next Five Years Group. An Essay in Political Agreement*. London: Macmillan.

——. 1935b. *A Plan for Britain*. London: Clarion Press.

Collini, S. 1979. *Liberalism and Sociology. L. T. Hobhouse and Political Argument in England 1880–1914*. Cambridge: Cambridge University Press.

Freeden, M. 1978. *The New Liberalism. An Ideology of Social Reform*. Oxford: Clarendon Press.

——. 1986. *Liberalism Divided. A Study in British Political Thought 1914–1939*. Oxford: Clarendon Press.

——. 1990. *Reappraising J. A. Hobson: Humanism and Welfare*. London: Unwin Hyman.

——, ed. 1989. *Minutes of the Rainbow Circle, 1894–1924*. London: Royal Historical Society.

Harris, J. 1972. *Unemployment and Politics. A Study in English Social Policy 1886–1914*. Oxford: Clarendon Press.

——. 1990. Society and the State in Twentieth-century Britain. In F. M. L. Thompson, ed., *The Cambridge Social History of Britain 1750-1950. Volume 3: Social Agencies and Institutions*, pp. 52–61. Cambridge: Cambridge University Press.

——. 1993. *Private Lives, Public Spirit: Britain, 1870–1914*. London: Penguin.

——. 1997. *William Beveridge. A Biography*. Oxford: Clarendon Press.

Hobson, J. A. 1891. *Problems of Poverty. An Enquiry into the Industrial Condition of the Poor*. London: University Extension Series.

Laski, H. J. 1919. *Authority in the Modern State*. New Haven: Yale University Press.

Lindsay, A. D. 1914. The State in Recent Political Theory. *Political Quarterly* 1: 128–45.

Mackenzie, N., ed. 1978. *The Letters of Sidney and Beatrice Webb. Volumes I–III*. Cambridge: Cambridge University Press.

Martin, K. 1938. *Fascism, Democracy and the Press*. London: New Statesman & Nation.

Marwick, A. 1964. Middle Opinion in the Thirties: Planning, Progress and Political Agreement. *English Historical Review* 79: 285–98.

Pugh, M. 1993. *The Making of Modern British Politics 1867–1939*. Oxford: Blackwell.

Stedman Jones, G. 1971. *Outcast London: A Study in the Relationship between Classes in Victorian Society*. Oxford: Clarendon Press.

Stevenson, J. and Cook, C. 1994. *Britain in the Depression: Society and Politics, 1929-1939*. London: Longman.

Tawney, R. H. 1978. The Abolition of Economic Controls, 1918–1921. In J. M. Winter, ed., *History and Society: Essays by R. H. Tawney*. London: Routledge & Kegan Paul.

Thorpe, A. 1997. *A History of the British Labour Party*. Basingstoke: Macmillan.

10

Physics: "A strange footprint"

Michael H. Whitworth

Description and Explanation

Isaac Newton famously belittled his achievements in physics, depicting his scientific pursuits as those of "a boy playing on the sea-shore," diverting himself with "a smoother pebble or a prettier shell than ordinary, whilst the great ocean of truth lay all undiscovered before me" (quoted in Eddington 1920: 93). Although Albert Einstein was popularly believed to have "dethroned" his eighteenth-century forebear by devising the general principle of relativity, Newton's phrase remained common currency, known to scientific and literary writers alike. As the border of the known and the unknown, the seashore is an appropriate place to begin a discussion of scientific theories and scientific method:

> The only thing that moved upon the vast semicircle of the beach was one small black spot. As it came nearer to the ribs and spine of the stranded pilchard boat, it became apparent from a certain tenuity in its blackness that this spot possessed four legs; and moment by moment it became more unmistakable that it was composed of the persons of two young men. (Wolf 1989: 102)

Virginia Woolf's short story " Solid Objects" (1920) goes on to focus on one of these young men, John, who uncovers not a smooth pebble or pretty shell on the beach, but an intriguing and worthless lump of sea-smoothed glass. John's fascination with the material particularity of such objects soon becomes an obsession, so much so that he throws away a promising political career to collect fascinating scraps of broken china and peculiar lumps of metal. The story primarily explores the question of how political action or even individual existence can be meaningful in mass society, but it is also a meditation on knowledge. The descriptions of John's solid objects suggest that he wants to reach out not only into the ocean of undiscovered truth, but also the depths of interstellar space: one appears to be "pirouetting through space, winking light like a fitful star," while another appears to originate in "one of the dead stars" or to be "the cinder of a moon." The question that arises is how these material particularities can be assembled into any sort of pattern without recourse to abstract generalizations; how we move from perceptions to conceptions. It is a problem that Woolf has implicitly posed to the reader at the opening of the story (in the sentences quoted above) by adopting a representational strategy similar to Conrad's "delayed decoding." The passage mimics a process of optical focusing, as if the narrator were watching through a telescope, but it also represents a process of conceptual focusing. We begin with the pure visual sensation of the small black spot, and only by reference to its visual qualities ("a certain tenuity in its blackness") does the narrator come to infer that the spot possesses legs; even then, the narrator momentarily reserves judgment about what these legs might belong to.

Although the seashore imagery had acquired a certain topicality in 1920, this representational strategy was not new; nor were the philosophical questions it raised. They had been raised by the movement in the philosophy of science known as descriptionism. Descriptionism had its roots in the theory and practice of several scientists, principally the Austrian "empirio-critic" Ernst Mach (1838–1916), and his British follower Karl Pearson (1857–1936). For Mach, human knowledge of the external world begins with an inchoate and potentially overwhelming mass of sense-impressions; to survive, the individual organism and the collective culture must find efficient ways of selecting the relevant sensations. Science, as Mach defined it, was "the economy of thought." When a "primitive man" hears "a noise in the underbrush," he correlates this with the possible presence of an enemy, and, without dwelling on the sense-impressions in themselves, moves out of danger. This instinctive reaction is economical, but it becomes science only when men invent concepts and symbols which allow sensations to be communicated economically. The narrator of "Solid Objects" begins by conveying sense-impressions, and then economizes with the phrase "two young men."

Such economy implies a loss. Mach argued that concepts and symbols

201

were, in an extended sense of the word, "metaphysical." Many nineteenth-century physicists would have accepted that theological concepts such as "God" were metaphysical, but would have insisted that such things as "space," "time," "force," and "matter" had a real existence. Mach argued that "matter" is metaphysical, a mental construct which allows us economically to describe the persistence of certain clusters of sense impressions. The concept of "force," as in "the force of gravity," is metaphysical: it allows us to attribute a property to inanimate bodies by analogy with our own experience; it is convenient to think of the earth "attracting" smaller bodies, but it is not necessarily true. Our concepts of "space" are influenced in everyday life by our bodies' physical apparatus, and in physics by our measuring apparatus. To say that an object is one meter long is simply to compare it to another, standard object, which is no less physical than the first.

Such "metaphysical" concepts had often been taken to *explain* certain sequences of events: if an apple falls to the ground, its fall is explained by "the force of gravity." The descriptionist school held that science should not aim to explain, but to describe. If "the force of gravity" allows an economical description of apples falling from trees, then it can be retained; but if it fails to describe a set of sense-impressions, or can do so only with the assistance of uneconomical supplementary hypotheses, then the scientist must search for a more economical mode of description.

Mach's work was not only translated, but was extensively promulgated in the English language by Karl Pearson. Pearson's most extensive exposition of the philosophy of descriptionism came in *The Grammar of Science* (1892). *The Grammar* was an unusual book, in that it assumed very little technical knowledge, and was readable by nonscientists; yet, by advancing a novel philosophy of science, it attracted the attention of very able scientists and philosophers. Einstein used it when he was working as a private tutor in Berne in 1902, though he also knew Mach's work directly; A. S. Eddington, who was later to test Einstein's theory and expound it for British readers, read *The Grammar* in 1911; Josiah Royce, the Harvard philosopher, made it prescribed reading for his postgraduate seminar.

Though Pearson's philosophy is deeply indebted to Mach's, and though Mach said they were in agreement in everything but terminology, Pearson's account underplayed the latent realism of Mach's philosophy, and emphasized its subjective idealism. For Mach: "The world consists of colors, sounds, temperatures, pressures, spaces, times, and so forth, which now we shall not call sensations, nor phenomena, because in either term an arbitrary, one-sided theory is embodied, but simply *elements*" (1910: 208–9).

Mach's "elements" are poised between an objective phenomenal existence, and a subjective perceptual existence. For Pearson, science deals only with sense-impressions: "We *know* ourselves, and we *know* around us an impenetrable wall of sense-impressions. There is no necessity, nay, not even logic, in the statement that behind sense-impressions there are 'things-in-themselves' *producing* sense-impressions" (1892: 82). That Pearson's subjective idealism could lead to a form of solipsism is most readily apparent in his metaphor of the "wall" of sensations: the metaphor entirely inverts the commonly accepted realist view of sensations. His extended metaphor of the self as the clerk in a telephone exchange emphasizes the isolation as much as the connectedness of the clerk (1892: 74). However, Pearson argues that intersubjective communication is possible, at least approximately, because "the organs of sense" and the "perceptive faculty" of all "normal human beings" are substantially the same. The "normal" human mind is like a machine for sorting stones: just as such machines separate stones of different sizes by passing them over a series of meshes, so "[s]ensations of all kinds and magnitudes" flow into the mind, "some to be rejected," others to be sorted into order "in place and time." We are capable of formulating laws about matter" and "causation" because the perceptive faculty has already filtered these things out from the chaos of sensations. Pearson appears to have been unaware or unconcerned that the concepts of "normality" and of "race" are also metaphysical. The "solidarity of humanity" obtains between "civilized men of European race," but not between those men and "a dark-skinned tribe" (1892: 437–8). Such concepts were to become more important as Pearson's interests turned, around 1906, to eugenics (see Chapter 2 of this volume).

The theory of mind advanced by Mach and Pearson was by no means completely original, nor restricted to science. Not only did it have roots in Darwinian ideas, but it had been anticipated in the 1870s by Walter Pater in his "Conclusion" to *The Renaissance*. Pater begins from a materialist position: the human body does not differ from its physical environment, being composed, like nature, of combinations of material elements; these elements are perpetually in a "flame-like" flux. The world for Pater consists not of solid "objects," but of "impressions, unstable, flickering, inconsistent, which burn and are extinguished with our consciousness of them"; any solidity that "objects" appear to possess is merely a quality "with which language invests them." Like the observer in Mach's and Pearson's philosophy, Pater's observer is potentially overwhelmed by a "flood" of external sensations, and so must select from them. But this process of selection brings the danger of solipsism, more acutely for Pater than for Pearson, as Pater does not have recourse to any normative idea of "the human": Pater's individual is trapped not by a wall of impressions, but by the "thick wall of personality" which filters them.

In the context of Oxford in the 1870s, Pater's subjective idealism was scandalous; but in the context of the sciences in the 1890s, Pearson's similar position was more readily assimilated. While the materialist science of the 1860s, 1870s, and 1880s, had asserted the reality of matter and motion, to the exclusion of "spirit" and "God," Pearson seemed to be making more modest claims for scientific knowledge. Although the rejection of "truth" in favor of "convenience" was disquietingly effeminate to some commentators, the softening of the claims of science allowed an accommodation between science and the humanities. Such compromises were particularly important when scientists needed money for new laboratories and equipment, given that the senior positions in universities were still dominated by classicists (Heilbron 1982: 70). The second edition of *The Grammar* applauded the replacement of a "crude materialism" by a "sound idealism," and noted the irony of the first edition having been attacked for its materialism (Pearson 1900: vii–viii).

The account of physical reality given by Pater, Mach, and Pearson, in which it appears as an overwhelming, unstructured flux, anticipates the presentation of a fragmentary reality in modernist fiction and poetry. The young T. E. Hulme argued about Pearson with his headmaster (Jones 1960: 19), and his fragmentary philosophical notes, although primarily indebted to Nietzsche and Bergson, also record the idea that "[t]he apparent scientific unity of the world" is due to man's being "a kind of sorting machine" (Hulme 1994: 13). In the case of Woolf's essay "Modern Novels" (1919), it is likely that the "myriad impressions" falling on the mind, "trivial, fantastic, evanescent, or engraved with the sharpness of steel," are derived most immediately from Pater; however, the coincident influence of Mach and Pearson cannot be ruled out. John in "Solid Objects" is himself a stone-sorting machine.

In February 1914, T. S. Eliot discussed Pearson's distinction between description and explanation as part of his contribution to Josiah Royce's seminar at Harvard. Although the subject matter of his paper, the interpretation of primitive religions, may appear anthropological, the methodological questions he faced were identical to those confronting the physicists. What is curious is the way that Eliot evaluates the methodological choices in a discourse derived from anthropology, thus blurring the distinction between discursive levels: "Explanation is more primitive," he said, "description more sophisticated"; a "craving" for explanations is a characteristic of the primitive mind, which "luxuriates in the feeling of explanation" (Smith 1963: 120-1). Eliot implies that science before descriptionism was itself a form of primitive religion. He is aware, however, that description is never perfect, as "the art of describing brings alteration of the object described" (Smith 1963: 121). The implications for Eliot's poetry are profound: the "sophisticated" detachment of "description," corresponding to the voyeurism of the Baudelairean dandy, is locked in tension with a primitivist craving for explanation in the form of myth and religion. The conflict between the savage and the city-dweller is recast in epistemological terms.

Not all modernist writers were in sympathy with the subjective idealism which followed from the work of Mach and Pearson. Hulme wanted to preserve the reality of "space," arguing that it was something more than "a mode of arranging sensations" (Hulme 1994: 19). This line of critique was pursued by Wyndham Lewis in *Time and Western Man* (1927), where he criticized the "idealo-materialism" of his scientific and philosophical contemporaries. Objections came from other quarters, most notably from V. I. Lenin, who considered Mach such a danger to Marxist materialism that he wrote *Materialism and Empirio-Criticism: Critical Notes Concerning a Reactionary Philosophy* (1909).

In spite of such critiques, the influence of the descriptionist philosophy spread in the 1920s, as it was adopted as a framework for interpretations of the "new physics" of relativity and quantum mechanics. Eddington, in *Space, Time and Gravitation*, saw the mind as a filter, filtering out "matter" from the "meaningless jumble" of qualities exhibited by the world. He followed Pearson in suggesting that "mind's search for permanence" had created "the world of physics" (Eddington 1920: 198). This idealist belief in the mind's creative power led him to a frequently quoted conclusion: "We have found a strange foot-print on the shores of the unknown. We have devised profound theories, one after another, to account for its origin. At last, we have succeeded in reconstructing the creature that made the foot-print. And Lo! it is our own" (1920: 201). The image is extraordinarily dense in its implications: Robinson Crusoe and Man Friday are found to be identical; subject and object, self and other, colonizing perceiver and colonized percept, collapse into an idealist unity.

The imagery of this passage was adopted directly by Herbert Read in the title poem to his collection *Mutations of the Phoenix* (1923). Read begins with a seemingly realistic narration in which "We have rested our limbs / in some forsaken cove," but he soon turns to explore the metaphysical implications of the "impress" that the limbs leave in the sand; the perceived world is "cast in the mould and measure / of a finite instrument." It is intriguing to return to the beach in Woolf's "Solid Objects" in the light of Eddington's imagery, though it is harder to determine whether Woolf intended the beach as a general symbol of the border between the finite and the infinite, or as a more specific reference; if she was thinking of Eddington's conclusion, she was less anxious than Read to flaunt it.

Atoms and Quanta

Scientific research into matter in the period 1880 to 1930 began with a world that was so minute as to be invisible, and ended with one that was so strange as to be unvisualizable. Developments in this area were rapid, but incremental; popularizers were reluctant to write about the latest developments, in case their expositions became obsolete between submission and publication. Whereas Einstein's relativity theory attracted a great deal of attention in periodicals and books, research into matter was commented on less widely. The exception to this general rule was W. Röntgen's discovery in 1895 of the rays which were briefly known by his name, and later known as X-rays: because of their potential medical applications, and because they were readily accommodated within an existing culture of public lectures, and the nascent visual culture of photography and cinema, X-rays were widely known about within months of their discovery. This discovery was soon followed by the discovery of radioactivity by Becquerel in 1896, and the isolation of the radioactive element radium by Pierre and Marie Curie in 1898. In 1900, Max Planck introduced the theory of quanta: he argued that matter does not absorb or radiate energy in continuously variable amounts, but in finite parcels, or "quanta." Matter can emit energy in multiples of Planck's constant, but can never emit fractional parcels of energy. It is only because the parcels are so minute, and the human sorting-machine so coarse-grained, that the everyday appearance is of continuous variation.

Planck had not recognized the relevance of his quantum theory to investigations of atomic structure, but others soon did. Ernest Rutherford had succeeded in splitting atoms of nitrogen late in 1910, an achievement he announced in 1911. This work, combined with the spectroscopic analysis of gases, led Rutherford to hypothesize that atoms had a "solar" structure, in which electrons orbited around a nucleus. The solid atom consisted mostly of empty space. Rutherford's model could not account for the stability of atoms, and it was left to his junior associate, Niels Bohr, to improve upon it by reference to Planck's theory. In Bohr's model of the atom, electrons were capable of moving from one "orbit" to another, with corresponding input or output of energy. However, Bohr hypothesized that, unlike planets, electrons did not move through intermediate positions between two orbits, but moved instantaneously and discontinuously in a "quantum leap." The intermediate positions were impossible by Planck's theory, because they would require fractional quanta.

Bohr's atom was still visualizable, but developments in the 1920s led to models which were too paradoxical and too abstract to be pictured. It was gradually realized that Bohr's 1913 model contained many contradictions (Holton 1973: 131). As early as 1914, it was recognized that, while the quantum rules adequately described the behavior of particles of matter, they could not be reconciled with the wave motion of light (Russell 1923: 148–9). Moreover, Bohr's 1913 theory employed a contradictory combination of classical continuity and quantum discontinuity: the former to describe electrons moving in their orbits, the latter to describe their leaps between. Louis de Broglie proposed in 1923 that light be treated as both wave and particle, and that, conversely, electrons should be treated as having wave as well as particle characteristics. Diverse models of the atom were proposed: in his "New Quantum Theory" of autumn 1925, Werner Heisenberg emphasized quanta and discontinuity, while in his theory of July 1926, Erwin Schrödinger attempted to describe the atom in terms of waves of probability (Holton 1973: 132).

These developments were followed by Heisenberg's articulation of the "uncertainty principle" in the summer of 1927, a principle which was generalized by Bohr, in "The Quantum Postulate" (1928) and subsequent papers, into the "principle of complementarity." Because our knowledge of electrons inside the atom comes only when they change orbital levels, and thus emit or absorb energy, they cannot be "observed" without an exchange of energy between the atom and the outside world. Such exchanges of energy alter the state of the very thing we wish to observe. Because of this interaction between observer and observed, the more accurately one measures the position of a particle, the less accurately one can measure its momentum, and vice versa; momentum and position exist in a complementary relationship. Bohr, extending this principle, recognized that the wave–particle duality was not contradictory, but complementary.

The extent to which modernist writers were familiar with these ideas is difficult to summarize, as we are dealing with a wide range of developments, and with writers from a wide range of backgrounds. Even though the earlier discoveries were more widely publicized, literary history has tended to emphasize the analogies between modernist literature and the conceptual developments of the 1920s. It is certain that Joseph Conrad, Virginia Woolf, James Joyce, and T. S. Eliot were familiar with X-rays; the image of "nerves" thrown "in patterns on a screen" in "The Love Song of J. Alfred Prufrock" derives from an 1897 newspaper article on the rays (Crawford 1987: 8–9); in *Ulysses* they form part of one of Bloom's techno-logical fantasies; in *To the Lighthouse* Lily Briscoe sees through Charles Tansley's "desire to impress" as if X-raying his body. Likewise, radium proved fascinating. In *Women in Love*, Gerald seems "wonderful" to Gudrun, "like a piece of radium"; in the drafts of *To the Lighthouse*, the "moment" is said to throw out its meaning "like radium."

Later developments also filtered out into the literary community. Through his presence at Josiah Royce's seminar, Eliot was unusually well informed about developments up to 1914: his fellow student L. T. Troland gave a paper on "statistical mechanics," referring specifically to Planck's theory of quanta (Smith 1963: 149). Aldous Huxley was kept up to date by J. W. N. Sullivan, the popular science writer, as were others in Huxley's circle; in *Those Barren Leaves* (1925), Calamy gives a reliable account of current atomic theory, emphasizing the contradiction between the classical rules which operate outside of the atom, and the quantum rules which operate within it (Bradshaw 1996: 357–8). Virginia Woolf was aware of these develop-ments, though apparently in less detail: her diary for May 8, 1932 records a discussion between Leonard Woolf and Roger Fry about the "break up of the atom"; and in *Between the Acts* (1941), one of the "stray voices" at the end of the play is heard to remark on "the very latest notion," that "noth-ing's solid." That this notion was at least thirty years old may be attributed to Woolf's satirical intent.

Knowledge of atomic structure would be of little use to a novelist or poet were it not for the circulation of metaphors between scientific dis-course and the discourse of everyday life. The early developments in the theory of matter acquire greater significance because of the ubiquity in everyday speech of half-forgotten metaphors of opacity and transparency, stability and instability, and solidity and porosity. These metaphors may be applied to questions of literary form, as in Woolf's ascription of "solid" craftsmanship to Arnold Bennett's work, or to metaphors of the self: the solidity of a body (in the scientific sense) is analogous to the solidity of a human body, which is in turn analogous to the solidity of the self. Bertrand Russell was conscious of these analogies when he wrote not only that "our old comfortable notion of 'solid matter' cannot survive," but that "the persistent ego seems as fictitious as the permanent atom"; although his argument for this point was rooted in a philosophy of perception rather than in scientific discoveries, the metaphorical connections between bodies and selves are equally relevant (1924: 288–9). Modernist writing, both fiction and poetry, is characteristically concerned with the permeability of the ego and of the text, their "semi-transparency," to adapt Woolf's phrase. The ego is open to the influence of memories, perceptions, and unconscious drives; the text is open to allusion, parody, pastiche, and other forms of intertextuality.

Modernist theory and practice were diverse, and not all writers embraced porosity with such enthusiasm. Hulme's aesthetic theories, derived from Wilhelm Worringer, valorized sculptural solidity and the maintenance of boundaries; these metaphors were adopted by many later writers, most prominently Pound and Lewis. Their expressed preference for solidity can be interpreted politically, as a reaction against the "fluidity" of mass society, and psychologically, as a reaction against the "softness" of the feminine; as metaphors derived from one sphere were so frequently applied to the other, such "explanations" are not mutually exclusive. However, even texts which ostensibly exemplify the ideal of "solidity," such as Eliot and Pound's quatrain poems (written by around 1918–19 in reaction against the "dilution" of *vers libre*) are still characterized by an extraordinary level of textual "porosity"; "Burbank with a Baedeker: Bleistein with a Cigar" (1919) is every bit as allusive as "Prufrock."

The significance of the new ideas of matter extended further than this. For many modernist writers, the new descriptions of matter provided a new vocabulary in which they could respond to the phenomenon of modernity. This vocabulary allowed them to avoid the perceived materialism and objectivity of industrial and technological modernity, without lapsing into an imprecise vocabulary involving the "soul" and other abstractions. It allowed them to create a world which was both material and yet miraculous. It allowed them to find "objective correlatives" for subjective states in words uncontaminated with literary associations. In Lawrence's 1916 drafts of *Women in Love*, Gerald looks like "fruit made to eat," an "apple of knowledge"; the new sciences allowed Lawrence to eliminate these biblical connotations in the published versions, replacing the apple with radium.

The expression of an ambivalent relation to modernity does not necessitate reference to the most recent scientific concepts; discredited ones may serve equally well, and in any case, a writer in the 1920s would have found it difficult to know which concepts were creditable and which had been declared bankrupt. The rapidity of developments in quantum theory was such that no authoritative account was available even for scientists. For non-specialists, reliant on popular expositions, the problem was exacerbated by Sir Oliver Lodge, who, in spite of great scientific achievements at the turn of the century (or perhaps because of them), was unsympathetic to the ideas developed in relativity theory and quantum mechanics; his widely acclaimed abilities as a broadcaster made his continuing promulgation of outdated ether theories all the more persuasive. *Ether and Reality* (1925), a book based on BBC broadcasts, gives an account of magnetism which dates back to Faraday, but which is peculiarly suggestive in connection with Virginia Woolf's imagery. For Lodge, all electrical phenomena are united by "lines of force"; he likens them to elastic threads, but cautions that they are threads "of infinitesimal length, capable of being stretched ad libitum, without limit; the lines never snap, nor do they ever shrink up into absolute nothingness" (1925: 109). When Woolf attempts to describe relationships which are too subtle to be described in conventional novelistic or social terms, and which in some cases defy physical or social distances, she is driven to using a vocabulary of "filaments," "fibres," and "threads." In *Mrs. Dalloway*, Lady Bruton, falling asleep after lunch with Richard Dalloway and Hugh Whitbread, is nevertheless connected to them by a "thin thread"; in *The Waves* Bernard describes himself as connected to Neville by one. Woolf does not follow the theory pedantically: contrary to Lodge's description, Lady Bruton's thread snaps as she falls asleep. Nevertheless, the instance suggests that modernity in literature is readily achieved with outdated conceptual materials.

Quantum theory has attracted far more attention than radium, X-rays, and Bohr's 1913 atom; in particular, the principles of uncertainty and complementarity have often been proposed as analogies for modernist form or for the experience of reading modernist literature. While all such analogies are open to question on the grounds of their "looseness" or "tightness," these particular analogies are open to more fundamental questions about their historical relevance. If the writers of the 1910s and early 1920s knew about complementarity, it was as a psychological theory derived from William James, not one about subatomic particles; as Holton has shown, James may well have been Bohr's source for this innovation (1973: 133–42). If the writers of those years were aware of complementary relations obtaining between two aspects of knowledge, it was as a general truth of human affairs, not as something pertaining to momentum and position. A further historiographical problem arises in connection with the texts most commonly cited by critics and cultural historians in support of claims about quantum mechanics: Heisenberg's *The Physicist's Conception of Nature* (1958), *Physics and Philosophy* (1959), and his autobiographical volume *Physics and Beyond* (1971); Fritjof Capra's *The Tao of Physics* (1975), David Bohm's *Wholeness and Implicate Order* (1980), and Gary Zukav's *The Dancing Wu Li Masters* (1979). In his 1958 book, Heisenberg drew attention to a new, holistic approach to nature which was then emerging from quantum mechanics, and quoted Bohr's often-repeated phrase, "we are not merely observers but also actors on the stage of life." However, such statements were clearly intended to pacify a Cold-War public who had come to identify science with the hydrogen bomb and the scientist with an attitude of inhumane detachment. The movement which made the word "quantum" synonymous with "holistic" and "ecological" was an ideological movement, and did not exist in a historical vacuum. Readings which associate texts of the 1920s and 1930s with postwar readings of quantum theory risk anachronism. Some have done so with frank acknowledgment of their speculative and ahistorical approach, relating prewar modernists to postwar cosmologies (Hussey 1995), while others have been less clear about the historical questions involved (Westling 1999).

This is not to say that modernist writers were wholly unaware of quantum theory, or that their appropriations of it were wholly dissimilar from those of the postwar period. Nevertheless, there were significant divergences. Michael Roberts, one of the few modernist poets and critics formally educated in science, brought quantum mechanics to the attention of the readers of the *Poetry Review* in 1928. His framework for understanding the new science derived indirectly from Mach, and explicitly from T. E. Hulme: Roberts quoted the latter on the idea of man as a "sorting machine," and his doing so suggests that much that is now attributed to "quantum philosophy" derived from descriptionism. Roberts, in this article, deemed quantum mechanics important not because of uncertainty or complementarity, but because it demanded that thinkers break with the idea of representation: Bohr had written on the difficulty felt by physicists in accepting "a limitation" on their "usual means of visualization" (Roberts 1928: 438). That Roberts was quoting from Bohr's 1925 paper and not from the 1928 "Quantum Postulate" suggests that there existed a time-lag in the cultural absorption of the new physics, even among the best-informed. By 1932, Roberts was drawing attention to the uncertainty principle, and implying an analogy with a philosophy of language in which language is "an instrument"; "not a disinterested and detached picture of things as they eternally are," but "part of the temporal pattern which it attempts to mirror" (Roberts 1932: 309). Here his position is closer to post-

1945 holism, but not identical to it.

Though the uncertainty principle provided support for man's continuity with nature, the notion of the quantum leap could be appropriated to support various aesthetics of discontinuity. For Herbert Read, it brought scientific credibility to the idea of an artwork consisting not simply of rhythmical patterns, but of patterns broken by unexpected ruptures, in which the artist asserts his will and takes "a leap into the unknown." The notion of formal discontinuity is relevant to the structure of most modernist works, whether as narrative leaps in *Ulysses* or *Jacob's Room*, or as psychological leaps in "The Love Song of J. Alfred Prufrock." However, the analogy is very broad: such "leaps" do not imply an input or output of energy from the system. If the phrase "fractured atoms" in Eliot's "Gerontion" suggests modernist selves and modernist texts, it does so in general terms: the fractures could have been created by alpha-particle bombardment in Rutherford's laboratory, or could be the discontinuities between orbits in a stable atom.

The idea of discontinuity was central to T. E. Hulme's influential aesthetic and political theorizing, and this case demonstrates the difficulties involved in tracing lines of conceptual descent. Hulme criticized liberal and democratic ideology for its "universal application of the principle of *continuity*" (1994: 423). In a world characterized by continuity, individuals could gradually progress from one physical or moral state to another. For Hulme, the principle of continuity had grown so dominant that it had come to seem "an inevitable constituent of reality itself. ... This shrinking from a *gap* or jump in nature has developed to a degree which paralyses any objective perception, and prejudices our seeing things as they really are." Hulme, who had enrolled at University College, London, in 1904 to study biology and physics, may well have known Planck's quantum theory: however, in so far as he justified his theory of discontinuity from science, he drew on the evolutionary "mutation theory" of Hugo de Vries. This theory held that new species came into existence, "not gradually by the accumulation of small steps, but suddenly in a jump" (Hulme 1994: 61). Hulme's recruitment of De Vries allows him to critique the Darwinian roots of liberal ideology far more directly than a reference to Planck would have done, but it need not imply that genetics was the sole influence. The themes of continuity and discontinuity manifested themselves in several different sciences simultaneously. Hulme's worldview is certainly not holistic; the equation of "quantum" with romantic ideals of harmony was by no means universal.

Relativity

As Alan Friedman has noted, histories of modernism sometimes treat relativity and the 1920s quantum theories as if they were fundamentally identical (1982: 199). Monroe K. Spears, for example, conflated not only these theories, but also Planck's, saying that they "all demonstrate the inseparability of subject and object" (1970: 55). Historians of science have been far more careful to distinguish the "classical" qualities of Einstein's theory from the postclassical tendencies of Heisenberg and Bohr: Einstein disliked the discontinuity implicit in Planck's theory, and could not accept the indeterminacy at the heart of the later quantum theories; God, as he famously wrote in December 1926, "does not play dice" (Holton 1973: 120). "Relativity" is a misleading label for Einstein's theory; although he rejected the absolute time and space of Newtonian theories, he replaced it with a new constant, the finite velocity of light. Chronologies of the early twentieth century often include a reference to Einstein's "Special Theory of Relativity" in 1905, italicizing it as if it were book-length publication. In fact the thirty-page paper that appeared in *Annalen der Physik* in that year was titled "Zur Elektrodynamik bewegter Körper" ("On the Electrodynamics of Moving Bodies"). As Holton notes, the phrase "relativity theory" does not appear in Einstein's manuscript papers until 1911, and for the first two years Einstein preferred the opposite: *Invariantentheorie* (1973: 197, 362). Nor was the idea of "invariant theory" or "irrelativity" private to Einstein: Bertrand Russell cautioned against the misunderstanding of "relativity" in his *ABC of Relativity* (1925). Frequent references to "the observer" had led to a misunderstanding about the theory supporting "subjectivity"; in fact the "subjectivity" of the theory is "a *physical* subjectivity," and would exist "if there were no such things as minds or senses in the world." Moreover, Russell noted, the theory did not say that "*everything* is relative," but rather it allowed the scientist to distinguish "what is relative from what belongs to a physical occurrence in its own right" (1925: 148). It is clear from Russell's account that he was cutting against the grain of contemporary expository writing, but though unrepresentative of popular science writing at the time, the *ABC* clarifies the issues significantly. While "relativity" was undoubtedly taken to support the subjectivism and perspectivism of modernist writing, those who treated it thus were building on the descriptionist tendency of the late nineteenth century. "[N]othing is, or can be rightly known, except relatively and under conditions": the words are not those of a post-Einsteinian physicist, but of Walter Pater writing in 1865 about Coleridge. There are instead other routes by which Einstein's special and general theories informed literary discourse, imagery, and form.

Einstein's 1905 special theory began as a comparison of the laws relating to the motion of a magnet around a conductor, and to the motion of a conductor around a magnet; however, it generalized these problems into a consideration of the relativity of all motion. Even light moves with a finite velocity: Einstein made this limitation of knowledge a central fact of physical theory. In consequence, the notion of "simultaneity" changed fundamentally, being newly understood as something relative to the position and movement of the observer. An astronomer may observe the sudden extinction of a star at the "same time" as the observatory clock chimes midnight, but the extinction may have happened many years previously; the light may have been traveling for many years before reaching the observatory. The "simultaneity" of the two events is apparent, not real. Though Einstein rejected many aspects of Mach's philosophy, there is a Machian element to this idea, in that it assumes that our knowledge of the world begins with sense-impressions (Holton 1973: 219–59).

The special theory held true only for bodies at rest or moving at a constant velocity; the general theory of 1916 accounts for bodies which are accelerating (changing speed or direction). In formulating it, Einstein was led to a radical new theory of space and gravitation. Newtonian theory had assumed that space was Euclidean, and that gravity was an attractive force that pervaded space. Left to its own devices, the earth would travel in a straight line through space, in accordance with Newton's first law; however, the sun's gravitational force causes it to travel in an elliptical orbit. Newton's theory accurately described most astronomical phenomena, including most of the orbits of the solar system, but it could not explain the anomalous orbit of Mercury. Einstein's theory described gravity as due to the non-Euclidean deformation of spacetime; the earth, as it orbits the sun, really is traveling in a straight line, but the straight line is embedded in distorted spacetime; the distortion is due to the mass of the sun. A straight line in a curved spacetime may sound paradoxical, but it is easily understood by analogy with the curved surface of the earth: someone traveling around the earth's equator is traveling along a straight line on a curved surface. Einstein's adoption of this geometry caused much concern among scientists and writers who had been taught to believe in the absolute truth of Euclid; for them, adopting a geometry simply on account of its convenience too closely resembled a form of moral relativism. However, such objections were essentially reprising the debate between description and explanation; geometry was simply one of many territories on which this battle was fought.

Though Einstein formulated the general theory in 1916, the war prevented its experimental proof, and consequently delayed its wider acceptance and dissemination. The theory predicted that light passing near a massive body would be deflected by the body's distortion of spacetime; Newton's theory had also predicted deflection, but to a measurably different extent. The deflection of light can most readily be measured by observing starlight passing near the sun during a total eclipse, and a suitable opportunity arose in May 1919. The British astronomer A. S. Eddington conducted the tests, and announced the results to the Royal Society on November 6, 1919. Some intelligent popular expositions of the theory had already appeared in the general press by this date; most notable among them was a series of articles by J. W N. Sullivan which had appeared in May and June in the *Athenaeum*; the journal included T. S. Eliot, Virginia Woolf, and Aldous Huxley among its other regular contributors (Whitworth 1996: 150–3; Bradshaw 1996: 194–5). However, it took Eddington's November announcement to stimulate wider public interest, and popular accounts subsequently appeared in a wide range of newspapers and literary journals. The years following the announcement saw the publication of many popular expositions, as well as the publication of specialist works. In the later 1920s, many popular expositions tried to provide an overview of all the developments in physics, and sought to relate these scientific developments to broader questions about the nature of human knowledge and existence.

This level of publicity meant that modernist writers had ample opportunity to learn of and about Einstein's work. T. S. Eliot had known of the special theory of relativity since 1913, and though the "Einstein" to whom he wrote in June 1922 was an art historian, the lack of direct contact is unimportant: he would have been brought up to date with the general theory through his contact with J. W. N. Sullivan; Ezra Pound was certainly informed about Einstein by Sullivan (Smith 1963: 51; Whitworth 1996: 153; Whitworth 2000: 336–7). D. H. Lawrence specifically wrote to his friend S. S. Koteliansky on June 4, 1921 to request "a simple book" on relativity, and received a copy of Einstein's nontechnical account, *Relativity, the Special and the General Theory* (1920). W. B. Yeats read Lyndon Bolton's *An Introduction to the Theory of Relativity* (1921), and quoted from it in the 1925 edition of *A Vision* (Chapter 2). Virginia Woolf wrote in 1938 that she had "not read Einstein," and would not have understood him if she had. However, her letter was intended to discourage the unwelcome attentions of a Ph.D. student with a fixation on relativity theory, and was unlikely to concede the other possibilities: that she had read about Einstein, or heard broadcasts about him, or discussed him. She had read James Jeans's *The Mysterious Universe* (1930), and, from the reference to Eddington in *Between the Acts*, it is clear that she knew of Eddington's eminence as a popularizer, though there is no unequivocal evidence that she had read him (*pace* Beer 1996a: 171). Leonard and Virginia Woolf's library contained James Rice's *Relativity: An Exposition without Mathematics* (1927), and though it is possible that this pamphlet was acquired after Virginia's death, it seems more likely that it was purchased in the late 1920s or early 1930s, when the theory was widely discussed.

What remained in the minds of these authors after such reading is available only through conjecture and imaginative reconstruction, and cannot be dealt with in detail here. In general terms, it seems that the imagery of popular science expositions was as influential as the abstract concepts of the new physics. Einstein himself had been fascinated by visualizations of hypothetical situations long before he turned to mathematical formulae: at the age of 16, in 1895–6, he asked himself what a beam of light would look like if he pursued it at the speed of light (Holton 1973: 358). More fantastic versions of this hypothesis had appeared in Camille Flammarion's *Popular Astronomy* (1880, translated 1894), and in his *Lumen* (1872, translated 1897). In the latter, Flammarion asked the reader to imagine the earth as seen by someone traveling away from it faster than light: because this traveler would be overtaking the light, historical events would appear in reverse chronology; the Battle of Waterloo would come before Austerlitz. T. S. Eliot's fellow Harvard postgraduate, Harry Costello, enjoyed similar semi-metaphysical speculations about taking "a ride on a light wave," believing that as one rushed past the earth, it would "flatten up like a pancake" (Smith 1963: 56). Light is imagined as a high-speed train, or, more fundamentally, as a carrier or messenger. Imagining it this way allows one to stand outside history, because, as Flammarion put it, the past becomes "an eternal present." The title of W. J. Turner's short lyric "In Time Like Glass" (c.1925) summarizes the poem's central conceit, according to which time is a solid transparent medium preserving events and images; although the poem could have been written at any time since 1674, it appeared to Turner's contemporaries to be Einsteinian (Rickword 1974: 186). A similar conceit appears fleetingly in *The Waves*, where Louis refers to "the lighted strip of history." In *Finnegans Wake*, the idea appears both in the "Willingdone Museyroom," with its implicit reference to Flammarion's illustrative instance, and again later, in the extended farewells to Haun (alias Jaun), where the scientific image of traveling starlight is indistinguishable from the older literary tradition of the stellification of the dead: Haun will be "looked after" like a "beam of light" on a "photophoric pilgrimage."

More fundamental than these localized images is the emergence in modernist literature of a new conception of simultaneity. Just as a ray of light unites the "now" of two distinct locations in spacetime, making it theoretically possible for the battle of Waterloo to be seen "now" on a distant planet, so the canonical works of high modernism fuse texts and characters from diverse periods into a single space: *Ulysses* merges Leopold Bloom with Odysseus, and Stephen Daedalus with Telemachus and Hamlet, while *The Waste Land* fuses texts from Ecclesiastes to Hermann Hesse. For Septimus Warren Smith in *Mrs. Dalloway*, the battles of 1914–18 are still happening, "now," while for Clarissa, more benignly, the hinges of Bourton in the 1890s can be heard squeaking "now" in London. The new form of simultaneity cannot be attributed solely to the new physics; indeed, many coinciding causes could be cited, including telecommunications, anthropology, museums, urbanization, and Bergson's theory of mind (see Chapter 5 of this volume). If physics was not a direct cause, it was a secondary cause in a particularly valuable way: it provided a system of concepts and imagery which articulated the experiences of urban modernity.

It is more difficult to identify connections between the general principle of relativity and modernist literature. It was used as the basis for at least one ingenious metaphysical conceit, in Herbert Read's "Equation" (1923), but the form of Read's poem owes nothing to relativity; its precision, greatly admired by Michael Roberts, may be a scientific quality of mind, but such qualities are not unique to poems using Einsteinian metaphors (Roberts 1933: 84–5). If any more general pattern of similarity is to be found, it might lie in non-Euclidean geometry. The notion of "distortions" or "wrinkles" in spacetime offers a compelling metaphor for modernist distortions of conventional forms. T. S. Eliot's teasing comparison of the world of Ben Jonson's plays to the world of non-Euclidean geometries provides one specific point of reference (Whitworth 2001: 214–18). Speculatively, I would suggest that non-Euclidean geometries provided a metaphor for a half-articulated feeling: that the experience of modernity could not be sufficiently accounted for by reference to the perceptible world; that there must be some additional distortion in the fabric of things to account for its strangeness. This metaphor emerged most often in references to the "fourth dimension," this being the most readily absorbed element of the new geometries, but the spiritualists who had recourse to this metaphor were not so exceptional as they liked to believe. The disconcerting experience of modernity – of "accelerating in the void," as Herbert Read had put it – was shared by many.

Coda: The 1930s

Few developments in physics in the 1930s were as striking as the discovery of X-rays in 1895, the "proof" of relativity theory in 1919, or the developments in quantum theory in the 1920s. From a literary and cultural perspective, the important changes lay in the reception of popular science writing. Many commentators in the 1920s had expressed hopes that science and humanism could converge, or at least reconcile their nineteenth-century differences. Such hopes had their basis in the writings of Poincaré and Pearson, who had both emphasized the role of the imagination in the formulation of scientific theories; they were further encouraged by Sullivan in his *Athenaeum* columns. Similarly, many commentators had expressed the belief that, at the very least, the scientific worldview was no longer a barrier to religious faith: at best, nature appeared to have recovered its miraculous qualities. Although some writers resisted such speculations throughout the 1920s – notably Bertrand Russell – it was only with the publication of James Jeans's *The Mysterious Universe* in 1930 that the opposition grew more vocal. Jeans's conclusion, that the "Great Architect of the Universe" was neither a biologist nor an engineer but a "pure mathematician," drew the ire of many reviewers and commentators. Both Christians and atheists expressed impatience with the vague religiosity of the popular physics writers. Increasingly, commentators argued for the separateness of religion, science, and literature. They professed admiration for the scientific achievements of Eddington and Jeans, but regretted their incursions into nonscientific territory. Marxist and socialist critics such as Christopher Caudwell, J. G. Crowther, and Herbert Samuel not only adopted these arguments, but also critiqued modern physics for its philosophical idealism. In a decade of social and political crisis, matter resumed its customary solidity, and thought-experiments about travel at the speed of light looked increasingly like escapist fantasies.

References and Further Reading

Beer, G. 1996a. *Open Fields: Science in Cultural Encounter*. Oxford: Clarendon Press.
——. 1996b. *Virginia Woolf: The Common Ground*. Edinburgh: Edinburgh University Press.
Bell, I. F. A. 1981. *Critic as Scientist: The Modernist Poetics of Ezra Pound*. London: Methuen.
Bradshaw, D. 1996. The Best of Companions: J. W. N. Sullivan, Aldous Huxley, and the New Physics. *Review of English Studies* 47: 188–206, 352–68.
Crawford, R. 1987. *The Savage and the City in the Work of T. S. Eliot*. Oxford: Clarendon Press.
Eddington, A. S. 1920. *Space, Time and Gravitation*. Cambridge: Cambridge University Press.
Friedman, A. J. 1982. *Ulysses* and Modern Science. In B. Benstock, ed., *The Seventh of Joyce*, pp. 198–206. Brighton: Harvester.
—— and C. C. Donley. 1985. *Einstein as Myth and Muse*. Cambridge: Cambridge University Press.
Hayles, N. K. 1984. *The Cosmic Web: Scientific Field Models and Narrative Strategy in Twentieth-Century Fiction*. Ithaca: Cornell University Press.
Heilbron, J. L. 1982. Fin-de-siècle Physics. In C. G. Bernhard, E. Crawford, and P. Sörbom, eds., *Science, Technology and Society in the Time of Alfred Nobel*, pp. 51–73. Oxford: Pergamon.
Henderson, L. D. 1985. *The Fourth Dimension and Non-Euclidean Geometry in Modern Art*. Princeton: Princeton University Press.
Holton, G. 1973. *Thematic Origins of Scientific Thought*. Cambridge, MA: Harvard University Press.
Hulme, T. E. 1994. *Collected Writings*. Ed. K. Csengeri. Oxford: Clarendon Press.
Hussey, M. 1995. *To the Lighthouse* and Physics: The Cosmology of David Bohm and Virginia Woolf. In H. Wussow, ed., *New Essays on Virginia Woolf*, pp. 79–97. Dallas: Contemporary Research Press.
Jones, A. 1960. *The Life and Opinions of T. E. Hulme*. London: Gollancz.
Lodge, O. 1925. *Ether and Reality*. London: Hodder & Stoughton.
Mach, E. 1910. *Popular Scientific Lectures*. Trans. Thomas J. McCormack. Chicago: Open Court.
Pearson, K. 1892. *The Grammar of Science*. London: Walter Scott.
——. 1900. *The Grammar of Science*, 2nd ed. London: A. & C. Black.
Rice, T. J. 1997. *Joyce, Chaos and Complexity*. Urbana: University of Illinois Press.
Richards, J. 1988. *Mathematical Visions: The Pursuit of Geometry in Victorian England*. San Diego: Academic Press.
Rickword, E. 1974. *Essays and Opinions 1921–31*. Ed. A. Young. Cheadle Hulme: Carcanet.
Roberts, M. 1933. *Critique of Poetry*. London: Jonathan Cape.
Roberts, M. 1928. On Mechanical Hallelujahs. *Poetry Review* 19: 433–8.

Michael H. Whitworth

——. 1932. Review of W. T. Stace, *The Theory of Knowledge and Existence. Adelphi* 5: 309–10.

——. 1933. *Critique of Poetry.* London: Jonathan Cape.

Russell, B. 1923. *The ABC of Atoms.* London: Kegan Paul, Trench, Trubner.

——. 1924. Philosophy in the Twentieth Century. *The Dial* 77 (4): 271–90.

——. [1925] 1997. *ABC of Relativity,* 5th ed. London: Routledge.

Ryan, J. 1991. *The Vanishing Subject: Early Psychology and Literary Modernism.* Chicago: University of Chicago Press.

Smith, G., ed. 1963. *Josiah Royce's Seminar, 1913–1914: As Recorded in the Notebooks of Harry T. Costello.* New Brunswick, NJ: Rutgers University Press.

Spears, M. K. 1970. *Dionysus and the City.* New York: Oxford University Press.

Vargish, T., and D. E. Mook. 1999. *Inside Modernism: Relativity Theory, Cubism, Narrative.* New Haven: Yale University Press.

Westling, L. 1999. Virginia Woolf and the Flesh of the World. *New Literary History* 30: 855–75.

Whitworth, M. H. 1996. *Pièces d'identité*: T. S. Eliot, J. W. N. Sullivan and Poetic Impersonality. *English Literature in Transition* 39: 149–70.

——. 2000. Eliot, Schiff and Einstein. *Notes and Queries* 47 (n.s.): 336–7.

——. 2001. *Einstein's Wake: Relativity, Metaphor, and Modernist Literature.* Oxford: Oxford University Press.

Woolf, V. 1989. *The Complete Shorter Fiction.* Ed. Susan Dick. rev. ed. [1st pub 1985] London: Hogarth Press.

11

Modernist Publishing: "Nomads and mapmakers"[1]

Peter D. McDonald

Where and how were the texts that constitute the literary culture of the period 1880 to 1939 first published? Questions of this kind have until recently been considered chiefly the preserve of bibliographers and scholarly editors, academic specialists in the material history of text production and transmission. For bibliographers, such questions direct one of their primary aims: to list and describe as comprehensively as possible the total output of a period, a publishing house, or, most commonly, a specific author. For scholarly editors, these questions are motivated, not necessarily by an interest in changing publishing venues *per se*, but by an editorial concern with the history of textual variation these changes evince. In the last two decades, however, questions of publishing provenance have come to interest a larger constituency within and beyond literary studies. This is in part because of developments in literary theory and criticism – the influence of Stephen Greenblatt's "new historicism," Janice Radway's feminist studies of women readers, and Raymond Williams's "cultural materialism" are especially pertinent – and in part due to the cross-disciplinary impact of revisionist bibliographers and scholarly editors themselves, most notably D. F. McKenzie and Jerome McGann. It is also a consequence of the new prominence given in the 1980s to the emergent interdisciplinary field of 'book history' (after the French *histoire du livre*) by

[1] *For Ann Wordsworth*

American and French historians, particularly Robert Darnton, Elisabeth Eisenstein, and Roger Chartier. These very different but intersecting initiatives transformed the study of text production, and opened up new modes of inquiry.

They also contributed, directly or indirectly, to the much vaunted "(re)turn to history" in the 1980s and 1990s, and in so doing they situated the more widespread preoccupation with publishing in a broader intellectual and institutional context. Asking the question "Where and how were texts first published?" – and, of course, many other "historical" questions – at that time not only meant, in a positive sense, rethinking the possibilities of bibliographical and editorial inquiry. It also frequently meant, in a negative sense, marshaling evidence against "theory" (poststructuralism in particular) which allegedly occluded the complex social, political, and economic conditions of reading and writing by promoting an empty, ahistorical textualism. For some – Greenblatt, for instance – slaying the dragon of poststructural ahistoricism (Derrida himself called this bogey a "monstrosity" in 1990) played a significant part in their successful quest for academic credibility (Carroll 1990: 79). For others, the bogey was more like an unwelcome ghost haunting the archives and present less directly in the style and tone of their writing. There were also those who favored the quiet life and who chose, sometimes conspicuously, to ignore the bogey altogether. This larger context – which is inevitably more complex than my brief account makes out – is worth bearing in mind, not least because all questions, even the seemingly modest, empirical one I am asking, bear witness to the concrete debates and institutional energies that define the time and place in which they are asked. And this is no less true of the answers they yield. What we need to consider, then, is why, at the beginning of the twenty-first century, we should want to ask where and how the novels and poems written at the outset of the twentieth century were first published. What is the value of this question? To whom? And what is at stake?

I would like to approach these large issues by examining one of the most important recent books in the field, Lawrence Rainey's *Institutions of Modernism: Literary Elites and Public Culture* (1998). In the first part of this essay, I shall evaluate what Rainey says about the possibilities for publishing history as a special mode of *cultural analysis*; in the second part, I shall briefly consider his resistance to *reading* before proposing an alternative perspective on the question of the relevance of publishing history to literary studies. Here I shall focus mainly on the first appearance of Ezra Pound's "In a Station of the Metro."

I

Institutions of Modernism is one of the most ambitious, stylish and richly researched studies of modernism and publishing to have emerged out of the reconsideration of text production as a field of study in the 1980s. Focusing mainly on the years 1912 to 1924 – conventionally identified as the zenith of "high modernism" – it is arranged as a series of closely observed microhistories detailing the 'institutional profile of modernism in the social spaces and staging venues where it operated' (1998: 5). To this extent it is not only about publishing. The first case study, for instance, contrasts F. T. Marinetti's loud championing of Futurism to large audiences in London's Coliseum theatre with Ezra Pound's lectures on medieval poetry to a select elite at the London home of Lord and Lady Glenconner. Yet the four remaining chapters – on the first appearance of *Ulysses* and *The Waste Land,* on the composition of Pound's Malatesta Cantos, and on H. D. and coterie culture – are centrally concerned with the role that publishing, especially in the form of the 'little review' and the limited deluxe edition, played in modernism's apparent 'withdrawal from the public sphere' (1998: 75). Hence Rainey's principal, and much reiterated, claim that modernist writers, "by restricting supply, could exploit the limited demand for modernist literature, turning each book into an objet d'art that acquired potential investment value for collectors" (1998: 154). This cultural generalization is contentious, as we shall see, but, stated thus baldly, it fails to capture the significance of *Institutions of Modernism* as a contribution to publishing history at the level of methodology.

According to Rainey's grandish narrative, modernism was poised in a precarious state of uncertainty between a mid-Victorian confidence in an expanding literary marketplace – he opens with Dickens's 1853 paean to "the people" who have "set Literature free" from patronage – and postmodernism's knowing embrace of culture as a commodity – he refers at one point to Andy Warhol and the *"tristes tropiques* of late capitalism" (1998: 1, 41). The exclusive modes of modernist publication are, then, of interest, he claims, as a particularly clear manifestation of, and means of understanding, this equivocal episode in the history of Anglo-American culture. More importantly, for Rainey the rigors of his methodology – all that archival digging – make possible new ways of challenging the mythologies of modernism invented by the writers themselves (and their publishers) and too often uncritically rehearsed by subsequent commentators. The most well known of these are the heroic authorial self-constructions encoded in the stock oppositions between "high" and "low," the "intellectuals" and the "masses," or "literary purists" and "commercial profiteers." Taking issue with Terry Eagleton's account in "Capitalism, Modernism, and Postmodernism" (1985), for instance, Rainey argues:

> Modernism is commonly considered a "strategy whereby the work of art resists commodification, holds out by the skin of its teeth" against the loss of aesthetic autonomy. But it may be that just the opposite would be a more accurate account: that modernism, among other things, is a strategy whereby the work of art invites and solicits its commodification, but does so in a way that it becomes a commodity of a special sort . . . integrated into a different economic circuit of patronage, collecting, speculation, and investment. (1998: 3)

Though Rainey often takes a little too much delight in the easy disenchantments this line of argument affords – the anti-commercial is *really* commercial after all – it does enable him to make a strong case for seeing publishing history as a sophisticated mode of cultural analysis and critique, an appealingly ambitious prospect.

Difficulties begin to arise, however, when we consider his account of the background to the crisis of cultural value which gives a larger significance to the local details he amasses so assiduously. In his view, three events "epitomized" the "growing complexity of cultural exchange and circulation in modern society" which put paid to any "rigorous opposition between 'high' and 'low'": the *Daily Mail's* (1896) record-breaking sales of a million copies a day in 1902; the construction, in 1904, of the Coliseum theatre, a new, upmarket version of the traditional music hall; and the first recorded appearance of the word "middlebrow" in 1906 (1998: 2–3). These are sound observations. The *Daily Mail* did, like the Coliseum, provide a forum for Marinetti's Futurist assault on the "high/low" divide. Later, as Rainey shows, the Sunday *Observer*, another of Alfred Harmsworth's popular papers, boomed the deluxe first edition of *Ulysses*, boosting its sales (1998: 57–8). These details reveal lines of diffusion more intricate and interconnected than any envisaged by critics, such as Andreas Huyssen and John Carey, who define modernism in terms of its hostility to "mass culture." Rightly resisting the rigid dichotomy between "high" and "low" that such definitions presuppose, Rainey argues that modernism's "ambiguous achievement" was "to probe the interstices dividing that variegated field and to forge within it a *strange* and *unprecedented* space for cultural production" (1998: 3, my italics). But just how odd or unique was this space? And just how definitive of modernism was it?

Part of the problem is that Rainey's emphasis on the four years from

1902 to 1906 gives the impression that the modernists were responding directly to a new set of conditions peculiar to the beginning of the twentieth century. The causality implied – the modernists' space was unique *because* the cultural conditions were unprecedented – seems less clear, however, if we take the longer history of cultural transformation in the late nineteenth century into consideration. In one of its most popular versions, this is a relatively simple story of the rapid and radical incursion of the market economy into every aspect of late Victorian literary culture. An enlarged reading public, created in part by the broad expansion of educational opportunities after 1870, attracted a new generation of modernizing publishers – George Newnes was the first, followed by Harmsworth and C. Arthur Pearson – who turned the gentlemanly world of Victorian publishing into a large-scale culture industry. Taking advantage of new printing technologies – Hoe rotary presses, linotype machines – and energetically adopting new promotional strategies (prize competitions, advertising stunts), they created a highly commercialized "mass culture" for a new socially diverse population of suburban consumers. Newnes pioneered its major forms first with *Tit-Bits* (1881), a penny weekly, and then with *The Strand Magazine* (1891), a sixpenny monthly. These changes in the magazine culture were echoed, in the book market, by the rise of the "bestseller" made possible, in part, by the death of the three-volume novel in the mid-1890s. At the same time, the Society of Authors, founded by Walter Besant in 1884, and the emergence of literary agents signaled a new era of literary professionalization. By the late 1880s, then, literary publishing in the dominant sector of the market was big business, and the gulf between "high" and "low," the purists and the profiteers, was plain and unbridgeable.

Or so it seemed, particularly to the established literary intelligentsia – George Gissing's *New Grub Street* (1891) is the clearest single expression of their apocalyptic view. In fact, things were not so straightforward. This was partly because the new mass-market publishers were not profiteers out to exploit the "low," as their detractors claimed. They were sometimes socially responsible entrepreneurs who, in effect, created the new cultural space later called the "middlebrow." (While quietly abandoning the piety of most mid-Victorian family periodicals, Newnes, for instance, was as averse to the "unwholesome" elements of the established popular press as he was to the latest risqué literary experiments.) The story of the advent of "mass culture" was also complicated by the fact that many other editors and publishers at the time took Matthew Arnold at his word. Though their motivations were always complex – some had political objectives, some were hoping to make money – they saw themselves as Arnold's "true apostles of equality," with a "passion for diffusing, for making prevail, for carrying from one end of society to the other, the best knowledge, the best ideas of their time" (1867: 79).

Some, like Archibald Grove, the founding editor of the *New Review* (1889), were not particularly successful – Grove wanted to democratize the Victorian review by pricing his at sixpence rather than two shillings and sixpence, but, despite some real achievements, this proved unsustainable. Others, most notably W. T. Stead and T. P. O'Connor, prospered. In 1890, Stead, the controversial former editor of the *Pall Mall Gazette*, launched the *Review of Reviews*, a popular digest of all the "high cultural" periodicals, priced at sixpence. And in 1902, T. P. O'Connor, another pioneering "New Journalist" of the 1880s, started the equally successful *T. P.'s Weekly*, a penny *Tit-Bits*-style miscellany intended "to bring to many thousands a love of letters." Each weekly issue included "Cameos from the Classics," extracts from, among others, Plutarch, Byron, Shelley, Wordsworth, Browning, and Carlyle. The book publishers' equivalent to this was the cheap "classic" reprint series, another important late Victorian initiative. This can be traced back at least to Cassell's "Library of English Literature" (1875), but it was given new life and popularity by the next generation of publishers, notably Grant Richards ("World's Classics"), Newnes ("Pocket Classics"), and J. M. Dent ("Everyman" and "Temple Classics").

Seen from the perspective of publishing history, then, the cultural dynamics of the period were neither quite as simple, nor as ominous, as *New Grub Street* made out. The late Victorian period did not see the abyss between "high" and "low" yawn ever wider, nor was it a time when a new, autonomous "mass culture" threatened to obliterate the literary elite. It was, as younger writers like Arnold Bennett and H. G. Wells recognized – the former most notably in *Fame and Fiction* (1901), the latter in *Anticipations* (1901) – the moment when instability became the most conspicuous feature of all cultural hierarchies, and new cultural spaces began to open up. What was, for some, an apocalyptic crisis of value was, for others, a new opportunity for cultural mobility and innovation. This longer history makes Rainey's emphasis on the special complexity of the Edwardian period arguable. It also weakens his claims about the uniqueness of the Georgian modernists' position. Culturally speaking – that is, in terms of their attitudes, career strategies, and publishing practices – the modernists were not responding to a wholly new set of conditions. They were the inheritors of a late-Victorian legacy which included both a highly volatile cultural climate and a range of possible reactions to it.

Rainey is right to remind us, especially in respect of Joyce, Pound, and H. D., that "much of the literature that we now designate 'modernist' was produced under the aegis of a revived patronage that flourished on a remarkable scale" (1998: 73). This was one effect of the late Victorian inheritance, representing one response, on the part of writers and publishers, to the complexities of cultural value. How unprecedented it was is another matter, however. Though it is true that few individual writers in the 1890s received the kind of lavish direct patronage Joyce or H. D. enjoyed, many of the boldest late Victorian cultural projects, and so, indirectly, their contributors, were privately financed. The most outspoken and important forum for the literary elite, W. E. Henley's *Scots* (later *National*) *Observer* (1888–94), was funded by a group of wealthy Scottish Tories; an elite circle of subscribers connected to Lady Randolph Spencer Churchill supported the stylish *Anglo-Saxon Review* (1899–1901); and John Lane, the most innovative publisher of the 1890s, was able to create the prestige of the Bodley Head, which published *The Yellow Book* (1894–7), *The Anglo-Saxon Review*, and, later, *BLAST* (1914–15), only by actively nurturing a network of private investors. True, these publications were still intended for a general readership, not just for a coterie of collectors, but their existence had little to do with the market economy, and they often traded on the idea of collectability. It could be argued, for instance, that John Lane pioneered the equivocal cultural position which Rainey identifies as peculiarly modernist. With *The Yellow Book* and his controversial "Keynotes" series in particular – both are still too often wrongly considered the emblems of aesthetic autonomy in the 1890s – he turned "high art" into a successful marketing strategy. Capitalizing on the prestige of the "limited edition," the "beautiful book," and the appeal of the risqué, he commodified and popularized 1890s aestheticism in a way that both manifested and fell foul of the contemporary instability of value. Pointing to one of the key problems, one group of high-minded critics remarked in response to a promotional announcement for the new *Yellow Book*: "we should like to know . . . what the promoters take to be the best sense of the word 'popular', and how they imagine that anything concerned with art or letters can be at once popular . . . and distinguished" (Unsigned, 1894: 588–9). Rainey's culturally ambiguous space which entailed neither "a straightforward resistance nor an outright capitulation to commodification" was, in other words, not news to late-Victorian writers, publishers, and readers (1998: 3).

What about Rainey's other central claim? If the modernist modes of publication were not as "strange and unprecedented" as he urges, did they still in some way define modernism? There is no doubt that Georgian mod-

ernism was shaped by a series of small magazines and publishing houses –
the *Dial*, Middleton Murry's *Rhythm* and *Blue Review*, Ford's *English Review*,
Lewis's *BLAST*, the *Little Review*, the *New Freewoman* (later the *Egoist*), Shakespeare & Co., The Hogarth Press – all of which existed outside or on the
margins of the market economy. They made the modernist movement vi-
able by providing (temporary) refuge from censorship; by creating a space
relatively free from the various constraints of large-scale commercial publishing; and by becoming centers of association, cultural solidarity, and self-
promotion. Yet does it follow from this that "literary modernism constitutes
. . . a retreat into a divided world of patronage, investment, and collecting"
and away from "public culture" (Rainey 1998: 75)? Part of the difficulty
here is conceptual, since it is not clear how Rainey's phrase "public culture" is related to Jürgen Habermas's influential concept of the "public
sphere" from which it derives. For Rainey the *act of publication* in, say, the
form of a limited deluxe edition targeted at collectors, seems sufficient in
itself to epitomize modernism's "tactical retreat" from "public culture" (1998:
5). Yet this either makes too much of publishing, or too little of the concept
of the public sphere. If the modernists did rely on the cultural economy of
the coterie to get their work in print – and it is not the case that they all did
– their books were also news that stayed news, even, as the case of *Ulysses*
and the Sunday *Observer* illustrates, for mass-market newspapers. Through
reviews, interviews, advertisements, high-profile court cases, and more,
their public presence in the 1920s and 1930s was marked, even if their
books were not being bought or read by most readers.

The other problem with Rainey's claim about the modernists' definitive
retreat is historical. Here the value of his methodological contribution –
making publishing history a lens for high-resolution cultural critique – is
qualified by his tendency to oversell his richly documented case studies.
His unparalleled narratives of the first appearance of *Ulysses* or *The Waste
Land* tell us an enormous amount about Joyce, Eliot, and their "agent,"
Pound; about the ironies and complexities of publishing; and about the
intricate, contradictory relationship between the literary elites of the 1920s
and "public culture." It is far from clear how much they tell us about "modernism," however, despite Rainey's assertions. The fact that the deluxe
first edition of *Ulysses* (1922) published by Shakespeare & Co. was less a
book than an investment opportunity is, for him, "the final and consummate paradox of modernism" (1998: 56). On this logic, we could argue
that the serialization of Conrad's *Nostromo* in *T. P.'s Weekly* in 1904, or
Chance in the *New York Herald* in 1912, is evidence of modernism's consummate populism.

More importantly, such generalizations sit uneasily with Rainey's narrow, focused approach, since his case studies inevitably obscure the modernists' many other publishing strategies and markets. For one thing, though some of their publishers – Elkin Mathews, John Lane, The Hogarth Press, Faber – were small and exclusive, they were not limited to the coterie. Conversely, others were larger-scale commercial publishers who, on occasion, took cautious risks, as Methuen did with Lawrence's *The Rainbow* (1915). For another, the diversity of contemporary English-language publishing markets – Britain, America, the Colonies, Europe – and the complexities of the trade meant that their works seldom remained fixed in one place or mode for long. By 1929, for instance, Bernard Tauchnitz, the Leipzig publisher who sold inexpensive paper-covered English-language books in Europe, had May Sinclair, Conrad, Woolf, and Lawrence as well as Conan Doyle, Edgar Wallace, Wells, and Bennett on his list. And if we include the illegal trade, the field becomes even larger, as Lawrence discovered to his cost when a host of pirated editions of the "privately printed" *Lady Chatterley's Lover* (1928) rapidly entered circulation. The pirating of the Florence edition, which was as exclusive as the first edition of *Ulysses*, forced him to bring out the cheap Paris edition in 1929.

Institutions of Modernism convincingly demonstrates that publishing history – still a marginal area in literary studies – can be used to rethink and rewrite cultural history. At the same time, its doubtful generalizations and historical gaps indicate how much work is left to be done. Given the diversity of modernist spaces, the multiplicity of publishing strategies, and the chanciness of the whole business, it is clear that the many cultural meanings of publishing in the period have yet to be fully deciphered.

II

Where does all this leave us as readers? Or, to put it more bluntly, does publishing history have anything to do with meaning? Rainey's position on this is bracingly uncompromising. One of his favorite devices is the witty, self-justifying punchline designed to put close readers in their place. "Reconsidering the publication history of *The Waste Land* might prompt us," he notes, "to question the dominant methodology of modern literary studies" (1998: 106). The fact that the editors of the *Dial* never actually read the poem before publishing it – they accepted Pound's opinion of it – leads him to wonder if "the best reading of a work may, on some occasions, be one that does not read it at all" (Rainey 1998: 106). In his introduction, he formulates this resistance to reading more programmatically: "I reject the idea that history or theory are acceptable only if they take on the role of humble handmaiden to the aesthetic artifact. Further, juxtaposing the analysis of specific works with discussion of institutional networks would encourage, however inadvertently, a vulgar materialism that I also disclaim" (1998: 6–7). Intended to justify his own work as a cultural historian – especially to skeptical literary theorists and critics – this is an admirably robust defense of publishing history as a mode of cultural analysis in its own right. Yet it also betrays an anxiety about reading – and hence criticism and "theory" – evident in the tone and style of the book as a whole and especially apparent in the final chapter on H. D. (In an unusually moralistic moment, Rainey dismisses her writing – and recent feminist reappraisals of it – largely because she was a coterie poet.) Though he has never been one to shy away from the urgent questions raised by "theory" – his first book *Ezra Pound and the Monument of Culture* (1991) engages with poststructuralism directly – his resolute rejection of reading says something about the polarized institutional context out of which his book emerged. Reading is for critics and theorists (who, it is assumed, dominate the field); the study of publishing provenance is for bibliographers, scholarly editors, and cultural historians (assumed to be the dominated). In the second half of this essay, I would like to question this hierarchical division of labor by looking at the first appearance of Pound's "In a Station of the Metro," not simply as a cultural historian, but as a reader interested in the history and formation of meaning. I have chosen this example in part because the lyric has traditionally been considered the form most amenable to rigorous close reading.

In a Station of the Metro

> The apparition of these faces in the crowd ;
> Petals on a wet, black bough.

For those trained in one or another tradition of detailed textual exegesis, this highly compressed, free-verse lyric would rightly demand careful critical scrutiny. Such readers might want to begin, for example, by asking about its peculiar, minimalist rhetoric and grammar (it contains no verbs, no logical connectives, no explicit lyric "I," no rhyme, no fixed meter, etc.). They would, in other words, approach the poem as a complex verbal icon, privileging its linguistic codes and anomalies. This classical reading protocol, which bibliographers and scholarly editors questioned to little avail throughout the twentieth century, came under concerted attack in the 1980s and 1990s from French book historians like Chartier and revisionist Anglo-American textual scholars like McKenzie and McGann. They insisted on seeing the text, not as an abstract linguistic form, but as a mediated material artifact, a redescription which, they urged, entailed a significant shift in our understanding of the scene of reading. If this scene was defined for close readers by their critical engagement with what we could call the transcendent "text-type" – the free-floating, idealized verbal text – *written* by the author, it was structured more immediately for materialist readers by their physical encounter with an immanent "text-token" – a particular material document – *produced* by various cultural mediators (editors, publishers, printers, etc.) for specific markets. For them, in other words, you are looking not so much at Pound's "Metro," but at my facsimile reproduction of a version abstracted from *Lustra* (1916), his seventh volume of poems.

Seen in the context of the theoretical debates of the 1980s, this determinedly anti-Platonic view of reading seemed to move in two opposite directions. On the one hand, by insisting on the role of cultural mediators, it seemed to endorse the critique of author-centered criticism formulated most persuasively by the poststructuralists; but, on the other, by privileging the self-contained document, it seemed to reject the new concept of "text" as the borderless space of writing that justified the "death of the author" in the first place. ("The idea of the book," Derrida wrote in *Of Grammatology*, "is profoundly alien to the sense of writing" [1976: 18].) This ambiguity, exacerbated by the contentious climate of debate, soon hardened into a polemical opposition as ahistorical textualists determinedly held out against historical documentalists, and vice versa. Predictably, few were willing to recognize any common ground. Yet what the textualists (who were not so ahistorical after all) and the documentalists (who were not all antiquarians) shared – albeit against the background of their radically different traditions – was a new interest in the problematics of dissemination and its implications for classical ideas of close reading.

For the poststructuralists, this was a broad conceptual issue central to their general theory of meaning: texts have meaning, they argued, only in a context, but since contexts are infinitely variable, meanings are never final. It followed that any attempt to police meaning, to contain it once and for all, was seen as a form of interpretative coercion. "Poststructuralism," as Derrida put it in 1990, "dislocates the borders, the framing of texts, everything which should preserve their immanence and make possible an internal reading" (Carroll 1990: 92). On the face of it, the documentalists were committed to the opposite view, given their investment in the preservation and analysis of the immanent "text-token." Yet, as many recognized, immanence did not entail stability, since, even in material terms, there is no end to the process of dissemination. Proliferation, not fixity, is the norm as texts are successively put to new uses in new forms. This is not, it should be stressed, simply a reassertion of the scholarly editor's traditional insistence on *textual* variation. It is a matter of recognizing the volatility of material *contexts* and the unpredictability of *readings*. Produced and reproduced by new cultural mediators, in new contexts, and for new readers, the successive versions of texts represent unique episodes in the constitution of meaning. This complements, rather than contradicts, the poststructuralists' primary insight. If the Derridean reader is a permanent nomad who refuses to accept the finality of any border, the documentalist's ideal reader is a stateless cartographer mapping the frontiers as they change. The point, then, is not to celebrate the document at the expense of writing – in Derrida's sense of the term – but to study its attempts to contain the disruptive energies of dissemination, and, in so doing, to make publishing history the foundation of a larger history of reading.

Even at the most elementary level – typographical format – the publication history of "In a Station of the Metro" illustrates these investigative opportunities well. Of course, in a relatively banal sense the poem has been in a constant state of typographical flux, through all its numerous printings and reprintings, from one publisher's house style to another, or as fashions changed. More compelling, however, is the fact that when it first appeared in *Poetry*, Harriet Monroe's Chicago monthly, in April 1913, and then again in Dora Marsden's the *New Freewoman* in London four months later (August 15), it was printed, at Pound's insistence, in this arresting format:

IN A STATION OF THE METRO.

The apparition   of these faces   in the crowd   :
Petals   on a wet, black   bough   .

In a letter to Monroe of March 30, 1913, he noted "In the 'Metro' hokku, I was careful, I think, to indicate spaces between the rhythmic units, and I want them observed" (Pound 1951: 53). The trouble is no other version printed in Pound's lifetime followed these strictures. This created a problem for subsequent editors and anthologists. Most quietly opted for the 1916 text as it appeared, in the form I cited first (note the changed punctuation as well), in *Lustra*, no doubt on the traditional grounds that this was the author's "final version." Peter Jones took this route in his still popular 1972 Penguin anthology *Imagist Poetry*. By the 1990s, however, those who kept up with developments in textual theory found ways of being more transparent about the problems. The editors of *The Norton Anthology of Poetry* (fourth edition), for instance, who "introduced notes" to "challenge and problematize the idea of textual 'authority,'" used the *Lustra* format but alerted their large, mainly undergraduate readership to the alternatives by dating it "1913, 1916" (Ferguson et al. 1996: lvii). By contrast, Thom Gunn in his slim Faber volume *Ezra Pound: Poems Selected by Thom Gunn* (2000) – part of a new series of contemporary poets editing canonical poets – explicitly opted for the more radical *Poetry* version.

In each of these books, then, we encounter a different "Metro," the mediated product not only of particular editors' decisions, but of changes in textual theory which reflect our historical moment more than any other. Knowing this does not only raise questions of textual authority, however. It also problematizes the scene of reading by fragmenting it and, more interestingly, by obliging us to consider the effects peculiar to the 1913 format. These seem fairly clear if Pound's letter to Monroe is anything to go by. In the absence of a fixed meter, the spaces were meant to indicate the poem's underlying phrasal rhythm (three unequal units per line). The visual cues advertise, more aggressively than the later versions, the aural aspect of Pound's new poetics by emphatically challenging readers to abandon received assumptions about poetic rhythm, and by foregrounding his desire to "compose in sequence of the musical phrase, not in sequence of a metronome" (West 1913: 87). Yet this can only be part of the story, since we still need to account for the spaces before the terminal punctuation marks of each line which have nothing to do with phrasal patterning. On the contrary, their effect seems exclusively visual. This was true of many other effects beginning to preoccupy Pound around 1913. About another poem ("The Garret") he remarked, in the same letter to Monroe, "I was careful . . . as to line ends and breaking *and capitals*" (1951: 53, emphasis in the original). Here, again, it is the physical appearance of the printed poem, as much as its musicality, that mattered. The visual dimension, of course, became a vital part of Pound's later poetics, particularly after he read Ernest Fenollosa (1853–1908) in late 1913 and discovered the rich potentialities of the Chinese ideogram. Yet what are we to make of it at this early stage in his career? Was it simply a self-conscious expression of prosodic experimentalism about which he later had second thoughts?

There is little doubt that the primary effect of the 1913 format is to draw attention to Pound's rejection of a fixed meter in favor of a loose, musical cadence. Yet the fact that it used visual cues to do so, coupled with the seemingly gratuitous spacing before the punctuation marks, opens up another possibility as well. As Vincent Sherry has argued, Pound's resistance to Symbolism – conventionally seen to be the driving force behind Imagism – was not conducted only at the level of poetic language (Pound's denotative directness versus, say, early Yeats's connotative suggestiveness) or epistemology (knowing the concrete directly via the "image," not the transcendent indirectly via the "symbol"). It also centered on his changing attitudes to the competing poetics of orality and print, the auditory versus the visual effect. Partly as a consequence of his reading Remy de Gourmont (1858–1915) – he probably first did so in 1911 – he began to move away from his early Provençal-influenced preoccupation with acoustic effects and to give increasing priority to what Sherry calls "visual values" (1993: 52). This happened gradually in the course of 1912 to 1914, and by 1915, with Fenollosa's backing, his association of Symbolism with a debased vagueness bred in part of its reliance on musical evocation for its effects was firmly entrenched. As his thinking began to change, he started to emphasize not only clear perception, but, increasingly, the visible modalities of the poems themselves. This makes the 1913 version of the "Metro" something of a paradox. It used visual cues both to underwrite its innovative musicality and to give new importance to the medium of print itself. Unlike the 1916 version, then, its unusual format manifests Pound's uncertain position in 1913 as a young poet – he was twenty-eight – determined to redefine his relationship to the oral traditions of the past while creating new forms appropriate to a culture dominated by print, a *vers libre* experimenter on his way to discovering a new poetry for the eye.

When we encounter "Metro" in *Poetry* or the *New Freewoman*, we cannot, of course, consider its format in isolation from the frames created by the periodical context itself which had other, often unexpected, effects. Unlike those produced by the format, these are inevitably erased in the process of dissemination. It could even be argued that a canonical text, like "Metro," is by definition one which is capable of countless, responsible recontextualizations in the various documents that constitute the cultural memory. The challenge is to delineate these changing material contexts and analyze their readerly effects.

In the *New Freewoman* – to keep to one particularly testing example – "Metro" appeared as part of a series of six poems Pound grouped together under the heading "The Contemporania of Ezra Pound." The significance of this general title is highlighted in "Salutation the Second," one of two explicitly metapoetic poems in the series. In it Pound reviews the first five years of his career as a published poet and looks to the future. "My books," he claims, were "praised" in part because "I was twenty years behind the times" (1913: 88). Now, however, he insists he has entered a new phase.

> Here they stand without quaint devices,
> Here they are with nothing archaic about them.

(Illustrating the shifting effects of context, the deictic "here" acquires a different force in each material document.) "Contemporania" referred, then, not simply to Pound's latest work, but to his own new engagement with modernity and its idioms. In "Salutation the Second" he drew attention to this change of direction, and, more importantly, attempted to control his readers' response to it by preempting criticism. He included direct references to the hostile "reporters," "professors," "practical people," and "pretty ladies" whose conventional ideas of poetry – "the Picturesque," the "vertigo of emotions," etc. – he gleefully anticipated affronting with his "little naked and impudent songs." His new poems were, he claimed, intended to "rejuvenate things" by dealing with sexuality ("the dance of the phallus"), exploiting the license of free verse ("with two light feet, if it please you!"), and reinventing poetic language even at the risk of writing what might appear "nonsense." "Metro," strategically placed as the last poem in the series, appeared immediately below this manifesto statement, presented as an exemplary instance of the risky new idiom. In this immediate context, then, its meaning is strongly determined by Pound's heroic narrative of his own poetic development which he sees in ethical as much as literary terms. The oddly formatted poem, in effect, becomes a testament not only to his new experimentalism, but to his own purist integrity. As he characteristically put it in "Tenzone,", the opening poem of the series, "I beg you, my friendly critics, / Do not set about to procure me an audience. // I mate with my free kind upon the crags" (1913: 87).

The general title and metapoetic surrounding poems were not the only explicit framing devices in the *New Freewoman*, however. Rebecca West (1892–1983) introduced the series as a whole with a headnote entitled "Imagisme." The main point of her piece was to explain that "the following are poems written by Mr Ezra Pound since he became an *imagiste*" (West 1913: 87). For the most part, she simply used extracts from F. S. Flint's essay "Imagisme" and Pound's "A Few Don'ts by an Imagiste," both of which had appeared in *Poetry* for March 1913 (i.e., a month before Pound's other, larger series of "Contemporania" appeared in Monroe's monthly). In borrowing from these pieces West started a critical trend, since they subsequently became canonical paratexts in the history of the Imagists, used and reused by critics and editors to comment on the group's poetics and on individual poems like "Metro." Yet West also had some, now forgotten, thoughts of her own which had a special resonance in the *New Freewoman*. Under economic pressure, she claimed, recent English poetry had become elitist and self-indulgent: "because the public will not pay for poetry it has become the occupation of learned persons, given to soft living among veiled things and unaccustomed to being sacked for talking too much."

> That is why from the beautiful stark bride of Blake it has become the idle hussy hung with ornament kept by Lord Tennyson, handed on to Stephen Phillips [1854–1915, a celebrated turn-of-the-century poet and playwright] and now supported at Devonshire Street by the Georgian School. [Edward Marsh's popular anthology, *Georgian Poetry, 1911–1912*, was first published in December 1912] (West 1913: 86)

Rather surprisingly – given Rainey's thesis and Pound's social attitudes and connections – she saw the Imagists as an answer to this decadent coterie culture and its over-elaborated forms. Unlike their indulgent drawing-room precursors and contemporaries, they were, according to West's socialist rhetoric, "a little band who desire the poet to be as disciplined and efficient at his job as the stevedore" (1913: 86). In a more high-minded gesture, she also associated them with "Taylor and Gilbreth," who wanted "to introduce scientific management into industry" – Frederick Taylor published *The Principles of Scientific Management* in 1911, and Frank Gilbreth's *Primer of Scientific Management* appeared in 1912 (see Chapter 8 of this volume).

With this colorful rhetoric West invited her readers to consider Pound's poems in a very particular light: as examples of a new literary movement produced by specific local conditions, as a reaction against decadent *English* poetic traditions, and as a manifestation of other extra-literary modern tendencies. Underlying her analysis was a grand narrative of national decline and regeneration which took Pound's new Imagist poems out of the relatively limited sphere of his personal narrative (as reflected in "Salutation the Second") and put them in a larger literary and sociopolitical context. With a stevedore's practical good sense – her outlook is noticeably egalitarian – the Imagists were, in her view, intent on bringing the same efficient, rational practices to poetry that Taylor and Gilbreth were applying in industry. As many articles – on topics ranging from masturbation to prostitution, taxation to women's rights – testified, this was very much in keeping with some dominant strains of thought in the *New Freewoman* itself. One article, in the same issue as Pound's "Contemporania," appealed, for instance, to the latest anthropological research into cultural taboo to explain the "primeval" resistance to the enfranchisement of women. It argued that the House of Commons was a "primitive Men's House," with all the associated rites and rituals, organized to "defend" men from "the natural sovereignty of the female sex" (F.R.A.I 1913: 85–6). On West's reading, then, the literary values reflected most clearly in the innovative form and sparse language of "Metro" embodied the new anti-elitist, scientific spirit of modernity, and echoed the *New Freewoman's* emancipatory call for a radical transformation of a decadent social and political order.

Despite Pound's editorial influence – he became the journal's literary editor in June 1913 – and though he, like T. S. Eliot, was himself not averse to justifying his poetics in scientific terms, it is unlikely that he would have endorsed West's framing of his poems unreservedly. This is a price many authors have to pay for periodical publication which is the product of numerous, sometimes unlikely, collaborations. For Pound it was almost inevitable given the personal and intellectual tensions within the *New Freewoman* in 1913. Pound, who never had a high opinion of Dora Marsden (1882–1960), was at odds with her from the start. Though he and his allies managed to shift its orientation away from feminism to a more inclusive individualism as early as December 1913, when they had it renamed the *Egoist*, he was still frustrated by his inability to veto Marsden's editorial decisions some months later. In a letter to Amy Lowell of March 18, 1914 he remarked: "I'm responsible for what I get into the paper but I am at present nearly, oh we might as well say quite powerless to keep anything out" (1951: 72). Marsden had very strong editorial views of her own. She had started the *Freewoman* – as it was called until June 1913 – in 1911 with the aim of taking the feminist debate beyond the narrow question of the vote. (A committed suffragette since 1908 – she was imprisoned in 1909 – she left the Women's Social and Political Union in 1910 after becoming disenchanted with the Pankhursts' leadership.) As her ideas evolved, however, the journal also became a forum for her radical individualism – the *New Freewoman* was subtitled "An Individualist Review." She, in fact, became England's most fervent advocate of Max Stirner, the obscure early nineteenth-century German philosopher whose controversial book *Der Einzige und sein Eigentum* (1844, translated as *The Ego and His Own*) remains one of the most uncompromising articulations of philosophical egoism. This resolute individualism created ideological tensions with established members of her stable like West. A dedicated socialist and suffragette in her early twenties – she was ten years younger than Marsden – West had been writing for the *Freewoman* from the start, and so her rhetoric, which commented directly on Imagism and "Contemporania," said more about the journal's past, as a campaigning feminist paper, than its future, as a celebrated modernist "little review."

In the *New Freewoman*, then, "Metro" – and Imagism itself – is explicitly inscribed into a series of multi-authored paratexts which bear witness to the diverse currents of opinion shaping the journal at that historical moment. Its possibilities do not end there, however. If we look beyond the poem's explicit framing devices at the readerly effects of the entire journal itself – considered as an implicit or co-textual frame – other, more challenging, questions arise. Reading the issue for August 15, 1913, it is not difficult to detect the conspicuous correspondences between, for instance, the extracts West cites from Pound's "A Few Don'ts" and Marsden's editorial, entitled "Thinking and Thought." His own maxim – "Go in fear of abstractions" – and his insistence on "presentation" resonate with her rousing conclusion: "When men acquire the ability to make and co-ordinate accurate descriptions, that is, when they learn to think, the empire of mere words, 'thoughts', will be broken, the sacred pedestals shattered, and the seats of authority cast down" (Marsden 1913: 83). Earlier in the same editorial she had called for the "purging of language," arguing that the "vitally true things are all personally revealed" in "experienced emotion" (Marsden 1913: 82). This again recalls Pound's definition of the "Image," also cited by West, as "that which presents an intellectual and emotional complex in an instant of time," and his claim that it is "better to present one Image in a life-time than to produce voluminous works" (West 1913: 86). As Marsden's conclusion indicates, however, her editorials, unlike Pound's poetic statements, are explicitly political. Her nominalist critique of abstract language was motivated by her radical libertarian politics. Indeed, language and authority, particularly in their elitist male forms, were among the main targets of her fierce editorials for both the *New Freewoman* and the *Egoist*. In "Thinking and Thought" she attacked the "cultured," especially the "pseudo-logicians," who "prefer to retain inaccurate thinking which breeds thoughts, to accurate thinking which reveals facts." Sharpening her focus, she set herself against "the mountain of culture which in the world of the West they have been assiduously piling up since the time of the gentle father of lies and deceits, Plato" (Marsden 1913: 82).

The co-textual links between Pound and Marsden inevitably raise the question of Imagism's own politics. For Michael Levenson and Robert von Hallberg, the resonances are not coincidental. They reveal, in their view, a lost frame of reference for understanding the historical complexity of Pound's political affiliations. Rightly challenging Donald Davie's unsubstantiated claim, first made in the 1950s, that there is a direct line between Pound's Imagist poetics and his later fascism, they have pointed to the historical connections with the *New Freewoman's* emancipatory, individualist politics. For Levenson, these correspondences, coupled with Pound's intellectual debts to other philosophical egoists like Allen Upward, reveal that "modernism was individualist before it was anti-individualist, anti-traditional before it was traditional, inclined to anarchism before it was inclined to authoritarianism" (Levenson 1984: 79). This is a useful corrective, not least because it reattaches modernism – and Imagism in particular – to the concrete debates of a time that mixed politics and poetics in uncertain measures.

Yet, seen in the context of *The New Freewoman*, Levenson's revisionist political reading looks too emphatic. For one thing, in its pages Pound insisted on Imagism's traditionalism. Through F. S. Flint – Pound had Flint interview him for the *Poetry* piece – he insisted that, unlike the Futurists, the Imagists were "not a revolutionary school; their only endeavour was to write in accordance with the best tradition" (West 1913: 85). In another instance of modernism's cultural mobility, he made the same point, with a more national inflection, in an article, entitled "Imagisme and England," in *T. P's Weekly* for February 20, 1915. For another, if the links between Pound's poetic statements and Marsden's editorials shed light on his prewar politics, they also tell us something about his inability, despite his best efforts, to control the contexts in which his poetry and his poetics might be understood. The extent to which he wished to do so is evident in a characteristic letter, again to Amy Lowell, dated August 1, 1914. He was responding critically to her suggestion that she might bring out another anthology like his own *Des Imagists* (1914), but in a more collaborative way.

> The present machinery [for promoting Imagism] was largely or wholly of my making. I ordered "the public" (i.e. a few hundred people and a few reviewers) to take note of certain poems. . . . I should like the name "Imagisme" to retain some sort of meaning. It stands, or I should like it to stand, for hard light, clear edges. I can not trust a democratized committee to maintain that standard. Some will be splay-footed and some sentimental. (Pound 1951: 78)

In the *New Freewoman*, this authoritarian desire to contain the meaning of Imagism was compromised. It was, after all, Marsden and West, not Pound, who in their different ways invoked the larger sociopolitical context. He restricted his own designs on the reader to the ethical and literary domains. Responding to the rigid historicism implicit in Levenson and von Hallberg's accounts, Sherry rightly maintains that "an understanding of this moment in cultural history is properly grounded when we see the radical Image standing poised – against the continental background impinging on Marsden – between opposite possibilities; between a turn left and a slide to the right" (1993: 46). Rereading "Metro" in the *New Freewoman* suggests we can take this further, since, even in this one material context, the meanings of the "radical Image" – which are not just political – shift unpredictably within a wide variety of implicit and explicit frames.

This is unsurprising, since, contrary to some of Rainey's claims, publication, even in a "little review," by definition marks the moment when a text becomes subject to the various, unstable forces that shape the public sphere. Even in the confines of one document, as we have seen with "Metro" in the *New Freewoman*, texts are caught within an intricate tangle of sometimes competing, sometimes converging interests. If we extend the analysis across a collection of documents, the picture becomes even more complex. Between 1913 and 1916 alone, "Metro" appeared in a remarkable range of other settings, which once again reveal the extraordinary cultural mobility of modernist texts. It forms part of Pound's short literary autobiography "How I began" for *T. P.'s Weekly* (June 6, 1913) – this was his contribution to the paper's long-running series designed to appeal to the literary aspirations of its large, frequently lower-middle-class readership. It then resurfaced in his article "Vorticism" published in the eminent *Fortnightly Review* for September 1, 1914 before also appearing in the *Catholic Anthology* (1915), Pound's self-consciously anti-movement (i.e., anti-Lowell and anti-Georgian) anthology, published by Elkin Mathews; in *Lustra* (1916), his seventh volume, published by Mathews in two editions, one unexpurgated and "privately printed" in September, the other censored version issued for general sale in October; and in *Gaudier-Brzeska* (1916), Pound's experimental biography of the sculptor, published by John Lane. Each of these material contexts created new, sometimes unique, readerly effects in a process that is, of course, ongoing.

Studying these effects, on the basis of the documentary evidence, is one task for publishing history, but it is only a beginning. A more comprehensive approach to the history of meaning also needs to examine the more elusive evidence detailing how readers themselves – reviewers, critics, and so-called ordinary readers – interpreted "Metro" by framing it in their own ways without necessarily acknowledging the designs of its material context. Asking where and how texts were first published is, then, a way into a much larger series of questions which challenge our understanding of how texts relate to their many, shifting contexts. It is also, as we have seen in the case of Levenson and von Hallberg, an analytical tool for critiquing later readings. Approached in this way publishing history makes possible a nuanced, responsible study of the formation of meaning which refuses to accept the assurances of traditional historicism, or to define itself against reading, criticism, and "theory."

References and Further Reading

Arnold, M. [1867] 1993. *Culture and Anarchy and Other Writings,* ed. Stefan Collini. Cambridge: Cambridge University Press.

Bourdieu, P. 1993. *The Field of Cultural Production.* Cambridge: Polity Press.

Carey, J. 1992. *The Intellectuals and the Masses.* London: Faber & Faber.

Carroll, D., ed. 1990. *The States of "Theory."* Stanford: Stanford University Press.

Chartier, R. and Cavallo, G., eds. 1999. *A History of Reading in the West.* Cambridge: Polity Press.

Darnton, R. 1990. *The Kiss of Lamourette.* London: Faber & Faber.

Derrida, J. 1976: *Of Grammatology.* Trans. Gayatri Chakravorty Spivak. Baltimore: Johns Hopkins University Press.

Eisenstein, E. 1979. *The Printing Press as an Agent of Change.* Cambridge: Cambridge University Press.

Ferguson, M. et al. 1996. *The Norton Anthology of Poetry.* New York: W. W. Norton.

F.R.A.I. 1913. The House of Commons. *New Freewoman* I/5 (August 15): 85–6.

Genette, G. 1997. *Paratexts: Thresholds of Interpretation.* Cambridge: Cambridge University Press.

Huyssen, A. 1986. *After the Great Divide: Modernism, Mass Culture, Postmodernism.* Bloomington: Indiana University Press.

Levenson, M. 1984. *A Genealogy of Modernism: A Study of English Literary Doctrine 1908–1922.* Cambridge: Cambridge University Press.

Marsden, D. 1913. Thinking and Thought. *New Freewoman* I/5 (August 15): 81–3.

McDonald, P. D. 1997. *British Literary Culture and Publishing Practice, 1880–1914.* Cambridge: Cambridge University Press.

McGann, J. J. 1983. *A Critique of Modern Textual Criticism.* Chicago: University of Chicago Press.

McKenzie, D. F. 1999. *Bibliography and the Sociology of Texts.* Cambridge: Cambridge

University Press.

Pound, E. 1913. Contemporania. *New Freewoman* I/5 (August 15): 87–8.

——. 1951. *The Letters of Ezra Pound, 1907–1941*, ed. D. D. Paige. London: Faber & Faber.

Rainey, L. 1998. *Institutions of Modernism: Literary Elites and Public Culture*. New Haven and London: Yale University Press.

Sherry, V. 1993. *Ezra Pound, Wyndham Lewis, and Radical Modernism*. Oxford: Oxford University Press.

Unsigned. 1894. ΨΑΥΜΑ ΨΕΑΣΨΑΙ. *National Observer* (April 21): 588–9.

Von Hallberg, R. 1995. Libertarian Imagism. *Modernism/Modernity* 2/2 (April): 63–79.

West, R. 1913. Imagisme. *New Freewoman* I/5 (August 15): 86–7.

Willison, I., Gould, W., and Chernaik, W., eds. 1996. *Modernist Writers and the Marketplace*. New York: St. Martin's Press.

12

Reading and Modernism: "'Mind hungers' common and uncommon"

Todd Avery and Patrick Brantlinger

In her final novel, *Between the Acts* (1941), Virginia Woolf worried that the generation that had been born during the twentieth century in Britain had grown up in a world where "the newspaper was a book" (20). This is especially true for Isa Oliver; in her father-in-law's library, in search of "a cure" for her "mind-hunger" (16) and general malaise, she wonders, "What remedy was there for her at her age – the age of the century, thirty-nine – in books? Book-shy she was, like the rest of her generation" (19). Isa Oliver's consternation is partly that of Woolf herself, who, besides being a prodigious reader, wrote more often about questions of reading and writer–reader relations than any other modernist. Woolf/ Isa's question is notable for its dual emphasis on the use-value of reading – and by implication, writing – both for individuals of the 1930s and for "the century" that they inhabited. It also raises other questions pertinent to the study of reading and modernism; for although literary modernism in Britain had almost run its course by 1941, Woolf's lingering concerns are those of the other modernists. For example: What value did literature possess, for the individual and for British society as a whole, at a time when, according to some modernists, the masses of readers preferred to satisfy their "mind-hunger" with newspapers? Did and could such readers satisfactorily quench their thirst for knowledge of something "real" by dipping into the expanding ocean of mass-culture texts? What was the nature of the modernist writer's obligation, if any, to her or his readers? Who were these intended readers anyway? And in what ways did the modernists resemble each other with respect to their views on readers and reading, and how did they differ?

In the first part of this essay, we discuss a range of the modernists' critical, fictional, and poetic responses to the presence of an unprecedented mass reading public; more specifically, we explore some of the ways that writers positioned themselves above this public or in opposition to it. The second part looks closely at one group of influential modernist intellectuals, the Bloomsbury group, and especially at Virginia Woolf, from an ethical perspective; drawing on recent thinking in this direction by Emmanuel Levinas, Gilles Deleuze, Elaine Scarry, Terry Eagleton, and others, our purpose is to show that while many modernists bristled at the threat to their aesthetic sovereignty posed by a mass reading public (and by the emergence of electronic mass telecommunications, specifically radio, during the 1920s), some celebrated the progressive ethical and political potential of this state of affairs by crossing the "Great Divide" of twentieth-century culture; they embraced their readers and invited them to participate in a cooperative effort, as Woolf put it, to "discover what new combinations make good wholes in human life" (1966: 34). We conclude with a brief discussion of two new perspectives on reading and modernism that promise to open fruitful avenues of investigation for literary and cultural studies and modernist historiography in general.

Modernism and the New Mass Readership

With the achievement of almost universal literacy in Britain by 1900, the age of the "common reader" had arrived. For many, the achievement was positive: a fully enlightened, democratic culture and society was dawning. For others, universal literacy entailed a range of problems and even apocalyptic terrors associated with mass culture and society. From the most negative perspective, the literacy of the masses did not mean enlightenment, but the opposite. Thus, F. R. Leavis contrasted a cultivated, discriminating elite with a rising tide of semi-educated barbarism (e.g., in *Mass Civilisation and Minority Culture*, 1930). So, too, G. M. Trevelyan announced that mass education "has produced a vast population able to read but unable to distinguish what is worth reading" (*English Social History*, 1942, Ch. 18).

Matching the expansion of the reading public was a burgeoning of texts of all sorts, from mass-readership newspapers and bestsellers to avant-garde "little magazines." Modernist authors frequently represent the proliferation of printed matter as a major threat to elite taste or knowledge, and they often figure printed mass culture – which was paralleled by the emergence of the early, non-print mass media (cinema, radio, the phonograph) – as a monolithic entity, opposed to high culture and the progress of civilization. But mass culture, although ruled for the most part by the logic of capitalist commodification, was internally fragmented in many ways – a fragmentation that is both reflected and critiqued in high modernist works of literature and art. Fragmentation (or atomization) and massification are the two poles governing that typical antihero of modernism, the mass man – for example, T. S. Eliot's J. Alfred Prufrock and "Apeneck" Sweeney, and James Joyce's Leopold Bloom.

Despite the increasing specializations and divisions among types of texts, publishers, and readerships, the compelling idea of a uniform, mass readership, generated in part by the emergence of totalitarian mass movements (communism and fascism), entailed a conception of false reading that could only be overcome by a sophistication which, by definition, few possessed. In "The Day of the Rabblement" (1901), Joyce declared that "No man . . . can be a lover of the true or the good unless he abhors the multitude" (69). *The Little Review*, edited by Ezra Pound, promised on its masthead to make "no compromise with the public taste." "The age is illiterate with periodicals," wrote L. C. Knights and Donald Culver in the manifesto that prefaced the first issue of the Leavisite journal, *Scrutiny*. Recognizing the irony of possibly contributing to this "illiteracy," they worried about making yet another "addition to the swarm." And Eliot's poems often stress the inability of ordinary individuals and therefore the masses to make sense of their lives, much less of modernist literature:

We are the hollow men
We are the stuffed men
Leaning together
Headpiece filled with straw. Alas!

Joyce, Pound, and Eliot, along with many other modernists, inherited from Victorian aesthetes and decadents such as Walter Pater and Oscar Wilde the idea of "art for art's sake." This aesthetic battle cry, adopted from Théophile Gautier, Charles Baudelaire, and Gustave Flaubert in France, expressed bohemian rebellion against middle-class philistinism, a theme that D. H. Lawrence makes explicit:

> How beastly the bourgeois is!
> Standing in their thousands, these appearances, in damp England
> what a pity they can't all be kicked over
> like sickening toadstools. . . .

For Lawrence, the problem with the individual bourgeois "toadstool" was not that she or he was uneducated or illiterate. Instead, superficial education produced repression and too much self-consciousness, causing people to lose touch with their unconscious vitality and sexuality. Whether literate or not, members of the working class and of primitive societies, he believed, lived in harmony with their bodies and "the life of the blood."

Similar versions of primitivism were expressed by other modernists. Thus, William Butler Yeats agreed with his countryman Joyce that education in Ireland had produced a repressed, superficial populace. Only a cultivated minority on the one hand, and the uneducated Irish peasantry on the other, remembered the myths and folklore of the Irish past, which for Yeats constituted the essence of Irishness. "Have not all races had their first unity from a mythology, that marries them to rock and hill?," Yeats asks in his *Autobiography* (131); "We had in Ireland imaginative stories, which the uneducated classes knew and even sang, and might we not make those stories current among the educated classes . . . ?" Paradoxically, for Yeats, as for Lawrence and Thomas Hardy, the "educated classes" needed to be re-educated, or somehow severed from their superficial rationality and literacy, in order to regain unconscious vitality and the folk wisdom and poetry of the past. In Hardy's *Jude the Obscure* (1895), literacy and consciousness operate almost like curses upon the central characters – Jude Fawley, Sue Bridehead, and their children.

The belief that modern, literate individuals were alienated from the mythic past and their unconscious selves was reinforced by psychoanalysis. Although British modernists often expressed reservations about Freud's ideas, the new paradigm of the self, according to which the conscious, rational ego exercises at best only a weak control over the forces of the unconscious, influenced fiction, poetry, and the other arts, and posed new questions about education and reading. Did reading a text, literary or otherwise, involve merely interpreting the conscious meanings and intentions of its author? Or did it involve revealing unconscious meanings? Or both? Freud's *Interpretation of Dreams* (1900) provided a powerful model for a new sort of reading, one suggesting that the common reader would never be able to delve below the surface of whatever she or he tried to read. Like the analysis of dreams and psychoses, the reading of texts was rapidly becoming a matter for the experts, especially through the increasingly professionalized, academic practice of literary criticism and interpretation.

To be expert and receive the attention of experts involved for the modernists various states of exile and alienation from the common reader. Joyce lived in voluntary exile from Ireland and also implied, in *A Portrait of the Artist as a Young Man*, that the artist must stand alone. Some critics have argued that, as with any fictional creation, we should be wary of conflating the young Stephen Dedalus with his creator. Nevertheless, Stephen does illustrate Joyce's general disbelief that a mass readership could or even should understand the complexities of the increasingly experimental style he developed in his fiction. The "aesthetic philosophy" that Stephen espouses in *Portrait* and continues to ponder in *Ulysses* makes no concessions to the common reader, or indeed to any concept of audience or readership outside the small circle of devotees who ensured the publication of two of the most radical fictional experiments in the English (or any other) language. The focus of this philosophy is solely on abstract "beauty." Stephen says that his aim will be "to forge in the smithy of my soul the uncreated conscience of my race," but he tells his friend Davin that he can do so only by leaving his "race" and "country" behind: "When the soul of a man is born in this country there are nets flung at it to hold it back from flight. You talk to me of nationality, language, religion. I shall try to fly by those nets."

Although he was not one of the signatories of the 1929 "Proclamation" by Eugène Jolas and other modernists associated with the Paris-based "little magazine" *transition*, Joyce clearly agreed with it. The twelfth statement in the "Proclamation" reads: "The plain reader be damned." Its sixth statement declares: "The literary creator has the right to disintegrate the primal matter of words imposed on him by text-books and dictionaries," and the seventh says: "He has the right to use words of his own fashioning and to disregard existing grammatical and syntactical laws." The artist's "rights" transcend those of the "plain reader," as embodied in common sense and everyday language. Joyce took these "rights" to literary extremes, especially in his final novel, *Finnegans Wake* (much of which first appeared in *transition* as "Work in Progress."

Jolas and *transition* published numerous defenses of and commentaries on Joyce's experimental, notoriously difficult fiction. And for his part, Joyce produced a book that, he declared, would keep the professors busy for at least a century, and that "as were it sentenced to be nuzzled over a full trillion times for ever and a night till his noddle sink or swim by that ideal reader suffering from an ideal insomnia" (*Finnegans Wake*: 120). Despite recording the quotidian experiences of such ordinary individuals as Leopold Bloom and H. C. Earwicker, Joyce had no faith in any common as opposed to "ideal" reader to understand his novels. *Finnegans Wake* is the dream-thoughts or "dark night of the soul" of H. C. Earwicker, who is also called "Here Comes Everybody." Joyce's Everyman protagonist is the unconscious producer of a text that he himself, though literate, would never be able to read and understand. Joyce's intended audience for *Ulysses* and *Finnegans Wake* resembles the audience that Ezra Pound imagined for his *Cantos* and other poetic experiments; this happy elite, as Mark Kyburz points out in a recent study of Pound's early audiences, was to comprise "'*voi altri pochi* [you other few] who understand,' and would, he believed, read his poetry on his specific – and specifically idiosyncratic – terms of poetic communication and, moreover, 'will love me better for my labor in proportion as you read more carefully'" (1996: 4).

Many early-twentieth-century readers balked at what they perceived to be the inordinate labor required by works like *Finnegans Wake*. While it was still "in progress," H. G. Wells warned Joyce against going too far:

> you have in your crowded composition a mighty genius for expression which has escaped discipline. [You] . . . have turned your back on common men, on their elementary needs and their restricted time and intelligence. . . . What is the result? Vast riddles . . . . Take me as a typical common reader. Do I get much pleasure from [your] work? No. Do I feel I am getting something new and illuminating . . . ? No. So I ask: Who the hell is this Joyce who demands so many waking hours of the few thousands I have still to live for a proper appreciation of his quirks and fancies? (*Correspondence* 3: 277)

Whether or not Wells was "a typical common reader," he probably felt empowered to criticize *Ulysses* and "Work in Progress" because he had earlier been one of Joyce's champions. But it is also no coincidence that Wells was one of Virginia Woolf's targets, in her 1924 essay "Mr. Bennett and Mrs. Brown," for practicing an outmoded realism or "materialism" in such novels as *Tono Bungay* and *Ann Veronica*.

According to Woolf, realist fiction like that by Wells, Arnold Bennett, and John Galsworthy failed to capture the fleeting, contingent nuances of human nature and experience. Indeed, in one of the essay's most caustic remarks, Woolf tells her readers (and other potential writers) that "to go to these men and ask them to teach you how to write a novel – how to create characters that are real – is precisely like going to a bootmaker and asking him to teach you how to make a watch" (240). Always keenly attuned to the needs of readers as well as writers, and to their interrelation, Woolf thought that, in a world where "all human relations have shifted" (235), the methods of Edwardian realism were inadequate tools of the literary imagination. Thus, "Grammar is violated; syntax disintegrated" (247). In common with Joyce and other modernist writers, Woolf experimented with narrative form and "stream of consciousness" in such works as *To the Lighthouse*, *Mrs. Dalloway*, and *The Waves*. In "Modern Fiction," first written in 1919, Woolf advised: "Let us record the atoms as they fall upon the mind, in the order in which they fall, let us trace the pattern, however disconnected and incoherent in appearance, which each sight or incident scores upon the consciousness." Taking Joyce as her model, Woolf adds:

> In contrast with those we have called materialists Mr. Joyce is spiritual; he is concerned at all costs to reveal the flickerings of that innermost flame which flashes its messages through the brain . . . he disregards with complete courage whatever seems to him adventitious, whether it be probability, or coherence or any other of these signposts which for generations have served to support the imagination of a reader when called upon to imagine what he can neither touch nor see. (288)

A defining feature of all modernisms is expressed by Ezra Pound's slogan, "make it new." In pursuing the "new," especially through experimentation with narrative and poetic forms and conventions, modernist writers inevitably defamiliarized the common reader. Many of them therefore wrote first for themselves and then, at most, for small coteries of kindred spirits. Their readers would, perforce, be "ideal." If none of the major modernists declared, as William Blake did toward the end of his career, "I am hid," that is because they so loudly and often successfully trumpeted their causes in their little magazines and beyond. Pound, for one, served as an indefatigable exponent of "the new." And sometimes modernist works – *Ulysses* and Lawrence's *Lady Chatterley's Lover* are the best-known examples – gained fame and readership through the censorship trials to which they were subjected.

Further, the renewal of patterns of patronage – for instance, Harriet Shaw Weaver's sponsorship of Joyce and Pound's of T. S. Eliot – as well as the avant-garde predilections of little magazines such as *transition*, Eliot's *Criterion*, Pound's *Egoist*, and Wyndham Lewis's *BLAST*, facilitated modernist aesthetic innovation and also created an atmosphere of anti-mass elitism. In many of the little magazines, as in F. R. Leavis's *Mass Civilisation and Minority Culture*, a key theme was the lowering or nonexistence of aesthetic, cultural values. The more educated and literate the general public grew, the more ignorant – according to many influential modernists – it became. Like Lawrence and Yeats, for example, Lewis thought that "Education . . . tends to destroy the creative instinct"; he therefore conceived *BLAST* as an effort "to make the rich of the community shed their education skin, to destroy politeness, standardization and academic, that is civilised, vision" (*BLAST*: 1, 7).

While decrying the decline of "minority culture" and the increasing dominance of "mass civilization," however, journals such as *BLAST* and *Scrutiny* continued the Victorian effort to educate what Matthew Arnold had called "the raw, unkindled masses." Even the most seemingly aloof modernists engaged in attempts to teach unsophisticated readers to read in more sophisticated ways. These attempts include such obviously instructional – if eccentric – efforts as Pound's *ABC of Reading*, a textbook that purports to get the "science" of poetry and reading right, and to instruct novice readers in the principles of aesthetic taste far better than the ordinary, academic textbook. Pound's intention is evident in his epigraph, where he offers to lead his readers *"gradus ad Parnassum"* – to the steps of Parnassus, the home of the Muses in Greek mythology. A similar instructional effort is evident in Eliot's addition of footnotes to *The Waste Land*. Joyce also, despite his disdain for the common reader, relished distributing clues about how to interpret *Ulysses* and *Finnegans Wake*, and he supplied Stuart Gilbert and Carlo Linati with schemas for reading *Ulysses*.

Further, reviews and criticism written by Joyce, Eliot, Pound, Woolf, and many other modernists, as well as those written by such professional educators as the Leavises and I. A. Richards in Britain and, in the United States, the so-called New Critics, aimed to bring the "common reader" up to speed. Richards's *Practical Criticism* (1929), the forerunner of what has come to be known as "reader-response" literary theory, examined the reading habits, errors, and "stock responses" of Cambridge undergraduates in order to devise ways to eliminate the errors and improve those habits. Richards's assertion that "all respectable poetry invites close reading" became a mantra for the American New Critics, who in such works as Cleanth Brooks's and Robert Penn Warren's *Understanding Poetry* (1938), sought to teach readers both how to read literary texts and how to appreciate the genuinely literary or poetic. Installed as academic orthodoxy after World War II, New Critical close reading is still *the* chief method of teaching literature to high-school and undergraduate students.

Virginia Woolf, the Bloomsbury Group, and the Ethics of Reading

Like most of her male contemporaries, Virginia Woolf wished to improve the taste of "common readers." However, while the male modernists espoused the idea of the writer as cultural prophet or creative hero in opposition to a mass of underdeveloped or improperly educated readers, Woolf neither disdained nor "damned" the "plain" or "common reader." Rather, in her essays, short stories, and novels, Woolf often honored those who read simply "for the love of reading." Also, as in the late essay "Reading," Woolf practiced a sort of autoethnography of her own reading habits that affirms the individual reader's prerogative to exercise her or his unique judgment in the determination of the meaning and value of a literary text, independent of academic or critical orthodoxy.

This affirmation was partly a result of Woolf's reading experiences as a child, and partly an expression of the aesthetic and ethical sensibility she developed through her membership of the Bloomsbury group. Despite being a member of Britain's "intellectual aristocracy," Woolf was denied a formal education because of her sex. This impediment did not prevent her, however, from becoming one of the century's most voracious, self-reflective readers; she also wrote about reading more often than any other modernist writer. Roaming freely through her father's library, she learned the affective power of books on the reader that she later wrote about in "Notes on an Elizabethan Play": "we are apt to forget . . . how great a power the body of a literature possesses to impose itself: how it will not suffer itself to be read passively, but takes us and reads us; flouts our preconceptions; questions principles which we had got in the habit of taking for granted, and, in fact, splits us into two parts as we read." Here, Woolf associates herself with the "ordinary reader" for whom reading is often "an ordeal, an upsetting experience which plys [*sic*] him with questions, harries him with doubts, alternately delights and vexes him with pleasures and pains." This multivalent response to literary texts was for Woolf an unavoidable effect of venturing into "that wilderness" of books. Written in 1925, "Notes" recalls the bookplate that the young Virginia Stephen pasted into her books; it contained a Latin motto which translates, "In such woods the hunting is never exhausted."

Woolf was exposed to the aesthetic and ethical ideals that male friends had learned in fin-de-siècle Cambridge from their philosophical mentor, G. E. Moore. Moore's *Principia Ethica* (1903), the "Bloomsbury Bible," valorized "personal affections" and "aesthetic enjoyments" – which comprised *all* the greatest, and *by far* the greatest, goods we can imagine" (189, emphasis in original). Woolf's Bloomsbury friends, including Clive Bell, E. M. Forster, John Maynard Keynes, Desmond MacCarthy, Lytton Strachey, and her husband Leonard Woolf, embraced Moore's ideas and applied them in diverse fields – art criticism, the novel, economics and probability, literary journalism, international politics, and biography. These friends flouted social conventions and mocked Victorian habits of conduct in their individual and collective efforts to "make it new" in aesthetics and politics – to establish what Keynes called "a renaissance, the opening of a new heaven on a new earth" ("My Early Beliefs," 85). Bloomsbury was in many ways an exclusive group; ironically, however, their exclusivity and intimacy as a group of friends, when combined with highly sophisticated aesthetic sensibilities, fostered in them an abiding concern with the complex nuances and subtle gradations of aesthetic habitation and of ethical responsiveness to others.

This concern manifested itself in the Bloomsburyans' many reflections on reading. Keynes's essay "On Reading Books," first delivered as a radio broadcast in 1936, extolled the sensuousness of reading. "A reader," Keynes advised his audience, "should acquire a wide general acquaintance with books *as such*. . . . He should approach them with all his senses; he should know their touch and their smell. He should learn how to take them in his hands, rustle their pages and reach in a few seconds a first intuitive impression of what they contain" (emphasis in original). In addition to this aesthetic appreciation, Keynes emphasized the ethical care that a reader should bring to books: "He should cast an eye over books as a shepherd over sheep." Forster, for his part, in a radio broadcast titled "In My Library," subsumed Keynes's aesthetic pleasure in the "outside" of books to the pleasure he takes in "the words in them." Keynes's approach, he implies, is "non-adult," because it fetishizes the physical book, however beautiful, as a mere commodity. Words for Forster are "the wine of life," and reading is a "spiritual" activity, one that enables an individual reader, in a library as "unregimented" as his own, to achieve a sort of consubstantiation with past and present writers.

Virginia Woolf's novels, in particular *Jacob's Room, To the Lighthouse*, and especially *The Waves*, place demands on readers equal to those of the difficult experimental texts of Joyce, Pound, Eliot, and other contemporaries. And Woolf also thought, as they did, that writers should "train our taste" and "make it submit to some control" in order to recognize the "common quality" that literary masterpieces possess. But despite these similarities to her male counterparts, Woolf sharply differs from them in her vision of readers and writers as intimate, symbiotically connected partners in an effort to increase human sympathy. For her, the reader and the (modernist) writer were – or *might be* – joined by an ethic that promoted sympathetic and noncoercive human relations, as opposed to one that affirmed the romantic individualism and patriarchal authoritarianism of those male modernists who demanded conformity to ostensibly transcendent aesthetic standards. In "The Patron and the Crocus," for example, Woolf expressed a keen recognition of the mutual responsibilities of reader and writer: "To know whom to write for is to know how to write," she reminded writers. For writers and readers "are twins indeed, one dying if the other dies, one flourishing if the other flourishes . . . the fate of literature depends upon their happy alliance."

Woolf's nonhierarchical, feminist, and politically egalitarian approach to reading is clearest in the essay, "How Should One Read a Book?" with which she concluded her collection, *The Second Common Reader* (1932). Emphasizing the interrogative uncertainty of the essay's title, as well as her inability sufficiently to "answer the question for myself," Woolf offered her readers a curious, paradoxical bit of advice about how to read: "The only advice, indeed, that one person can give another about reading is to take no advice, to follow your own instincts, to use your own reason, to come to your own conclusions." By doing this, Woolf thought, "unprofessional" or inexpert readers could become more adept at negotiating, and thus help to improve the quality of, the books being written in a time of increasingly prodigious publishing, when "books written in all languages by men and women of all tempers, races, and ages jostle each other on the shelf."

More importantly, however, from a political perspective, in this essay Woolf alludes to her feminist polemic *A Room of One's Own* (1929) when she argues for the necessary independence of readers from the opinions of male academics who insisted on readers' acquiescence to some version of the Arnoldian standard of "the best that has been thought and said." Woolf writes:

> To admit authorities, however heavily furred and gowned, into our libraries and let them tell us how to read, what to read, what value to place upon what we read, is to destroy the spirit of freedom which is the breath of those sanctuaries. Everywhere else we may be bound by laws and conventions—there we have none. (234)

A Room of One's Own, one of the germinal texts of twentieth-century feminism, is also an example of the narrative criticism that Woolf wrote in order to "seduce" her (female) audience into a practice of reading, writing, and critical evaluation that would foster the development of an alternative, female literary tradition and thus liberate women from the literary and social "laws and conventions" imposed on them by their canon-building fathers.

Throughout her adult life, Woolf's continual meditations on the art of reading also adumbrated poststructuralist ideas about language and ethics; she emphasized the textuality of human character and individuals' potential for empathy toward others. For her, reading literary texts was similar to reading the "character," "personality," or "soul" of another human being. Her short story "An Unwritten Novel" and her essay "Mr. Bennett and Mrs. Brown" contain two of Woolf's most famous attempts at reading character in this way. Her most experimental novel, *The Waves* (1931), anticipates poststructuralist notions of identity and the deconstructionist critique of metaphysics (that is, of the transcendental signified) in its representation, through the form of six interlaced soliloquies, of "the ceaseless interplay of linguistic deferral and difference" (Moi 1985: 111). Woolf's writer-figure in *The Waves,* Bernard, notes the linguistic constructedness of individual and group identity: "we melt into each other with phrases" (16). Another character, Jinny, whose fascination with physical and sartorial appearances places her in a unique position to decode surfaces, voices Woolf's ideas about the textuality of personality, and thus about the similarity between reading texts and reading people: "we decipher the hieroglyphs written on other people's faces" (175).

Additionally, the act of reading was an ethical activity for Woolf in that the discovery of beauty in works of literature and the recognition of individuals' textual interrelatedness carried a distributional imperative: "perhaps one of the invariable properties of beauty," Woolf writes in "Reading," "is that it leaves in the mind a desire to impart. Some offering we must make; some act we must dedicate." Woolf seems to have in mind an idea similar to that which Elaine Scarry has recently expressed in *On Beauty and Being Just* (1999), where she writes of "the pressure beauty exerts toward the distributional. . . . Through its beauty, the world continually recommits us to a rigorous standard of . . . care" (80–1).

The Bloomsbury group has often been criticized for being a clique of social and aesthetic elitists. However, along with that of many other modernist writers (Eliot, Pound, Yeats, Wells, Shaw, Lewis, Vita Sackville-West and Harold Nicolson, to name a few), their involvement with early radio broadcasting calls into question the neatness of this Manichaean separation of "the intellectuals" and "the masses." Their participation in radio also illuminates the democratic beliefs that informed their ideas about reading. As Allison Pease notes, "the relationship between mass culture and modernis[m] . . . was more fluid and more complicated than we have yet to recognize" (2000: 77). When the British Broadcasting Company (later Corporation) took to the airwaves in late 1922, near the end of that *annus mirabilis* of modernist literature, it brought into being a new type of reading public – one christened in the title of the BBC's publication, the *Listener*. The BBC's founders and first administrators, led by John Reith, its first Director-General, envisioned radio as an unprecedented means of diffusing cultural touchstones to a mass listening public. The mass culture that the BBC sought to create was to be different from American mass culture, in that state-sponsored public service broadcasting in the national interest would resist the logic of capitalist commodification, and the concomitant pressure to cater to existing popular taste, which characterized privately funded American broadcasting from its own beginnings a few years earlier.

But despite their best efforts, public service radio in Britain instead contributed to what the radio historian Paddy Scannell has called "the democratization of everyday life, in public and private contexts" (1989: 136). It did so by mixing the public and private spheres and by expanding access to "elite" cultural and social venues and activities – thereby removing them from elite control. At the same time that the BBC's founders wanted to use the airwaves to regulate British morality by subsuming individual tastes to a universal norm, wireless technology allowed some eager broadcasters to cross social borders, trouble social distinctions, and promote countercultural reading habits. Such broadcasters – or "Talkers" – Scannell notes, "brought into the public domain the experiences and pleasures of the majority in ways that had been denied in the dominant traditions of literature and the arts" (141).

Many conservative politicians and cultural arbiters – the Leavises, for example – thought the BBC represented a dangerous "radiocracy" that offered a range of ideas to ill-educated people who might just *use* them – that is, promiscuously, without concern for the national health. The Bloomsbury writer Desmond MacCarthy, a favorite target of the *Scrutiny* gang, relished this opportunity to be a little promiscuous. In a series of eighteen radio talks he delivered in late 1932 and early 1933 titled "The Art of Reading," MacCarthy celebrated the ideologically disruptive uses of "reading for pleasure." Like Woolf's "How Should One Read a Book?" and

"The Patron and the Crocus," MacCarthy's talks represent Bloomsbury's effort to enlist an audience of common readers – or in this case, common listeners – into what we might call a "conspiracy of intimacy" against cultural pretensions. In "The Art of Reading," MacCarthy champions, in Peter Stansky's words, "the 'democracy' of art, of sensibility, the equality of the aesthetic reaction" (250).

In his first "Art of Reading" talk, MacCarthy explains the purpose of the series:

> I do not want to lecture. . . . Nor do I want you to agree with the general judgment upon famous books. It is no doubt a sign of education to hold approved opinions about the comparative merit of authors. . . . But . . . art and literature stand in a different relation to man. The study of literature is as much a matter of feeling and perceiving as of knowing. ("Art of Reading": 1–2)

Later in the decade, Virginia Woolf would criticize the "paid-for" culture and morality of men of the "educated class" (Woolf 1966: 4). Here, MacCarthy anticipates Woolf's argument by criticizing a mode of reading that requires the abdication of empathy in favor of conformity to traditional judgment.

For MacCarthy and his Bloomsbury friends, reading was a paradigmatic ethical activity on an intimate, everyday scale. In his "Art of Reading" talks, he elaborated a type of "ethical pedagogy" that countered the "uplifting" moral agenda of the BBC's administration during the 1920s and 1930s. In his view, readers' enjoyment of literary works precedes and encourages inventive responses to them, and fosters (in the way that Elaine Scarry describes) an increased sensitivity to and sense of responsibility for other individuals. This approach to reading also marks MacCarthy's effort to distance himself from modes of literary valuation such as T. S. Eliot was propounding, in his Norton lectures at Harvard (published in 1932 as *The Use of Poetry and the Use of Criticism*), during the same months that he was delivering his "Art of Reading" talks. His most emphatic affirmation of his central critical principles comes in his talk on "Milton's Shorter Poems":

> It is best to enjoy any author before one understands him. Indeed, in my opinion, it is little use trying to understand him before one has enjoyed him. That is what often seems to me wrong with the teaching of literature. Students learn all about a famous book or a famous author except what they

could have found out for themselves. . . . Take then . . . from every book what belongs to you in it. . . . I'm sure that this is the right way to set about studying literature. True, this method won't necessarily help you to pass examinations or impress others by your cultured conversation, but it is the best way of making literature part of your life and that after all is the most important thing. ("Art of Reading": 4)

In this talk, MacCarthy criticizes the same "unreal loyalties" – such as "college pride" and "school pride" – that Virginia Woolf later connected to fascism and the patriarchal "infantile fixation" in *Three Guineas*. Examinations, Woolf thought, encouraged young men to embrace "the old poisoned vanities and parades which breed competition and jealousy," "the arts of dominating other people . . . of ruling, of killing." For her, the "common reader" was, as Molly Abel Travis writes, "the last line of defense against fascisms both foreign and domestic" (1998: 40). So, too, Desmond MacCarthy envisioned a "common reader" or "common listener" who read "for pleasure" and not to discover "the true and the good" or to become the cooked and kindled consumer of high cultural values. Like many of their contemporaries, Woolf, MacCarthy, and the other Bloomsburyans wanted to help educate the "masses" – but on the masses' own promiscuous terms. Unlike many of the modernists, they approached reading as a unique ethical and political opportunity; instead of promoting a homogeneity of consent, they agitated, often in the space of modern mass technoculture, for a "heterogeneity of dissensus" among the multitude of ordinary, plain, raw, general, low, unkindled, novice, or common readers and "listeners-in."

Reading Modernism/Modernism's Readers

As one of the most prominent literary journalists in Britain during the first half of the twentieth century, Desmond MacCarthy frequently corresponded with many of the modernist era's illuminati. The MacCarthy archives at Indiana University's Lilly Library contain dozens of letters to him from these literary "prophets" and "priests." Many of these letters refer to details about the editing and publication of articles for the various journals he served in editorial capacities; others are friendly letters; some contain gossip about the intricate web of Anglo-American literary relationships; and a few, from aspiring writers, solicit expert opinion on the critical craft. Equally fascinating, however, with respect to modernism's "common reader," are a handful of the fan letters that MacCarthy saved over the course of his career. One of these letters suggests the extent of MacCarthy's reach as a "purveyor" of modernism and a radio celebrity into the reading – or in this case, listening – public. "Dear Sir," the letter, written on July 7, 1943, begins:

> I wonder if there may be a book or some trifle which you would enjoy the more if it came to you with the gratitude of a blind listener who has derived much pleasure & profit from your delightful broadcasts. If so will you accept the enclosed cheque for £20 with warmest of good wishes.
>
> Yours very sincerely
H. C. Russell (blind)
Per E. M. H. Russell

Who were – and are – modernism's readers? And in what ways and to what ends did – and do – modernism's readers read modernist literature? Two recent developments in modernist criticism promise to extend ongoing efforts to contextualize the experience of reading modernism. The nature of the "pleasure & profit" that "common readers" took from modernist literature is the subject of new work by such Woolf scholars as Anna Snaith and Melba Cuddy-Keane. In respective, archival studies of the working-class women readers of *Three Guineas* (Snaith), and of "individual readers who were reading high modernist literature in the interwar period but who were not themselves of the privileged British upper-middle class" , they are, in Cuddy-Keane's words, "exploring the ways in which high culture was welcomed and embraced – though perhaps also transformed – by predominantly middle-class or working-class readers." Their underlying goal, she continues, is "to break down categories that have identified high culture with high class and to pay respect to both the intellectual impulse and the intellectual accomplishment of non-privileged, non-specialist readers" (Imbricated Voices: 5).

Snaith's and Cuddy-Keane's interests are primarily historical as they focus on the recuperation of forgotten readers and neglected histories of reading. The types of pleasure and profit to be gained from modernist literature in a postmodern age is also the focus of recent work by such critics as Derek Attridge and Kevin Dettmar. The current "ethical turn" in literary and cultural studies prompts Attridge, for example, in *Joyce Effects: On Language, Theory, and History* (2000), to speculate about how to escape the exegetical limitations of the New Critical assumptions that still pervade much writing on modernism, in order "to create space for alternative approaches that may bring with them new ways of enjoying, and experiencing the vivid and lasting effects of, Joyce's writing" (xvi). In a related vein, Dettmar, in *The Illicit Joyce of Postmodernism: Reading Against the Grain* (1996), constructs a series of loosely connected "incursions" into *Dubliners*, *A Portrait of the Artist as a Young Man*, and *Ulysses* (xii) – incursions which together comprise a "postmodern" method of reading intended to sidestep the "global strategies" and "philosophical consistency" characteristic of "modern" readings of Joyce (xii). Attridge regards such postmodern approaches to Joyce – and indeed to literature in general, modernist or otherwise – as also evidence of a renewed commitment to the ethics of literary study. Urging his readers to "make a leap of trust" before (or into) literature, he harbors the hope that such a leap will foster individual readers' "openness to an alterity that would challenge cherished habits or assumptions" (165). Attridge also sees the ethical responsibility of reading modernism as a microcosm of ethical responsibility in general. "The parallels," he writes, "with the kinds of commitment we make to other persons, or, sometimes, institutions or communities, will be evident" (165). Snaith, Cuddy-Keane, Dettmar, Attridge, and other recent critics are developing a type of critical practice that, through the unceasing historical contextualization of canonical and less-read modernist texts, together with increased attention to a post-reader-response notion of literature's aesthetically and emotionally provocative effects on readers, may engender a clearer recognition of these texts' ethical and political stakes and of the challenges and opportunities they present to readers with respect to those readers' individual and collective negotiation of their own everyday relationships.

References and Further Reading

Attridge, Derek. 1999. Innovation, Literature, Ethics: Relating to the Other. *Proceedings of the Modern Language Association (PMLA)* 114 (1): 20–31.

——. 2000. *Joyce Effects: On Language, Theory, and History*. Cambridge and New York: Cambridge University Press.

Brantlinger, Patrick. 1998. *The Reading Lesson: The Threat of Mass Literacy in Nineteenth-Century British Fiction*. Bloomington: Indiana University Press.

Brooker, Jewel Spears and Joseph Bentley. 1990. *Reading the Waste Land: Modernism and the Limits of Interpretation*. Amherst: University of Massachusetts Press.

Caws, Mary Ann. 1985. *Reading Frames in Modern Fiction*. Princeton: Princeton University Press.

Corcoran, Neil. 1997. *After Yeats and Joyce: Reading Modern Irish Literature*. Oxford: Oxford University Press.

Cuddy-Keane, Melba. 1999. Imbricated Voices: Modernism's Historical Readers. Unpublished paper read at the inaugural conference of the Modernist Studies Association, Penn State University, October 7–10.

Dettmar, Kevin J. H. 1996. *The Illicit Joyce of Postmodernism: Reading Against the Grain.* Madison: University of Wisconsin Press.

——, ed. 1992. *Rereading the New: A Backward Glance at Modernism.* Ann Arbor: University of Michigan Press.

—— and Stephen Watts, eds., 1996. *Marketing Modernisms: Self-promotion, Canonization,Rereading.* Ann Arbor: University of Michigan Press.

Eagleton, Terry. 2000. *The Idea of Culture.* Oxford: Blackwell.

Kyburz, Mark. 1996. *"Voi Altri Pochi": Ezra Pound and His Audience, 1908–1925.* Basel, Boston, and Berlin: Birkhäuser Verlag.

Lindberg, Kathryne. 1987. *Reading Pound Reading: Modernism after Nietzsche.* New York and Oxford: Oxford University Press.

MacCarthy, Desmond. 1932. The Art of Reading. Desmond and Mary MacCarthy Papers, Lilly Library, Bloomington, Indiana. Box 7, folder 41, 10 pp.

Marcus, Jane. 1994. Sapphistry: Narration as Lesbian Seduction in *A Room of One's Own*. In Eleanor McNees, ed., *Virginia Woolf: Critical Assessments*, Vol. 2, pp. 221–50. Mountfield, East Sussex: Helm Info.

Moi, Toril. 1985. *Sexual/Textual Politics: Feminist Literary Theory.* London: Methuen.

Natoli, Joseph. 1996. Meditating on a Postmodern Strategy of Reading. *Yearbook of English Studies* 26: 260–6.

North, Michael. 1999. *Reading 1922: A Return to the Scene of the Modern.* New York and Oxford: Oxford University Press.

Pease, Allison. 2000. Readers with Bodies: Modernist Criticism's Bridge Across the Cultural Divide. *Modernism/Modernity* 7 (1): 77–97.

Rosenberg, Beth Carole. 1995. *Virginia Woolf and Samuel Johnson: Common Readers.* London: Macmillan.

Scannell, Paddy. 1989. Public Service Broadcasting and Modern Public Life. *Media, Culture & Society*, 11 (2): 135–66.

Scarry, Elaine. 1999. *On Beauty and Being Just.* Princeton: Princeton University Press.

Snaith, Anna. 2001. "Stray Guineas": Virginia Woolf, Women Readers and the Marsham Street Library. In Jane Goldman and Mark Hussey, eds., *Virginia Woolf Out of Bounds: Selected Papers from the Tenth Annual Virginia Woolf Conference.* New York: Pace University Press.

——, ed. 2000. Wide Circles: The *Three Guineas* Letters. *Woolf Studies Annual*, 6: 1–168.

Stansky, Peter. 1996. *On or About December 1910: Early Bloomsbury and Its Intimate World.* Cambridge, MA: Harvard University Press.

Travis, Molly Abel. 1998. *Reading Cultures: The Construction of Readers in the Twentieth Century.* Carbondale: Southern Illinois University Press.

Tuma, Keith. 1998. *Fishing by Obstinate Isles: Modern and Postmodern British Poetry and American Readers.* Evanston: Northwestern University Press.

Vincent, David. 2000. *The Rise of Mass Literacy: Reading and Writing in Modern Europe.* Malden, MA: Polity Press.

Wells, H. G. 1998. *The Correspondence of H. G. Wells,* 4 vols. Ed. David C. Smith. London: Pickering & Chatto.

Woolf, Virginia. [1938] 1966. *Three Guineas.* New York: Harcourt Brace Jovanovich.

Select Bibliography

Abraham, Julie. *Are Girls Necessary? Lesbian Writing and Modern Histories.* New York: Routledge, 1996.

Altick, Richard. *The English Common Reader.* Chicago: University of Chicago Press, 1957.

Ardis, Ann. *New Women, New Novels: Feminism and Early Modernism.* New Brunswick, NJ: Rutgers University Press, 1990.

Beach, Sylvia. *Shakespeare and Company.* New York: Harcourt, Brace, 1959.

Bell, Michael. *Literature, Modernism and Myth: Belief and Responsibility in the Twentieth Century.* Cambridge: Cambridge University Press, 1997.

—, ed. *The Context of English Literature, 1900–1930.* London: Methuen, 1980.

Benstock, Shari. *Women of the Left Bank: Paris, 1900–1940.* Austin: University of Texas Press, 1986.

Bornstein, George. *Material Modernism: The Politics of the Page.* Cambridge: Cambridge University Press, 2001.

Bradbury, Malcolm and James McFarlane, eds. *Modernism 1890–1930.* Harmondsworth: Penguin, 1976.

Butler, Christopher. *Early Modernism: Literature, Music and Painting in Europe 1900–1916,* 1994.

Childs, Peter. *Modernism.* London: Routledge, 2000.

Clark, Suzanne. *Sentimental Modernism: Women Writers and the Revolution of the Word.* Bloomington: Indiana University Press. 1991.

Cox, C. B. and A. E. Dyson, eds. *The Twentieth-Century Mind: History, Ideas and Literature in Britain,* vol. I, 1900–1918. Oxford and New York: Oxford University Press, 1972.

——. *The Twentieth-Century Mind,* vol. II, 1918–1945. Oxford and New York: Oxford University Press, 1972.

Daly, Nicholas. *Modernism, Romance and the Fin de siècle: Popular Fiction and British*

Culture, 1880–1914. Cambridge: Cambridge University Press, 1999.

DeKoven, Marianne. *Rich and Strange: Gender, History, Modernism*. Princeton: Princeton University Press, 1991.

Delany, Paul. *Islands of Money: English Literature and the Financial Culture*. Andover: University of Massachusetts Press, 1998.

Dettmar, Kevin J. H. and Stephen Watts, eds. *Marketing Modernisms: Self-promotion, Canonization, Re-reading*. Ann Arbor: University of Michigan Press, 1996.

DiBattista, Maria and Lucy McDiarmid, eds. *High and Low Moderns: Literature and Culture, 1889–1939*. New York and Oxford: Oxford University Press, 1996.

Douglas, Ann. *Terrible Honesty: Mongrel Manhattan in the 1920s*. New York: Farrar, Straus, & Giroux, 1995.

DuPlessis, Rachel Blau. *Writing Beyond the Ending: Narrative Strategies of Twentieth-Century Women Writers*. Bloomington: Indiana University Press, 1985.

Eksteins, Modris. *Rights of Spring: The Great War and the Birth of the Modern Age*. London: Bantam, 1989.

Elliott, Bridget and Jo-Ann Wallace. *Women Artists and Writers: Modernist (Im)positionings*. New York: Routledge, 1994.

Ellmann, Richard and Charles Feidelson, eds. *The Modern Tradition*. Oxford and New York: Oxford University Press, 1965.

Felski, Rita. *The Gender of Modernity*. Cambridge, MA: Harvard University Press, 1996.

Ferrall, Charles. *Modernist Writing and Reactionary Politics*. Cambridge: Cambridge University Press, 2001.

Fussell, Paul. *The Great War and Modern Memory*. New York and London: Oxford University Press, 1975.

Gilbert, Sandra and Susan Gubar. *No Man's Land, vol. I, The War of the Words*. New Haven: Yale University Press, 1988.

——. *No Man's Land, vol. II, Sexchanges*. New Haven: Yale University Press, 1989.

——. *No Man's Land, vol. III, Letters from the Front*. New Haven: Yale University Press, 1994.

Hanscombe, Gillian and Virginia L. Smyers. *Writing for Their Lives: The Modernist Women, 1910–1940*. Boston, MA: Northeastern University Press, 1987.

Hutchinson, George. *The Harlem Renaissance in Black and White*. Cambridge, MA: Belknap Press of Harvard University Press, 1995.

Huyssen, Andreas. *After the Great Divide: Modernism, Mass Culture, Postmodernism*. Bloomington: Indiana University Press, 1986.

Hynes, Samuel. *A War Imagined: The First World War and English Culture*. London: The Bodley Head, 1990.

Jensen, Robert. *Marketing Modernism in Fin de siècle Europe*. Princeton: Princeton University Press, 1994.

Kaestle, Carl. *Literacy in the United States: Readers and Reading Since 1880*. New Haven and London: Yale University Press, 1991.

Keating, Peter. *The Haunted Study: A Social History of the English Novel 1875–1914*. London: Secker & Warburg, 1989.

Kenner, Hugh. *The Pound Era*. Berkeley: University of California Press, 1971.

Levenson, Michael. *A Genealogy of Modernism: A Study of English Literary Doctrine 1908–1922*. Cambridge: Cambridge University Press, 1984.

Levenson, Michael H., ed. *The Cambridge Companion to Modernism*. Cambridge: Cambridge University Press, 1999.

Lidderdale, Jane and Mary Nicholson. *Dear Miss Weaver, Harriet Shaw Weaver, 1876–1961*. New York: Viking Press, 1970.

Manganaro, Marc, ed. *Modernist Anthropology: from Fieldwork to Text*. Princeton: Princeton University Press, 1990.

McAleer, Joseph. *Popular Reading and Publishing in Britain, 1914–1950*. Oxford: Clarendon Press, 1992.

Naremore, James and Patrick Brantlinger. *Modernity and Mass Culture*. Bloomington: Indiana University Press, 1991.

Nicholls, Peter. *Modernisms: A Literary Guide*. Basingstoke and London: Macmillan, 1995.

North, Michael. *The Political Aesthetic of Yeats, Eliot and Pound*. Cambridge: Cambridge University Press, 1991.

——. *Reading 1922: A Return to the Scene of the Modern*. New York and Oxford: Oxford University Press, 1999.

Ohmann, Richard. *Selling Culture: Magazines, Markets and Class at the Turn of the Century*. London and New York: Verso, 1996.

Rainey, Lawrence. *Institutions of Modernism: Literary Elites and Public Culture*. New Haven and London: Yale University Press, 1998.

Reid, B. L. *The Man from New York: John Quinn and His Friends*. Oxford and New York: Oxford University Press, 1968.

Schwartz, Sanford. *The Matrix of Modernism: Pound, Eliot and Early Twentieth Century Thought*. Princeton: Princeton University Press, 1985.

Scott, Bonnie K., ed. *The Gender of Modernism*. Bloomington: Indiana University Press, 1990.

——. *Refiguring Modernism*. Bloomington: Indiana University Press, 1995. Vol. I, *The Women of 1928*. Vol II, *Postmodern Feminist Readings of Woolf, West and Barnes*.

Smith, Stan. *The Origins of Modernism: Eliot, Pound, Yeats and the Rhetorics of Renewal*. Hemel Hempstead: Harvester Wheatsheaf, 1994.

Stevenson, Randall. *Modernist Fiction: An Introduction*. Rev. ed. London: Prentice Hall, 1997.

Sutherland, John. *Victorian Novelists and Publishers*. London: Athlone Press, 1976.

Trotter, David. *Paranoid Modernism: Literary Experiment, Psychosis, and the Professionalization of English Society*. Oxford: Oxford University Press, 2001.

Wall, Cheryl A. *Women of the Harlem Renaissance*. Bloomington: Indiana University Press, 1995.

Waugh, Patricia, ed. *Revolutions of the Word: Intellectual Contexts for the Study of Modern Literature*. London and New York: Arnold, 1997.

Wexler, Joyce Piell. *Who Paid for Modernism? Art, Money and the Fiction of Conrad, Joyce and Lawrence*. Fayetteville: University of Arkansas Press, 1997.

Whitworth, Michael. H. *Einstein's Wake: Relativity, Metaphor, and Modernist Litera-*

ture. Oxford: Oxford University Press, 2001.

Williams, Raymond. *The Politics of Modernism: Against the New Conformists*. London: Verso, 1989.

Willison, Ian, Warwick Gould, and Warren Chernaik, eds. *Modernist Writers and the Marketplace*. London and New York: Macmillan and St. Martin's Press, 1996.

Wilson, Edmund. *Axel's Castle, a Study in the Imaginative Literature of 1870–1930*. New York: Scribner's, 1931.

Index

Lightning Source UK Ltd.
Milton Keynes UK
UKOW05f0446130214

226362UK00001B/65/P